ART AS INVESTMENT

A RESEARCH ANTHOLOGY FROM THE PAST 100 YEARS

Robert L. Lewis, Esq.
315 West 70th Street
New York, N.Y. 10023
(646) -753-0450
RobertLewisESQ@aol.com

TABLE OF RESEARCH PAPERS

Does it Pay to Invest in Art? A Selection-corrected Returns Perspective by Arthur Korteweg, Roman Kraussl and Patrick Verwijmeren (Current Draft: October 15, 2013)

Economics of the Arts: Sale Rates and Price Movements in Art Auctions by Orley Ashenfelter and Kathryn Graddy, *The American Economic Review*, Vol 101, No. 3 (May 2011) pp. 212-216

Art and Money by William N. Goetzmann, Luc Renneboog and Christophe Spaenjers, *The American Economic Review*, Vol. 101, No.3 (May 2011) pp. 222-226

Investment in Visual Arts: Evidence from International Transactions by Benjamin R. Mandel (November 2010)

Art as an Investment and Conspicuous Consumption Good by Benjamin R. Mandel, *The American Economic Review*, Vol. 99, No. 4 (September 2009) pp. 1653-1663

Asset Pricing Theory and the Valuation of Canadian Paintings by Douglas J. Hodgson and Keith P. Vorkink, *The Canadian Journal of Economics*, Vol. 37, No. 3 (August 2004) pp. 629-655

Pre-sale Estimates, Risk Analysis, and the Investment Quality of Fine Art by Clare McAndrew and Rex Thompson (September 2003)

Art as an Investment: The Market for Modern Prints by James E. Pesando, *The American Economic Review*, Vol. 83, No. 5 (December 1993) pp. 1075-1089

Accounting for Taste: Art and the Financial Markets Over Three Centuries by William N. Goetzmann, *The American Economic Review*, Vol. 83, No. 5 (December 1993) pp. 1370-1376

Rate of Return to Investment in American Antique Furniture by Paul Graeser, *Southern Economic Journal*, Vol. 59, No. 4 (April 1993) pp. 817-821

Art as a Commodity? Aspects of a Current Issue by Lisa Koenigsberg, *Archives of American Art Journal*, (Published by The Smithsonian Institution) Vol. 29, No. ¾ (1989) pp. 23-35

Art Investment: An Empirical Inquiry by Bruno S. Frey and Werner W. Pommerehne, *Southern Economic Journal*, Vol. 56, No. 2 (October 1989) pp. 396-409

Unnatural Value: Or Art Investment as Floating Crap Game by William J. Baumol, *The American Economic Review*, Vol. 76, No. 2 (May 1986) pp. 10-14

Contemporary Modern Art as an Investment by Evelyn Marie Stuart, *Fine Arts Journal*, Vol. 35, No. 4 (April 1917) pp 243-257

Does it Pay to Invest in Art?
A Selection-corrected Returns Perspective

Arthur Korteweg, Roman Kräussl, and Patrick Verwijmeren*

Abstract

This paper shows the importance of correcting for sample selection when investing in illiquid assets with endogenous trading. Using a large sample of 20,538 paintings that were sold repeatedly at auction between 1972 and 2010, we find that paintings with higher price appreciation are more likely to trade. This strongly biases estimates of returns. The selection-corrected average annual index return is 6.5 percent, down from 10 percent for traditional uncorrected repeat sales regressions, and Sharpe Ratios drop from 0.24 to 0.04. From a pure financial perspective, passive index investing in paintings is not a viable investment strategy once selection bias is accounted for. Our results have important implications for other illiquid asset classes that trade endogenously.

JEL classification: D44, G11, Z11

Keywords: Art investing; Selection bias; Portfolio allocation

First Draft: December 13, 2012
Current Draft: October 15, 2013

---

* Arthur Korteweg (korteweg@stanford.edu) is from Stanford Graduate School of Business, Roman Kräussl (r.g.w.kraussl@vu.nl) is from Luxembourg School of Finance and the Center for Alternative Investments at Goizueta Business School, Emory University, and Patrick Verwijmeren (verwijmeren@ese.eur.nl) is from Erasmus University Rotterdam, University of Melbourne, University of Glasgow, Duisenberg School of Finance and the Tinbergen Institute. We thank Andrew Ang, Les Coleman, Elroy Dimson, Bruce Grundy, Bryan Lim, George Parker, Christophe Spaenjers, Mark Westerfield, and participants at the 2013 European Finance Association meetings for helpful comments.

Over the last two decades investors are allocating increasingly larger shares of their portfolios to alternative assets. Many of the alternative asset classes, such as private equity and real estate, and even certain traditional assets such as corporate bonds, are highly illiquid. This complicates return evaluation, especially when trades are endogenously related to the performance of the asset, giving rise to a sample selection problem. This paper demonstrates the empirical first-order importance of correcting for sample selection when evaluating performance and constructing optimal portfolios that include alternative assets.

Among the alternative assets, paintings (and other collectibles) are often considered a comparatively safe investment in times of financial turmoil (Dimson and Spaenjers, 2011). Finding low or negative correlations between art[1] and public equity markets, several recent academic studies argue that art investments should be included in optimal asset allocations (see, for example, Mei and Moses, 2002; Taylor and Coleman, 2011). Indeed, investors allocate about 6 percent of their total wealth to so-called passion investments[2], and several art funds have been created to allow for diversified investments in art.

The returns and risks of art investments are, however, not beyond debate, and indeed not well known. Constructing an art index and computing the return to art investing is a non-trivial exercise, as prices are not observed at fixed intervals, but only when the artwork trades. Goetzmann (1993, 1996) argues that these trades are endogenous, and he conjectures that paintings that have appreciated in value are more likely to come to market, resulting in high observed returns for paintings that sell, relative to the population. As a result, the observed price appreciation is not representative of the entire market for paintings. In fact, in periods with few

---

[1] Following the literature, we use the terms "art" and "paintings" interchangeably throughout the paper.
[2] See the article "Follow your heart" in the Wall Street Journal on September 20, 2010. Passion investments include art, wine, and jewelry.

trades, it is possible to observe high and positive returns even though overall values of paintings are declining.

We present an econometric model of art indices, based on the framework developed by Korteweg and Sorensen (2010, 2013), that generalizes the standard repeat sales regression (RSR; see Bailey et al., 1963, and Case and Shiller, 1987) to correct for selection bias in the sample of observed sales. This model explicitly specifies the entire path of unobserved valuation and returns between sales, as well as the probability of observing a trade at each point in time, and estimates the selection-corrected price for each individual artwork at each point in time, even when it is not traded. We estimate the model using a unique proprietary auction database from which we construct one of the largest samples of repeat sales of paintings in the literature to date, with 20,538 paintings being sold a total of 42,548 times between 1972 and 2010.

We find that selection bias is of first-order importance. Paintings are indeed more likely to sell when they have risen in value, consistent with Goetzmann's hypothesis. The difference between our selection-corrected index and the standard (non-corrected) RSR index is economically and statistically large, and robust across specifications. Normalizing indices at 100 in 1972, the RSR index is 4,278 in 2010, the end of our sample period, whereas the selection-corrected index ends around 1,000 to 1,300, depending on the specification of the selection model.

The selection correction has important implications for asset allocation decisions. The annual return to the standard RSR art index over the period 1972 to 2010 is on average 10 percent, with volatility of 17 percent, a Sharpe Ratio of 0.24, and a correlation with world equity returns of 0.3. Given these statistics, a mean-variance investor would allocate roughly equal fractions of her portfolio to art and to public equities, and she would appear to earn a portfolio

Sharpe Ratio of 0.31, which is 17% higher than the Sharpe Ratio of 0.26 on a portfolio of equities only.

However, these returns are not what a passive art investor actually earns, unless she is able to pick a portfolio of "winners" that rise in value in similar fashion to the paintings that come to auction (such that the RSR index is representative for her portfolio). Instead, it is the selection-corrected returns that are more representative for the experience of an investor who has invested in a well-diversified, passive portfolio of paintings.[3] After correcting for selection bias we find an average annual art index return of 6.5 percent, which is 3.5 percentage points lower than the non-corrected index, and a Sharpe Ratio of 0.04, down from 0.24 without the selection correction. This reduces the attractiveness of art as an investment to the point that the passive index investor optimally assigns zero weight to art in her portfolio. If the investor chooses to ignore the sample selection problem and assigns equal weight to art and stocks instead, she ends up reaping a portfolio Sharpe Ratio that is 18% lower than what she would earn by investing in stocks alone. This main portfolio allocation result is robust to broadening the investment opportunity set to other asset classes, to the effects of illiquidity and transaction costs on portfolio allocations, and to considering higher moments of art returns.

Our model also allows us to separately assess various styles of paintings. We distinguish between five styles: Post-war and Contemporary, Impressionist and Modern, Old Masters, American, and 19th Century European. In addition, we consider returns to top selling artists. Although we observe interesting differences between the selection-corrected returns per style,

---

[3] Index investing is a feasible strategy for investors who cannot afford a diversified exposure to the art market through the purchase of individual, often expensive paintings. With this view, we ignore any aesthetic return on art, i.e., we assume no consumption utility of owning art, since the investor does not have access to the artworks underlying the index.

and positive portfolio allocations to either Post-war and Contemporary paintings or paintings from top artists, the portfolio weights and improvements in Sharpe ratios are small at best.

To our knowledge, this is the first paper to show the statistical and economic importance of selection effects for price indices of collectibles, and the first to show the importance of selection bias for performance evaluation and portfolio allocation for any asset class. A number of papers in the literature estimate art returns and assess their usefulness for optimal portfolio construction without accounting for selection bias (see Ashenfelter and Graddy, 2003, for an excellent overview of this literature). The real estate literature on the other hand has recognized the sample selection problem for index construction (for example, Case et al., 1997, and Korteweg and Sorensen, 2013, show that appreciating properties trade faster), but the impact on performance and portfolio allocations has not been examined.

In summary, our results suggest that sample selection can be of first-order importance for performance evaluation and portfolio allocation in illiquid markets with endogenous trading. Exploring the severity of this effect in other asset classes is an important avenue for future research.

The remainder of the paper is organized as follows. In Section 1, we describe our model for prices and trades of artworks. Section 2 describes our data. We discuss the art indices in Section 3, both with and without correcting for sample selection, and perform additional tests on the existence and strength of the selection problem in Section 4. In Section 5 we analyze optimal asset allocations, and Section 6 concludes.

1. A selection model of prices and sales of artworks

1.1. Selection model

We decompose the log return of an artwork, *i*, from time *t-1* to *t*, into two components,

$$r_i(t) = \delta(t) + \varepsilon_i(t). \tag{1}$$

The first return component, $\delta(t)$, is the log price change of the aggregate art market from time *t-1* to *t*. We show below how to use the time series of δ to construct a price index for the market. The second return component, $\varepsilon_i(t)$, is an idiosyncratic return that is particular to the individual artwork. We assume that ε has a normal distribution with mean zero and variance σ^2, and is independent over time and across artworks.

If we observe sales of artworks at both time *t-1* and *t*, then the returns are observed, and estimation is straightforward. However, art is sold very infrequently. Typically, years pass between consecutive sales. With a sale at time *t-h* and at time *t*, the observed *h*-period log return is derived from the single-period returns in equation (1) by summation:

$$r_i^h(t) = \sum_{\tau=t-h+1}^{t} \delta(\tau) + \varepsilon_i^h(t). \tag{2}$$

The error term $\varepsilon_i^h(t)$ is normally distributed with mean zero and variance $h\sigma^2$. By defining indicator variables for the periods between sales, the δ's can be estimated by standard generalized least squares (GLS) regression techniques, scaling return observations by $1/\sqrt{h}$ to correct for heteroskedasticity. This is the repeat sales regression (RSR) technique that is standard in the literature (Bailey et al., 1963, and Case and Shiller, 1987).

The δ estimates are consistent as long as the indicator variables in the RSR regression are uncorrelated with the error term, i.e., if the probability of a sale is unrelated to the idiosyncratic return component. However, in their survey of the literature, Ashenfelter and Graddy (2003) highlight the concern that art prices may be exacerbated during booms as "better" paintings may come up for sale. Similarly, Goetzmann (1993, 1996) argues that selection biases are important in art data because the decision by an owner to sell a work of art may be conditional on whether or not the value of the artwork has increased, either for rational reasons or due to the disposition effect.[4]

To correct the repeat sales model for selection bias of this nature, we specify the sales behavior of art following the model of Korteweg and Sorensen (2010, 2013) that was developed for venture capital and real estate. Suppose a sale of artwork i at time t occurs whenever the latent variable $w_i(t)$ is greater than zero, and remains untraded otherwise, i.e.,

$$w_i(t) = W_i(t)'\alpha_0 + r_i^0(t)\alpha_r + \eta_i(t), \tag{3}$$

where $r_i^0(t)$ is the return since the last sale of the artwork, and is mostly unobserved, except when $w_i(t) > 0$. The vector $W_i(t)$ contains observed covariates. The error term, $\eta_i(t)$, is i.i.d. normal with mean zero and variance normalized to one, and independent of $\varepsilon_i(t)$.[5]

The selection model, consisting of the observation equation, (1), and the selection equation, (3), nests the classic RSR model: If the selection coefficient, α_r, equals zero, then trades occur for reasons unrelated to price, there is no selection bias, and we recover the standard RSR model. Conversely, if Goetzmann's conjecture is correct and artworks that have risen in value are more likely to sell, then we should find a positive selection coefficient.[6] By estimating and testing the selection coefficient, we allow the data to speak to the direction and importance of selection bias.

---

[4] The disposition effect states that investors are more likely to sell assets that have risen in price since purchase while holding on to those that have dropped in value, and has been documented in real estate (e.g., Genesove and Mayer, 2001) and public equities (e.g., Odean, 1998, though Ben-David and Hirshleifer, 2012, offer a different and more nuanced view of the empirical evidence for stocks).
[5] The normalization is necessary, but without loss of generality, because the parameters in equation (3) are only identified up to scale, as in a standard binary probit model.
[6] We follow Goetzmann's conjecture and model the selection process as a function of the return since prior sale. Similar selection effects occur if selection is on price rather than return, as suggested by Pénasse et al. (2013).

From an econometric perspective, the model is a dynamic extension of Heckman's (1979, 1990) selection model. As in Heckman's model, our model adjusts not only for selection on observable variables, such as the size or style of a painting, but also controls for selection on unobservable variables. However, Heckman's model assumes that observations are independent, implying that observations for which price data are missing, are only informative for estimating the selection model, (3), in the first stage, but do not carry any further information for the price index in equation (1) in the second stage. Since prices are path-dependent, this independence assumption fails to hold. Each observation carries information about not only the current price, but also about past and future prices of a painting, even at times when the artwork does not trade. Unlike the standard selection model, our model does not impose the independence assumption, and uses all information to make inference about the price path of individual artworks, and the parameters of interest, α, δ, and σ^2.

The downside of allowing for the dependencies between observed and missing data is that it makes estimation more difficult relative to the standard selection model. We use Markov chain Monte Carlo (MCMC), a Bayesian estimation technique, to estimate the model parameters (see Korteweg and Sorensen, 2013, for details).

Our model extends Korteweg and Sorensen (2013) by allowing for separate indices for different styles of artwork, or whether the artist belongs to the top 100 artists. For these specifications, we replace equation (1) with

$$r_i(t) = X_i' \cdot \delta(t) + \varepsilon_i(t). \tag{4}$$

The vector X_i is a set of dummy variables that indicate to which category the painting belongs. The categories need not be mutually exclusive. For example, a painting can belong both to the "Old Masters" style and be in the "Top 100 Artists" category (to be defined below).

1.2. Price index construction

The art literature defines the price index, $\Pi(t)$, across N artworks relative to base year 0 as

$$\Pi(t) \equiv \sum_{i=1}^{N} P_i(t) \Big/ \sum_{i=1}^{N} P_i(0), \tag{5}$$

where $P_i(t)$ is the price of painting i at time t. Goetzmann (1992) and Goetzmann and Peng (2002) show that the index can be constructed from the model estimates in a sequential manner starting from the base year index normalized at 100,

$$\Pi(t) = \Pi(t-1) \cdot \exp\left(\delta(t) + \frac{1}{2}\sigma^2\right). \tag{6}$$

The $\frac{1}{2}\sigma^2$ adjusts for the Jensen inequality term due to the log operator in (1).[7]

2. Art data

We construct a sample of repeat sales from the Blouin Art Sales Index (BASI), an online database that provides data on artworks that are sold at auction at over 350 auction houses worldwide.[8] The BASI database is presently the largest known database of artworks, containing roughly 4.6 million works of art by more than 225,000 individual artists over the period 1922 to 2010. We solely focus on paintings, which represent 2.3 million artworks in the database.

For each auction record, the database contains information on the artist, the artwork, and the sale. We observe the artist's name, nationality, year of birth, and year of death (if applicable). For the artwork, we know its title, year of creation, medium, size, and style, and whether it is

---

[7] Shiller (1991) develops a repeat sales index estimator that corrects for the Jensen inequality term in the estimation, but in our model it is computationally more convenient to do the adjustment post-estimation as it preserves the linearity of the state space in the filtering problem.

[8] Art is not only sold in auction but also privately, for example through dealers. Renneboog and Spaenjers (2013) note that it is generally accepted that auction prices set a benchmark that is also used in the private market.

signed or stamped. For the sale, we have data on the auction house, date of the auction, lot number, hammer price (the price for which the artwork was sold, excluding any premiums paid from the buyer to the auction house, and converted to U.S. dollars at the prevailing spot price), and whether the artwork has been "bought in" or was withdrawn.[9]

We identify repeat sales by matching auction sales records using artists' names, artwork names, painting size, medium, and signature (similar to the matching procedures in Taylor and Coleman, 2011, and Renneboog and Spaenjers, 2013). We start our search in 1972, due to the limited coverage of the database before that time. We drop buy-ins to avoid Goetzmann's (1993) concern that particular auction records are wrongly classified as sales when the painting fails to meet the seller's reservation price. To eliminate false matches, we remove paintings from the same artist with the generic titles "untitled" and "landscape." We further check whether the remaining potential repeat sales are true repeat sales by manually searching for the artwork's provenance, which shows the chronology of the artwork's earlier sales. The provenance is typically found on the websites of the auction houses. For instance, Christie's and Sotheby's provide online provenance information on all auction sales since 1998. When we are in doubt about whether we are dealing with a true repeat sale, we delete it from our sample. Our final sample includes 42,548 sales of 20,538 unique paintings.

Panel A of Figure 1 shows the number of sales in the repeat sales sample, broken down by the number of first, second, and third or more sales for the artworks in our repeat sales sample.[10] For comparison, Panel B shows the number for the full BASI dataset since 1972. The full sample shows substantial growth in sales over time, peaking in 2006, whereas the repeat sales sample has the highest number of sales in 1989. This difference is due to the drop in the number of first

---

[9] An artwork is "bought in" when the bidding does not reach the reserve price, and the artwork goes unsold.
[10] Observing more than three sales is extremely rare in our sample period: we only observe 26 paintings with four sales, and one painting with five sales.

sales, as paintings that sell for the first time in the later part of our sample period have a smaller probability of being sold for a second time by the end of the sample period and thus have a smaller chance of being included in the repeat sales sample.

[Please insert Figure 1 here]

Panel A of Table 1 shows descriptive statistics of the paintings in our repeat sales sample. The average hammer price in the full sample is $61,939, with a long right tail of extremely expensive paintings. The average surface of the paintings is about 547,000mm^2, or 0.55m^2. Around 22 percent of sales take place at Christie's auction house, and 25 percent at Sotheby's. For 20 percent of sales, the auction house is located in London, and another 20 percent are sold in New York. Using the same style classifications as Christie's and Sotheby's, the BASI database distinguishes between six broad styles. The Impressionist and Modern style accounts for one third of sales, followed by European 19th Century paintings with one fourth of sales. About 16 percent of sales are of the Post-war and Contemporary style, 12 percent are American paintings, and 5 percent are Old Masters. The residual "Other style" category makes up the remaining 9 percent of sales. Nearly 10 percent of sold paintings are by artists with total dollar sales in the top 100 of the BASI database over the sample period.[11] Finally, more than two percent of sales occur within two years after the artist has deceased.

[Please insert Table 1 here]

Panel A also shows the descriptive statistics for the full BASI sample over the same period. Compared to the full sample, more expensive paintings of higher quality are more likely to be sold repeatedly, underscoring the importance of correcting for sample selection. It should be noted that even if the repeat sales sample were statistically indistinguishable from the full sample

---

[11] We keep the artists in the top 100 category fixed throughout the sample period.

of sales, the sample selection issue that we address in this paper may still be present, as even the full sample of sales may not be representative of the underlying population of paintings.

Panel B of Table 1 provides information about the sale-to-sale returns in the repeat sales sample. The arithmetic price increase between two consecutive sales of the same painting is 123.5 percent on average. The median return is 42.4 percent, and the standard deviation is 368.5 percent. With an average time between sales of 7.6 years, this translates to an average (median) annualized return of 16.5 percent (7.5 percent), with a standard deviation of 32.7 percent. Log returns are lower, on average 43.9 percent (6.9 percent annualized), with a median of 35.3 percent (5.7 percent annualized) and a standard deviation of 78.1 percent (16.7 percent annualized).

[Please insert Figure 2 here]

Figure 2 shows the distribution of the annualized sale-to-sale returns. Although the average return is positive, the distribution shows negative returns occur regularly. Annualized returns below –30 percent or above 70 percent are rare.

3. Art indices

In this section we first present the results of estimating art indices without taking selection into account. Then we turn to our selection-corrected indices.

3.1. Art indices without selection correction

Figure 3 plots two estimated art price indices that ignore selection bias. The first index is constructed from the standard repeat sales regression estimated by GLS, weighing each observation by the inverse of the square root of the time between trades, to correct for potential heteroskedasticity (the "GLS index"). The second is a MCMC specification that ignores selection by forcing α_r in equation (3) to equal zero (the "MCMC index"). We assign an index value of 100 to the year 1972 and construct annual end-of-year arithmetic indices as shown in equations (5) and (6).

[Please insert Figure 3 here]

The GLS and MCMC indices practically coincide, mitigating concerns about distributional assumptions of the MCMC estimator. Over the early part of the sample period, the indices rise until they peak at 1,300 in 1990. After bottoming out at 900 in 1993, following the Japanese real estate collapse in the early 1990s, the indices climb again until peaking at around 4,300 in 2007, showing particularly high growth after 2001. In 2010, the end of our sample period, the price indices have largely recovered from the dip in the global financial crisis of 2008-2009, and are nearing the 4,300 level again.

3.2. Selection models

The selection models require us to take a stance on what drives the sale of an artwork. We estimate three specifications of the selection equation. All models include the log return since last sale, to capture the direction and strength of the sample selection effect. We also include the time since the last sale, both linearly and squared, in all specifications. Time since last sale functions as an instrument to identify the model from more than distributional assumptions alone: it changes the probability of a sale in the next period without affecting the return on the artwork going forward, based on the common-place assumption that prices incorporate all available public information, which includes the date that the painting last sold. Other variables that may be important for the probability of sale are the size of the painting, an indicator whether the artist deceased in the past two years, and the growth in worldwide GDP. The size of the painting may be related to the probability of sale, because smaller paintings are easier to hang and transport. The death of the artist might be relevant as there is a popular belief that artworks are more likely to be sold when the artist has recently deceased. We include worldwide GDP growth since Goetzmann (1993), Hiraki et al. (2009), Goetzmann et al. (2011), and Pownall et al. (2013) establish an important relation between art and wealth.

[Please insert Table 2 here]

Table 2 shows the estimated coefficients of the selection models. Model A only includes the log return and the time variables. Most importantly, paintings with higher returns since the prior sale are more likely to sell, and hence appear more frequently in the sales data, confirming that selection is important in evaluating art returns. As a result, standard indices exaggerate the price appreciation of the overall market.

The magnitude of the selection coefficient is not only statistically significant, it is also economically meaningful. For example, a painting that was last sold one year ago and has not changed in value since, has a 3.6 percent probability of being sold in the next year. Had the painting increased in value by one standard deviation of the annualized return, then the probability of sale in the next year would be 4.1 percent. For a two standard deviation increase in price, the sale probability in the next year is 4.7 percent.

Controlling for price appreciation, the time since the prior sale has a non-linear relation to the probability of a sale. An artwork is less likely to sell again in the first year after a trade, but as the time since last sale increases, the probability of a sale rises as the coefficient on the squared time since sale starts to dominate. All time effects are significant at the one percent significance level, indicating that the time variables improve the statistical identification of the model.

The estimates for Model B show that our main finding that returns and the probability of sale are positively related, is robust to adding additional variables to the selection model. The coefficients on these variables provide further insight into what drives sales behavior. A painting is more likely to sell within two years after the artist deceases, and when world GDP is declining. The latter result is not straightforward to interpret given that we also control for price appreciation separately, but it is in line with situations in which owners are forced to sell in bad times (Campbell, 2008). We do not find a significant effect of a painting's size.

Model C in Table 2 allows for different selection coefficients and intercepts by decade, where we group the 1970s with the 1980s (due to data sparseness), and we split the 2000s in the pre and post financial crisis years. Thus, our periods are 1972 to 1989, 1990 to 1999, 2000 to 2006, and 2007 to 2010. We find evidence for selection bias in every sub-period. The effect of returns on the probability of trade is especially large in the two periods after 2000. This could indicate that the selection bias has become more important since the turn of century. However, it may also mean that, although sample selection is important even in the earliest years of the sample, the selection problem is worse in more recent periods, as many paintings with slow price appreciation have not yet been sold. This is related to the well-known problem of revision bias in repeat sales indices (Clapham et al., 2006), which the selection correction model helps to ameliorate (as shown in Korteweg and Sorensen, 2013).

We use Models A, B, and C to construct three selection-corrected indices, which we denote Indices A, B, and C, respectively. Panel A of Figure 4 shows the selection-corrected price indices over time. The selection correction is quite robust across models, as the differences among the three selection-corrected indices are not very large. Panel A also includes the MCMC model without selection correction. The differences between the non-corrected and the selection-corrected indices are striking. First, the selection-corrected indices are considerably lower than the non-corrected indices, conform the intuition of the effect of a positive selection coefficient. The peak in 1990, which occurred at a 1,300 index level in the non-selection-corrected model, occurs at around 850 in the corrected indices. The 2007 peak is around 1,300 (or 1,000 for model C), rather than the 4,300 index level of the non-corrected model. Second, the selection-corrected indices show an additional peak around the year 2003, which does not occur in the non-corrected indices. Third, the selection-corrected indices do not recover after the global financial crisis of 2008, unlike the non-corrected indices.

[Please insert Figure 4 here]

In Panel B, we plot the difference between the natural logarithm of the non-selection-corrected index and each of the selection-corrected indices. As foreshadowed by the time-varying selection coefficients in model C, the graph shows that the deviation between the non-selection and the selection-corrected indices already starts in the first years of our sample period, increases steadily over time, and accelerates in the new millennium.

Next, we consider potential differences between art styles. Buelens and Ginsburgh (1993) find differential performance among styles, and possibly, different styles are in favor in different periods. Figure 5 plots the estimated selection-corrected indices.

[Please insert Figure 5 here]

We observe that the price index of Post-war and Contemporary paintings peaks around 1990 and 2007. Impressionist and Modern paintings show large increases in the early period but are hit heavily in 1990, which is in line with the popular interpretation of art observers that the Japanese real estate bubble (which burst in 1990) and the corresponding strong yen in the 1980s had strong effects on the prices of Impressionist paintings (see for example Wood, 1992). Old Masters do not increase as much in value as the other styles over the sample period.

Figure 5 also shows the selection-corrected price index for paintings of the top 100 artists in terms of the total dollar value of sales in our sample period. Top artists outperform all of the styles, and the index peaks both around the years 1990 and 2007. This result relates to the "masterpiece effect", the general belief among art dealers and critics that highly priced paintings are the best buy (e.g., Adam, 2008). Several prior academic studies examine masterpieces, but generally find that masterpieces underperform (Pesando, 1993; Mei and Moses, 2002; 2005).[12] Our results suggest that selection bias is an important determinant of this discrepancy, as not controlling for selection biases artificially drives up the returns for artworks with which masterpieces are compared. Paintings from top artists do experience relatively volatile returns, so it is not clear whether they should get higher weights in optimal portfolios. We discuss portfolio allocations after we present further evidence in support of the sample selection problem in the next section.

4. Further supporting evidence for sample selection

The results from the econometric model show that paintings are more likely to trade when they have experienced a high return since prior sale, and that correcting for the sample selection problem is economically important for index construction. In this section we show further corroborating evidence of the existence and strength of the selection problem in the raw data, without relying on the econometric machinery of the selection model.

---

[12] A notable exception is Renneboog and Spaenjers (2013), who find no evidence that masterpieces underperform.

First, we consider the relationship between the time between sales and the annualized sale-to-sale return. For each painting in the repeat sales sample, we compute the annualized log return between two adjacent sales, and the number of years between the two sales. Both these quantities are observed in the raw data. In Figure 6, we graph the average annualized sale-to-sale return against the return horizon. For example, for all sale-to-sale returns that occurred over a span of one year or less, the average annualized return is 13 percent, compared to 8 percent for sales that took place between one and two years apart. For longer return horizons the average annualized return is even lower. We also show the median annualized return against the return horizon, which follows a nearly identical pattern.

[Please insert Figure 6 here]

If there were no sample selection problem (i.e., if the selection coefficient, α_r, equals zero in the econometric model), then there should be no systematic relation between annualized returns and the time between sales, and Figure 6 should show a flat, horizontal line. Instead, the line is downward-sloping, which is consistent with a sample selection problem in which paintings with high returns are more likely to trade. To take an oversimplified example, suppose that paintings trade as soon as the return since last sale hits a fixed threshold, say, 10 percent (not annualized). Then the paintings that happen (by chance) to have a high return soon after the prior sale, will trade quickly and show a high annualized return. The paintings that are slower to hit the threshold will trade at a later date and exhibit lower annualized returns.

Figure 6 also shows that the selection problem is plausibly large. The mean annual index return from the RSR regressions is essentially an average of the annualized observed returns over all horizons. In a selected sample where the paintings with higher returns are more likely to sell, the selection-corrected average annualized return must be lower than the observed returns, and thus lower than even the long-horizon returns. Based on Figure 6, a difference of a few percentage points in the mean annual return between the RSR and the selection-corrected indices is not surprising.

The second piece of evidence suggesting sample selection is the relation between annualized returns and trading intensity. In Figure 7, we plot the time series of annualized log returns, where we take the average sale-to-sale returns for all second sales of a sales pair in a given year. We only show the time series starting in 1980, because for many sales in the 1970s the first sale takes place prior to the start of our sample in 1972, and we see only the short-horizon returns in the 1970s. In the same graph, we show the time series of trading intensity, defined as the percentage of paintings that sold in the calendar year, calculated from the full BASI dataset of 2.3 million observations (the results are very similar if we use the repeat sales sample instead).

[Please insert Figure 7 here]

Without selection, i.e. when paintings trade for reasons unrelated to returns, there should not be a systematic relation between trading intensity and annualized returns. This is clearly not what we observe in Figure 7, which shows a strong positive correlation between trading intensity and the annualized returns. This relation is consistent with the sample selection problem identified in this paper, where a positive shock to the value of paintings results in more paintings that are likely to trade, and a higher average (annualized) realized return, and vice versa for negative shocks.

Our third exercise further exploits the variation in the data, by considering the relation between trading intensity and annualized returns for individual styles of paintings. Consistent with the aggregate results, Table 3 Panel A shows that both the average and median annualized return of a specific style of painting are strongly positively correlated with the market share of that style, where market share is defined as the number of paintings of the style that sold over the year relative to the total number of paintings that traded across all styles. Panel B shows that this correlation is highly statistically significant in a pooled regression analysis that controls for style fixed effects.

[Please insert Table 3 here]

To summarize, the evidence in this section is supportive of the result from the econometric model that the probability that a painting trades is positively related to its return since the prior sale.

5. Optimal portfolio allocation

In this section, we show that our estimated indices provide important insights regarding the role of paintings for diversification and optimal portfolio allocation. More broadly, the results underscore the importance of adjusting for sample selection for performance evaluation and portfolio optimization in the presence of illiquid assets when trading is endogenous.

5.1 Descriptive Statistics

We start our analysis by describing the returns to the art indices. We follow the art-investments literature (e.g., Campbell, 2008, and Renneboog and Spaenjers, 2013) and use the technique pioneered in real estate by Geltner (1991) to unsmooth the index to deal with spurious first-order autocorrelation caused by time-aggregation of sales (Working, 1960, and Schwert, 1990). The unsmoothing procedure causes us to lose the first observation, so all returns in this section start in 1973.[13] Table 4 reports means, standard deviations and Sharpe Ratios of the

---

[13] The portfolio allocation results are qualitatively the same if we do not unsmooth the returns and use the original index returns instead. We discuss this in more detail in the robustness section below.

annual arithmetic returns on the art indices. For clarity, it should be noted that these are the returns to the indices, and thus are different from the sale-to-sale returns reported in Table 1 and Figures 2, 6, and 7.

[Please insert Table 4 here]

Panel A shows that the standard repeat sales GLS index that does not correct for selection has an average annual return of 10.1 percent with a standard deviation of 16.7 percent, and an annual Sharpe ratio of 0.24. The non-selection-corrected MCMC index returns are nearly identical to the GLS index. In contrast, the selection-corrected indices have considerably lower average returns, standard deviations and Sharpe Ratios. The average return ranges from 6.0 percent to 6.6 percent depending on the selection model specification. The standard deviations are in the range of 12.8 percent to 13.0 percent, and Sharpe Ratios range from -0.01 to 0.04.

It is important to point out that, as a measure of performance, the standard non-selection-corrected indices implicitly assume that an investor can either pick "winners" that rise in value and are thus more likely to sell, or assume that there is no selection problem and that all other holdings of the investor follow the same price path as the paintings that are auctioned off. The selection-corrected indices do not make such assumptions but rather measure the rise in value of the overall portfolio of paintings, both those that sold and those that did not. The selection-corrected returns are therefore more representative of the experience of an investor who has invested in a well-diversified, passive portfolio of paintings.

Panel A of Table 4 also presents the descriptive statistics for sample period returns of a broad portfolio of global equities (the MSCI world total return index, which includes distributions), corporate bonds (the Merrill Lynch US Corporate Master Bond index), commodities (the GSCI Commodity total return index for commodity futures), and real estate (the U.S. residential real estate index from Shiller, 2009). For the risk-free asset we use the one-year U.S. Treasury bill rate at the beginning of the year. Being our risk-free asset, we do not report the Sharpe Ratio on Treasuries in Table 4.

Despite the low Sharpe Ratios on the selection-corrected art indices relative to the Sharpe Ratios on stocks, corporate bonds, and commodities of 0.26, 0.33, and 0.18, respectively[14], investing in paintings may still be useful for constructing optimal portfolios if the correlations between art and the other asset classes are low. Panel B of Table 4 shows that the art indices have a correlation of 0.32 with world stock returns. The correlations of art with commodities and real estate are of similar magnitude, and the correlation with corporate bonds is negative, although not statistically significant.

5.2 Optimal Portfolio Allocations

To examine the portfolio allocation decision formally, we construct optimal portfolios based on the following base case assumptions that are common in the literature. First, investors have mean-variance utility, and allocate their portfolio among the risk-free asset, a well-diversified stock index, and a well-diversified, passive art index (we will consider other assets below). Second, borrowing and short sales are not allowed. Third, there are no transaction costs to constructing the indices. Fourth, there is no illiquidity return premium on paintings. Fifth, investing in the art index does not provide the investor with access to the artworks underlying the index, and we therefore do not consider any consumption utility of owning art.

[Please insert Table 5 here]

---

[14] Real estate had a Sharpe Ratio of -0.15 over the period, though this ignores any dividends from consuming housing.

Panel A of Table 5 shows the portfolio weights for the tangency portfolio of stocks and art (i.e., the portfolio with the maximum Sharpe Ratio in the presence of a risk-free asset). An investor who does not correct for selection bias in art returns would want to assign considerable weight to art. Based on the GLS returns, art receives a portfolio weight of 47 percent, with the remainder assigned to stocks. The perceived portfolio Sharpe ratio of 0.31 is 17% higher than the Sharpe Ratio of 0.26 that is achieved with stocks alone, an economically significant improvement. The MCMC index that ignores selection gives weights that are nearly identical to the GLS index, and for brevity we omit them from the portfolio weights tables. The non-selection-corrected indices thus suggest that paintings should play an important role in asset allocation.

In contrast, an investor who corrects for sample selection optimally assigns zero weight to paintings across all selection model specifications, as the diversification benefit from investing in art as an asset class does not outweigh its low Sharpe Ratio. This stark result underscores the importance of correcting for sample selection when making optimal portfolio decisions, as the results can be dramatically different. Had the investor allocated 47% of her portfolio to art, her realized portfolio Sharpe Ratio would be only 0.21, based on the selection-corrected art returns, rather than the 0.26 Sharpe Ratio that she would have earned on an all-stock portfolio, which corresponds to a loss of 18% (this result is not tabulated).

Panels B, C, and D of Table 5 show the portfolio allocations to paintings, stocks, and the risk-free asset for a mean-variance utility investor with a risk aversion coefficient equal to two, five, and ten, respectively. The results are similar to the tangency portfolio results and underscore our main result: an investor who does not correct for sample selection would allocate roughly the same fraction of her portfolio to paintings as to public equity. With the selection correction, the same investor would put all her weight on stocks and Treasuries, and zero weight on paintings. The Sharpe Ratios are naturally the same across all panels of Table 5.

We explore two extensions of the base case scenario. In the first extension we broaden the investment opportunity set of risky assets to include corporate bonds, commodities, and real estate in addition to stocks and art.

[Please insert Table 6 here]

Table 6 shows that the results are similar to the base case. A benchmark portfolio that includes all assets except art earns a Sharpe ratio of 0.41. Adding art to the investment opportunity set would appear to raise the portfolio Sharpe ratio by 0.05 to 0.46, a 13% increase, if selection is ignored. However, with the selection correction the optimal weight on art is again zero, and the optimal portfolio is identical to the benchmark portfolio.

In the second extension we consider whether investing in particular styles of paintings, or in top-selling artists, would be beneficial for forming portfolios. Panel A of Table 7 reports the results when restricting the set of risky assets to stocks and art only. Panel B extends the opportunity set to incorporate corporate bonds, commodities, and real estate. All results in this table are based on the selection-corrected returns.

[Please insert Table 7 here]

Across the two panels, the only style that receives a non-zero portfolio allocation is the Post-war and Contemporary style. Investing in this style and stocks yields a portfolio Sharpe Ratio of 0.28 if we only consider stocks and art (compared to 0.26 for stocks only), and 0.43 if we consider the broader opportunity set (compared to 0.41 for the benchmark portfolio that excludes art). Including the index of the Top 100 artists as a separate asset drives out the allocation to Post-war and Contemporary paintings, while raising the Sharpe Ratio slightly to

0.29 and 0.45 in panels A and B, respectively. Thus, there appears to be a small improvement in performance when considering narrower categories of paintings. Still, we should be careful in drawing strong conclusions from this exercise, as the styles do not show consistent performance relative to each other (as seen in Figure 5), and the Top 100 index is defined rather endogenously: it might not be surprising that the top-selling artists over the sample period outperformed, but it is not obvious that these artists could be identified ex ante.

5.3 Robustness

In this section we show that the zero portfolio allocation to art after selection correction is robust to various measurement and other issues. First, Ang et al. (2013) show that allocation to an illiquid asset is lower when the illiquid nature of the asset is taken into account. For example, using their model and our non-selection-corrected returns, a power utility investor with risk aversion of two allocates 10% of the tangency portfolio to art and 90% to stocks, down from roughly equal allocations. Not surprisingly, the allocation to art after correcting for selection remains at zero for all levels of risk aversion.[15]

Second, if investors have, for example, power utility rather than mean-variance utility, they may care about higher moments of returns such as skewness (e.g. Ball et al., 1995, and Harvey and Siddique, 2000) and kurtosis. However, art returns are negatively skewed and exhibit excess kurtosis (results not tabulated), which only serves to make art less attractive relative to stocks.

Third, there are sizeable transaction costs in the art market: the typical buyer's premium in art is up to 17.5 percent of the hammer price, and on top of that there are storage and insurance

---

[15] We thank Andrew Ang, Dimitris Papanikolaou, and Mark Westerfield for generously sharing their code for the portfolio optimization problem in their paper.

fees. These costs make paintings less appealing for optimal portfolio allocation and hence reinforce our main result.

In other robustness tests, we confirm robustness to the choices we made regarding assets and methodology. As an alternative to unsmoothing the art returns, we correct for non-synchronous trading using Dimson's (1979) method with one year leads and lags of stock returns. Our main result holds: correcting for sample selection, an investor would optimally not invest in art. We also reran the portfolio allocations without unsmoothing the returns (i.e., using the original index returns). Without unsmoothing, the volatility of art returns is lower and the correlation of art with stocks is closer to zero. This makes art more attractive as an investment, but after controlling for sample selection we find that there is still virtually no gain in the Sharpe Ratio when including art in the investor's opportunity set.

Next, we take a U.S.-centric approach and use the value-weighted or the equally-weighted CRSP index (both including distributions) or the S&P composite index instead of the MSCI world total return index. The correlation between art and U.S. stock returns is around 0.09, considerably lower than the 0.32 correlation with global stock returns, making art more attractive for diversification to an investor with a U.S. focus. For comparison, Renneboog and Spaenjers (2013) find a correlation coefficient of -0.03 between art and the S&P 500 index, and Taylor and Coleman (2011) find a negative correlation (of about -0.30) between Australian stocks and aboriginal art. Our finding underscores that art is truly a global asset and its return is more closely linked to the global economy than to the U.S. economy. Still, despite the lower correlation with U.S. stocks, our main result carries through, and investors correcting for sample selection optimally forego investing in art.

Finally, our portfolio allocation result is also robust to using the longer 1926 to 2010 period to estimate the average market return and its standard deviation (computing the covariance with art from the correlation over the 1972 to 2010 period but using the standard deviation from the longer time series)[16], to using the return to the Citigroup World Government Bond Index instead of the one-year T-bill rate as the risk-free asset, and to using logarithmic rather than arithmetic returns.

6. Conclusion

We estimate an empirical model that adjusts for selection bias in illiquid asset markets with endogenous trading, using a large dataset of auction sales of paintings. We find a large selection effect of the kind hypothesized by Goetzmann (1993, 1996), namely that paintings that have increased in value are more likely to sell. This has a first-order impact on art indices, lowering the average annual price increase from 10 percent for a standard repeat sales index to 6.5 percent for selection-corrected indices, and resulting in a drop in annual Sharpe Ratios from 0.24 to 0.04.

If passive index investors ignore the sample selection problem, they would allocate roughly equal fractions of their portfolios to art and stocks, and they would appear to reap large portfolio Sharpe Ratios on the order of 0.31 annually, or 17% more than the 0.26 Sharpe Ratio on a portfolio of stocks only. However, this strategy turns out to hurt them as they in fact reap Sharpe Ratios that are 18% lower than what they would earn on a portfolio of only stocks, once sample selection is accounted for. In summary, the diversification benefits of art do not outweigh its lower Sharpe Ratio. Our results show that investors should optimally forego investing in paintings, even without considering transaction and insurance costs, and the risks of forgeries,

---

[16] For the 1926 to 2010 period we use the CRSP stock return index (including distributions) and the one-month T-bill rate to compute excess market returns, as the MSCI world index is only available starting 1969, and the one-year T-bill rate is only available starting 1959.

thefts, and physical damage, unless they are able to pick winners or there is substantial non-monetary utility from owning and enjoying art. This result is robust to considering a broader investment opportunity set that includes corporate bonds, commodities, and real estate, as well as to considering the effects of illiquidity and higher moments of art returns on optimal portfolio allocations.

To our knowledge, this is the first paper to show the importance of the endogenous trading sample selection problem for performance evaluation and optimal portfolio allocation. It stands to reason that other illiquid asset classes exhibit a similar selection problem, and evaluating the returns to these other asset classes is an important task for future work.

References

Adam, G., 2008. When Brueghel met Schnabel. *Financial Times* (21-04-2008).

Ang, A., Papanikolaou, D., and Westerfield, M., 2013. Portfolio choice with illiquid assets. *Working paper*, Columbia University, Northwestern University and University of Washington.

Ashenfelter, O. and Graddy, K., 2003. Auctions and the price of art. *Journal of Economic Literature* 41, 763-786.

Bailey, M.J., Muth, R.F., and Nourse, H.O., 1963, A regression method for real estate price index construction. *Journal of the American Statistical Association* 58, 933–942.

Ball, R., Kothari, S.P., and Shanken, J., 1995, Problems in measuring portfolio performance: An application to contrarian investment strategies. *Journal of Financial Economics* 38, 79-107.

Ben-David, I., and Hirschleifer, D., 2012. Are investors really reluctant to realize their losses? Trading responses to past returns and the disposition effect. *Review of Financial Studies* 25, 2485-2532.

Buelens, N. and Ginsburgh, V., 1993. Revisiting Baumol's "Art as a floating crap game". *European Economic Review* 37, 1351-1371.

Case, K.E., Pollakowski, H.O., and Wachter, S.M., 1997. Frequency of transaction and house price modeling. *Journal of Real Estate Finance and Economics* 14, 173-187.

Case, K.E. and Shiller, R.J., 1987, Prices of single family homes since 1970: New indexes for four cities. *New England Economic Review Sept/Oct*, 46–56.

Campbell, R.A.J., 2008. Art Finance. In: Fabozzi, F.J., Handbook of Finance: Financial Markets and Instruments, pp. 605-610, John Wiley & Sons, New Jersey.

Clapham, E., Englund, P., Quigley, J.M., and Redfearn, C.L., 2006, Revisiting the past and settling the score: Index revisions for house price derivatives, *Real Estate Economics* 34, 275–302.

Dimson, E., 1979. Risk measurement and infrequent trading. *Journal of Financial Economics* 7, 197-226.

Dimson, E., and Spaenjers, C., 2011. Ex post: The investment performance of collectible stamps. *Journal of Financial Economics* 100, 443-458.

Geltner, D.M., 1991. Smoothing in appraisal-based returns. *Journal of Real Estate Finance and Economics* 4, 327-345.

Genesove, D., and Mayer, C., 2001. Loss aversion and seller behavior: Evidence from the housing market. *Quarterly Journal of Economics* 116, 1233-1260.

Goetzmann, W., 1992. The accuracy of real estate indices: Repeat sales estimators. *Journal of Real Estate Finance and Economics* 5, 5-53.

Goetzmann, W., 1993. Accounting for taste: Art and financial markets over three centuries. *American Economic Review* 83, 1370-1376.

Goetzmann, W., 1996. How costly is the fall from fashion? Survivorship bias in the painting market. In *Economics of the Arts: Selected Essays.* Vol. 237, Contributions to Economic Analysis, ed. Victor A. Ginsburgh and Pierre-Michel Menger, 71–84. New York: Elsevier.

Goetzmann, W., and Peng, L., 2002. The bias of the RSR estimator and the accuracy of some alternatives. *Real Estate Economics* 30, 13-39.

Goetzmann, W., Renneboog, L., and Spaenjers, C., 2011. Art and money. *American Economic Review* 101, 222-226.

Harvey, C.R., and Siddique, A., 2000, Conditional skewness in asset pricing tests. *Journal of Finance* 55, 1263-1295.

Heckman, J., 1979, Sample selection bias as a specification error. *Econometrica* 47, 153-162.

Heckman, J., 1990, Varieties of selection bias. *American Economic Review* 80, 313-318.

Hiraki, T., Ito, A., Spieth, D.A., and Takezawa, N., 2009, How did Japanese investments influence international art prices? *Journal of Financial and Quantitative Analysis* 44, 1489-1514.

Korteweg, A., and Sorensen, M., 2010. Risk and return characteristics of venture capital-backed entrepreneurial companies. *Review of Financial Studies* 23, 3738-3772.

Korteweg, A., and Sorensen, M., 2013. Estimating loan-to-value distributions. *Working paper*, Stanford University and Columbia University.

Mei, J. and Moses, M., 2002. Art as an investment and the underperformance of masterpieces. *American Economic Review* 92, 1656-1668.

Mei, J. and Moses, M., 2005. Vested interest and biased price estimates: Evidence from an auction market. *Journal of Finance* 60, 2409-2435.

Odean, T., 1998. Are investors reluctant to realize their losses? *Journal of Finance* 53, 1775-1798.

Pénasse, J., Renneboog, L., and Spaenjers, C., 2013. Speculative dynamics and sentiment in the art market. *Working paper*, ESSEC Business School.

Pesando, J.E., 1993. Art as an investment: The market for modern prints. *American Economic Review* 83, 1075-1089.

Pownall, R., Satchell, S., and Srivastava, N., 2013. A random walk through Mayfair: Dynamic models of UK art market prices and their dependence on UK equity prices. *Working paper*, Maastricht University and University of Cambridge.

Renneboog, L., and Spaenjers, C., 2013. Buying beauty: On prices and returns in the art market. *Management Science* 59, 36-53.

Schwert, G.W., 1990. Indexes of U.S. stock prices from 1802 to 1987. *Journal of Business* 63, 399-442.

Shiller, R.J., 1991, Arithmetic repeat sales price estimators, *Journal of Housing Economics* 1, 110-126.

Shiller, R.J., 2009, *Irrational Exuberance*, 2nd ed., Princeton University Press, Princeton, NJ.

Taylor, D., and Coleman, L., 2011. Price determinants of Aboriginal art, and its role as an alternative asset class. *Journal of Banking and Finance* 35, 1519-1529.

Wood, C., 1992. The Bubble Economy. The Japanese Economic Collapse. London: Sidgwick & Jackson.

Working, H., 1960. Note on the correlation of first differences of averages in a random chain. *Econometrica* 28, 916-918.

Figure 1: Number of sales

This figure shows the number of auction sales of paintings in the repeat sales sample (panel A) and the full sample (panel B) by calendar year. In the repeat sales sample in panel A, we distinguish between the first, second, and third or more sales of an artwork.

Panel A: Repeat sales sample

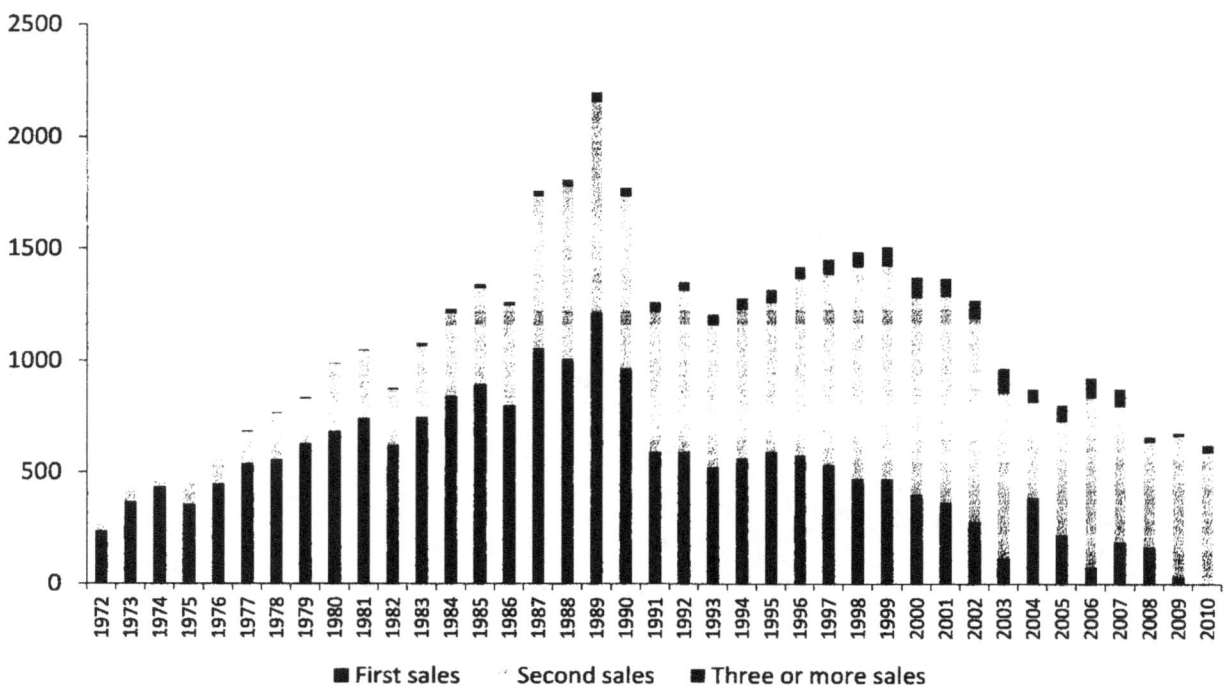

■ First sales   Second sales   ■ Three or more sales

Panel B: Full sample

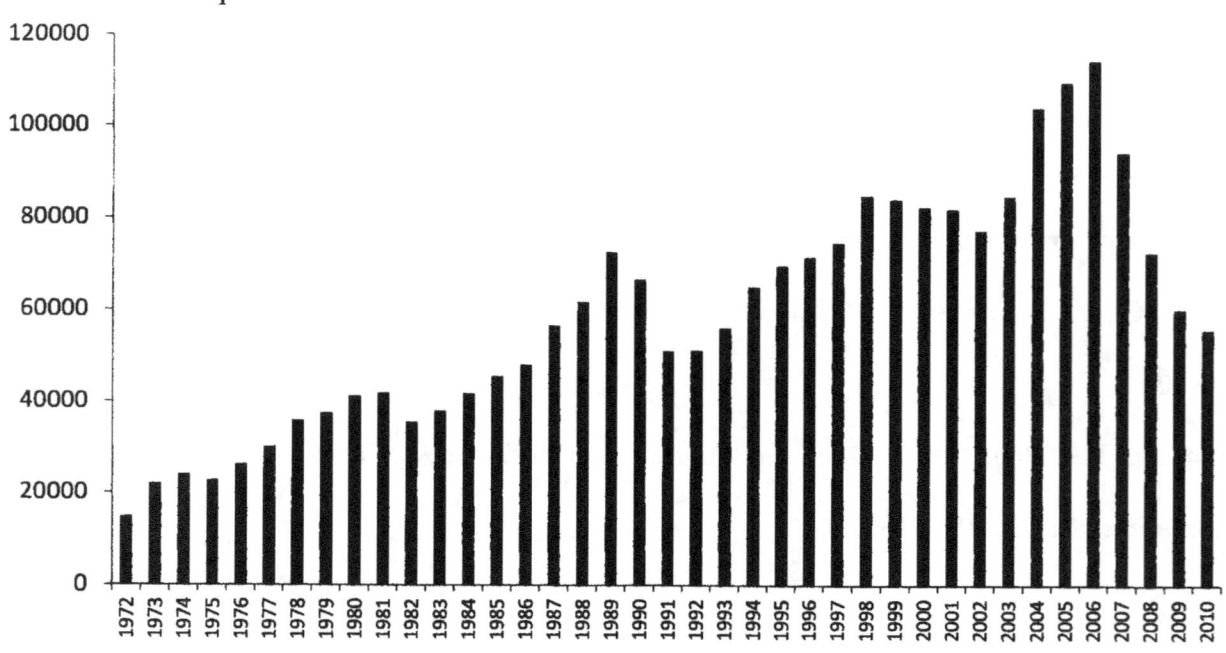

Figure 2: Annualized sale-to-sale return distribution

This figure shows histograms of the annualized sale-to-sale returns of paintings in the repeat sales sample. Panel A shows the annualized arithmetic sale-to-sale returns, and Panel B shows the natural logarithm of the annualized sale-to-sale returns.

Panel A: Arithmetic returns

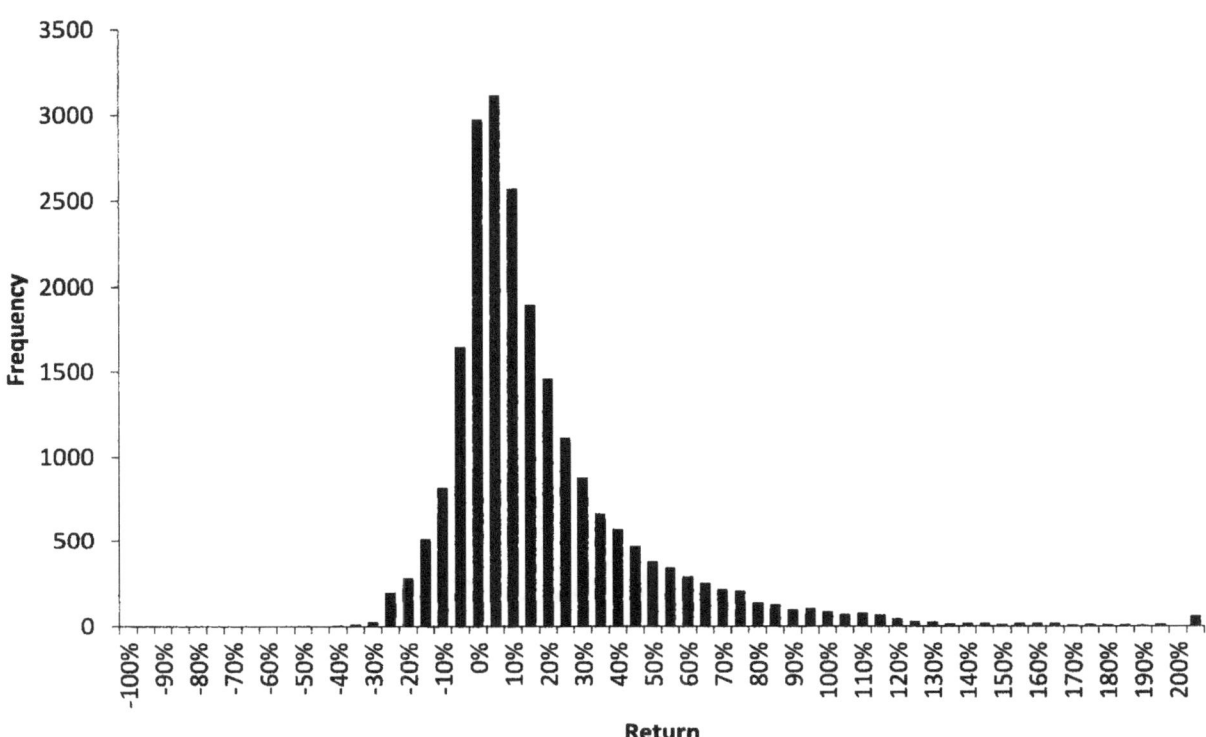

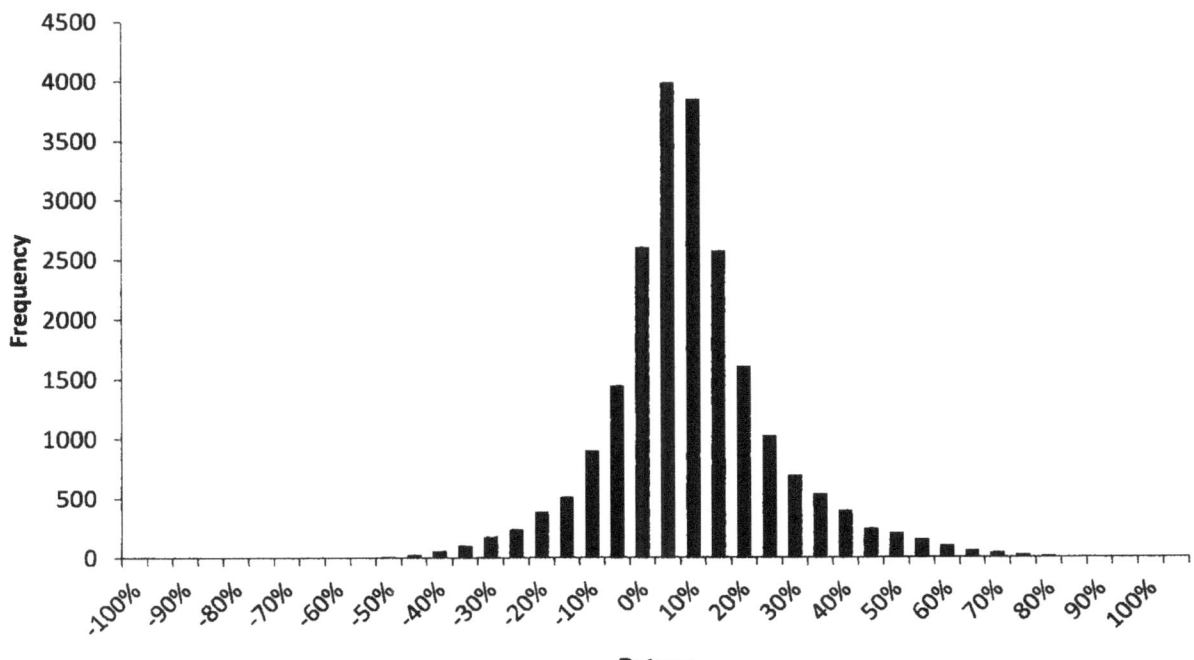

Figure 3: Non-selection-corrected price indices

This figure shows repeat sales arithmetic price indices that do not correct for sample selection. The indices are normalized to an index value of 100 in 1972. The *GLS* index is the standard repeat sales regression indices as estimated by generalized least squares, with weights that are inverse proportional to the square root of the time between sales. The *MCMC* index is the index estimated by the Markov chain Monte Carlo algorithm when the sample selection problem is forcibly ignored, i.e., α_r in equation (3) is set to zero.

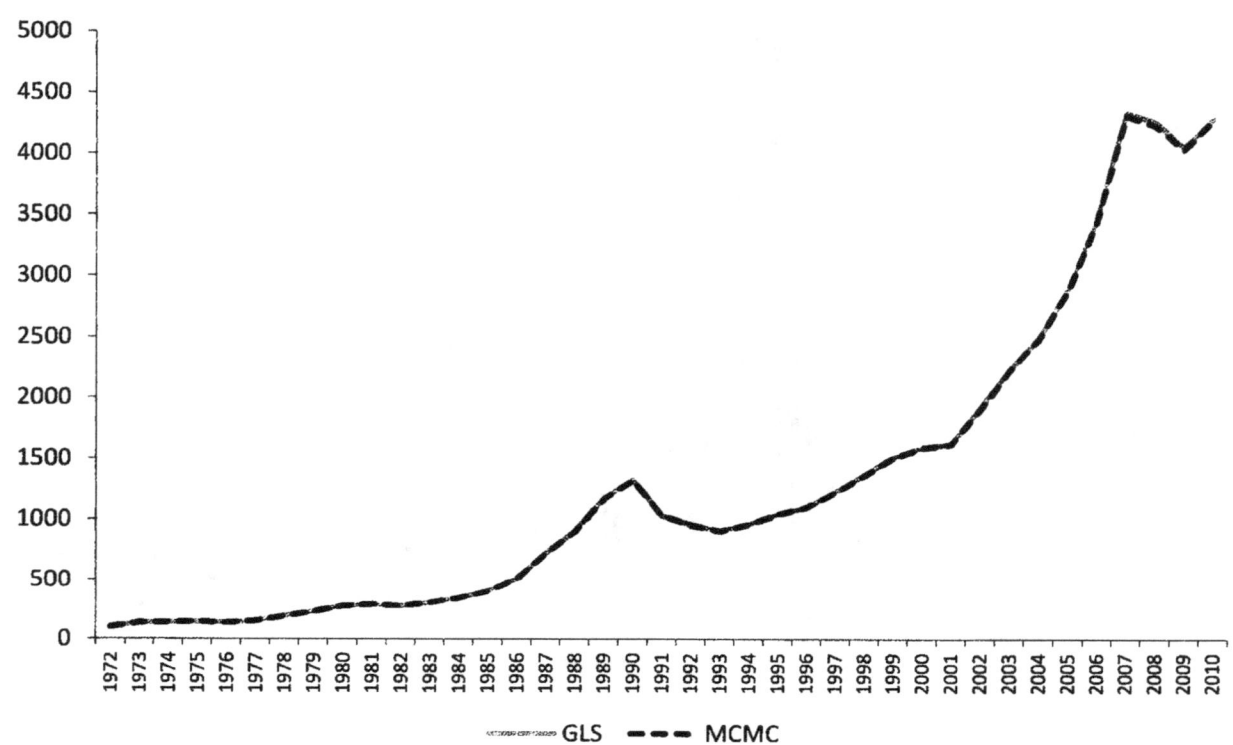

Figure 4: Selection-corrected price indices

Panel A shows price indices corrected for sample selection, and normalized to an index value of 100 in 1972. Models A through C correspond to the specifications of the selection equation as shown in Table 2. For comparison, the figure also shows the MCMC non-selection-corrected index over this same period (denoted *No selection*. This is the same index as the *MCMC* index in Figure 3). Panel B graphs the difference between the natural logarithm of the *No selection* index and the selection-corrected indices.

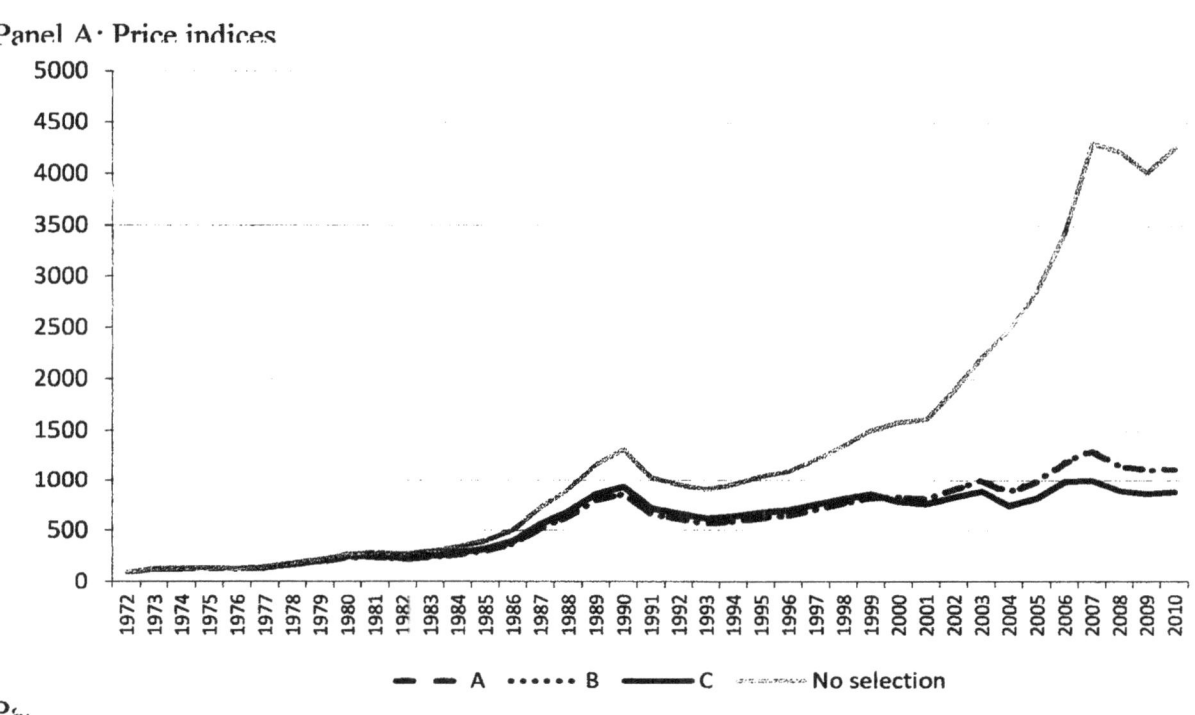

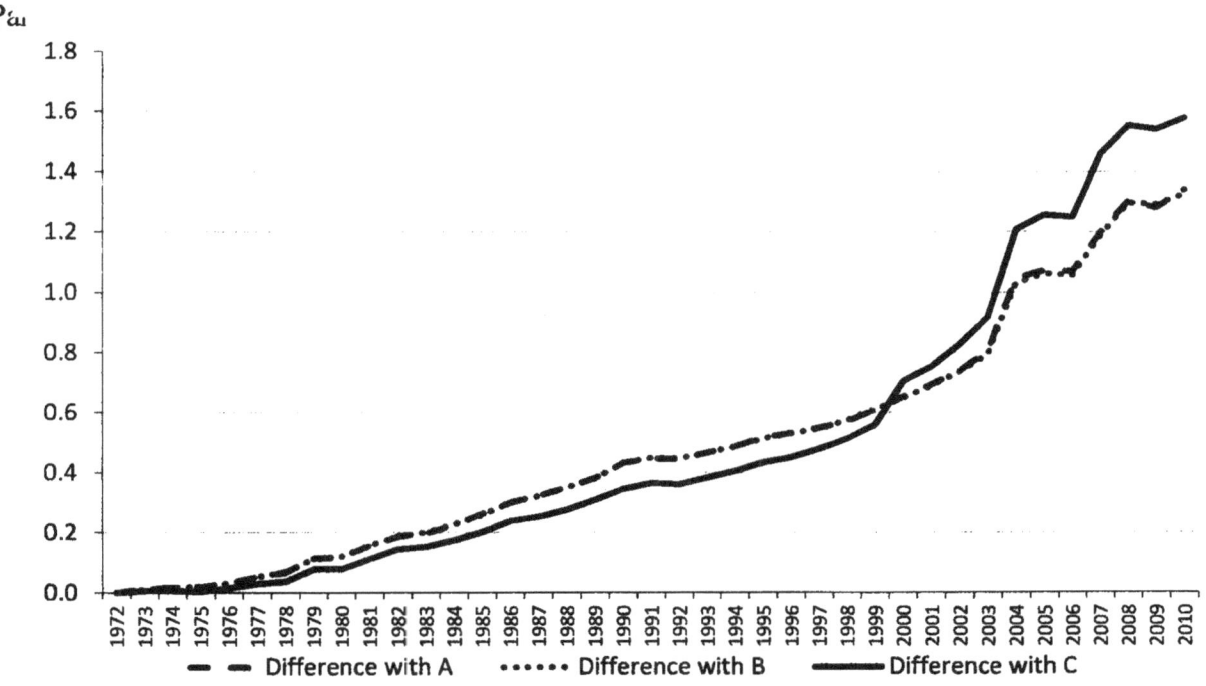

Figure 5: Selection-corrected price indices per style

This figure shows selection-corrected price indices for each style classification, normalized to an index value of 100 in 1972. *Top 100* refers to the index of paintings by top 100 artists based on the total value of sales (in U.S. dollars) of all paintings by the artist over the sample period.

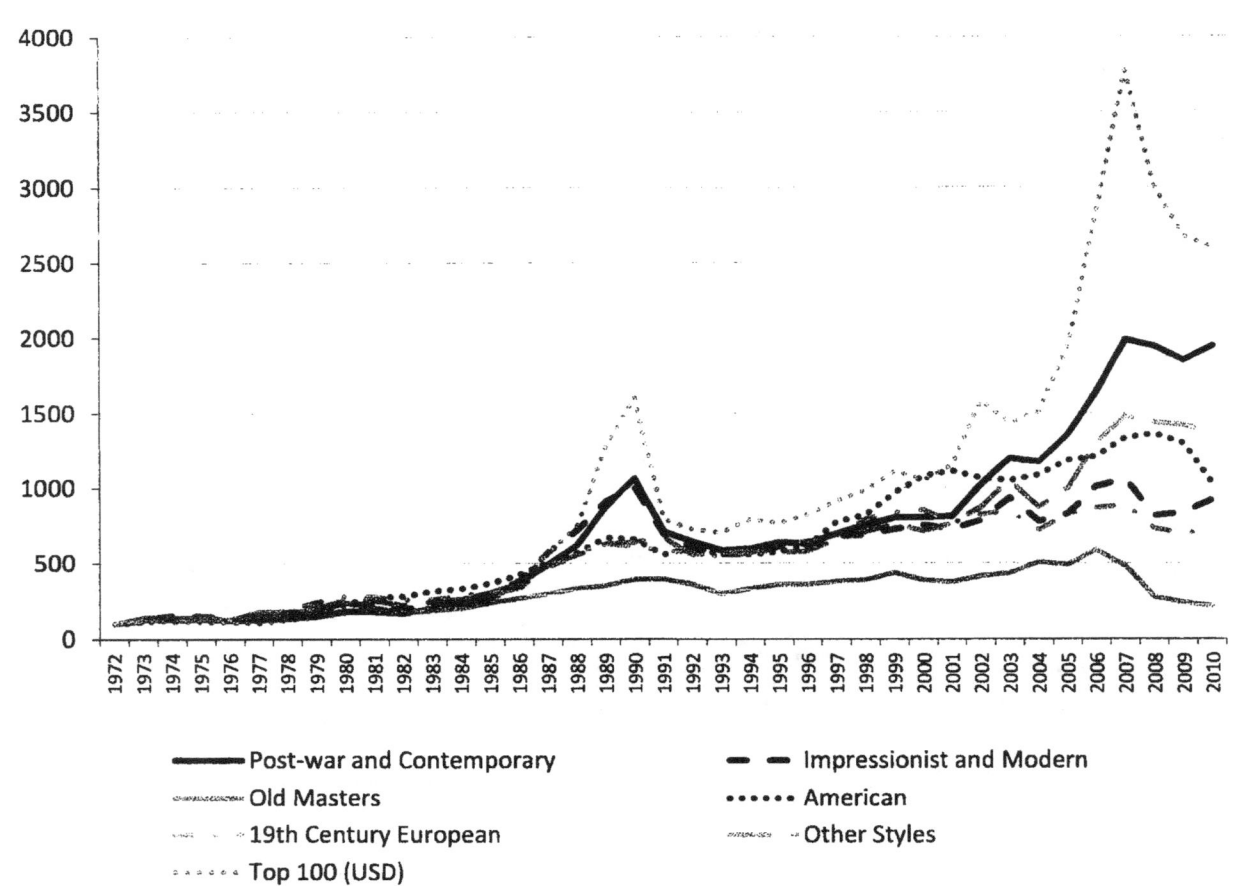

Figure 6: Annualized sale-to-sale returns by return horizon

This figure shows the relation between the annualized log sale-to-sale returns (on the left-hand vertical axis) and the time between sales (in years, on the horizontal axis) in the repeat sales data. The solid and striped lines represent the average and the median annualized log return between observed sales, respectively. The vertical bars are the number of observations in each bin, measured on the right-hand vertical axis.

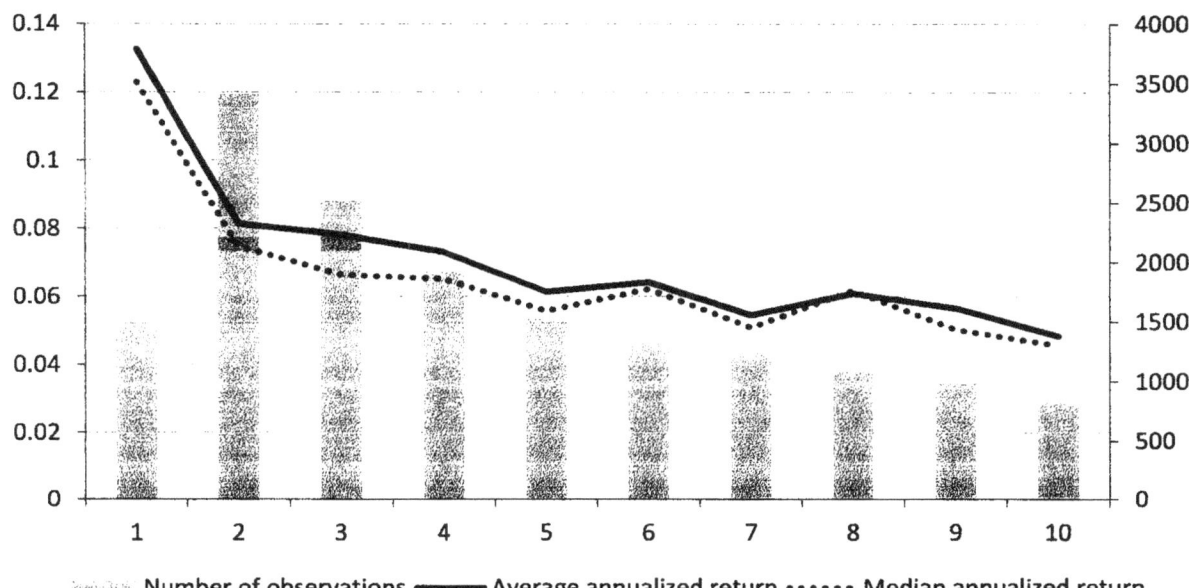

Figure 7: Time series of annualized returns and trading intensity

This figure graphs the time series of the average annualized log sale-to-sale returns (represented on the left-hand vertical axis) and trading intensity (on the right-hand axis). The average log sale-to-sale return is computed over consecutive sales of paintings for which the second sale falls in the given year. Trading intensity is calculated as the number of sales in a calendar year as a percentage of all sales over the 1980 to 2010 period.

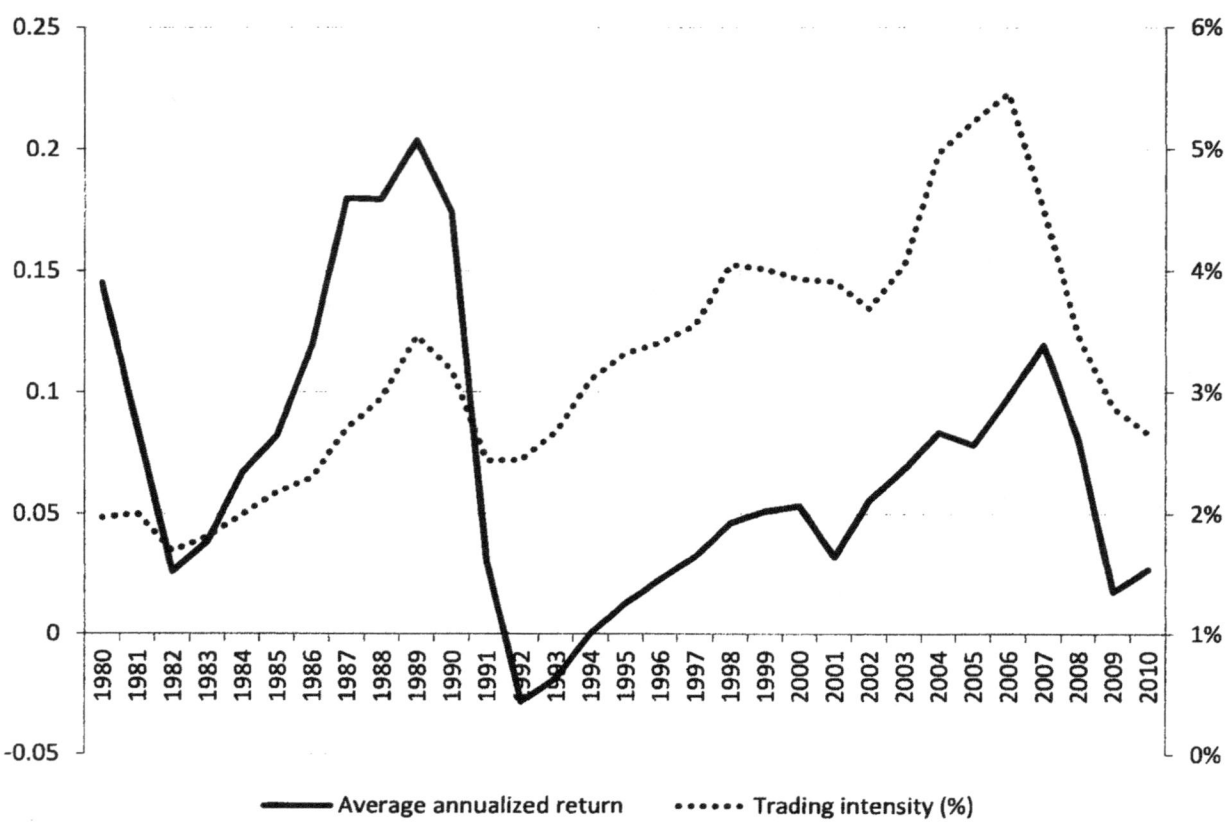

Table 1: Summary statistics

This table reports summary statistics for the sample of paintings in the Blouin Art Sales Index (BASI) dataset from 1972 to 2010. Panel A presents descriptive statistics for the repeat sales sample that contains paintings that sold at least twice during the sample period (left columns), and the full BASI dataset (right columns). The unit of observation is a sale of a painting at auction. *Hammer price* is the auction price in thousands of U.S. dollars. *Surface* is the surface of the painting in thousands of squared millimetres. *Deceased < 2 yrs* is a dummy variable equal to one when the sale occurs within two years after the artist deceases, and zero otherwise. *Christie's* and *Sotheby's* are dummy variables that equal one if the painting is auctioned at Christie's or Sotheby's, respectively, and *London* and *New York* are dummy variables that equal one if the painting is auctioned in London or New York, respectively. *Top 100 Artists* is a dummy variable equal to one when the artist is in the top 100 in terms of total value of sales (in U.S. dollars) over 1972 to 2010, and zero otherwise. The remaining variables in Panel A represent style classifications. The last column shows *t*-statistics for difference in means tests (for Hammer price and Surface) and *z*-statistics for difference in proportions tests (for the other variables) between the full and the repeat sales samples. The sale-to-sale returns in Panel B are for the repeat sales sample only, and calculated as the natural logarithm of the ratio of the current and prior hammer price of a painting. ***, ** and * indicate statistical significance at the 1, 5 and 10 percent level, respectively.

Panel A. Descriptive statistics for the full and repeat sales sample

	Repeat sales sample (42,548 sales)			Full sample (2,302,738 sales)			Difference statistic
	Mean	Median	St. Dev.	Mean	Median	St. Dev.	
Hammer price ($000s)	61.9	6.2	444.2	28.6	3.0	395.5	-15.39***
Surface	546.9	331.0	792.1	491.8	306.5	811.8	-14.19***
Deceased < 2yrs	2.12%			1.59%			-8.71***
Christie's	21.54%			15.57%			-33.59***
Sotheby's	25.46%			15.82%			-53.75***
London	19.47%			14.15%			-31.07***
New York	21.12%			9.75%			-77.66***
Top 100 Artists	9.62%			2.77%			-83.52***
Post-war and Contemporary	15.81%			11.75%			-25.69***
Impressionist and Modern	34.03%			22.32%			-57.29***
Old Masters	5.32%			9.87%			31.26***
American	11.57%			7.29%			-33.47***
European 19th Century	23.83%			31.28%			32.89***
Other Style	9.44%			17.49%			43.46***

Panel B. Sale-to-sale returns for the repeat sales sample (22,010 returns for 20,538 paintings)			
	Mean	Median	St. Dev.
Sale-to-sale return			
Arithmetic return	123.50%	42.37%	368.54%
Log return	43.94%	35.33%	78.08%
Years between sales	7.61	5.55	6.28
Annualized sale-to-sale return			
Arithmetic return	16.50%	7.53%	32.68%
Log return	6.90%	5.65%	16.69%

Table 2: Selection equation coefficients

This table presents the parameter estimates of three specifications of the selection equation (equation (3) in the text). *Log return* is the natural logarithm of the return since the prior sale of a painting. *Time* is the time in years since the prior sale. *Log surface* is the natural logarithm of the painting's surface in thousands of mm^2. *World GDP growth* is the yearly increase in worldwide GDP, obtained from Historical Statistics of the World Economy. The other variables are as defined in Table 1. *Sigma* is the standard deviation of the error term in equation (1). Standard errors are in parentheses. ***, ** and * indicate statistical significance at the 1, 5 and 10% level.

	A	B	C
Log return	0.375***	0.372***	
	(0.008)	(0.008)	
1972-1989			0.300***
			(0.014)
1990-1999			0.278***
			(0.009)
2000-2006			0.581***
			(0.013)
2007-2010			0.772***
			(0.027)
Time (yrs)	-0.401***	-0.033***	-0.022***
	(0.019)	(0.002)	(0.002)
Time squared	0.090***	0.001***	0.000***
	(0.009)	(0.000)	(0.000)
Log surface		0.005	0.002
		(0.007)	(0.008)
Deceased < 2yrs		0.104***	0.094***
		(0.031)	(0.031)
World GDP growth		-1.008***	-1.273***
		(0.253)	(0.309)
Intercept	-1.517***	-1.512***	
	(0.007)	(0.042)	
1972-1989			-1.487***
			(0.044)
1990-1999			-1.490***
			(0.044)
2000-2006			-1.518***
			(0.045)
2007-2010			-1.660***
			(0.046)
Sigma	0.282***	0.282***	0.288***
	(0.001)	(0.001)	(0.001)

Table 3: Relation between annualized returns and market shares by style

Panel A shows the correlation between the yearly market share of each style and the mean (left column) and median (right column) annualized log sale-to-sale return for the style, computed over the returns for which the second sale falls in the given year. The market share of a specific style is the total sales of this style in a given year relative to all sales in that year, calculated from the full BASI dataset. Panel B shows the coefficients of a regression of the yearly style market shares on the annualized sale-to-sale returns by style, and dummy variables representing the styles (*Other Style* is the omitted variable). Standard errors are in parentheses. ***, ** and * indicate statistical significance at the 1, 5 and 10% level, respectively.

Panel A. Correlation coefficients between market shares and returns per style

	Mean annualized sale-to-sale return	Median annualized sale-to-sale return
Post-war and Contemporary	0.235	0.257
Impressionist and Modern	0.411	0.426
Old Masters	0.083	-0.053
American	0.391	0.467
European 19th Century	0.224	0.295
Other Style	-0.080	-0.178
Top 100 Artists	0.373	0.296

Panel B. Regression analysis (Dependent variable = Yearly market share by style)

	I	II
Mean annualized sale-to-sale return	0.116***	
	(0.035)	
Median annualized sale-to-sale return		0.130***
		(0.034)
Post-war and Contemporary dummy	0.069***	0.069***
	(0.009)	(0.009)
Impressionist and Modern dummy	0.240***	0.240***
	(0.009)	(0.009)
Old Masters dummy	-0.033***	-0.033***
	(0.009)	(0.009)
American dummy	0.019**	0.019**
	(0.009)	(0.009)
European 19th Century dummy	0.145***	0.144***
	(0.009)	(0.009)
Top 100 Artists dummy	-0.001	-0.001
	(0.009)	(0.009)
Intercept	0.086***	0.087***
	(0.007)	(0.007)
Adjusted R^2	83.7%	83.7%
Number of observations	264	264

Table 4: Descriptive statistics of annual index returns

Panel A reports descriptive statistics of the annual arithmetic returns to indices of paintings and other assets over the period 1973 to 2010. *GLS* is the standard repeat sales index of paintings as estimated by generalized least squares. The *MCMC* index is the non-selection-corrected index from our Markov chain Monte Carlo estimator. The selection-corrected art indices *A* through *C* are as described in Table 2. All art returns are unsmoothed using the Geltner (1991) method. *Stocks* is the MSCI world total return index including distributions. *Corporate bonds* is the Merrill Lynch US Corporate Master Bond index. *Commodities* is the GSCI Commodity total return index for commodity futures. *Real estate* is the U.S. residential real estate index from Shiller (2009). *Treasuries* are one-year U.S. Treasury bills. The *Sharpe Ratio* is annualized. Panel B reports correlation coefficients between excess returns on the various art indices and the other assets. ***, ** and * indicate statistical significance at the 1, 5 and 10% level, respectively.

Panel A. Descriptive statistics of annual returns

	Mean	St. dev.	Sharpe Ratio
Returns on non-selection-corrected art indices:			
GLS	10.08%	16.70%	0.235
MCMC	10.07%	16.85%	0.232
Returns on selection-corrected art indices:			
A	6.53%	12.83%	0.035
B	6.57%	12.83%	0.038
C	5.95%	13.00%	-0.012
Returns on other assets:			
Stocks	10.95%	18.49%	0.261
Corporate bonds	8.94%	8.75%	0.332
Commodities	10.21%	23.44%	0.175
Real estate	5.03%	6.66%	-0.150
Treasuries	6.09%	3.38%	-

Panel B. Correlation coefficient between annual excess returns on art and other assets

Art	Stocks	Corporate bonds	Commodities	Real estate
GLS	0.327**	-0.189	0.367**	0.397**
MCMC	0.341**	-0.185	0.364**	0.403**
A	0.324*	-0.250	0.354**	0.357**
B	0.326**	-0.246	0.358**	0.360**
C	0.317*	-0.269*	0.275*	0.300*

Table 5: Optimal asset allocation between art and stocks

Panel A shows the mean-variance tangency portfolio weights on paintings (using the non-selection-corrected GLS index, and the selection-corrected indices A, B, and C from Table 2) and stocks (the MSCI world total return index including distributions). Panels B, C and D show the optimal weights for a one-period mean-variance utility investor with risk aversion (γ) equal to two, five, and ten, respectively, where one-year Treasuries are the risk-free asset. Short sales and borrowing are not allowed. Returns are measured over 1973 to 2010. Sharpe Ratios are annualized.

	GLS	Selection-corrected		
		A	B	C
Panel A. Tangency portfolio weights				
Paintings	0.470	0	0	0
Stocks	0.530	1	1	1
Sharpe Ratio	0.305	0.261	0.261	0.261
Panel B. Mean-variance utility, risk aversion $\gamma = 2$				
Paintings	0.470	0	0	0
Stocks	0.530	0.706	0.706	0.706
Treasuries	0	0.294	0.294	0.294
Sharpe Ratio	0.305	0.261	0.261	0.261
Panel C. Mean-variance utility, risk aversion $\gamma = 5$				
Paintings	0.208	0	0	0
Stocks	0.225	0.284	0.284	0.284
Treasuries	0.566	0.716	0.716	0.716
Sharpe Ratio	0.305	0.261	0.261	0.261
Panel D. Mean-variance utility, risk aversion $\gamma = 10$				
Paintings	0.104	0	0	0
Stocks	0.113	0.142	0.142	0.142
Treasuries	0.783	0.858	0.858	0.858
Sharpe Ratio	0.305	0.261	0.261	0.261

Table 6: Optimal asset allocation between art and other assets

Panel A shows the mean-variance tangency portfolio weights on art (using the non-selection-corrected GLS index, and the selection-corrected indices A, B, and C from Table 2) and other assets (as defined in Table 4). The *Benchmark* portfolio leaves art out of the opportunity set. Panels B, C and D show the optimal weights for a one-period mean-variance utility investor with risk aversion (γ) equal to two, five, and ten, respectively. Short sales and borrowing are not allowed. Returns are measured over 1973 to 2010. Sharpe Ratios are annualized.

	Benchmark	GLS	Selection-corrected A	Selection-corrected B	Selection-corrected C
Panel A. Tangency portfolio weights					
Paintings	-	0.231	0	0	0
Corporate bonds	0.692	0.677	0.692	0.692	0.692
Commodities	0.164	0.073	0.164	0.164	0.164
Real estate	0	0	0	0	0
Stocks	0.144	0.018	0.144	0.144	0.144
Sharpe Ratio	0.409	0.461	0.409	0.409	0.409
Panel B. Mean-variance utility, risk aversion $\gamma = 2$					
Paintings	-	0.222	0	0	0
Corporate bonds	0.441	0.392	0.441	0.441	0.441
Commodities	0.210	0.127	0.210	0.210	0.210
Real estate	0	0	0	0	0
Stocks	0.350	0.259	0.350	0.350	0.350
Treasuries	0	0	0	0	0
Sharpe Ratio	0.380	0.409	0.380	0.380	0.380
Panel C. Mean-variance utility, risk aversion $\gamma = 5$					
Paintings	-	0.243	0	0	0
Corporate bonds	0.674	0.620	0.674	0.674	0.674
Commodities	0.169	0.083	0.169	0.169	0.169
Real estate	0	0	0	0	0
Stocks	0.155	0.055	0.155	0.155	0.155
Treasuries	0.001	0	0.001	0.001	0.001
Sharpe Ratio	0.409	0.458	0.409	0.409	0.409
Panel D. Mean-variance utility, risk aversion $\gamma = 10$					
Paintings	-	0.163	0	0	0
Corporate bonds	0.333	0.440	0.333	0.333	0.333
Commodities	0.084	0.050	0.084	0.084	0.084
Real estate	0	0	0	0	0
Stocks	0.078	0.014	0.078	0.078	0.078
Treasuries	0.506	0.333	0.506	0.506	0.506
Sharpe Ratio	0.409	0.461	0.409	0.409	0.409

Table 7: Optimal asset allocation to painting styles

This table shows mean-variance tangency portfolio weights (in the column *Tang ptf*), and optimal weights on paintings of different styles, for a one-period mean-variance utility investor with risk aversion γ. Painting styles are as described in the text, and the assets are described in Table 4. *Top 100 Artists* is based on total value of sales over the sample period. Short sales and borrowing are not allowed. Returns are over 1973 to 2010. Sharpe Ratios are annualized.

Panel A. Painting styles and stocks only

	Tang ptf	Risk aversion (γ) 2	5	10	Tang ptf	Risk aversion (γ) 2	5	10
Post-war and Contemporary	0.306	0.289	0.117	0.058	0	0	0	0
Impressionist and Modern	0	0	0	0	0	0	0	0
Old Masters	0	0	0	0	0	0	0	0
American	0	0	0	0	0	0	0	0
European 19th Century	0	0	0	0	0	0	0	0
Other Styles	0	0	0	0	0	0	0	0
Top 100 Artists	-	-	-	-	0.276	0.240	0.094	0.048
Stocks	0.694	0.656	0.618	0.133	0.725	0.651	0.260	0.130
Treasuries	-	0.052	0.278	0.810	-	0.110	0.646	0.822
Sharpe Ratio	0.278	0.278	0.278	0.278	0.292	0.292	0.292	0.292

Panel B. Painting styles and all assets

	Tang ptf	Risk aversion (γ) 2	5	10	Tang ptf	Risk aversion (γ) 2	5	10
Post-war and Contemporary	0.033	0	0.067	0.030	0	0	0	0
Impressionist and Modern	0	0	0	0	0	0	0	0
Old Masters	0	0	0	0	0	0	0	0
American	0.075	0	0	0.012	0.052	0	0	0
European 19th Century	0	0	0	0	0	0	0	0
Other Styles	0.107	0	0.063	0.070	0.064	0	0.012	0.043
Top 100 Artists	-	-	-	-	0.082	0.134	0.108	0.053
Corporate bonds	0.644	0.441	0.623	0.399	0.670	0.418	0.653	0.400
Commodities	0.098	0.210	0.133	0.075	0.090	0.151	0.119	0.069
Real estate	0	0	0	0	0	0	0	0
Stocks	0.042	0.350	0.113	0.043	0.044	0.297	0.108	0.043
Treasuries	-	0	0	0.371	-	0	0	0.392
Sharpe Ratio	0.432	0.380	0.424	0.432	0.448	0.402	0.443	0.448

American Economic Association

Sale Rates and Price Movements in Art Auctions
Author(s): Orley Ashenfelter and Kathryn Graddy
Source: *The American Economic Review*, Vol. 101, No. 3, PAPERS AND PROCEEDINGS OF THE One Hundred Twenty Third Annual Meeting OF THE AMERICAN ECONOMIC ASSOCIATION (MAY 2011), pp. 212-216
Published by: American Economic Association
Stable URL: http://www.jstor.org/stable/29783741
Accessed: 05/02/2014 12:35

Your use of the JSTOR archive indicates your acceptance of the Terms & Conditions of Use, available at
http://www.jstor.org/page/info/about/policies/terms.jsp

JSTOR is a not-for-profit service that helps scholars, researchers, and students discover, use, and build upon a wide range of content in a trusted digital archive. We use information technology and tools to increase productivity and facilitate new forms of scholarship. For more information about JSTOR, please contact support@jstor.org.

American Economic Association is collaborating with JSTOR to digitize, preserve and extend access to *The American Economic Review.*

ECONOMICS OF THE ARTS[†]

Sale Rates and Price Movements in Art Auctions

By Orley Ashenfelter and Kathryn Graddy*

While much attention has been given to studying price movements in the art market, little attention has been given to studying sale rates.[1] Because of the presence of sellers' reserve prices, not all items that are put up for sale are sold. The variability in sale rates provides a quantity signal that plays a large role in public discussions of the current state of the art market. In this regard art markets, where the products on sale display considerable heterogeneity, are similar to housing and labor markets, where quantity signals also play an important role in discussions of the state of the market. An understanding of sale rates, as measured by the number of items that actually change hands as a proportion of items that are put up for sale, shows how quantity signals are formed even in the purest form of auction market transaction.

Sellers of individual art works usually set a confidential reserve price, and if the bidding does not reach this level, the items will go unsold. An item that has not been sold may be put up for sale at a later auction, sold elsewhere, or taken off the market. We begin our study by looking in detail at sale rates, prices, and unexpected price movements. Unexpected price movements are defined as the average percentage difference between the sale price and the presale estimate as produced by auction house experts and published in the presale catalogue. We show that sale rates have shown no discernible trend or consistent correlations with current price levels, but that sale rates and unexpected price movements have a strong visible relationship, despite the efforts of auctioneers to produce accurate estimates.

The confidential reserve price is commonly thought to be related to an auctioneer's presale estimated price. Indeed, the convention in art auctions is that the reserve price is set at or below the auctioneer's low estimate. We use this relationship to interpret our graphical relationship between sale rates and unexpected price movements. Using a dataset on contemporary art in which we have prices for sold items and high bids for unsold items, we estimate the average discount that the reserve is set below the low estimate. Our results indicate that the reserve price is set at about 70 percent of the low estimate, which is consistent with what little is known about reserve prices.

In Section I of the paper we describe the auction market and summary statistics on sale rates, prices, and unexpected price movements. In Section II we interpret the relationship between sale rates and unexpected price movements. In Section III we use sale rates and unexpected price changes to estimate the relation between the auctioneer's observable low estimate and the seller's observable reserve price.

I. Sale Rates and Prices in Art Auctions

Art auctions are ascending price auctions, where the bidding starts out low and the auctioneer subsequently calls out higher and higher prices. When the bidding stops, the item is said to be "knocked down" or "hammered down," and the final price is the "hammer price." Not all

---

[†]*Discussants:* Benjamin Mandel, Federal Reserve Board; Marie Conolly Pray, University of Quebec-Montreal; Bruce Weinburg, Ohio State University; Cédric Ceulemans, ECARES, Université Libre de Bruxelles.

*Ashenfelter: Industrial Relations Section, Princeton University, Firestone Library, Princeton, New Jersey 08544 (e-mail: c6789@princeton.edu); Graddy: Department of Economics and International Business School, Brandeis University, 415 South Street, Waltham, MA 02454 (e-mail: kgraddy@brandeis.edu). The authors would like to thank Jianping Mei, Mike Moses, Lara Shore, and Margaret Stevens for useful comments. The authors would also like to thank Ly Tran and Huong Nguyen for their research assistance.

[1] Studies of price movements in art markets include William J. Baumol (1986), James E. Pesando (1993), William N. Goetzmann (1993), Madeleine de la Barre, Sophie Docclo, and Victor Ginsburgh (1994), and Jianping Mei and Michael Moses (2002). Ashenfelter and Graddy (2003, 2006) provide a survey.

TABLE 1—SUMMARY STATISTICS

Year	Observations	Number of auctions	Price (sold items)	High bid (unsold items)	Average estimate	Sale rate
Impressionist art						
1980–1984	4,585	79	87,275	—	78,475	0.707
1985–1989	9,403	130	287,285	—	206,160	0.749
1990–1994	7,583	114	400,202	—	437,829	0.612
1995–1999	11,976	141	340,141	—	253,927	0.693
2000–2004	8,443	124	326,189	—	288,791	0.686
2005–2007	6,647	63	84,117	—	340,459	0.773
Contemporary art						
1982–1984	698	6	4,210	1,991	3,445	0.745
1985–1989	1,566	12	25,428	11,520	19,511	0.819
1990–1994	1,993	17	26,081	30,443	32,638	0.740

items that have been put up for sale and knocked down have been sold. Sellers of individual items typically set confidential reserve prices, and if the bidding does not reach this level, the items will go unsold. Auctioneers say that an unsold item has been "bought-in."

Prior to the sale, a presale catalogue is published which includes high and low estimates of the art work to be auctioned. The auction house does not publish, and indeed is very secretive about, the seller's reserve price for the work of art. The auction houses observe an unwritten rule of setting the secret reserve price at or below the low estimate.[2]

Our first dataset consists of objects sold in auctions of impressionist art at Christie's and Sotheby's in London and New York. For the period 1980 to 1990, the dataset on impressionist and modern art auctions was constructed by Orley Ashenfelter and Andrew Richardson by looking through public price lists and auction catalogues from Christie's and Sotheby's. For the period 1990 to July of 2007, the dataset was constructed by Kathryn Graddy with the help of Ly Tran and Huong Nguyen by using a combination of Hislop's art sales index database and the ARTNET database. Our dataset includes sales of 58 selected impressionist and modern artists that took place at Christie's and Sotheby's auction houses in London and New York. The artists in this sample were selected because their art is well represented at auction.

Our second dataset on contemporary art was constructed by Kathryn Graddy and includes all sales of contemporary art at Christie's auction house on King Street in London between 1982 and 1994. The data were gathered from the archives of Christie's auction house, and for each item, the observable characteristics were hand-copied from the presale catalogues. For this dataset, we have observations both on the sale price for sold items and on the high bid for unsold items, as reported in Christie's internal property system.

Table 1 presents summary statistics on the number of observations, the number of auctions, the average prices for sold items, the high bids for unsold items in the contemporary art dataset, the average of the high and low presale estimates, and the sale rates for five-year periods. There are many more impressionist art auctions than contemporary art auctions because of the way the datasets were constructed. The sale rate is largely stationary over these five-year intervals in both datasets.[3] The average sale rate over the entire 27-year period is 69.8 percent for impressionist art, while it is 77 percent for contemporary art for the period 1982–1994. For comparison, the impressionist art sale rate is 68.5 percent over the same 1982–1994 period, suggesting the "normal" sale rate is higher for contemporary than impressionist art.

Figure 1 presents sale rates and a yearly hedonic price index plotted over time, and

[2] For a description of art auctions, please see Ashenfelter (1989), who shows that auctioneer's presale price estimates are highly correlated with the prices of subsequently sold items.

[3] Price estimates for impressionist art are missing for 105 out of 651 auctions; 80 of 105 of these missing price estimates occur in the years 1992 to 1994.

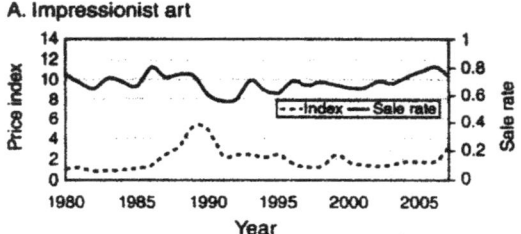
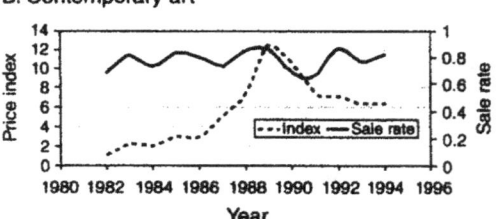

FIGURE 1. SALE RATES AND PRICE INDICES

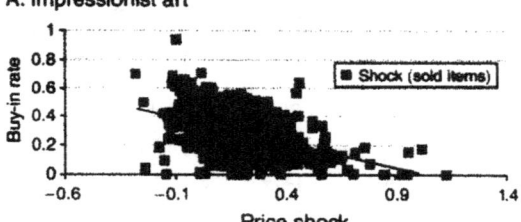
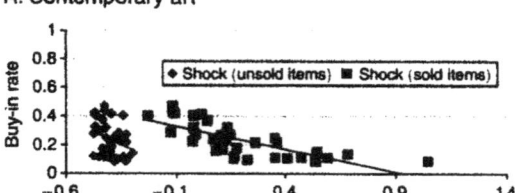

FIGURE 2. BUY-IN RATES AND PRICE SHOCKS

demonstrates that these sale rates fluctuate around a stable level, with no consistent correlation with an index of prices.[4] The correlation of yearly sale rates with the current impressionist index is -0.24, and the correlation of yearly sale rates with the current contemporary index is 0.26. There is a higher correlation of the lagged price indices with sale rates: for impressionist art the correlation is -0.60 and for contemporary art the correlation is -0.58. During the 1989 crash, in both datasets prices and sale rates fell. The negative correlations with the lagged yearly price index suggests that price surprises, or "price shocks," might be driving sale rates. We have a very good measure of price shocks on an item by item basis because of the presale estimates placed on items by experts at the auction houses.

In Figure 2, we plot the buy-in rate (which is calculated as one minus the sale rate) against the price shock, by auction, for both impressionist and contemporary art. Price shocks are calculated as the ratio of the sale price to the average estimate minus one for each painting, and then averaged over each auction. For contemporary art, we separate the unexpected shock for sold items from the unexpected shock for unsold items (using the high bid price in place of a sold price). As would be expected, the price shock for unsold items is consistently negative.

The figures show a strong relationship between buy-in rates and price shocks. A regression of the buy-in rate on the price shock for sold items for impressionist art yields a slope coefficient of -0.345 and a standard error of just 0.029. A regression of the buy-in rate on the price shock for sold items for contemporary art yields a slope coefficient of -0.322 with a standard error of 0.050. The slope of the relationship is steeper for unsold items at -0.759, but with a standard error of 0.399 it is not significantly different from the slope for sold items.

This strong observed correlation between unexpected price shocks and our measure of volume—the sale rate—is suggestive of a Phillips curve. Dale T. Mortensen (1970) sets out an elegant model of reservation price determination in a labor market context and uses it to explain the nature of a Phillips curve. With art, one can think of the buy-in rate as the unemployment rate for paintings. An unexpected positive price shock raises the sale rate because more owners of paintings receive price offers above their reservation price.

---

[4] The impressionist art index is constructed by regressing log prices on 57 artist dummies, log height, log width, and 27 year dummies. The contemporary art index is constructed by regressing log price on 119 artist dummies, log height, log width, 20 medium dummies, log of years since painting was constructed, whether the painting was subject to VAT, and 13 year dummies.

II. An Empirical Explanation of the Relationship of Sale Rates to Unexpected Price Movements

Before the auction, the auction house publishes a range of estimates of the value of each item for sale, but does not reveal the reserve price, which by convention is at or below the low estimate. Consistent with the common perception in art auctions, each reserve price, R_{it}, which is both item specific and time specific, is related to each low estimate, LE_{it}, by an individual reserve factor, θ_{it}, where $R_{it} = \theta_{it} LE_{it}$.[5]

An item is sold when $p_{it} > R_{it}$ or $p_{it} > \theta_{it} LE_{it}$. Now define the price shock ps_{it} for that item as $ps_{it} = \ln p_{it} - \ln LE_{it}$ and let $y_{it} = 1$ if the item is sold, and $y_{it} = 0$ otherwise. Then, $y_{it} = 1$ when $ps_{it} > \ln \theta_{it}$, where θ_{it} is the reserve factor of the seller of item it. We model the reserve factors for individual sellers as $\ln \theta_{it} = \ln \bar{\theta} + \mu_{jt} + \omega_{it}$, where $\bar{\theta}$ is an "average" reserve factor for all sellers and $\mu_{jt} \sim IN(0, \sigma_\mu^2)$ is a cluster effect. We allow paintings to be clustered by auction date (t), artist (j), and jointly by artist and auction date. An individual seller effect is represented by $\omega_{it} \sim IN(0, \sigma_\omega^2)$. Therefore,

$$y_{it} = 1 \leftrightarrow ps_{it} > \ln \bar{\theta} + \mu_{jt} + \omega_{it}.$$

Thus, we have a random effects probit model (REPM) specification, which we can use to estimate the average reserve factor $\bar{\theta}$ and the standard deviation σ_ω across sellers. In the special case of no auction/artist-specific reserve factor effects ($\mu_{jt} = 0$), we have the standard probit model for which

$$\Pr[y_{it} = 1] = \phi\left(\frac{ps_{it} - \ln \bar{\theta}}{\sigma_\omega}\right),$$

where ϕ is the standard normal distribution function.

TABLE 2—SALE RATES AND UNEXPECTED PRICE SHOCKS FOR CONTEMPORARY ART

	Probit	REPM (auction)	REPM (artist)	REPM (artist and auction)
$\ln P_{it}/LE_{it}$	3.397 (0.107)	3.490 (0.112)	3.452 (0.117)	3.859 (0.172)
			1.172 (0.044)	
constant	1.145 (0.036)	1.183 (0.057)		1.312 (0.060)
RE: auction SD		0.253 (0.045)		
RE: artist SD			0.194 (0.082)	
RE: artist and auction SD				0.548 (0.081)
rho		0.060 (0.020)	0.037 (0.030)	0.231 (0.052)
Log likelihood	−1,315	−1,296	−1,314	−1,304
reserve factor (θ)	0.714	0.713	0.712	0.712
reserve factor SD (σ_ω)	0.294	0.286	0.290	0.259

Notes: Standard errors in parentheses. There are 4,257 observations in each regression.

III. Estimation

In column 1 of Table 2 we present the standard probit estimates, and in columns 2–4 we present the REPM estimates. The coefficients are highly significant in all models, and the results for both the standard probit and the random-effects probit indicate that the reserve price is on average 71 percent of the low estimate.[6] The estimates of the standard deviation across sellers, σ_ω, are also similar in the four models, ranging from 0.259 to 0.290. The intra-auction correlation (rho in column 2) equals 0.060 with an estimated error of 0.020, the intra-artist correlation (rho in column 3) equals 0.037 with a standard error of 0.030, and the intra-auction/artist correlation (rho in column 4) equals 0.231 with an estimated error of 0.052. Thus, in column 4, approximately 23 percent of the variance is attributable to the same artist within an auction.

How reasonable are our estimates of the average reserve factor, $\bar{\theta}$? In the contemporary art dataset, out of 3,295 sold items, 1,263 items (or 38 percent) sold at or below the low estimate. In this sample, the mean price was 87 percent of the low estimate. The high bid for unsold items was on average 72 percent of the low estimate. In impressionist and modern art, 37 percent sold at or below the low estimate, and the mean price

---

[5] Ashenfelter, Graddy, and Margaret Stevens (2004) show that, under certain assumptions, the seller has an optimal reserve price which is a constant proportion of the expected price. This proportion depends upon a seller's discount factor, the expected price growth of art, and the variance of the unexpected price shock.

[6] The coefficient on the constant in the probit model is equal to $(-1/\sigma_\omega)(\ln \bar{\theta})$ and the coefficient on the price shock is equal to $1/\sigma_\omega$.

was 90 percent of the low estimate. The only evidence we could find on any actual reserve prices is contained in a book by Peter Watson (1992) that documents the selling of Portrait of Dr. Gatchet. For this picture, the secret reserve was $35,000,000, 87.5 percent of the low estimate of $40,000,000.[7]

IV. Conclusion

Unexpected price movements regularly occur in art auctions, and these price shocks are highly correlated with art auction sale rates. The probability an item is sold in an auction depends upon how low the reserve price is set. In data on contemporary art auctions, we estimate the confidential reserve price to be set at approximately 70 percent of the low estimate. Our results explain why sale rates in art auctions are considered so significant to market observers: they indicate how aggregate prices are evolving.

REFERENCES

Ashenfelter, Orley. 1989. "How Auctions Work for Wine and Art." *Journal of Economic Perspectives*, 3(3): 23–36.

Ashenfelter, Orley, and Kathryn Graddy. 2003. "Auctions and the Price of Art." *Journal of Economic Literature*, 41(3): 763–87.

Ashenfelter, Orley, and Kathryn Graddy. 2006. "Art Auctions." In *Handbook of the Economics of Art and Culture*. Vol. 25, Handbooks in Economics, ed. Victor A. Ginsburgh and David Throsby, 909–45. New York: Elsevier.

Ashenfelter, Orley, Kathryn Graddy, and Margaret Stevens. 2004. "Sale Rates and the State of the Art Market: A Study of Impressionist and Contemporary Art Auctions." Unpublished.

Baumol, William J. 1986. "Unnatural Value: Or Art Investment as Floating Crap Game." *American Economic Review*, 76(2): 10–14.

de la Barre, Madeleine, Sophie Docclo, and Victor Ginsburgh. 1994. "Returns of Impressionist, Modern and Contemporary European Paintings 1962–1991." *Annales d'Economie et de Statistique*, 35(7): 143–81.

Goetzmann, William N. 1993. "Accounting for Taste: Art and the Financial Markets over Three Centuries." *American Economic Review*, 83(5): 1370–76.

McAndrew, Clare, James L. Smith, and Rex Thompson. Forthcoming. "The Impact of Reserve Prices on the Perceived Bias of Expert Appraisals of Fine Art." *Journal of Applied Econometrics*.

Mei, Jianping, and Michael Moses. 2002. "Art as an Investment and the Underperformance of Masterpieces." *American Economic Review*, 92(5): 1656–68.

Mortensen, Dale T. 1970. "Job Search, the Duration of Unemployment, and the Phillips Curve." *American Economic Review*, 60(5): 847–62.

Pesando, James E. 1993. "Art as an Investment: The Market for Modern Prints." *American Economic Review*, 83(5): 1075–89.

Watson, Peter. 1992. *From Monet to Manhattan: The Rise of the Modern Art Market*. New York: Random House.

---

[7] Using a very different method, Clare McAndrew, James L. Smith, and Rex Thompson (forthcoming) estimate that the reserve price is set at 73 percent of the low estimate.

American Economic Association

Art and Money
Author(s): William N. Goetzmann, Luc Renneboog and Christophe Spaenjers
Source: *The American Economic Review*, Vol. 101, No. 3, PAPERS AND PROCEEDINGS OF THE One Hundred Twenty Third Annual Meeting OF THE AMERICAN ECONOMIC ASSOCIATION (MAY 2011), pp. 222-226
Published by: American Economic Association
Stable URL: http://www.jstor.org/stable/29783743
Accessed: 05/02/2014 12:37

Your use of the JSTOR archive indicates your acceptance of the Terms & Conditions of Use, available at
http://www.jstor.org/page/info/about/policies/terms.jsp

JSTOR is a not-for-profit service that helps scholars, researchers, and students discover, use, and build upon a wide range of content in a trusted digital archive. We use information technology and tools to increase productivity and facilitate new forms of scholarship. For more information about JSTOR, please contact support@jstor.org.

American Economic Association is collaborating with JSTOR to digitize, preserve and extend access to *The American Economic Review*.

Art and Money

By William N. Goetzmann, Luc Renneboog, and Christophe Spaenjers*

Beauty is commonly a gratification of our sense of costliness masquerading under the name of beauty.
—Thorstein Veblen

Unless cast in platinum and covered with diamonds, as in the case of a 2007 Damien Hirst sculpture, a work of art has little intrinsic value. Nevertheless, works of art have from time to time fetched shockingly high prices, at least from the perspective of ordinary wage earners. The highest amounts have been paid for creations of deceased artists, but also living artists—Hirst being the exemplar—have commanded multi-million dollar or pound sums for their work. It is still largely a puzzle what determines these prices and their pattern over time.

Yet it is clear that the price of an art object is limited only by the amount that collectors are willing and able to pay for it. Given the interest of many high net worth individuals in art, we analyze the impact on art prices of time variation in how much money the wealthiest members of society can spend.

One way to measure changes in wealthy individuals' buying power is to look at stock market returns. Equities are typically held more widely among the most affluent. A number of studies have indeed looked at the relation between stock market and art market trends.[1] In this paper, we extend this work over a much longer time frame, starting our study in the first half of the nineteenth century.

A complementary approach to proxying for collectors' ability to purchase art consists of studying the evolution of top incomes over time, especially if the highest incomes also go to the wealthiest individuals. We therefore empirically investigate the link between the income distribution on the one hand and art prices on the other, a relationship which has not been analyzed before.[2]

I. Data

In this section, we first construct a long-run art price index. Since the index is largely based on London sales and is expressed in British pounds (GBP), we also collect equity market and income data for Great Britain. Insofar as it was mostly British individuals who bought the considered artists at British auctions over our time frame, this procedure seems justified.

A. Art Prices

We start by building a long-term art price index. To do so, we go back to the auction sales data collected by Gerard Reitlinger (1961), who investigated the history of the British paintings and drawings market. Despite the

---

* Goetzmann: Yale School of Management, 135 Prospect Street, New Haven, CT 06511 (e-mail: william.goetzmann@yale.edu); Renneboog: CentER, Tilburg University, P.O. Box 90153, Tilburg, 5000 LE, the Netherlands (e-mail: luc.renneboog@uvt.nl); Spaenjers: CentER, Tilburg University, P.O. Box 90153, Tilburg, 5000 LE, the Netherlands (e-mail: c.spaenjers@uvt.nl). The authors would like to thank Anthony Atkinson, Fabio Braggion, Elroy Dimson, Marc Goergen, Richard Grossman, Benjamin Mandel, Kim Oosterlinck, Emmanuel Saez, Darius Spieth, Radomir Todorov, John Turner, and seminar participants at Cardiff Business School, Erasmus University Rotterdam, Queen's University of Belfast, Tilburg University, and the Financial History Workshop at the University of Antwerp for helpful comments and data. Spaenjers thanks the Netherlands Organisation for Scientific Research (NWO) for financial support. Part of this paper was written while Spaenjers was visiting Columbia University, whose hospitality is appreciated.

[1] For example, William N. Goetzmann (1993) documents a lagged relationship between art prices and the stock market. Olivier Chanel (1995) presents evidence that stock markets Granger-cause art prices. Takato Hiraki et al. (2009) show that positive wealth shocks to Japanese investors affected their art purchases in the 1980s, lifting the price level in the global art market. While the latter authors treat art as a luxury consumption good, Benjamin R. Mandel (2009) constructs a model in which a positive correlation between equity returns and art returns is induced by the use of art as a savings asset.

[2] In contrast, in the real estate literature, Joseph Gyourko, Christopher Mayer, and Todd Sinai (2006) and Stijn Van Nieuwerburgh and Pierre-Olivier Weill (2010) have recently acknowledged the importance of the distribution of income in determining housing price levels.

well-documented selection issues with the Reitlinger data (Guido Guerzoni 1995), they still constitute a unique historical overview of auction sales since the eighteenth century. The artists whose sales are listed in this source mostly conform to English standards of taste. All transaction prices are expressed in GBP.

Reitlinger's data have previously been used to estimate the returns on art by, among others, William J. Baumol (1986) and Goetzmann (1993). In line with these studies, we identify all repeated sales within Reitlinger's book. This gives us a dataset of 1,096 sales pairs until 1961, excluding buy-ins (i.e., items for which the reserve price has not been met).

We then look up all 6,661 works listed in Reitlinger (1961) in the dataset constructed by Luc Renneboog and Christophe Spaenjers (2009), which contains more than one million auction sales until 2007, and try to identify resales of those same works in Great Britain. We treat a transaction as a resale only when there is a unique match of a nonambiguous title, which occurs in 253 cases.[3] In total we thus end up with a dataset containing 1,349 repeated sales. Since the data are very sparse for the first decades covered by Reitlinger, we delete the 13 pairs for which the purchase occurred prior to 1765. This leaves us with 1,336 repeated sales.

To estimate a price index, we follow the Bayesian formulation of a repeat sales regression, which imposes some additional restrictions on the estimation, outlined in Goetzmann (1992, 1993). The Bayes formulation avoids spurious negative autocorrelation in the estimated return series and is particularly useful when the number of observations is relatively small. Prior to applying the regression to our dataset, we deflate all transaction prices to real GBP. More details on our estimation methodology can be found in Goetzmann, Renneboog, and Spaenjers (2010).

We show the time series of the index values since 1830 in Figure 1. The figure suggests a relationship between the real economy and art prices. For example, we see significant

[3] We classify a transaction in Renneboog and Spaenjers (2009) as a match to a sale in Reitlinger's list if we find strong evidence of the existence of only one work with the same title by the same artist. Also, we exclude objects with attribution classifications and with very general titles (or titles that point to a much-used subject of the artist), and objects that went to museums according to Reitlinger.

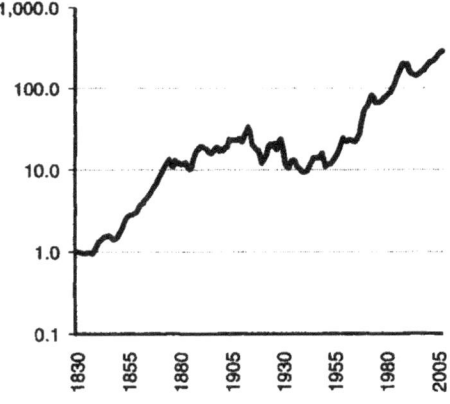

FIGURE 1. ART PRICES IN REAL GBP 1830–2007

Notes: This figure shows the annual art price index in real GBP for the period 1830–2007, on a logarithmic scale. The index value in 1830 is put equal to 1.

price drops during World War I, over the Great Depression in the 1930s, and after the oil crisis in 1973. In contrast, we find strong price appreciations throughout the 1960s, during the art market boom at the end of the 1980s, and in the 2000s (at least until 2007). However, art prices stayed remarkably low for many years in the middle of the twentieth century. In real terms, the price level of 1913 was not reached again until 1968, despite decades of economic growth.

We will henceforward refer to our log price index as *Art*. The first differences of this index constitute our estimates of the log returns on art. A concern with any art index is that survivorship issues can put an upward bias on the estimated returns (Goetzmann 1996). However, since our focus is not on estimating returns but on identifying what determines the variation in art returns, this does not have to be a major problem here.

B. *Equity Returns and Income Data*

We build a history of British stock price returns for the period 1830–2007, based on Richard S. Grossman (2002), Graeme G. Acheson et al. (2009), and Elroy Dimson et al. (2009). We create yearly indices covering total return, capital appreciation, and dividend yield, transformed into real terms. We call the natural log series *Equities*, *Equities* (*cap.*), and *Equities* (*div.*).

A recent literature has investigated the evolution of top incomes over the course of the twentieth century. We use data from A. B. Atkinson and T. Piketty (2010), who themselves rely on tax data, to build a consistent series of the share of total income received by the top 0.1 percent of all income earners in the UK for the period 1908–2005.[4] This series will be referred to as *Inequality*. Interestingly, income inequality generally decreased through the first half of the twentieth century and has increased over the last few decades, which is roughly in line with the pattern observed for art prices. We also construct the series *Income* and *Top income*, which measure the logs of deflated total personal income and deflated income of the top 0.1 percent earners in every year.

II. Results

We first present the results of comovement regressions that relate art returns to equity returns and changes in the income distribution. Thereafter, we undertake a cointegration analysis to investigate whether we can identify a long-run driver of art prices.

A. Comovement Regressions

In Table 1, we present the results of ordinary least squares (OLS) regressions that relate the log returns on art to equity returns, changes in total personal income, and changes in the income distribution. Below each coefficient, we present the Newey-West standard error that accounts for heteroskedasticity and first-order autocorrelation in the error terms. We also show the number of observations and the R^2 for each regression.

Model (1) regresses the returns on art on equity capital growth rates and dividend yields over the 1830–2007 period. Because of potential nonsynchroneity between our art price index (which aggregates information per calendar year) and equity prices, we also include lagged equity capital returns. Model (2) relates art returns to the growth of personal income and changes in income inequality. Data for these

[4] Data on the top 0.1 percent income share are missing for a limited number of years. For the periods 1908–1912 and 1987–1992, we impute the share of the top 0.1 percent, based on the available income shares. For the years 1961 and 1980, we linearly interpolate the top 0.1 percent income share.

TABLE 1—COMOVEMENT REGRESSIONS

	1830–2007 (1)	1908–2005 (2)	1908–2005 (3)
Δ Equities (cap.)	0.13* (0.07)		0.11 (0.07)
Δ_{-1} Equities (cap.)	0.21*** (0.05)		0.21*** (0.06)
Δ Equities (div.)	−0.01 (0.21)		
Δ Income		0.14 (0.26)	0.20 (0.26)
Δ Inequality		14.35*** (4.18)	9.59*** (4.13)
Observations	176	97	96
R^2	0.13	0.12	0.23

Notes: The returns on art are regressed on a constant and a changing set of independent variables, listed in the first column. All models are estimated using OLS. Newey-West standard errors are in parentheses below the coefficients.

*** Significant at the 1 percent level.
** Significant at the 5 percent level.
* Significant at the 10 percent level.

variables are only available over the 1908–2005 time frame. In model (3), we check how the results on the income variables change once we control for equity returns. In this last specification, we exclude the dividend variable, because dividends should already be captured by the personal income variables.

The results in Table 1 show that equity capital growth, and especially lagged stock price appreciation, has a statistically and economically significant impact on art prices. However, we also find that art prices rise when inequality goes up, even when controlling for equity market trends. The coefficient on *Inequality* in model (3) suggests that a 1 percentage point increase in the share of total personal income earned by the top 0.1 percent triggers an increase in art prices of about 10 percent. The R^2 of this model is substantially higher than when considering the impact of equities or the income distribution separately.

B. Cointegration Analysis

The above evidence on comovement between equity markets and income inequality on the one hand and art markets on the other is based on relatively short-term effects. The long-term

TABLE 2—COINTEGRATION TESTS

	Trace	Max. eigenvalue
Equities	5.67	5.66
Equities (cap.)	8.28	8.27
GDP	7.29	7.25
Income	10.18	9.54
Top income	20.27***	17.82**

Notes: This panel shows the results of Johansen's cointegration tests over the period 1908–2005. In each case, the null hypothesis is that of no cointegrating relation with *Art*. No trend is assumed in the cointegrating equation. The test statistics of both the trace and the maximum eigenvalue tests are reported.

*** Significant at the 1 percent level.
** Significant at the 5 percent level.
* Significant at the 10 percent level.

nature of our data series (and the fact that the series are integrated of order one) allows further exploration of the factors that drive art prices over the long run. If it is really the high-income individuals who determine the price level in the art market, then one would expect *Top income* (but not necessarily *Income*) to be cointegrated with art prices.

Table 2 shows the results of Johansen's cointegration tests applied to our time series since 1908. We report the results of trace and maximum eigenvalue tests, assuming no trend in the cointegrating equation and including one lagged first difference in the model.

We find that the null hypothesis of no cointegration between *Art* and the series in the first column can never be consistently rejected, except in the case of *Top income*.[5] Over the long run, the income of the wealthy, or at least of the highest earners, seems a key factor in the price formation in the art market.

III. Analysis per Subperiod

Profound changes have taken place in the art market since the middle of the previous century. Without doubt, the art market has become more globalized, or at least reached the level of international integration it enjoyed in the late nineteenth century. One may thus expect the relation between our UK art price index on the one hand and the British equity market and income distribution on the other to be weaker after World War II than before. Therefore, we repeat our main analyses, but differentiate between the 1908–1945 and the post-1945 period.

The results of the comovement regressions, which are reported in Goetzmann, Renneboog, and Spaenjers (2010), indicate that lagged British equity capital growth has a similar positive impact on our art price index in both subperiods. In contrast, the previous findings on the impact of income inequality on art prices seem attributable to trends in the early twentieth century, when substantial decreases in inequality eroded the relative buying power of the wealthiest. Our results are consistent with the hypothesis that the income concentration in Great Britain mattered less in the second half of the twentieth century in determining art prices.

Still, even for the postwar period, we can reject the hypothesis that top incomes are not cointegrated with art prices.

IV. Conclusion

This article has investigated how equity returns and personal income—more generally, money—determines the price of art. We are able to confirm and strengthen previous evidence that equity market movements affect art prices, using a newly constructed art price index. We find weaker evidence for the impact of income inequality. Although there is evidence that changes in income inequality had an important effect on British art prices in the first half of the twentieth century, and that this effect is significant for the overall time frame, we do not confirm the result for the postwar period. We conjecture that this may be due to the globalization in the demand for high-quality art in the later era. Arguably more important, however, is that we find cointegrating relationships between top incomes and art prices, both for the complete 1908–2005 period and since 1945. These relationships support the Veblenian view of art as an instrument of social competition among the very rich.

REFERENCES

Acheson, Graeme G., Charles R. Hickson, John D. Turner, and Qing Ye. 2009. "Rule Britannia! British Stock Market Returns, 1825–1870." *Journal of Economic History*, 69(4): 1107–37.

---

[5] We find similar results when allowing for a linear trend in the cointegration equation or when including lagged equity capital growth as an exogenous variable.

Atkinson, A. B., and T. Piketty, ed. 2010. *Top Incomes: A Global Perspective*. New York: Oxford University Press.

Baumol, William J. 1986. "Unnatural Value: Or Art Investment as Floating Crap Game." *American Economic Review*, 76(2): 10–14.

Chanel, Olivier. 1995. "Is Art Market Behaviour Predictable?" *European Economic Review*, 39(3–4): 519–27.

Dimson, Elroy, Paul Marsh, Mike Staunton, and Jonathan Wilmot. 2009. *Credit Suisse Global Investment Returns Yearbook 2009*. Zurich: Credit Suisse Research Institute.

Goetzmann, William Nelson. 1992. "The Accuracy of Real Estate Indices: Repeat Sale Estimators." *Journal of Real Estate Finance and Economics*, 5(1): 5–53.

Goetzmann, William N. 1993. "Accounting for Taste: Art and the Financial Markets over Three Centuries." *American Economic Review*, 83(5): 1370–76.

Goetzmann, William N. 1996. "How Costly Is the Fall from Fashion? Survivorship Bias in the Painting Market." In *Economics of the Arts: Selected Essays*. Vol. 237, Contributions to Economic Analysis, ed. Victor A. Ginsburgh and Pierre-Michel Menger, 71–84. New York: Elsevier.

Goetzmann, William N., Luc Renneboog, and Christophe Spaenjers. 2010. "Art and Money." Yale International Center for Finance Working Paper 09–26.

Grossman, Richard S. 2002. "New Indices of British Equity Prices, 1870–1913." *Journal of Economic History*, 62(1): 121–46.

Guerzoni, Guido. 1995. "Reflections on Historical Series of Art Prices: Reitlinger's Data Revisited." *Journal of Cultural Economics*, 19(3): 251–60.

Gyourko, Joseph, Christopher Mayer, and Todd Sinai. 2006. "Superstar Cities." National Bureau of Economic Research Working Paper 12355.

Hiraki, Takato, Akitoshi Ito, Darius A. Spieth, and Naoya Takezawa. 2009. "How Did Japanese Investments Influence International Art Prices?" *Journal of Financial and Quantitative Analysis*, 44(6): 1489–1514.

Mandel, Benjamin R. 2009. "Art as an Investment and Conspicuous Consumption Good." *American Economic Review*, 99(4): 1653–63.

Reitlinger, Gerald. 1961. *The Economics of Taste: The Rise and Fall of Picture Prices 1760–1960*. London: Barrie and Rockliff.

Renneboog, Luc, and Christophe Spaenjers. 2009. "Buying Beauty: On Prices and Returns in the Art Market." Tilburg University CentER Discussion Paper 2009-15.

Van Nieuwerburgh, Stijn, and Pierre-Olivier Weill. 2010. "Why Has House Price Dispersion Gone Up?" *Review of Economic Studies*, 77(4): 1567–1606.

Investment in Visual Arts:
Evidence from International Transactions

Benjamin R. Mandel*

November 2010

Preliminary

Abstract

This paper uses international trade data to discern between competing theories of visual art markets. We begin by documenting the growth and international distribution of painting, print and sculpture sales volumes over the past two decades. U.S. art exports and imports are highly concentrated in about 10 countries and the real value of cross-border transactions is very sensitive to importer national income. An import share that increases with income is consistent with art objects being either superior consumption goods or increasingly attractive investments. We use a stylized prediction of the permanent income hypothesis to discern which narrative is more pervasive in the data, and conclude that visual arts look most like consumption goods.

Keywords: art investment, permanent income hypothesis, painting, print, sculpture

JEL classification: Z11

---

* Division of International Finance, Board of Governors of the Federal Reserve System, Washington, D.C. 20551 U.S.A. Email: Benjamin.R.Mandel@frb.gov. A special thanks is owed to Seth Pruitt for providing Matlab code for the unobserved components model, as well as to Robert Vigfusson and Joseph Gruber for constructive conversations. Nathaniel Dau-Schmidt and Mallory Nobles provided superb research assistance. The views in this paper are solely the responsibility of the author and should not be interpreted as reflecting the views of the Board of Governors of the Federal Reserve System or any other person associated with the Federal Reserve System.

I.   Introduction

There has been broad interest in measuring the evolution of art prices, seeing how they relate to the returns of other assets, as well as vigorous debate of the question: are artworks 'good investments'? A slice of the literature on art investment investigates whether artworks are worthwhile investments from the perspective of asset pricing theory. In those works, the moments of painting, print or sculpture returns from the measurement literature are compared to what CAPM, consumption CAPM or an options pricing model would predict. However, notwithstanding varying degrees of success in matching the empirics to theory, are we putting "the cart before the horse" in attempting to rationalize patterns of investment returns without a firm grasp of the relationship between art buyers and artworks? Specifically, how do we interpret the financial returns for objects that are not pure investment goods?

Part of the gap in our understanding comes from the breadth of data we have at hand. While previous studies have carefully assembled prices from auction houses into aggregate index numbers, we have very little notion of the quantities of art flows, and hence the real consumption and investment services embodied in visual arts. In this paper, we take a preliminary step to address this shortcoming by focusing on detailed trade volume data for the international flows of paintings, prints and sculptures. Another issue with our assessment of the quality of art as an asset derives from our *a priori* assumption that art provides any type of investment service at all. Often this claim is justified by the mere existence of structured markets for art or the trend in financial markets towards securitization of unconventional stores of value. We argue below that the investment nature of visual arts is often dominated by its consumption nature. Hence, we may want to consider instead the factors contributing to art's success at embodying consumption services. That is, why are visual arts such compelling consumer goods?

To begin, it is important to acknowledge that our understanding of art price dynamics has grown substantially recently due to important empirical contributions to the literature. A more or less typical narrative in that strand begins with the presentation of a novel dataset of prices from auctions or collector catalogues, chooses the most appropriate index estimation technique – usually repeated sales or hedonic – and then reports the moments of the art returns series and their covariance with those of other assets. Detailed surveys of the index estimation literature are provided by Ashenfelter and Graddy (2003) and Ginsburgh, Mei and Moses (2006). Some of the main findings are that art returns: (i) tend to be low on average, often underperforming risk-free bonds, (ii) are quite volatile, more so than a basket of equities (iii) by some accounts, are below average for rare masterpieces, (iv) by some accounts, are correlated with the returns of equities, and (v) are very heterogeneous across artists, genres and time periods. Similar methods and empirical observations have radiated outwards from paintings to related media and types of collectible goods such as prints (Pesando, 1993, Pesando & Shum, 1999, 2008), sculptures (Locatelli-Biey & Zanola, 2002), stamps (Dimson & Spaenjers, 2009), and even violins (Graddy & Margolis, 2007). Therefore, much has been said about the intriguing price dynamics of artworks and collectibles, motivating theoretical constructions that fit their rather unusual profile of returns.

How does one rationalize investment in an asset seemingly dominated by other assets (i.e., arts tend to have lower average returns, higher variance, and a positive beta)? One common riposte is that artworks embody consumption services that are priced into their financial returns. That is, owners require lower pecuniary returns due to the dynamic flow of utility that they get from owning and enjoying a work of art. Our understanding of the dual nature of consumption and investment hinges upon observing real flows of art objects. In contrast to prices, however, precious little information is available about the quantities of art investments, the scope and depth of art markets, as well as the cross-sectional characteristics of investors.

The key piece of information employed below is the variation in art consumption across importing countries and over time, measured using detailed international trade volume data for U.S. exports of paintings, prints and sculptures. We analyze the characteristics of art trade in Section II, with an eye towards identifying the drivers of growth in art purchases: Who are art consumers? What are their characteristics? We find that the composition of art consumers is fairly stable over the past two decades, with a few exceptions, and concentrated in about 10 countries that play an outsized role in the level of international trade flows. To see whether international art flows are more similar to consumption or investment goods, we then analyze the extent to which bilateral U.S. exports of visual arts are correlated with U.S. sectoral exports of consumer and investment goods. As a proxy for investment goods, we use aggregate 'capital goods' exports, as defined by the U.S. Bureau of Economic Analysis, as an imperfect measure. Notwithstanding certain qualifications about the definition of investment goods, in the vast majority of cases nominal art flows are more closely correlated with consumer goods than capital goods. This is our first indication that, on average, consumption motives trump investment motives.

In Section III, we use the dataset of international real art flows and a stylized prediction of Milton Friedman's permanent income hypothesis (PIH) to identify consumption and investment more precisely. The PIH has very different implications for consumption and investment based on whether innovations to income are temporary or permanent: temporary shocks are mostly saved to smooth out consumption, while permanent shocks are consumed in their entirety. We can implement these predictions empirically by using a common econometric technique, called unobserved components, to separate transient and permanent innovations in national income and then measuring the correlations of these series with art imports. For example, we can test whether changes in the UK's imports of paintings is more correlated with changes in the UK's permanent or transient income. If real art imports increase due to a transient increase in real GDP it means that art is being demanded as a store of value. If, on the other hand, real art imports increase due to a permanent increase in real GDP it means that art is being demanded for its flow of consumption services.

We also measure the responsiveness of art purchases to income changes *relative* to overall consumption and investment. This responsiveness tells us in greater detail what type of consumption or investment services agents receive. Specifically, should we find that art demand is highly responsive to permanent changes in income (i.e., a consumption good), an increasing share of consumption would indicate that it is a superior consumption good. Should we find that art demand is highly responsive to temporary changes in income (i.e., an investment) then an increasing share of investment flows for other vehicles would indicate that the portfolio share of artworks is not constant with respect to income.

To summarize the empirical findings, art behaves very much like a superior consumption good. There is little indication that art demand responds to temporary income shocks or that it even moves in tandem with other investment vehicle flows, suggesting that the investment motive for purchasing art is rather weak. Additionally, we find that the responsiveness of art purchases to income is highly concentrated in countries with large nominal trade flows in cultural goods.

Finally, Section IV employs an alternative identification scheme to discern permanent and temporary innovations in income. The seminal work of Gali (1999) decomposes national productivity and hours data into either components driven by technology or components driven by non-technology factors in the context of a structural vector autogregression. Using an analogous identification assumption, we estimate the correlation between art imports and the portion of national productivity driven by technology (i.e., permanent innovations to national income). Using the logic of the PIH, a positive correlation between art demand and a permanent income innovation indicates that art is being treated as a consumption good. Although the results are somewhat mixed across art products and countries, we find suggestive evidence consistent with that prediction. Section V concludes.

II. International trade data for paintings, prints and sculptures

i. Art volume measures

We begin our exploration of international art flows by defining what constitutes visual art in the U.S. international trade data. The U.S. Census Bureau compiles monthly export and import statistics from U.S. customs reports. The export statistics consist of goods valued at more than $2,500 per commodity shipped by individuals and organizations (including exporters, freight forwarders, and carriers) from the U.S. to other countries.[1] The available statistics include the free alongside ship (FAS) nominal monthly value of exports for a given

---

[1] For more information on the collection and compilation of U.S. trade data, as well as for statistics updated monthly, see: www.census.gov/foreign-trade/index.html.

trading partner within a narrowly defined product category.[2] Narrowly defined product categories, in turn, are among the roughly 15,000 Harmonized System 10-digit (HS10) product classifications defined by the U.S. International Trade Commission.[3]

For the purposes of our analysis, we focus on three HS10 categories for paintings, prints and sculptures. The exact names of these categories are shown in the top panel of Table 1. The painting product code, 9701100000 (i.e., "Paintings, drawing and pastels other than of heading 4906"), is part of the broader 2-digit category 97 (i.e., "Works of art, collectors' pieces and antiques") and 4-digit category 9701 (i.e., "Paintings, drawings and pastels, executed by hand as works of art; collages and similar decorative plaques"). The description of the print (9702000000) and sculpture (9703000000) codes are: "Original engravings, prints and lithographs, framed or not framed" and "Original sculptures and statuary, in any material," respectively.

The specificity of these descriptions strongly suggests that these codes comprise trade in fine art. First, we can use the detail of the trade data to be concrete about what the codes do *not* contain. For paintings, the only other 10-digit code within 9701, 9701900000, is a catch-all category for items not elsewhere specified or indicated (NESOI). This suggests that collages and decorative plaques falling under 9701 are not grouped in with our category of interest. Further, the painting category is discerned by its functionality from professional renderings in code 4906; for instance, architectural blueprints, hand-drawn maps and cartoon advertisements would not be classified as paintings, drawings or pastels. As shown in the bottom panel of Table 1, paintings also excludes: other types of painted materials, textile wall

---
[2] Generally, information is also available on physical quantities of items imported and exported. However, for the categories focused on herein those data are not collected.
[3] Harmonized System codes are comparable across countries at the 6-digit level. The extra four digits are particular to the description of U.S. traded goods. The 10-digit codes are also referred to collectively as the Harmonized Tariff Schedule.

hangings and folklore products. Similarly, prints and sculptures exclude an array of lithographs, photographs, statuettes and ornaments, in some cases even those produced as original works by professional sculptors. Finally, given the transportation costs (shipping and otherwise) associated with sending an artwork abroad, trade in low-value, 'no name' works of art is less worthwhile. In sum, we expect that the trade data consists of a selection of high-value fine arts transactions.[4]

Table 2 provides a snapshot of bilateral export data in 2009; the U.S. exported about $6 billion of art, over 80 percent of which consisted of paintings. Within each product group, it is striking that trade is extremely concentrated geographically, with the top 10 exporters accounting for over 90 percent of total U.S. exports of paintings and sculptures. Across countries, there is also a substantial degree of skewness, with the top 3 destination countries (Switzerland, UK and France) accounting for 75 percent of total painting exports. This distribution has remained roughly constant over the 21 year sample, as evidenced by the top three importing countries growing in line with the overall average annual growth rates of 5.8 percent for paintings, 6.4 percent for prints and 9.5 percent for sculptures.[5] At the extremes, we see evidence that art demand is linked to national income growth. On one hand, the importer with the fastest growth in art purchases, Korea, was also among the fastest growing economies. On the other, the sharp decline in Japanese art imports likely reflects the fallout of Japan's drop in relative income growth since the late 1980's. Further, the fact that these

---

[4] The U.S. Census Bureau is careful to count only sales in its export data. If there is a reasonable expectation that the good is not being sold, then it is excluded from the trade records. Such a situation might arise if galleries or museums are transferring artworks on loan, if auction houses are sending an unsold work to a foreign affiliate, or if private individuals are moving their collection without a change in ownership.
[5] The compound annual growth rates are a few percentage points higher if we instead compute them over period ending in 2008. However, the other patterns are qualitatively similar.

trends are the same across art products suggests that they do, in fact, mirror the growth profile of the importing country.

Table 3 documents the same statistics for U.S. imports of painting, prints and sculptures. Again, we see a high degree of concentration in the top ten countries and, within those, the top four. In contrast to exports, however, we do not observe a strong link between the export growth rates of foreign economies and their rates of overall output growth. For instance, top exporters such as Italy and Spain did not register particularly high GDP growth over the same period, while the growth rate of Japanese sculpture exports was actually above average. We also do not observe as strong a correlation in growth rates across products for a given country. Taken together, U.S. export and import statistics imply that importer GDP appears to be more pertinent in determining art trade flows than exporter GDP.

ii. <u>The covariance of art, consumer goods and capital goods exports</u>

A well-defined measure of art volume gives rise to a simple atheoretical test of the similarity of art demand to that of consumption or investment products. A sensible empirical starting point is to take the U.S. Bureau of Economic Analysis' definitions of broad sector categories and to examine the extent to which art trade movements coincide with contemporaneous bilateral exports in those sectors. Of particular relevance will be the correlation of art exports with Consumer Goods and Capital Goods, where the former is a proxy for consumption demand and the latter is more closely related to investment demand.[6] Indeed, Consumer Goods contains many sub-categories which are intuitive final goods intended for consumption (e.g., household goods, recreational equipment, home

---

[6] The BEA categorizes goods trade according to the End Use classification scheme. Here we use 1-digit End Use codes as the sectoral trade measures.

entertainment, coins, gems and jewelry).[7] Capital Goods contains goods more typically associated with business investment (e.g., electricity generation equipment, industrial and agricultural machinery, computers, business machines, aircraft and other vessels). Figure 1 illustrates an index of U.S. painting volume compared to those of four large sectors. With the exception of a surge in painting exports in the late 1980's, all series are characterized by relatively steady growth through the 1990's, accelerating growth in the 2000's, and varying degrees of reversal due to the financial crisis. We can see that the features of the aggregate Consumer Goods series lines up reasonably well with the painting series; it accelerated rapidly in the 2000's without a major pull-back in the wake of the crisis.

We proceed to quantify these correlations conditioning further on destination country, global shocks and seasonal patterns in the following reduced form least squares regression:

$$\ln M_{jkt} = \alpha_0 + \sum_s \alpha_s \ln M_{skt} + \sum_z \alpha_z z + \varepsilon_{jkt}$$

where M_{jkt} is the nominal flow of U.S. exports of art HS10 product j, to country k in quarter t. Depending on the specification, the vector of z's contains either dummy variables for destination country or for the time period, controlling for destination-specific and global levels of U.S. exports, respectively. We implement the regression on non-seasonally adjusted, quarterly data ranging from Q1 1989 through Q1 2010.[8] Tables 4-6 show the resulting estimates for α_s across an array of specifications. Table 4 illustrates the results using time period fixed effects and pooling across destination countries. The first column in each product category shows the results for the full sample. The flows of artworks tend to be negatively correlated with Foods, Feeds, Beverages and Industrial Supplies, negatively or

---

[7] Artworks are classified as consumer goods by the BEA, and thus what we refer to as Consumer Goods hereafter is the BEA measure net of a smoothed series for paintings, prints, sculptures, stamps and antiques.
[8] Sectoral U.S. export data by country was downloaded from the USITC Dataweb application.

uncorrelated with Capital Goods, and positively correlated with Consumer and Military Goods. The largest absolute correlation coefficient is between art and Consumer Goods, where a one percent increase in consumer goods exports corresponds to an increase of art exports of greater than one percent. In other words, when importers demand more consumption goods, they also increase the share of art imports relative to consumption goods. All other estimates are less than one.

We test the linear prediction that art and Consumer Goods, the proxy for consumption demand, are correlated more positively than art and Capital Goods, the proxy for investment demand. The resulting difference, shown in the memo line, tends to be large, positive and statistically significant. To control for the size composition of trading relationships as well as the lumpiness of art trade flows, each of which may induce a selection bias in the estimates, we constrain the sample to those quarters where bilateral art flows have values larger than $1 million (shown in the second column). And, finally, to control for the possibility that intra-auction house transfers are being mistakenly counted as art trade, we exclude the UK and France from the sample (shown in the third column). In each case, art remains more positively correlated with Consumer Goods than Capital Goods.

While one can make intuitive sense of the coefficients for Consumer and Capital Goods, the interpretation of art's correlation with primary commodities and military goods is less clear. Table 5 shows that these correlations are an artifact of our specification. When using importer fixed effects and pooling across time periods, the Foods coefficient loses all of its significance and the Industrial Supplies correlation switches signs. The Consumer Goods coefficients remain positive and statistically significant, albeit with lower magnitudes. The Consumer-Capital ordering remains robust for prints and sculptures, though we can no longer reject the null hypothesis that the estimate for Consumer Goods is greater than for Capital Goods in the paintings category. Additionally, to allay concerns that the series are not stationary, and hence giving rise to spurious positive correlations, we rerun the estimation in first differences under the alternative hypothesis that the series are difference stationary. Table 6 shows the results for these regressions. Indeed, the only consistently significant (and positive) estimates are those of Consumer Goods, with the difference between Consumer and Capital Goods significant for the two larger product categories of paintings and sculptures. Finally, since the data do not adjust for seasonality, the results may simply reflect the fact that the quarterly seasonality of consumption goods is most similar to that of artworks. While this would be telling in and of itself, we test the robustness of the results using a smoothed series for bilateral art exports and find the outcomes to be very similar.[9]

Albeit suggestive that arts are demanded more for consumption services than investment services, a few caveats need to be applied to the interpretation of the measured correlations. First, the data are nominal flows and hence conflate price and quantity changes; high inflation rates for both art and consumption goods could be contributing to the results. In the empirical applications below, the art trade data are deflated by various price series to generate measures of real flows. These are the appropriate units with which to measure consumption versus investment demand. Second, using Capital Goods as a measure of investment demand is not completely appropriate. A primary motive for investing in assets is the smoothing out of consumption. However, the demand for capital goods by firms is presumably driven by many other factors besides the consumption smoothing behavior of the

---

[9] The smoothing algorithm used is double exponential, which models the trend of a variable whose difference between changes from the previous values is serially correlated. More precisely, it models a variable whose second difference follows a low-order, moving-average process. The resulting smoothed series has the added effect of increasing the sample size by providing non-zero quarterly flows for those trade series which are lumpy.

firm's owners; it will depend on the firm's technological process, the quantities of other inputs in production and also the idiosyncrasies of capital markets. Ideally, what one would like to identify in the data is a pure measure of savings demand. The following sections use the logic of the permanent income hypothesis to that end.

III. PIH predictions in a state-space model

With the international trade data for artworks in hand, we proceed to explore the fundamental question of whether art is demanded for consumption or investment services. Friedman's (1957) permanent income hypothesis offers a stylized behavioral prediction based on whether shocks to wealth are permanent or transient: agents will consume all of a permanent shock and save most of a transient one. In this section, we combine this insight with an econometric strategy for disentangling permanent and temporary innovations in real GDP. The resulting decomposition will vary with real art purchases in a manner depending on the nature of the service demanded. Table 7 provides a review of the key PIH predictions. The first column shows the correlation signs of art trade with importer income if art is a consumption good. Real art demand will be positively correlated with permanent innovations in real income and uncorrelated with temporary ones. The prediction is even more refined if we consider the share of art in total imports, as shown in the second column of Table 7; a normal consumption good's share of total consumption should be unrelated to a permanent income innovation while a superior consumption good's share will be positively correlated.[10] Analogous predictions hold if art is an investment (columns three and four). Demand for

---

[10] In stark contrast to the previous section, the application of this argument assumes that all traded goods are a form of consumption good. If some import goods such as Capital Goods are in fact investment, then this would increase the sensitivity of share to a permanent income innovation (i.e., the denominator would rise by less). We thus see our results as an upper bound estimate of the elasticity of art's consumption share.

consumption-smoothing investment will be correlated with transient income shocks but uncorrelated with permanent income shocks. Further, if art's portfolio weight is variable, then only the share of art in total investment will be sensitive to those income changes. We employ estimates of temporary and permanent real GDP changes to see which of these predictions fits best for paintings, prints and sculptures.

i. Art deflator measures

Since the art trade values are measured in nominal terms, the statistics computed in Tables 2 through 6 conflate growth in both quantities and prices. To properly measure the real services embodied in paintings, prints and sculptures, and to test our PIH predictions, an appropriate deflator should be employed. Information on art prices, in turn, can be gleaned from a variety of sources in the empirical fine arts literature as well as from an additional source of international trade data. Figure 2 shows the evolution of two hedonic indexes for paintings estimated by Renneboog and Spaenjers (2009). A lot of popular interest in art as an investment has stemmed from the observation that painting prices, driven largely by oil paintings, have climbed considerably since 2001, re-attaining levels last seen in the late 1980's. While Renneboog and Spaenjers use a large amount of auction data and a hedonic methodology to come up with their index, we can garner additional information on art prices from sources that are perhaps less careful about art quality and vintage though even more broad in their coverage of art items. Those sources include government statistical agencies which collect price data on international transactions. The U.S. Bureau of Labor Statistics (BLS) International Price Program (IPP) surveys a sample of U.S. importing and exporting firms to construct indexes of prices for traded goods. Given the international nature of art markets documented above as well as the geographic concentration of sellers, we might expect that goods crossing a popular border like that of the United States would provide a representative sample of current transactions. Indeed, when we look at U.S. import prices from the IPP for the product category: Coins, Gems, Jewelry, & Collectibles (3-digit End Use product code 413), we see that much of the recent dynamic in painting markets is captured by the broader index of collectibles.[11] It is rather remarkable that painting prices are so similar to those of collectible goods, many of which we would not consider to be a class of investment. We proceed using these two indexes as deflators for the art trade volume data.

ii. Model

Our test of the PIH predictions also requires measures of temporary and permanent income innovations. Our empirical bifurcation of real GDP into these two components components follows Clark (1987), and applies the unobserved components econometric model. The idea in this class of models is to specify a measurement equation, describing the relationship between observed data and unobserved state variables, and a transition equation, describing the dynamics of the state variable, and then to use the Kalman filter to estimate the unobserved component of the state variable using information available at any given time t. A common application of this estimation technique is to decompose the log of GDP into a stochastic trend component and a cyclical component. Following the exposition of Clark (1987) in Kim and Nelson (1999), we specify the following unobserved components model:

$$y_t = n_t + x_t$$

$$n_t = g_{t-1} + n_{t-1} + v_t, \quad v_t \sim i.i.d. N(0, \sigma_v^2)$$

$$g_t = g_{t-1} + w_t, \quad w_t \sim i.i.d. N(0, \sigma_w^2)$$

---

[11] The poor performance of the BLS index to capture the large decline in art prices at the beginning of the sample may reflect changes in the IPP sampling and index construction protocol, which evolved considerably during the 1990's. For further information on how IPP constructs its price indexes see the BLS Handbook of Methods, published online at: http://www.bls.gov/opub/hom/.

$$x_t = \theta_1 x_{t-1} + \theta_2 x_{t-2} + e_t, \quad e_t \sim i.i.d.\, N(0, \sigma_e^2)$$

where y is the log of real GDP, x is a stationary cyclical component, and n is the stochastic trend (i.e., permanent) component. The drift term, g, is modeled as a random walk. This system of equations and its state-space representation are estimated by country to recover the cyclical dynamics (θ_i) as well as the variance of each innovation (σ_l). With these estimates we construct series for x and n for each country. Figure 3 shows the resulting decomposition for the United Kingdom. We see that the permanent component rises steadily since 1993 with more rapid growth in the 1990's than the 2000's. The cyclical component is, as we would expect, stationary about zero. That series has four peaks with the most recent one preceding the financial crisis of 2008.

To implement our PIH test, the correlations between changes in bilateral real art flows and changes in the components of real GDP are estimated. We implement these predictions by running the following least squares regression:[12]

$$\Delta \ln\left[\frac{M_{jkt}}{P_t}\right] = \alpha_0 + \alpha_1 \Delta \ln RGDP_{kt}^i + \varepsilon_{jkt}$$

where M is the flow of nominal U.S. exports of product j (paintings, prints or sculptures) to country k at time t deflated by an index of art prices (P_t).[13] The changes in the real GDP of importing nations are of three types: $i\epsilon\{overall, temporary, permanent\}$.

As above, real art imports are measured at the quarterly frequency for each of the three HS 10-digit products: paintings, prints and sculptures. Nominal imports are deflated by the import price index computed by the BLS for the 3-digit End-use product 413: Coins, gems,

---

[12] Since the permanent component of GDP is typically non-stationary, the dataset is first converted to first differences.
[13] Due to data limitations on prices, it is assumed that the deflator is common to products and destination countries.

jewelry, & collectibles, from Figure 2.[14] On the right-hand side, seasonally adjusted real GDP for 32 countries is obtained at the quarterly frequency from Haver, and decomposed into temporary and permanent components as described above. In one of the specifications below, we will use an alternative measure of international investment demand from the U.S. Treasury International Capital (TIC) system. TIC data document monthly U.S. transactions in long-term securities and we will use "Gross Sales by U.S. Residents to Foreigners" of U.S. stocks and treasury bonds, aggregated to the quarterly frequency, as a measure of foreign investment demand.

iii. Results

Table 8 shows the baseline estimates of α_1. The left panel (columns 1-4) includes all bilateral quarterly flows greater than $5,000, a total of just over 6,000 observations. In column 1, a percent increase in national real GDP translates into a 3.4 percent increase in contemporaneous art imports, significant at the 5 percent level. An elasticity of above 1 implies that the share of art in income is increasing over time, which suggests that art is either a superior consumption good or becoming an increasingly attractive investment. Decomposing this coefficient into permanent and temporary components in columns 2-4, we see that there is little discernable correlation between the temporary component of income changes and art imports while the permanent component is very strongly correlated with art purchases; a percent increase in the permanent component of income increases art purchases by 24 percent. That permanent innovations in income stimulate art purchases while temporary

---

[14] No U.S. export price index is available for this product category however, as shown above, the price deflator does a good job of tracking price movements in an auction-based, international painting index. For this exercise, the trade price index is slightly favored since it encompasses more products and is particular to the selection of artworks traded internationally. The results are not qualitatively different if instead we use the painting index as the deflator.

innovations do not is consistent with the PIH prediction that art is a consumption good and not an investment.

In the right panel, the regressions are rerun only for countries whose art imports for a product within a given quarter exceeded $1 million. It is immediately apparent that all of the estimated coefficients are magnified. The overall responsiveness of art imports to GDP for this subset is 11 percent. While the response of art purchases to temporary income innovations is still zero, the elasticity of purchases with respect to permanent innovations increases to a staggering 89 percent. Therefore, it is not just that art behaves like a consumption good, but that the correlation of income and art demand is concentrated in countries with relatively high levels of quarterly purchases. This observation could be driven by a number of factors. Countries with higher levels are likely wealthier, have a larger proportion of art consumers and have 'deeper ties' to art markets; all of these factors would contribute to import flows being more sensitive to income.

Tables 9 and 10 explore the hypothesis that art demand changes with income *relative* to other consumption and investment goods. Recall that these correlations are informative about the type of a given consumption good or investment vehicle. In Table 9, the dependent variable is the quarterly change in real art exports from the United States, again at the HS10 level, normalized by the total amount of U.S. exports to each country in a given period. For example, in the first quarter of 2009 Germany imported $530 million worth of paintings from the U.S., a 39 percent decline relative to the previous year; over the same period real GDP was down about 6 percent. However, the decline in art purchases is less pronounced relative to total German imports from the U.S., which dropped by 17 percent, than it is to total GDP. In other words, it is important to additionally control for factors that affect overall trade flows.

In this example, we find that art demand is sensitive to income at a rate of greater than one-for-one, even after controlling for total imports as a gauge of other consumption goods. As such, art consumption is not only increasing relative to income but increasing as a share of all goods. This pattern is supported, albeit with lower statistical significance, by the data. In the left panel of Table 9 we find that art imports behave much like superior consumption goods: the relative consumption of artworks increases with income, specifically with permanent increases in income. The right panel, looking at the large importer set, is more precisely estimated with an elasticity of art imports to permanent GDP of 62 percent. This suggests that much of the increase in the consumption of art in the wake of an innovation to income is a relative increase.

Table 10 shows the analogous results for investment flows using TIC data for U.S. stocks and treasury bonds. The dependent variable is the quarterly change in real product-level art exports (similar to the Table 8 results), but we now include on the right-hand side an additional control for the quarterly change in bilateral foreign purchases of U.S. securities. The coefficients on the TIC variables tell us whether art flows are correlated with investment flows, e.g., whether German purchases of U.S. stocks rise and decline in tandem with art purchases. We find only weak evidence that art flows are related to the nominal flows of these investment goods. For a percent increase in foreign purchases of U.S. treasury bonds, art imports rise by a modest 0.14 percent, significant at the 5 percent level, while art flows are uncorrelated with foreign purchases of U.S. equities.

Using the data on aggregate bilateral international investment and trade flows we can check that the PIH predictions hold for purchases of products that we know to be either investments or consumption goods. Table 11 shows the results of regressions of the form:

$$\Delta \ln Z_{kt} = \alpha_0 + \alpha_1 \Delta \ln RGDP^i_{kt} + \varepsilon_{jkt}$$

where Z is the nominal flow of a given investment (i.e., stocks and t-bills) or consumption product (i.e., aggregate trade flows). In columns 1-3, the dependent variable is the bilateral foreign purchase of U.S. stocks. If stocks are pure investments, then the PIH would predict that their purchase is correlated with temporary innovations to GDP, though less so for permanent ones. Foreign purchases of U.S. equities are indeed correlated with temporary and permanent changes to real GDP. T-bills in columns 4-6 behave much like the canonical PIH investment vehicle: they are strongly correlated with temporary innovations to GDP but with a coefficient indistinguishable from zero on the permanent ones. In columns 7-9, aggregate trade flows (e.g., all of the U.S. exports to Germany) are positively correlated with both the temporary and permanent components of GDP, with a much stronger correlation with the permanent component. This observation conforms with some of our prior notions about the composition of trade; most of it is likely for consumption but with some of it being accounted for by investment. Finally, we investigate the possibility that income may operate with a lag on art purchases. In Table 12 we rerun our Table 8 results with 4 quarter lags of the independent variables and find that the results to be quite similar.

IV. PIH predictions in a structural VAR

A separate method for identifying permanent income innovations is developed in the literature on real business cycles. The dynamics in the canonical RBC model are driven by shocks to the technology parameter in production, which in turn, have first order effects on the level of national output and income. Gali (1999) evaluates the conditional correlations of the model in national data using an identification strategy that distinguishes technology from non-technology drivers of productivity and employment. The intuition of that strategy is that only permanent changes in the stochastic technology parameter can be the source of a unit root in productivity. In other words, the high degree of persistence of labor productivity is driven by the high degree of persistence in the underlying technology process, and not by other factors which can have only a transient impact. For our purposes, an identified permanent technology shock is tantamount to a permanent innovation in income. Thus, we mimic Gali's strategy and measure the conditional correlation of art demand with permanent income. Again, the PIH associates a positive conditional correlation with the consumption for art purchases.[15]

Following Gali, we specify the following bivariate system for national labor productivity (X_{kt}) and U.S. real bilateral art exports:

$$\begin{bmatrix} \Delta X_{kt} \\ \Delta \left(\frac{M_{jkt}}{P_t} \right) \end{bmatrix} = \begin{bmatrix} C_{jk}^{11}(L) & C_{jk}^{12}(L) \\ C_{jk}^{21}(L) & C_{jk}^{22}(L) \end{bmatrix} \begin{bmatrix} \varepsilon_{kt}^z \\ \varepsilon_{kt}^n \end{bmatrix}$$

where the left-hand side vector is assumed to be I(1) with a stationary VAR representation in first differences. The right-hand side is a distributed lag of disturbances of technology (ε_{kt}^z) and non-technology (ε_{kt}^n) components, which are allowed to vary by country. Gali's identifying assumption above is implemented as $C_{jk}^{12}(L) = 0$; that is, the only source of permanent fluctuations in labor productivity is ε_{kt}^z.

Data for national labor productivity are the log differences of quarterly seasonally-adjusted series for output per worker hour by country.[16] The real trade flows are the nominal U.S. export volumes deflated by the BLS price index for collectibles. Under the assumptions

---

[15] A zero or negative correlation is not necessarily due to the investment motive for purchasing art, since we have not identified a temporary innovation to technology. Temporary changes to the technological process will affect labor productivity along with a host of other factors and hence it is more difficult to isolate.
[16] Productivity data by country was downloaded from Haver.

that the technology and non-technology disturbances are orthogonal to one another and that the reduced form VAR innovations are a linear combination of those disturbances, we can consistently estimate $C_{jk}^{(.)}(.)$ and the corresponding impulse response functions for technology and non-technology shocks.

The impulse responses of painting, print and sculpture purchases to technology shocks (i.e., permanent income shocks) are shown for the four largest importers in Figures 4-6.[17] For paintings (Figure 4), the point estimates on impact are positive for the UK, Germany and France, and negligible for Switzerland. For the UK and France in particular, permanent income innovations lead to significant increases in art purchases on the order of $7 million and $4 million per quarter, respectively, for each percentage point increase in productivity. For prints (Figure 5), the results are decidedly weaker with none of the shocks registering significant changes on impact and with several of the point estimates below zero. For sculptures (Figure 6), we see several positive point estimates on impact, with the increase significantly different from zero for France. The impact for Germany, the smallest of the four importers, is negligible. Overall, the balance of estimates of the conditional correlation between permanent income and art purchases are positive for the larger painting and sculpture categories. However, this result is qualified by the lack of response in prints and, in some instances, our inability to reject the null hypothesis of no effect.

V. Conclusions

This paper presents an exploration of the global flows and dynamics of painting, print and sculpture markets. In contrast to the bulk of previous studies, our focus has been on the

---

[17] Also shown are bootstrapped 90% confidence bands for the impulse responses.

quantity of art purchases which, as opposed to prices alone, provides a more complete measure of the flow of real services from visual arts. Using a battery of novel measures, we have found that these services most closely resemble consumption services. International art trade varies closely with trade in Consumer Goods, with the income of destination countries, and specifically with the permanent component of income innovations. The interpretation of the results is also robust to variations in country characteristics. For instance, countries with larger, more stable art flows exhibit stronger correlations with permanent income. This is consistent with the notion that network effects and information flows play key roles in the export success of highly distinct final goods. Moreover, the high concentration of art importers over time suggests that it is indeed the incumbents driving the result rather than the entry and exit of smaller market participants.

Certain qualifications are in order for the preeminence of consumption versus investment motives in buying art. First, the effects identified here are average effects within and across countries. Using country data, it is indeed difficult to reject the hypothesis that a portion of the art buying population is composed of 'pure' investors. The distributional characteristics of art buyers and returns are investigated more thoroughly in Goetzmann, Renneboog and Spaenjers (forthcoming) and Scorcu and Zanola (2010). Further, pooling across countries likely smoothes over differences in the balance of consumers and investors. The trade data suggest, however, that the *average* art buyer is a consumer. Second, the focus on international data ignores a possible selection bias of traded visual arts versus those consumed domestically. While the characteristics of cross-border art purchases relative to domestic flows is beyond the scope of the data, one might conjecture that in order to bear the higher costs of international transactions, such as taxes or shipping, international sales are predominantly up market sales. If true, the selection induced by only considering international trade would be consistent with previous studies that have found masterpieces to be poorer investments. Finally, it is important to acknowledge that fine art sales are quite distinct from other trade goods due to the manner in which they are sold, primarily through auctions. Here we abstract from the idiosyncrasies and vagaries of auctions, such as those identified in Ashenfelter and Graddy (2006), but are cognizant of the possibility that the process of selling visual arts may itself be a function of the state of the economy, and hence a factor in determining trade flows.

References

Ashenfelter, Orley & Kathryn Graddy (2003). "Auctions and the Price of Art." *Journal of Economic Literature*, American Economic Association, 41(3), 763-787.

Ashenfelter, Orley & Kathryn Graddy (2006). "Art Auctions." In: Victor A. Ginsburg and David Throsby, Editor(s), Handbook on the Economics of Art and Culture, Elsevier, 1, 909-945

Clark, Peter K. (1987). "The Cyclical Component of U.S. Economic Activity." *Quarterly Journal of Economics*, 102: 797-814.

Dimson, Elroy & Christophe Spaenjers (2009). "Ex Post: The Investment Performance of Collectible Stamps." CentER Discussion Paper Series No. 2009-64.

Friedman, Milton (1957). *A Theory of the Consumption Function*. Princeton University Press.

Gali, Jordi (1999). "Technology, Employment, and the Business Cycle: Do Technology Shocks Explain Aggregate Fluctuations?" *American Economic Review*, American Economic Association, 89(1), 249-271.

Ginsburgh, Victor, Jianping Mei & Michael Moses (2006). "The Computation of Prices Indices." In: Victor A. Ginsburg and David Throsby, Editor(s), Handbook on the Economics of Art and Culture, Elsevier, 1, 947-979.

Goetzmann, William N., Luc Renneboog & Christophe Spaenjers (forthcoming). "Art and Money" *American Economic Review Papers and Proceedings*, American Economic Association. Yale ICF Working Paper No. 09-26; TILEC Discussion Paper No. 2010-002; CentER Discussion Paper Series No. 2010-08.

Graddy, Kathryn & Philip Margolis (2007). "Fiddling with Value: Violins as an Investment?" CEPR Discussion Papers 6583, C.E.P.R. Discussion Papers.

Kim, Chang-Jin and Charles R. Nelson (1999). State-Space Models with Regime Switching: Classical and Gibbs-Sampling Approaches with Applications. Massachusetts Institute of Technology.

Locatelli-Biey, Marilena & Roberto Zanola (2002). "The Sculpture Market: An Adjacent Year Regression Index," *Journal of Cultural Economics*, Springer, 26(1), 65-78.

Pesando, James E. (1993). "Art as an Investment: The Market for Modern Prints." *American Economic Review*, American Economic Association, 83(5), 1075-89.

Pesando, James E. & Pauline M. Shum (1999). "The Returns to Picasso's Prints and to Traditional Financial Assets, 1977 to 1996." *Journal of Cultural Economics*, Springer, 23(3), 181-190.

Pesando James E. & Pauline M. Shum (2008). "The Auction Market For Modern Prints: Confirmations, Contradictions, And New Puzzles." *Economic Inquiry*, Western Economic Association International, 46(2), 149-159.

Renneboog, Luc & Christophe Spaenjers (2009). "Buying Beauty: On Prices and Returns in the Art Market." CentER Discussion Paper Series No. 2009-15; TILEC Discussion Paper No. 2009-004.

Scorcu, Antonello E. & Roberto Zanola (2010). "The 'Right' Price for Art Collectibles. A Quantile Hedonic Regression Investigation of Picasso Paintings." Working Paper Series 01_10, Rimini Centre for Economic Analysis.

Visual art is identified as the following HS trade products:

	HS Code	Description
Paintings	9701.10.0000	Paintings, drawing and pastels other than of heading 4906
Prints	9702.00.0000	Original engravings, prints and lithographs, framed or not framed
Sculptures	9703.00.0000	Original sculptures and statuary, in any material

The following categories are *not* included in visual art trade:

	4906	Plans and drawings for architectural, engineering, industrial, commercial, topographical or similar purposes, originals and specific reproductions
Paintings	5805.00	Hand-woven tapestries of the type Gobelins, Flanders, Aubusson, Beauvais and the like, and needle-worked tapestries (for example, petit point, cross stitch), whether or not made up
	5907.00	Textile fabrics otherwise impregnated, coated or covered; painted canvas being theatrical scenery, studio back-cloths or the like: Other Made Up Textile Articles; sets; worn clothing and worn textile articles; rags
	6304.99.1000	Certified hand-loomed and folklore products
	6304.99.2500	Wall hangings of jute
	9701.90.0000	Painting, drawing and pastels, NESOI
	9810.00.1000	Painted, colored or stained glass windows and parts thereof, all the foregoing valued over $161 per square meter and designed by, and produced by or under the direction of, a professional artist
Prints	4911.91	Pictures, designs and photographs
	4911.91.20	Lithographs on paper or paperboard not over 0.51 mm in thickness
	4911.91.2020	Posters
Sculptures	4420.10.0000	Statuettes and other ornaments, of wood
	6913.10	Statuettes and other ornamental ceramic articles, of porcelain or china
	6913.10.1000	Statues, statuettes and handmade flowers, valued over $2.50 each and produced by professional sculptors or directly from molds made from original models produced by professional sculptors
	8306.10.0000	Bells, gongs and the like, and parts thereof Statuettes and other ornaments, and parts thereof
	9601	Worked ivory, bone, tortoise-shell, horn, antlers, coral, mother-of-pearl and other animal carving material, and articles of these materials (including articles obtained by molding)

Table 1: U.S. trade data categories for visual arts

	Paintings (9701100000)		Prints (9702000000)		Sculptures (9703000000)	
	2009 Value	89 - 09 CAGR	2009 Value	89 - 09 CAGR	2009 Value	89 - 09 CAGR
1. Switzerland	1591	3.7%	18	10.5%	230	9.7%
2. United Kingdom	1325	6.7%	22	4.0%	252	10.0%
3. France	572	5.9%	8	3.2%	73	5.8%
4. Germany	217	4.3%	14	7.0%	47	7.1%
5. Belgium	152	11.9%	3	17.8%	55	14.3%
6. Netherlands	126	8.5%	1	4.1%	20	14.6%
7. Korea	125	23.3%	2	25.1%	18	14.5%
8. Japan	106	-9.9%	4	-14.2%	7	-10.3%
9. Canada	59	2.3%	18	6.0%	36	4.0%
10. Italy	72	9.3%	3	13.5%	23	7.2%
Top 10	**4,345**	**5.7%**	**94**	**6.4%**	**760**	**9.3%**
All Countries	**4,640**	**5.8%**	**113**	**6.8%**	**826**	**9.5%**

Table 2: U.S. exports of visual arts, 1989-2009 ($ millions)

Notes: Shown are nominal U.S. exports and annual growth rates by country and HS10 category.
Source: USITC and author calculations.

	Paintings (9701100000)		Prints (9702000000)		Sculptures (9703000000)	
	2009 Value	89 - 09 CAGR	2009 Value	89 - 09 CAGR	2009 Value	89 - 09 CAGR
1. France	835	6.2%	15	1.6%	118	8.3%
2. United Kingdom	645	3.4%	18	2.2%	125	6.9%
3. Italy	351	13.9%	2	9.9%	85	8.4%
4. Germany	297	7.1%	17	7.3%	59	5.5%
5. Netherlands	217	11.9%	3	10.3%	5	5.8%
6. Switzerland	159	-4.5%	3	0.4%	53	2.7%
7. Spain	181	15.0%	2	5.0%	27	10.2%
8. Austria	85	16.0%	1	9.9%	5	5.1%
9. Japan	46	1.7%	4	-5.1%	13	7.2%
10. Belgium	55	8.3%	1	11.8%	4	1.6%
Top 10	2,873	7.3%	67	3.8%	492	7.0%
All Countries	3,020	7.2%	73	4.1%	528	7.1%

Table 3: U.S. imports of visual arts, 1989-2009 ($ millions)

Notes: Shown are nominal U.S. imports and annual growth rates by country and HS10 category.
Source: USITC and author calculations.

Dependent variable - Bilateral U.S. exports of:

	Paintings			Prints			Sculptures		
	Full Sample	Large Value	Ex. UK & France	Full Sample	Large Value	Ex. UK & France	Full Sample	Large Value	Ex. UK & France
Foods, Feeds & Beverages	-0.416 *** (0.036)	-0.503 *** (0.044)	-0.331 *** (0.035)	-0.190 *** (0.035)	0.057 (0.051)	-0.105 *** (0.035)	-0.271 *** (0.039)	-0.407 *** (0.040)	-0.166 *** (0.039)
Industrial Supplies	-0.168 ** (0.067)	0.367 *** (0.076)	-0.085 (0.066)	-0.354 *** (0.064)	-0.164 (0.117)	-0.258 *** (0.065)	-0.313 *** (0.072)	0.030 (0.077)	-0.189 *** (0.071)
Capital Goods	-0.273 *** (0.065)	0.096 (0.077)	-0.473 *** (0.065)	-0.020 (0.059)	-0.262 *** (0.100)	-0.190 *** (0.061)	-0.313 *** (0.066)	0.054 (0.067)	-0.550 *** (0.068)
Automotive Products	0.044 (0.034)	-0.264 *** (0.033)	0.074 ** (0.033)	0.113 *** (0.029)	-0.193 *** (0.047)	0.140 *** (0.029)	0.010 (0.033)	-0.160 *** (0.033)	0.054 * (0.032)
Consumer Goods	1.550 *** (0.064)	0.594 *** (0.073)	1.469 *** (0.064)	1.170 *** (0.057)	0.699 *** (0.116)	1.075 *** (0.058)	1.433 *** (0.064)	0.610 *** (0.074)	1.316 *** (0.064)
Military Goods	0.375 *** (0.023)	0.277 *** (0.031)	0.348 *** (0.023)	0.251 *** (0.023)	0.233 *** (0.041)	0.209 *** (0.023)	0.376 *** (0.025)	0.211 *** (0.032)	0.339 *** (0.025)
R-squared	0.540	0.300	0.510	0.520	0.320	0.490	0.480	0.370	0.450
Observations	3154	1533	2984	2451	423	2281	2632	849	2462
Memo: Consumer minus Capital	1.8229 *** (0.104)	0.4986 *** (0.115)	1.9419 *** (0.103)	1.1895 *** (0.091)	0.9614 *** (0.167)	1.2651 *** (0.091)	1.7455 *** (0.102)	0.5564 *** (0.108)	1.8658 *** (0.102)
Period fixed effects	Yes	Yes	Yes	Yes	Yes	Yes	Yes	Yes	Yes
Importer fixed effects	No	No	No	No	No	No	No	No	No

Table 4: The correlation of U.S. art exports with aggregate sector exports (period fixed effects).

Notes: Each column shows the log of quarterly bilateral U.S. art exports regressed on the log of aggregate U.S. exports by broad sector. Consumer goods exports are net of painting, print, sculpture, stamp and antique sales. The full sample consists of all quarterly, non-zero observations for the period 1989q1-2010q1; the subset of large-value observations are quarterly bilateral art exports greater than $1 million. Also included as controls are period fixed effects. Standard errors are shown in parentheses. * denotes significant at the 10% level; ** denotes significant at the 5% level; *** denotes significant at the 1% level.

Dependent variable - Bilateral U.S. exports of:

	Paintings			Prints			Sculptures		
	Full Sample	Large Value	Ex. UK & France	Full Sample	Large Value	Ex. UK & France	Full Sample	Large Value	Ex. UK & France
Foods, Feeds & Beverages	-0.023 (0.047)	-0.003 (0.055)	-0.019 (0.048)	-0.052 (0.055)	0.205 (0.129)	-0.054 (0.057)	-0.105 * (0.057)	-0.075 (0.075)	-0.107 * (0.059)
Industrial Supplies	0.342 *** (0.071)	0.313 *** (0.073)	0.332 *** (0.074)	0.516 *** (0.082)	0.514 *** (0.131)	0.519 *** (0.086)	0.361 *** (0.087)	0.467 *** (0.094)	0.340 *** (0.090)
Capital Goods	0.200 *** (0.071)	0.284 *** (0.082)	0.215 *** (0.074)	-0.185 ** (0.083)	-1.034 *** (0.177)	-0.163 * (0.086)	-0.042 (0.085)	-0.476 *** (0.115)	-0.002 (0.089)
Automotive Products	0.013 (0.041)	-0.022 (0.040)	0.011 (0.043)	0.184 *** (0.046)	0.099 (0.088)	0.172 *** (0.047)	0.032 (0.048)	0.154 *** (0.057)	0.028 (0.050)
Consumer Goods	0.416 *** (0.070)	0.283 *** (0.056)	0.397 *** (0.073)	0.371 *** (0.079)	0.298 ** (0.130)	0.331 *** (0.084)	0.830 *** (0.082)	0.625 *** (0.082)	0.805 *** (0.088)
Military Goods	0.003 (0.026)	-0.002 (0.032)	-0.001 (0.027)	-0.017 (0.032)	-0.019 (0.073)	-0.017 (0.033)	0.001 (0.034)	-0.010 (0.046)	-0.005 (0.035)
R-squared	0.790	0.760	0.760	0.700	0.390	0.660	0.700	0.540	0.650
Observations	3154	1533	2984	2451	423	2281	2632	849	2462
Memo: Consumer minus Capital	0.216 * (0.113)	-0.001 (0.111)	0.183 (0.118)	0.556 *** (0.129)	1.332 *** (0.249)	0.495 *** (0.136)	0.871 *** (0.134)	1.101 *** (0.162)	0.806 *** (0.141)
Period fixed effects	No	No	No	No	No	No	No	No	No
Importer fixed effects	Yes	Yes	Yes	Yes	Yes	Yes	Yes	Yes	Yes

Table 5: The correlation of U.S. art exports with aggregate sector exports (importer fixed effects).

Notes: Each column shows the log of quarterly bilateral U.S. art exports regressed on the log of aggregate U.S. exports by broad sector. Consumer goods exports are net of painting, print, sculpture, stamp and antique sales. The full sample consists of all quarterly, non-zero observations for the period 1989q1-2010q1; the subset of large-value observations are quarterly bilateral art exports greater than $1 million. Also included as controls are importer fixed effects. Standard errors are shown in parentheses. * denotes significant at the 10% level; ** denotes significant at the 5% level; *** denotes significant at the 1% level.

Dependent variable - Bilateral U.S. exports of:

	Paintings			Prints			Sculptures		
	Full Sample	Large Value	Ex. UK & France	Full Sample	Large Value	Ex. UK & France	Full Sample	Large Value	Ex. UK & France
Foods, Feeds & Beverages	-0.081 (0.074)	-0.081 (0.077)	-0.078 (0.077)	0.074 (0.089)	0.174 (0.177)	0.054 (0.094)	-0.005 (0.091)	0.054 (0.115)	-0.006 (0.095)
Industrial Supplies	0.322 ** (0.140)	0.375 ** (0.147)	0.328 ** (0.146)	0.163 (0.170)	-0.283 (0.254)	0.16 (0.180)	-0.678 *** (0.175)	-0.423 ** (0.186)	-0.698 *** (0.185)
Capital Goods	-0.019 (0.101)	-0.015 (0.143)	-0.024 (0.104)	0.012 (0.144)	0.979 ** (0.412)	0.009 (0.150)	-0.088 (0.136)	-0.286 (0.249)	-0.09 (0.142)
Automotive Products	0.072 (0.096)	0.162 (0.101)	0.066 (0.100)	-0.215 * (0.117)	0.293 (0.220)	-0.239 * (0.123)	0.387 *** (0.117)	0.241 (0.156)	0.4 *** (0.123)
Consumer Goods	0.873 *** (0.141)	0.433 *** (0.130)	0.864 *** (0.147)	0.388 ** (0.173)	0.65 ** (0.275)	0.35 * (0.183)	0.404 ** (0.166)	0.472 ** (0.196)	0.366 ** (0.175)
Military Goods	-0.035 (0.040)	0.056 (0.051)	-0.037 (0.042)	0.048 (0.053)	0.097 (0.098)	0.037 (0.056)	0.124 ** (0.053)	0.155 ** (0.077)	0.121 ** (0.056)
R-squared	0.020	0.310	0.020	0.010	0.420	0.010	0.020	0.280	0.020
Observations	2860	1513	2692	2040	417	1872	2251	827	2083
Memo: Consumer minus Capital	0.892 *** (0.187)	0.447 ** (0.210)	0.888 *** (0.194)	0.375 (0.240)	-0.329 * (0.542)	0.341 (0.251)	0.492 ** (0.227)	0.758 ** (0.350)	0.456 * (0.238)
Period fixed effects	No	No	No	No	No	No	No	No	No
Importer fixed effects	Yes	Yes	Yes	Yes	Yes	Yes	Yes	Yes	Yes

Table 6: The correlation of U.S. art exports with aggregate sector exports (first differences, importer fixed effects).

Notes: Each column shows the log of quarterly bilateral U.S. art exports regressed on the log of aggregate U.S. exports by broad sector. Consumer goods exports are net of painting, print, sculpture, stamp and antique sales. The full sample consists of all quarterly, non-zero observations for the period 1989q1-2010q1; the subset of large-value observations are quarterly bilateral art exports greater than $1 million. Also included as controls are period fixed effects. Standard errors are shown in parentheses. * denotes significant at the 10% level; ** denotes significant at the 5% level; *** denotes significant at the 1% level.

		Art consumption	Art consumption as a share of total	Art investment	Art investment as a share of total
Permanent change in GDP	Normal consumption good	+	0	0	0
	Superior consumption good	+	+	0	0
Temporary change in GDP	Constant weight in investment Portfolio	0	0	+	0
	Variable weight in investment portfolio	0	0	+	+/-

Table 7: Permanent income hypothesis predictions.

	Nominal Art Value > $5,000				Nominal Art Value > $1,000,000			
	(1)	(2)	(3)	(4)	(5)	(6)	(7)	(8)
Δ Real GDP	3.382 ** (1.483)				10.906 *** (2.335)			
Δ Temporary GDP		0.011 (0.018)		0.012 (0.018)		-0.011 (0.020)		-0.001 (0.025)
Δ Permanent GDP			24.131 *** (8.350)	22.555 ** (11.166)			89.892 *** (16.771)	134.225 *** (21.510)
Observations	6324	2545	3394	2545	2606	1195	1502	1195

Table 8: The elasticity of real artwork exports to temporary and permanent innovations in foreign GDP.

	Nominal Art Value > $5,000				Nominal Art Value > $1,000,000			
	(1)	(2)	(3)	(4)	(5)	(6)	(7)	(8)
Δ Real GDP	1.249 (1.542)				9.48 *** (2.394)			
Δ Temporary GDP		0.008 (0.018)		0.008 (0.017)		-0.012 (0.620)		-0.004 (0.020)
Δ Permanent GDP			16.173 (10.502)	19.098 (14.468)			62.73 *** (18.183)	109.678 *** (23.587)
Observations	5896	2265	2999	2265	2484	1109	1385	1109

Table 9: The elasticity of real artwork export share to temporary and permanent innovations in foreign GDP.

Notes: For Table 8 the dependent variable is the real bilateral U.S. export value of paintings, prints and sculptures. For Table 9 the dependent variable is the real bilateral U.S. export value of paintings, prints and sculptures as a share of total bilateral exports. Standard errors are shown in parentheses. ** significant at 5%; *** significant at 1%.

	Nominal Art Value > $5,000				Nominal Art Value > $1,000,000			
	(1)	(2)	(3)	(4)	(5)	(6)	(7)	(8)
Δ Real GDP	2.424 (2.164)				9.211 *** (2.430)			
Δ Temporary GDP		0.009 (0.016)		0.011 (0.017)		0.004 (0.014)		0.012 (0.016)
Δ Permanent GDP			10.805 (16.371)	15.629 (17.175)			81.43 *** (21.096)	88.939 *** (22.346)
Δ Stock purchases	0.004 (0.067)	0.113 (0.099)	0.054 (0.090)	0.108 (0.100)	-0.13 (0.080)	0.023 (0.105)	-0.104 (0.095)	-0.004 (0.100)
Δ T. bond purchases	0.078 (0.055)	0.197 ** (0.077)	0.145 ** (0.069)	0.192 ** (0.077)	-0.047 (0.063)	-0.026 (0.087)	-0.013 (0.076)	-0.064 (0.085)
Observations	2806	1327	1668	1327	1951	982	1216	982

Table 10: The elasticity of real artwork exports to temporary and permanent innovations in foreign GDP, controlling additionally for foreign asset purchases.

Notes: The dependent variable is the real bilateral U.S. export value of paintings, prints and sculptures. Standard errors shown in parentheses. ** significant at 5%; *** significant at 1%.

	Δ U.S. stocks purchased by foreigners			Δ U.S. t-bills purchased by foreigners			Δ U.S. exports purchased by foreigners		
	(1)	(2)	(3)	(4)	(5)	(6)	(7)	(8)	(9)
Δ Real GDP	2.902 *** (0.451)			2.246 *** (0.524)			1.835 *** (0.127)		
Δ Temporary GDP		7.809 *** (1.022)			3.604 *** (1.189)			1.559 *** (0.343)	
Δ Permanent GDP			8.368 *** (3.231)			4.919 (3.843)			5.23 *** (1.014)
Observations	2811	1683	1683	2668	1606	1606	7651	3830	3830

Table 11: The elasticity of nominal asset and aggregate trade flows to temporary and permanent innovations in foreign GDP.

Notes: The dependent variables are the nominal foreign assets purchases (foreign purchases of stocks and foreign purchases of Treasury Bills, respectively) as well as nominal aggregate U.S. exports. Standard errors shown in parentheses. ** significant at 5%; *** significant at 1%.

	Nominal Art Value > $5,000				Nominal Art Value > $1,000,000			
	(1)	(2)	(3)	(4)	(5)	(6)	(7)	(8)
Δ Real GDP (-4)	2.734 (1.519)				9.81 *** (2.535)			
Δ Temporary GDP (-4)		0.02 (0.018)		0.022 (0.018)		0.006 (0.018)		0.013 (0.018)
Δ Permanent GDP (-4)			27.664 *** (8.672)	29.797 ** (11.824)			106.358 *** (17.464)	106.353 *** (20.894)
Observations	6086	2483	3318	2483	2537	1171	1485	1171

Table 12: The elasticity of real artwork exports to temporary and permanent innovations in foreign GDP (lagged independent variables).

Notes: The dependent variable is the real bilateral U.S. export value of paintings, prints and sculptures. Standard errors are shown in parentheses. ** significant at 5%; *** significant at 1%.

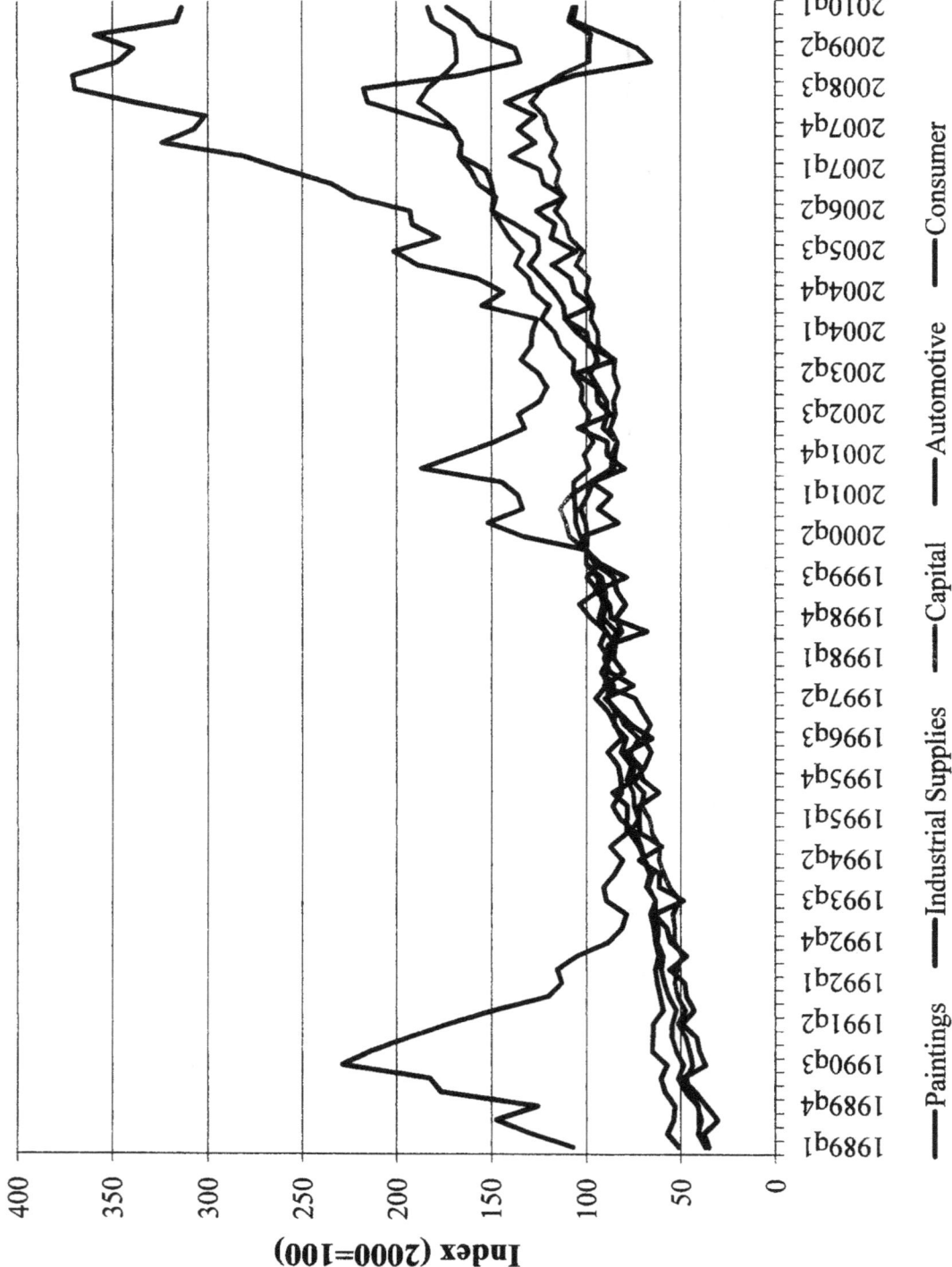

Figure 1: U.S. painting exports relative to broad sectors.

Source: USITC.

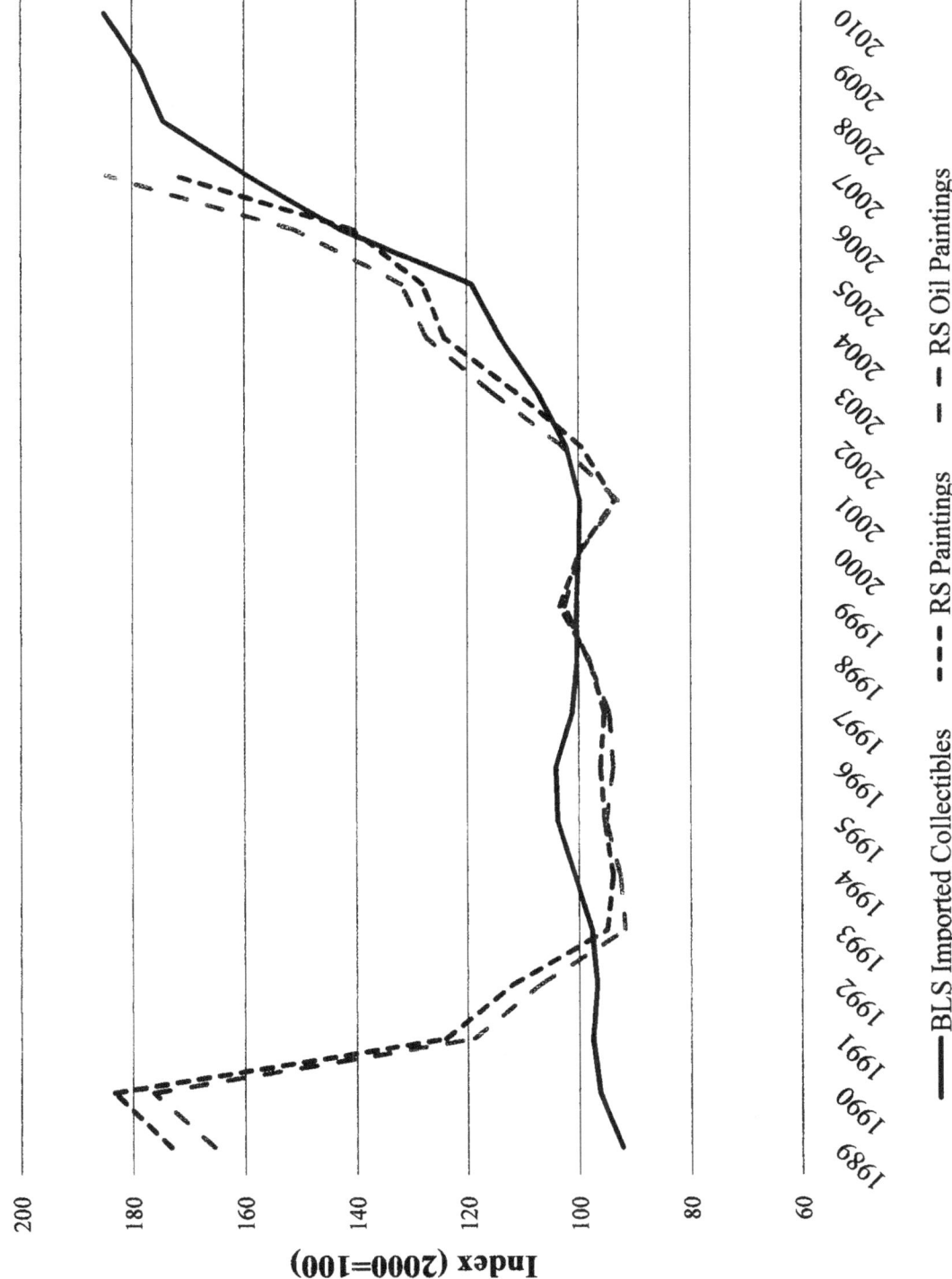

Figure 2: Painting and collectible prices.

Source: U.S. Bureau of Labor Statistics and Renneboog and Spaenjers (2009).

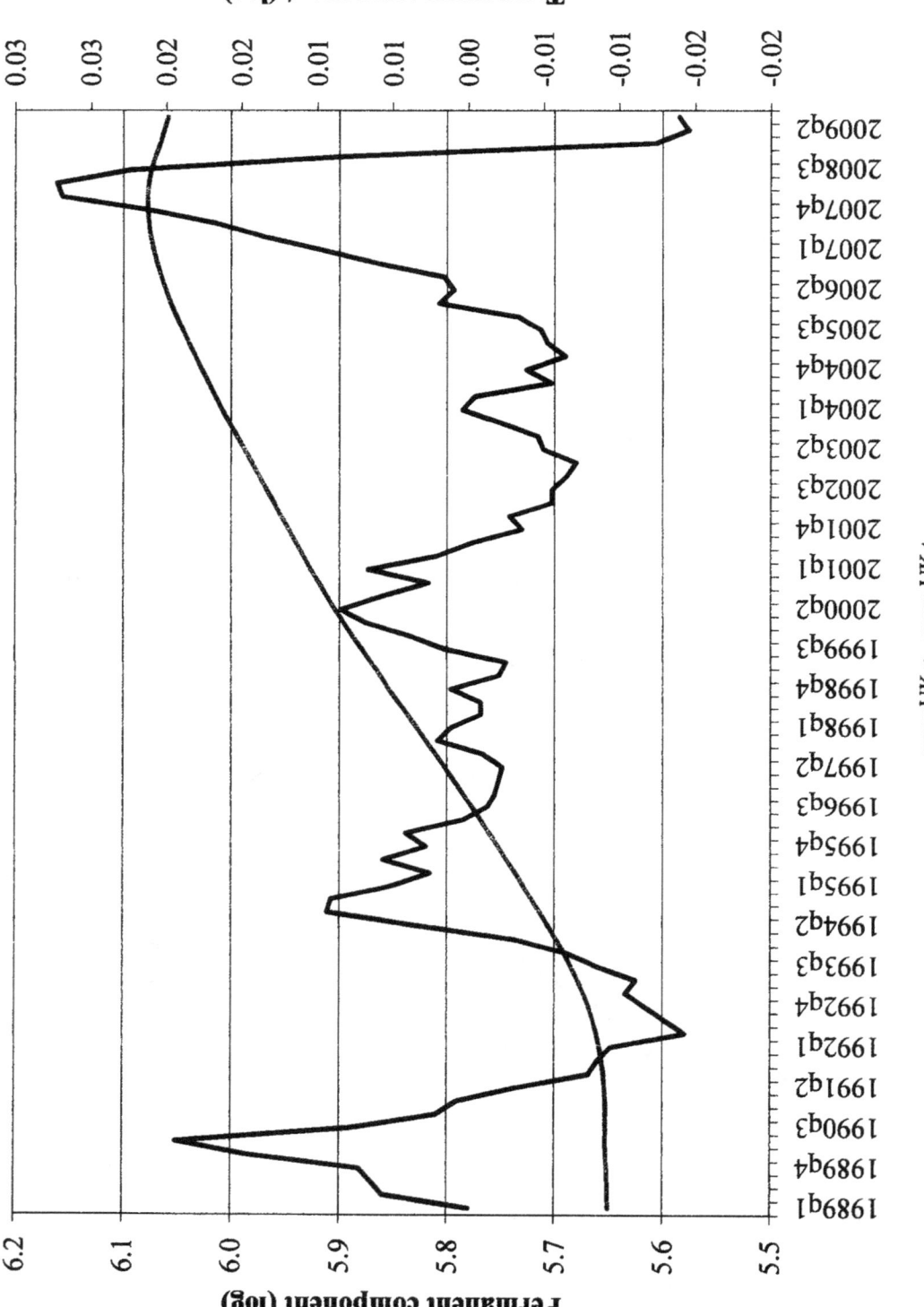

Figure 3: Temporary and permanent components of UK real GDP.

Source: Author calculations.

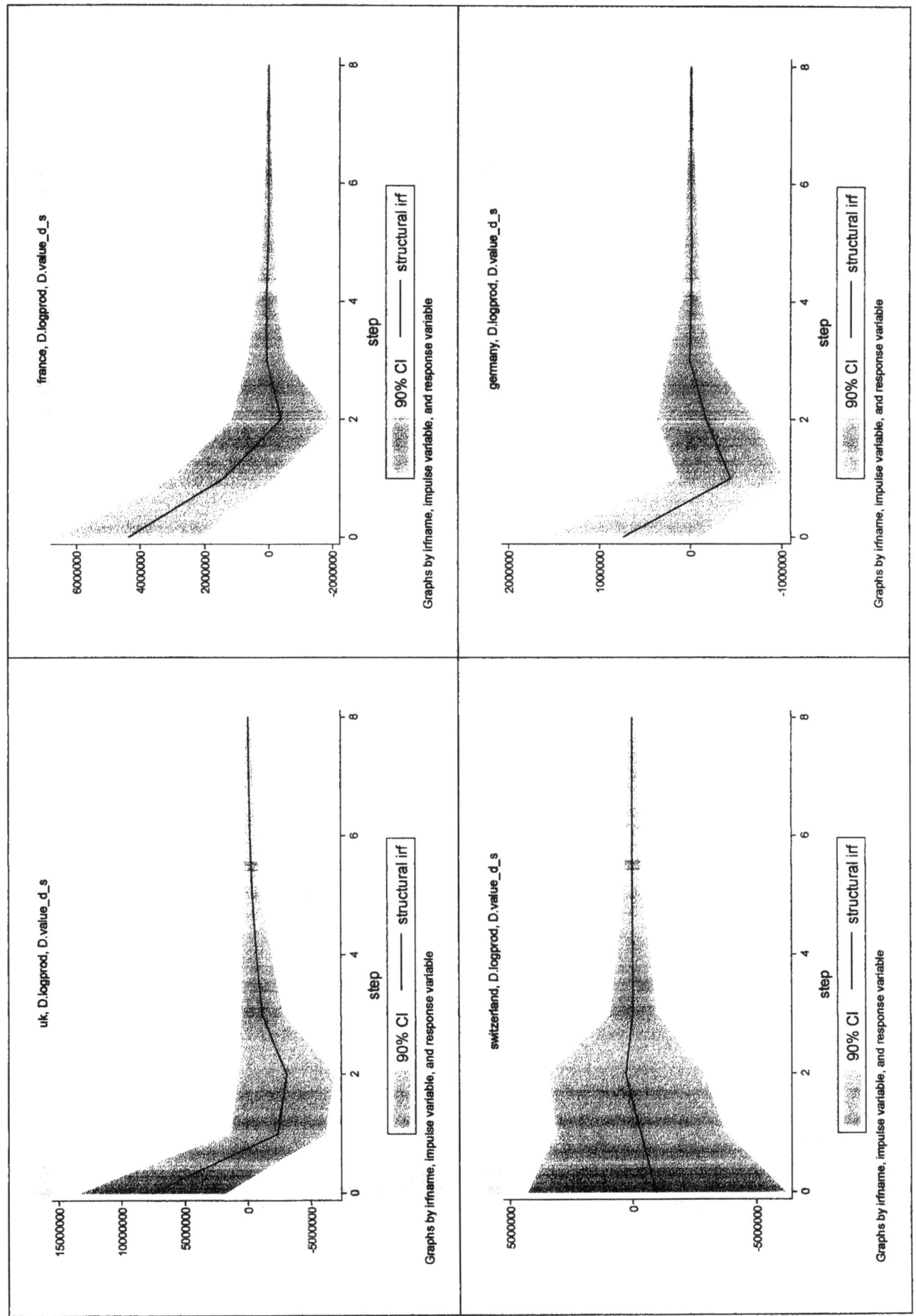

Figure 4: Estimated impulse responses of painting purchases to an identified permanent income shock

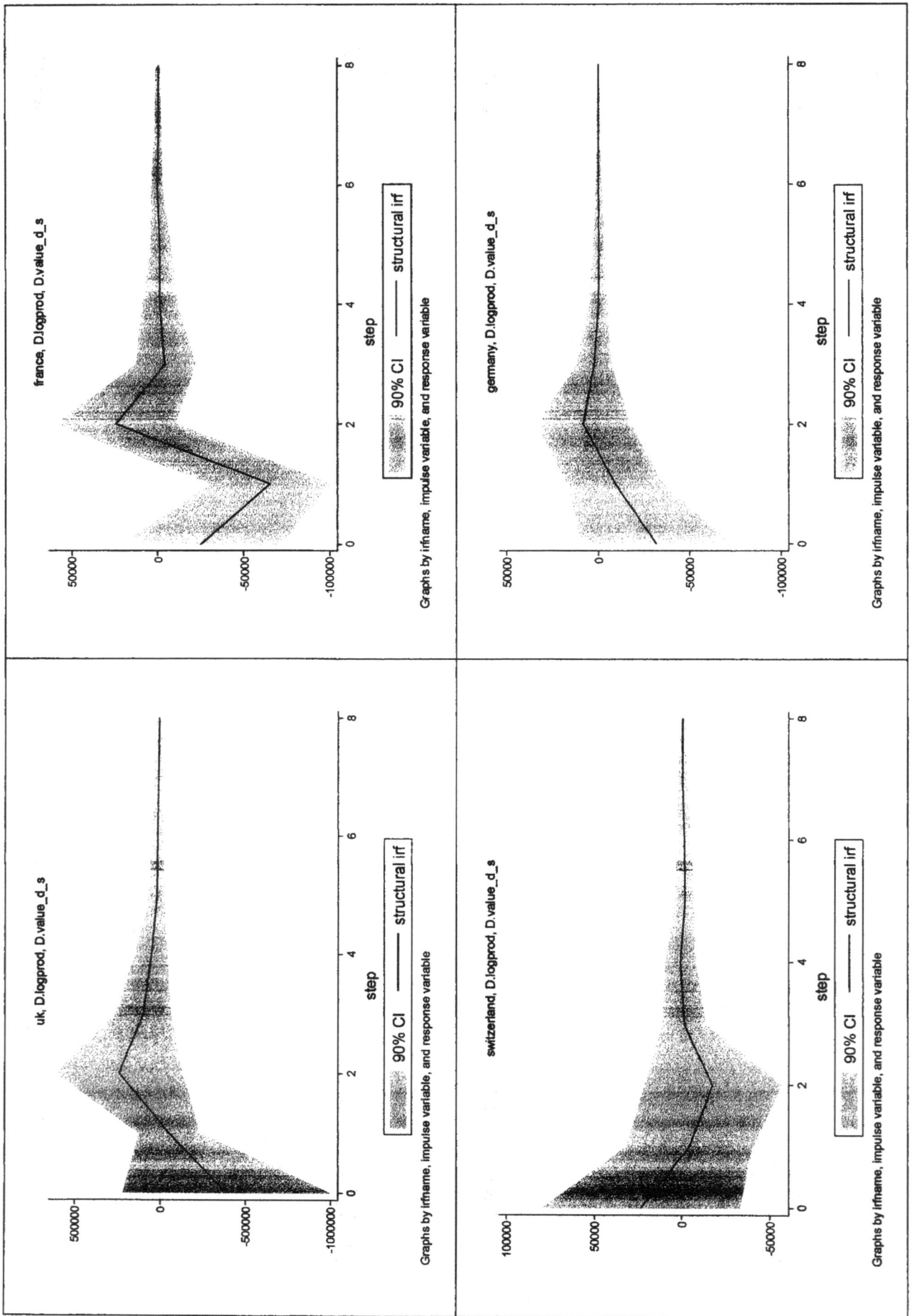

Figure 5: Estimated impulse responses of print purchases to an identified permanent income shock

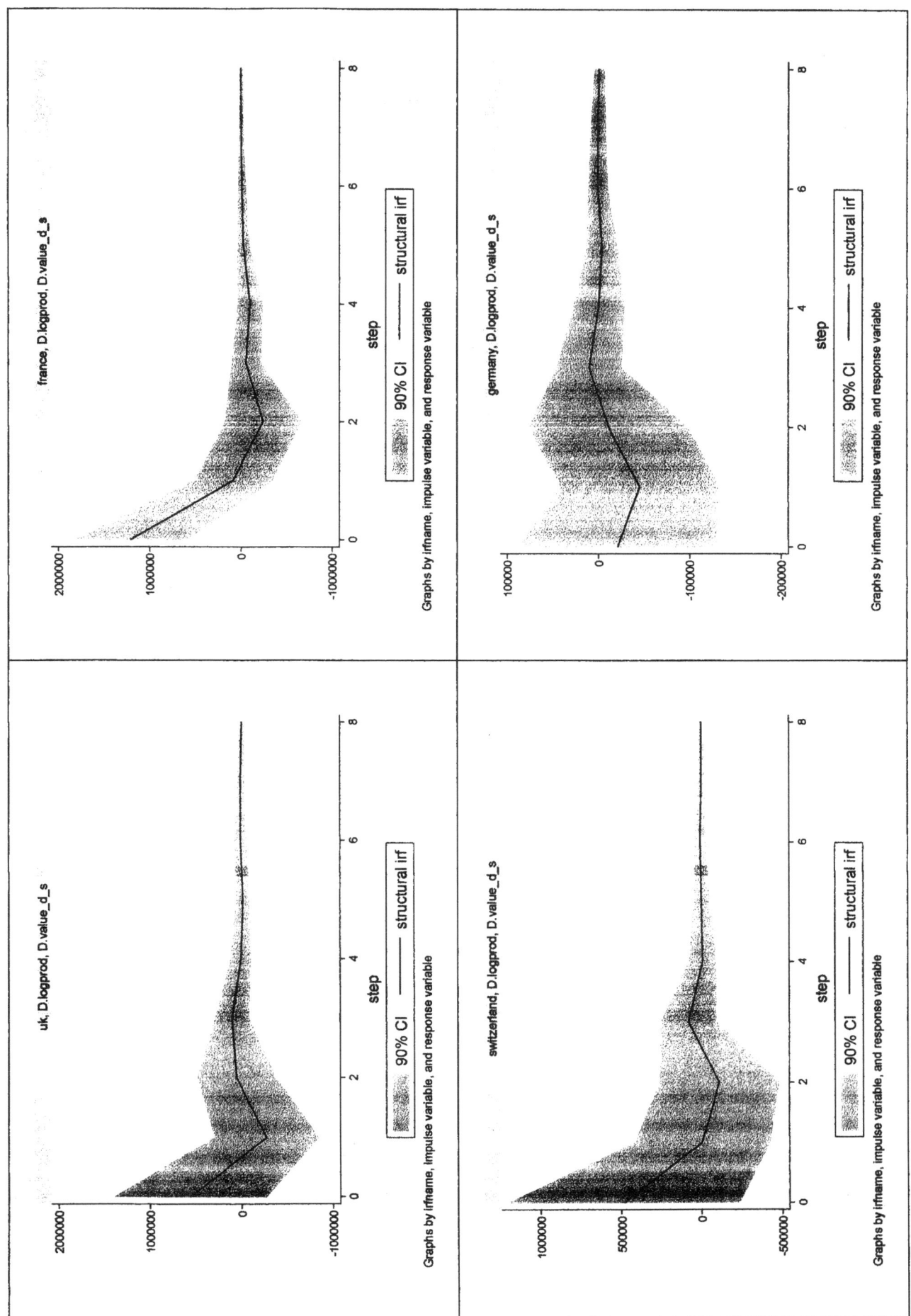

Figure 6: Estimated impulse responses of sculpture purchases to an identified permanent income shock

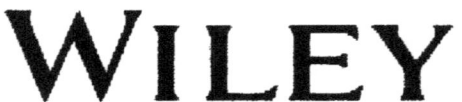
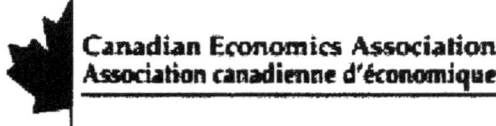

Asset Pricing Theory and the Valuation of Canadian Paintings
Author(s): Douglas J. Hodgson and Keith P. Vorkink
Source: *The Canadian Journal of Economics / Revue canadienne d'Economique*, Vol. 37, No. 3 (Aug., 2004), pp. 629-655
Published by: Wiley on behalf of the Canadian Economics Association
Stable URL: http://www.jstor.org/stable/3696009
Accessed: 05/02/2014 12:40

Asset pricing theory and the valuation of Canadian paintings

Douglas J. Hodgson *Département des sciences économiques, Université du Québec à Montréal*
Keith P. Vorkink *Marriott School of Management, Brigham Young University*

Abstract. The valuation of Canadian paintings is analysed empirically. Using a sample of auction prices for major Canadian painters for the period 1968–2001, we run hedonic regressions to analyse the influence of various factors, including painter identity, on auction prices, as well as to construct a market price index. This index is used in a second-stage analysis in which we analyse the properties of Canadian art viewed as an investment asset. We apply standard asset pricing theory, as incorporated in the capital asset pricing model (CAPM), to the analysis of price movements in the market for Canadian paintings.

Théorie du prix des actifs et évaluation de peintures canadiennes. Les auteurs font une étude empirique de l'évaluation de peintures canadiennes. A partir d'un échantillon de prix d'encan pour la période 1968–2001, ils estiment une régression hédonique qui leur permet d'analyser l'effet sur le prix de quelques variables comme l'identité du peintre, et de construire un indice de prix dans le temps. Cet indice est utilisé pour étudier les rendements sur les peintures considérées comme des investissements. On utilise le modèle d'évaluation des actifs financiers (MÉDAF) pour analyser ces mouvements de prix.

1. Introduction

It is not unusual to find the mass news media reporting the latest blockbuster sale of a high-priced painting, a frequent occurrence, for example, during the

For their comments, we thank Georges Dionne, Pascal St-Amour, anonymous referees, and seminar participants at Toronto, Rice, Rochester, Journées du CIRPÉE (Montreal 2002), the 2003 CEA and SCSE Meetings, the 2003 European Workshop on Applied Cultural Economics, and the Montreal Econometrics Workshop. Financial support from the Montreal Institute of Mathematical Finance and the Social Sciences and the Humanities Research Council of Canada is also acknowledged. Email: hodgson.douglas-james@uqam.ca art market boom of the late 1980s. There is a general interest in the value of art works, which can even lead to political controversy, as happened in 1990 when a work by Barnett Newman was purchased by the National Gallery of Canada. One argument made by those in favour of the acquisition was that the painting could be thought of as an investment – it was an asset being added to the capital stock of the nation, the monetary value of which had the potential for substantial future appreciation.

Although the price of any painting incorporates a portion that can be thought of as being paid in exchange for immediate consumption by the purchaser, it cannot be ignored that paintings are durable, capable of surviving in close to their original condition for centuries, and that therefore some portion of the price can be thought of as representing the discounted present value of the sums that may be paid by potential future owners in exchange for the consumption they may obtain from the painting. Two elements of uncertainty thus enter into consideration for the potential buyer of a painting: uncertainty over the future evolution of one's own taste and uncertainty over the future evolution of tastes of society in general. This dependence of the price of a painting on the expected present value of a future consumption stream of uncertain monetary value is analogous to that of a stock on the expected present value of a sequence of uncertain future dividend payments.

The latter consideration suggests the analysis of art prices within the context of asset pricing theory. The valuation of art works is an area that has received considerable attention from economists (see the books of Reitlinger 1961 and Grampp 1989), with the investment properties of paintings being a particular focus of academic investigation (see, for example, Stein 1977; Baumol 1986; Goetzmann 1993; Pesando 1993). The existing literature is focused on a few questions regarding the statistical properties of time series of art returns, in particular the first two moments of the return distribution. A time series index of prices and returns, for a given category of art work, is generally estimated from individual sale data at auctions using either the 'repeat-sale regression' or the 'hedonic regression' method, described in more detail in section 2. The sample average returns and return variances are compared with those of financial assets such as bonds and stocks. Covariances with the stock market and the associated market betas are also often computed.[1] Results in the literature vary, depending on the time period and the 'portfolio' of paintings under consideration, with some studies finding the return on art to be low on average relative to stocks and bonds and some finding it to be high. One feature of art returns that does seem to be robust is that they are at least as variable as stocks or bonds, so that art tends to be a risky investment. The

---

1 The 'beta' of a financial asset is the ratio between the covariance of the asset's return with that of a general market portfolio and the market variance. Beta represents the degree of non-diversifiable risk incurred in the holding of the asset and is, according to the capital asset pricing model (CAPM), the sole factor that should influence the equilibrium price of an asset.

correlations of art portfolios with the stock market tend to be positive, but are often close to zero. A non-positive correlation would suggest that art, despite its high variance, can serve a useful function in a diversified portfolio as an element that counters, or is at least neutral to, general market risk.

Most of the existing literature on art as an investment is concerned with European and American paintings. In the present paper, we conduct an empirical analysis of the valuation of Canadian paintings. We consider the behaviour of prices of oil and acrylic paintings, over the period 1968–2001, for a portfolio of major Canadian painters. We begin by estimating a price index and a return series using hedonic methods, reported in section 2. The results of our hedonic regression allow us to gauge the influence on auction prices of a number of separate factors, including the identity of the artist, the auction house, the size of the painting, and the medium and support. We depart from the literature in estimating the hedonic regression using the semi-parametric efficient adaptive estimator of Bickel (1982), motivated by the high leptokurtosis present in our auction price data and by our sample size of nearly 13,000 sales. The resulting estimates of returns are more precise than would be obtained using ordinary least squares, an important consideration because these *estimated* returns are treated as being *observed* returns when we proceed to the analysis of the investment properties of paintings. The results of the latter analysis are presented in section 3. We compare the investment properties of Canadian art with those of Canadian government bonds and stocks. We estimate the capital asset pricing model (CAPM) and also apply the conditional CAPM of Bollerslev, Engle, and Wooldridge (1988), in which conditional covariances and conditional betas are permitted to vary over time.

2. The hedonic regression

In this section, we compute a time series representing general movements in the market for Canadian art. Such an index is not readily available, but must be inferred from the individual sales of paintings that occur over time. Each painting is, to a certain extent, a unique object, and therefore the price at which it sells cannot be taken as a general indicator of the level of the market. The price will also be affected by factors such as the identity of the artist, the size, medium, and support of the painting, the location of the sale (the auction house, or city, for example), the condition and quality of the work itself, and a host of idiosyncratic factors.

The various approaches that have been taken to address this problem can be placed into two general classes, the 'repeat-sale regression' method and the use of hedonic regression. The former approach, used, for example, by Baumol (1986), Goetzmann (1993), Pesando (1993) and Pesando and Shum (1999), is based on a comparison of the prices at which an identical art work was sold in different time periods in order to compute a rate of return for the given art work and time interval; it then effectively averages over all art works for which such repeat-sales occurred to obtain an average rate of return in each time period. The application of the method to obtain a price index for paintings has obvious data problems – the identification of repeat sales of the same painting may be difficult to make based on published sale data, and the number of such repeat sales may be too small to construct an accurate price index. These problems are significantly mitigated in the work of Pesando (1993) and Pesando and Shum (1999), who analyse the valuation of prints, for which multiple impressions of the same image can effectively be considered as identical objects.

Hedonic regressions have been estimated in many previous studies, a few recent examples being Chanel, Gérad-Varet, and Ginsburgh (1996), Czujack (1997), and Locatelli-Biey and Zanola (2002). The essential approach is to gather data on a number of art sales through time (auction sales, for example), and to then regress the price of each work (or its logarithm) on other available characteristics of the work, such as the artist, the size, the medium, the auction house, the time period, and so forth. Many of the regressors, such as those associated with the time period, will take the form of a set of dummy variables. The estimated time period dummy parameters can be thought of as representing an index of variation of the price of an 'average' painting, within the class under consideration, after controlling for the art-work-specific variables represented by the other included variables. In our study, this would be the average price of a painting by a 'major' Canadian painter, as defined below. Such an index would be a relatively accurate reflection of the return to be earned by a collector holding a large, well-diversified collection of works by several painters. It would, of course, provide a less accurate reflection of the price variation of a single painting, or of the works of a single painter, or even of a specific school of painters, such as, for example, the Automatistes or the Group of Seven. An analysis of returns at such disaggregated levels would be desirable and is under consideration for future research, but data availability makes the analysis of returns at these levels problematic. For more discussion of the use of hedonic methods in the estimation of art prices, see Chanel, Gérad-Varet, and Ginsburgh (1996).

It should also be emphasized that the hedonic regression estimates a reduced-form model of price determination at auctions, with no attempt to disentangle supply and demand influences. We are not aware of existing efforts to separately model supply and demand functions in art auctions, but it seems to be a very difficult, if not impossible, task. This is principally because the sellers and buyers in this market are very similar – being a secondary market, both sides of the market consist of collectors. Indeed, the same individuals may be both buyers and sellers (of different works) at the same auction. What work has been done on supply and demand in art markets tends to focus on primary markets, where currently active artists market their new works through galleries (see, for example, Caves 2000).

2.1. Data

Records of sales of Canadian paintings at auction from 1968 to 2001 were collected by the authors from Campbell (1973–75, 1980), Sotheby's (1975, 1980), and Westbridge (1981–2002). Sales are recorded in these publications for an enormous number of artists, including quite minor ones. We chose to restrict our analysis to artists considered to have made contributions of some lasting importance to the development of Canadian art, so that we can claim to have assembled a sample of paintings by 'major' artists that should be expected to have solid long-term investment value. Our criterion for an artist to be 'important' is that his or her work be mentioned in Reid's (1973) survey of the history of Canadian painting. In addition to being a principal reference on Canadian painting, Reid (1973), having been published near the beginning of our sample period, provides us with a list of painters who had achieved some degree of renown, and presumably of investment value, by this time. This emphasis on 'blue-chip' artists is not unusual in the literature. As our focus is on art as an investment, we would like to consider paintings the current price of which can largely be considered as representing investment, as opposed to consumption, value. For relatively unknown artists or young contemporary artists, whose paintings are generally low priced, the investment motivation will generally be much less important than the consumption motivation for purchasers. As noted by Grampp (1989), the vast majority of paintings sold in the art market eventually become valueless.

We consider only oil and acrylic paintings – the vast majority of our observations are for oils. The number of painters listed in Reid (1973) and for whom we have at least one recorded sale of an oil or acrylic painting is 152, and the total number of sales in our data set is 12,821. We have included only sales for which the auction house's attribution is confident, so that paintings listed as being 'school of' or 'in the manner of,' say, Cornelius Krieghoff are excluded. For each painting, we recorded, in addition to the identity of the artist, the height and width in centimetres, the medium and support, the auction house, and the half-year of the sale. Since most auctions occur in fairly concentrated time periods (autumn auctions are mostly in October and November, and spring auctions in April and May), we have followed the standard practice in the literature on art pricing by using a semi-annual time index.

Throughout the empirical study, we use hammer prices as recorded in the publications listed above. No effort has been made to adjust or correct our numbers to account for costs such as auctioneers' commissions, taxes, insurance premia, maintenance and restoration costs, and so on. All these factors act to reduce the monetary returns of owning paintings below the levels recorded here. Factors acting to augment the monetary returns to art owners, such as reproduction fees and exhibition lending fees, are also omitted.

2.2. Econometric model

Our auction data are used to estimate a hedonic regression with time-period dummy variables, the associated parameter estimates being used to construct semi-annual and annual price indices. The econometric model is written:

$$p_i = \sum_{t=1}^{T} \gamma_t z_{it} + \sum_{j=1}^{J} \alpha_j w_{ij} + u_i, \quad i = 1, \ldots, n, \tag{1}$$

where p_i is the logarithm of the price of sale i, the number of sales is $n = 12{,}821$, z_{it} is the value of a period-t dummy variable, equal to 1 if painting i was sold in period t and zero otherwise, with the number of time periods T being 66 when the data are grouped semi-annually and 33 when they are grouped annually. All auctions held during the months from January to June of a given year are considered to belong to the first half of the year, with the year's remaining auctions belonging to its second half. The semi-annual dummies thus run from 1968:2 to 2001:1. Owing to the low incidence of auctions during the summer months, we will consider an auction year in the same way as one would consider a school year or a hockey season, so that, for the purposes of forming an annual price series, the auction year is considered to run from July 1 of a given calendar year to June 30 of the following one. We thus have 33 annual dummies, starting with the 1968–69 auction year, followed by 1969–70 and concluding with 2000–2001. Our estimates of the vector of associated parameters $\{\gamma_t\}_{t=1}^{T}$ will form our price indices, to be used in the asset pricing analysis of the following section.

The regressors $\{w_{ij}\}$ in (1) represent the other characteristics of painting i. These include 151 dummy variables for the painting's artist, 19 medium/support dummies, and 35 auction house dummies (in all three cases, one dummy was omitted to avoid collinearity with the time period dummies; hence, 151 painter dummies corresponds to a set of 152 painters). Three additional variables reflecting a painting's dimensions – height, width, and surface area – were included. Equation (1) can be written more concisely as

$$p_i = x_i'\beta + u_i, \quad i = 1, \ldots, n, \tag{2}$$

where $x_i' = (z_{i1}, \ldots, z_{iT}, w_{i1}, \ldots, w_{iJ})$ and $\beta = (\gamma_1, \ldots, \gamma_T, \alpha_1, \ldots, \alpha_J)'$. Note that we have $J = 208$ and $T = 66$ or $T = 33$ for semi-annual and annual dummies, respectively, giving us a dimension K for the parameter vector β of 274 or 241.

A note should be added on the interpretation of the dummy parameters. If we knew the time period dummies $\{\gamma_t\}_{t=1}^{T}$, we could compute the rate of return between, say, periods t and $t+1$ as follows:

$$r_{t+1} = \exp(\gamma_{t+1} - \gamma_t) - 1.$$

We can proceed similarly for the characteristic-related dummies. We will see below that the dummy for A.Y. Jackson was omitted from the regression (1), in other words it was arbitrarily set equal to zero. The dummy parameters α_j for each of the remaining painters can then be seen as reflecting their market values vis-à-vis Jackson. The percentage difference between the value of a work by painter j and a Jackson, controlling for all the other factors in our analysis, will be

$$\exp(\alpha_j) - 1.$$

The regression (1) and (2) can be, and usually is, estimated by ordinary least squares (OLS). Under the standard assumptions, OLS will be consistent and asymptotically normal and will be asymptotically efficient if the disturbances $\{u_i\}$ are normally distributed. An application of the Jarque-Bera (1980) normality test to our OLS residuals yielded an enormous statistic of 10,537 (the test has a chi-squared null distribution with two degrees of freedom), with an associated $\chi^2(1)$ kurtosis statistic of 10,033. Hence, there is reason to suppose that a substantial efficiency loss is borne when the model is estimated by OLS, relative to maximum likelihood or to a robust estimator such as least absolute deviations. For our purposes, efficiency is a major concern. This is because our estimates of the time period dummies $\{\gamma_t\}_{t=1}^T$ and, more specifically, of the associated returns $\{r_t\}_{t=2}^T$, will be treated in our analysis of the following section as being observed series of prices and returns. Thus, these parameters should be estimated as precisely as possible. To this end, we estimate (2) adaptively, according to the procedure of Bickel (1982), designed to deliver asymptotically efficient estimates when the distribution function of the disturbances $\{u_i\}$ is unknown, and described in more detail in appendix A.

2.3. Results

The results of our estimation of the hedonic regression (1)–(2) are discussed here and reported in tables 1–3 and in appendix B.

2.3.1. Time series price index and estimated returns

In tables 1 and 2 are reported the semi-annual and annual dummy estimates, respectively. For each time period, we have provided the number of observations, with the estimated dummy parameter and its standard error, the estimated rate of return with standard error, and the real rate of return.[2] The returns are plotted in figures 1 and 2. Striking is the high volatility of the market, particularly prior to 1988, a phenomenon present in both data periodicities. Perhaps not merely coincidentally, the reduction in return volatility apparent in the late 1980s corresponds with a general increase in the number of observations. The latter is to an extent due to problems of data availability, particularly in the very early years of the period, but it probably also represents a general thickening and maturation of the Canadian art market in these years. The higher estimated volatility prior to 1988 may be partially due to imprecise

---

2 Computed using the CPI deflator, obtained from Bloomberg.

TABLE 1
Time period dummies and estimated returns (semi-annual)

Time period	Number Of Obs.	Log-price dummy	Std error	Estimated nominal return (%)	Std error	Estimated real return (%)
68:2	39	7.21	.092			
69:1	61	7.57	.075	43.19	15.97	40.12
69:2	57	7.81	.077	27.78	12.76	26.08
70:1	130	7.29	.055	−40.38	5.15	−41.64
70:2	68	7.22	.071	−7.47	7.52	−7.47
71:1	168	7.28	.054	6.46	8.55	3.98
71:2	120	7.44	.061	17.59	7.63	15.17
72:1	170	7.48	.053	4.37	6.80	2.80
72:2	155	7.45	.056	−2.90	5.85	−6.39
73:1	134	7.63	.058	19.08	7.61	14.59
73:2	132	7.63	.057	−0.10	6.65	−4.76
74:1	145	7.89	.055	30.21	8.52	23.70
74:2	132	7.95	.057	5.65	6.94	0.18
75:1	58	7.99	.076	4.44	9.07	−0.13
75:2	47	7.96	.084	−2.91	10.36	−7.58
76:1	138	7.80	.057	−14.89	7.97	−17.96
76:2	92	8.09	.065	34.29	9.89	31.59
77:1	114	8.03	.059	−6.10	7.18	−11.10
77:2	91	8.17	.064	15.21	8.80	10.94
78:1	137	8.24	.055	7.24	7.88	2.44
78:2	126	8.45	.056	22.37	8.21	18.93
79:1	120	8.61	.057	18.35	8.20	13.02
79:2	123	8.68	.057	7.31	7.52	3.10
80:1	131	9.04	.055	42.71	9.75	37.26
80:2	195	9.04	.048	−0.10	6.12	−5.46
81:1	225	9.23	.046	20.50	6.39	13.41
81:2	205	9.09	.048	−12.52	4.61	−17.28
82:1	189	8.74	.049	−29.47	3.87	−35.80
82:2	116	8.46	.058	−24.49	4.85	−27.24
83:1	124	8.45	.057	−1.15	6.95	−3.82
83:2	121	8.67	.057	24.26	8.62	22.39
84:1	115	8.53	.058	−13.06	6.13	−15.32
84:2	131	8.66	.055	14.22	7.91	12.83
85:1	208	8.74	.047	8.08	6.54	5.48
85:2	223	8.83	.046	9.31	5.73	7.58
86:1	252	8.71	.044	−11.31	4.42	−13.28
86:2	342	9.08	.042	46.29	6.63	44.10
87:1	337	8.95	.041	−13.12	3.64	−15.63
87:2	303	9.17	.043	24.48	5.34	22.88
88:1	420	9.22	.041	5.99	4.48	3.69
88:2	336	9.28	.041	6.15	4.36	4.49
89:1	356	9.26	.041	−2.40	4.03	−6.00
89:2	324	9.31	.042	5.15	4.42	3.58
90:1	325	9.24	.042	−6.51	4.00	−9.27
90:2	294	9.16	.043	−8.14	4.02	−10.29
91:1	187	9.04	.049	−10.62	4.60	−14.62
91:2	220	9.03	.047	−1.35	5.40	−1.15
92:1	218	8.99	.048	−3.71	5.17	−5.03
92:2	218	9.07	.047	8.65	5.80	7.85
93:1	179	8.94	.050	−12.35	4.82	−13.14

(Continued)

Table 1 *Concluded*

Time period	Number Of Obs.	Log-price dummy	Std error	Estimated nominal return (%)	Std error	Estimated real return (%)
93:2	177	8.95	.050	0.14	5.77	−0.74
94:1	183	9.20	.050	28.97	7.39	29.85
94:2	229	9.10	.046	−9.26	4.91	−10.35
95:1	235	8.91	.046	−17.36	4.17	−19.02
95:2	217	8.99	.048	7.92	5.59	7.83
96:1	233	8.96	.047	−3.07	4.98	−4.41
96:2	236	9.01	.046	5.09	5.34	4.24
97:1	221	9.05	.047	4.59	5.37	3.74
97:2	275	9.10	.044	4.94	5.23	5.03
98:1	254	9.06	.045	−3.95	4.58	−5.06
98:2	335	9.08	.042	2.15	4.68	2.24
99:1	225	9.07	.047	−1.26	4.67	−2.92
99:2	278	9.19	.045	13.03	5.51	12.13
00:1	251	9.27	.046	8.10	5.11	6.13
00:2	298	9.33	.043	6.65	4.97	6.24
01:1	322	9.27	.043	−6.16	4.11	−7.17

estimates resulting from sparser data – the estimation error is clearly higher in this period – but cannot be entirely, or even predominantly, ascribed to this cause. Rather, we would contend that the thinness and immaturity of the market, coupled with an atmosphere of general macroeconomic instability in Canada during these years, would provide more likely explanations. Deeper investigation of this issue is warranted. We can also see that grouping the data annually leads to substantial reductions in standard errors. Similarly, the standard errors reported here for the adaptive estimator are generally about 30% below the OLS standard errors (not reported), suggesting that our precision gains in using the adaptive estimator are not negligible.

Looking at the annual returns, we can see that the market value grew very rapidly during the 1970s, with an average annual return between 1971 and 1981 of over 21% in nominal terms and 13% in real terms. A deep dip in the early 1980s can probably be ascribed to the general recession of this period, but the market gradually recovered during the remainder of the decade, with a moderate dip in the early 1990s, probably also due to the macroeconomic slowdown of these years. The market was generally stable during the 1990s.

2.3.2. Painters

The 152 painters included in the study are identified in appendix B, with information on the number of works sold for each painter and the estimated regression dummy parameter and standard error. As mentioned above, one dummy variable, that representing A.Y. Jackson, was omitted to prevent collinearity with the time period dummies. Thus, each painter's dummy estimate can be interpreted as representing his/her market value vis-à-vis that of Jackson. In table 3, we provide results on the 'Top 25' Canadian painters, that

TABLE 2
Time period dummies and estimated returns (annual)

Time period	Number Of Obs.	Log-price dummy	Std error	Estimated nominal return (%)	Std error	Estimated real return (%)
68–69	100	7.43	.062			
69–70	187	7.47	.048	3.65	7.06	0.67
70–71	236	7.27	.047	−17.68	4.57	−20.16
71–72	290	7.48	.046	22.65	5.91	18.62
72–73	289	7.55	.047	7.14	4.88	−1.00
73–74	277	7.78	.046	26.16	5.85	14.69
74–75	190	7.97	.049	20.97	6.33	10.68
75–76	185	7.85	.051	−11.09	5.06	−18.97
76–77	206	8.07	.049	24.02	6.92	16.18
77–78	228	8.22	.047	16.82	6.20	7.54
78–79	246	8.53	.045	35.92	6.95	26.97
79–80	254	8.87	.044	40.44	6.93	30.55
80–81	420	9.14	.039	31.18	5.72	18.35
81–82	394	8.93	.040	−18.97	3.14	−30.34
82–83	240	8.46	.045	−37.59	2.82	−43.08
83–84	236	8.61	.046	15.67	5.82	11.48
84–85	339	8.71	.041	11.61	5.19	7.58
85–86	475	8.77	.038	5.84	4.16	2.10
86–87	679	9.02	.036	24.43	4.23	23.67
87–88	723	9.21	.036	20.30	3.63	16.37
88–89	692	9.28	.036	7.54	3.21	2.22
89–90	649	9.28	.036	0.43	3.02	−3.94
90–91	481	9.12	.038	−14.79	2.82	−21.02
91–92	438	9.02	.040	−9.68	3.43	−10.79
92–93	397	9.02	.040	0.13	3.86	−1.47
93–94	360	9.08	.041	5.92	4.25	5.92
94–95	464	9.02	.039	−6.22	3.64	−8.98
95–96	450	8.98	.040	−3.44	3.60	−4.88
96–97	457	9.04	.039	5.83	3.93	4.13
97–98	529	9.09	.038	5.18	3.72	4.16
98–99	560	9.08	.038	−0.34	3.35	−1.19
99–00	530	9.24	.039	16.64	3.91	13.75
00–01	620	9.31	.037	7.28	3.50	5.84

is, those with the 25 highest dummy point estimates, ranked in descending order. For each of these painters, we compute the percentage difference between the value of one of his/her works and a work of Jackson, controlling for the other variables included in the regression. In the following discussion of these results and of the artists, we will often rely on information provided by Reid (1973), without specific citation in each case.

When analysing table 3, a few considerations should be borne in mind. First, the ranking is not necessarily statistically significant. The reported standard errors allow us to infer the significance of the parameter estimate relative to A.Y. Jackson, but not relative to any of the other artists on the list. Secondly, the precision of these estimates varies widely by artist, depending on the number of observations available, the latter varying from a low of 1 for

Asset pricing theory

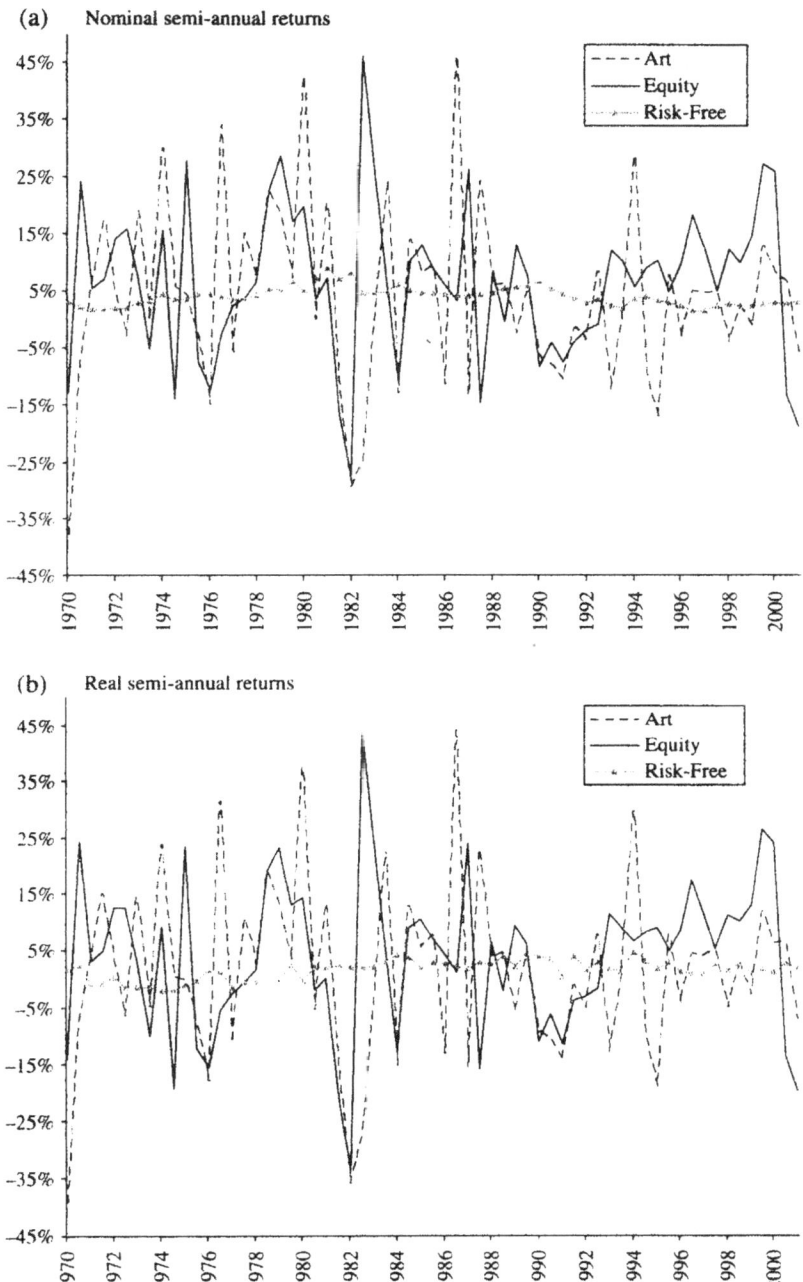

FIGURE 1 A time series of semi-annual Canadian art price, equity, and risk-free returns from the period July 1970 through June 2001

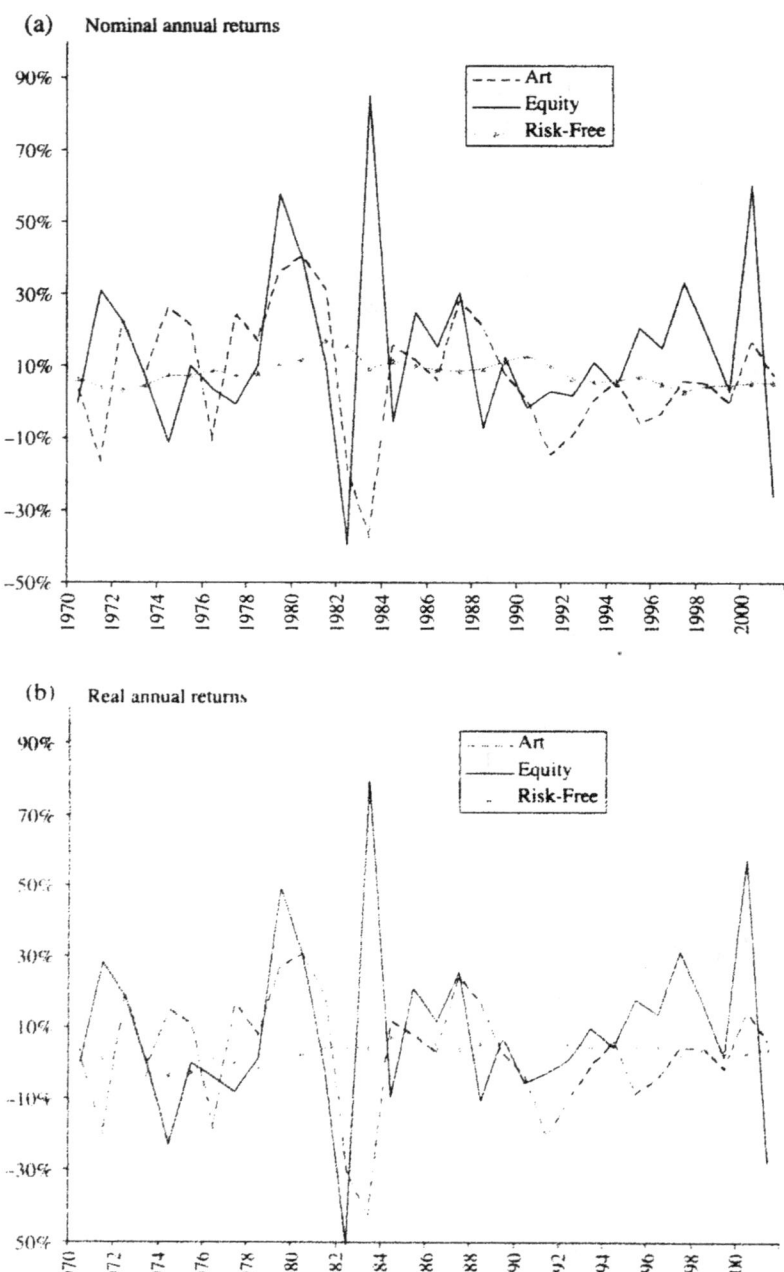

FIGURE 2 A time series of annual Canadian art price, equity, and risk-free returns from the period July 1970 through June 2001

TABLE 3
Dummy estimates for top 25 painters

Rank	Artist	No. obs.	Dummy estimate	Std Err.	% change rel. A.Y. Jackson	Std Err.
1	Tom Thomson	95	1.7381	.0578	468.68	32.90
2	William Berczy	2	1.2258	.3817	240.69	130.04
3	Frank Carmichael	68	1.1390	.0676	212.35	21.13
4	Cornelius Krieghoff	472	1.0400	.0311	182.92	8.81
5	James Duncan	2	0.9118	.3831	148.87	95.35
6	Lawren S. Harris	364	0.8866	.0329	142.68	7.99
7	J.W. Morrice	191	0.7704	.0427	116.07	9.23
8	David Milne	98	0.7502	.0579	111.74	12.26
9	Emily Carr	182	0.7177	.0489	104.98	10.01
10	Paul-Emile Borduas	56	0.6804	.0748	97.47	14.77
11	Christopher Pratt	3	0.5187	.3120	67.99	52.42
12	J.-B. Roy-Audy	1	0.3384	.5398	40.26	75.71
13	J.-P. Riopelle	150	0.3102	.0485	36.37	6.62
14	Fred Varley	121	0.2981	.0519	34.74	7.00
15	Paul Kane	7	0.1248	.2053	13.29	23.26
16	J.-P. Lemieux	142	0.1061	.0491	11.19	5.46
17	W.G.R. Hind	2	0.0984	.3827	10.34	42.22
18	A.J. Casson	579	0.0700	.0290	7.25	3.11
19	J.E.H. Macdonald	406	0.0672	.0326	6.95	3.49
20	Clarence Gagnon	234	0.0592	.0389	6.10	4.13
21	A.Y. Jackson	1246	–	–	0	0
22	Alex Colville	5	−0.0304	.2436	−2.99	23.63
23	Paul Peel	78	−0.1055	.0645	−10.01	5.80
24	Maurice Cullen	204	−0.1570	.0414	−14.53	3.54
25	Edwin Holgate	104	−0.2250	.0552	−20.15	4.41

Jean-Baptiste Roy-Audy to a maximum of 1246 for A.Y. Jackson. Thirdly, the hedonic regression estimates a reduced-form model in which no attempt is made to distinguish between supply and demand influences on price.

The painter by far the most highly valued in the Canadian art market is Tom Thomson (1877–1917). This is not surprising, since Thomson is considered by many to be Canada's greatest painter. He is credited as being the first painter to develop a characteristic national style, which responds in an intuitive manner to the country's rugged landscape. His work provided the impetus for the development of the Group of Seven, whose members included Frank Carmichael, Lawren S. Harris, Fred Varley, A.J. Casson, J.E.H. MacDonald, A.Y. Jackson, and Edwin Holgate.

Among the painters on our list for whom very few observations are available, many were early pioneers of Canadian art. In this category fall William Berczy (1744–1813), James Duncan (1806–81), Jean–Baptiste Roy-Audy (1778–c.1848), Paul Kane (1810–71), and W.G.R. Hind (1833–89). Aside from their inherent quality, these painters' works are valued for their historical interest and their scarcity, the latter factor highlighting the importance of distinguishing between supply and demand influences on the art market.

Most of the painters on our list are associated with one or another of the two major Canadian urban centres during the period when most of the artists considered here were active, viz., Montreal and Toronto. Thomson and the Group of Seven were mostly based in Toronto, and the lion's share of their paintings depict the rural wilderness of the province of Ontario. The regional aspect is worth stressing for a couple of reasons. First, Canada is large and sparsely populated, with regional identifications tending to be strong. Second, the existence of a dominant region such as Ontario can have an important impact, from a purely economic standpoint, on the style and content that is valued in the art market as a whole. In this context, it is worth citing the work of Valsan (2002), whose comparison of the markets for Canadian and American paintings finds a relation of the latter to the former analogous to the relation of Ontario to the rest of Canada noted here.

Nevertheless, a number of painters associated with the province of Quebec find their way onto our list. Aside from the aforementioned Duncan, one can cite the Group of Seven painters Jackson and Holgate, as well as Cornelius Krieghoff, James Wilson Morrice, Maurice Cullen, and the francophones Paul-Emile Borduas, Jean-Paul Riopelle, Jean-Paul Lemieux, and Clarence Gagnon. Setting aside the early figure of Roy-Audy, the most highly valued francophone artists are Borduas (1905–60) and Riopelle (1923–2002). This is not surprising, since these two represent the pillars of the fecund abstract and surrealist school that emerged in Montreal in the late 1940s and 1950s. What may initially seem surprising is the placement of Borduas ahead of Riopelle. After all, Riopelle is the most internationally well known Canadian painter, and the only one mentioned in Arnason's (1986) comprehensive survey of the history of modern art.

One can nevertheless posit several hypotheses to explain Borduas's higher market valuation. First, from the standpoint of Canadian art history, he is arguably of greater importance than Riopelle. Secondly, from a supply-side standpoint, his lifespan was over two decades shorter than that of Riopelle, and his paintings are therefore presumably harder to come by, a hypothesis consistent with the fact that, in our sample, there were three times as many Riopelles as Borduases sold at auction. There is a third potential explanation, perhaps more compelling than the first two. It derives from the structure and functioning of the post-war market for avante-garde art, as analysed and interpreted by Galenson (2000). In a study of American modern artists, Galenson (2000) finds that the function relating the auction value of an artist's work with the artist's age at the time of the execution of the work has a shape that depends heavily on whether the artist was born before or after 1920, that is, on whether or not the artist's professional career commenced before or after the mid-1940s. For artists born after 1920, the function is tilted more significantly in favour of paintings executed early in the artist's career. Galenson (2000) interprets this finding as reflecting changes that occurred in the American art world in the post-war era, with an emphasis among critics and collectors on craftsmanship gradually being replaced by one on formal innovation.

Galenson's (2000) conclusions are relevant to us because a comparison of the careers of Borduas (born in 1905) and Riopelle (born in 1923) conforms in large measure with his analysis. Borduas received a classical training and worked for many years as an assistant of the 'Old Master' Ozias Leduc. He was well into his thirties before turning to a modern idiom in painting, but once doing so, he continued to produce important, original, high-quality work until the very end of his life. Riopelle, on the other hand, came of age in the post-war avant-garde climate of abstract formal innovation, and his best-known works by a large margin are his abstract-expressionist canvases of the late 1940s and 1950s. The critical reputation of the works produced during the remaining four decades of his life is much lower than his early work. We therefore hypothesize that the overall lower market value of Riopelle's work relative to that of Borduas is due to a declining age profile in the former, with many low-priced late works more than compensating for the presence of some high-priced early works. A more complete and formal analysis of this hypothesis is left for future work.

2.3.3. Other factors

We do not report the parameter estimates for the remaining hedonic variables,[3] but briefly remark on some of the results. We found that medium and support can significantly affect price, with a large premium for oil on canvas. The identity of the auction house also has a large effect. In both cases, these variables are proxies for quality. Oils on canvas tend to be more finished and carefully worked than, for example, oils on board or panel, which are often quick preparatory sketches and are discounted relative to canvas by 30% and 25%, respectively. As for auction houses, certain ones are known to deal in works of relatively high quality, such as Sotheby's, which holds two auctions each year, whereas Empire (discounted by 26% relative to Sotheby's), for example, holds monthly auctions at each of its three locations and is presumably less discriminating in what it chooses to sell.

Regarding size, we find that greater height can add somewhat to the value of a painting, whereas width and surface area have negligible marginal effects. This could be because landscapes, usually of horizontal format, are in great supply on the market, which may lead to a scarcity-driven premium on compositions of vertical format.

3. Asset pricing tests

We conduct tests of the returns to our art index in the framework of the capital asset pricing model (CAPM) of Sharpe (1964) and Lintner (1965). The following equation demonstrates the main result of the CAPM, stating that the

---

[3] Available on request from the authors.

expectation of the return on asset i, denoted as $R_{i,t}$, in excess of the return on a risk-free security, $R_{f,t}$, is a linear function of the expected excess return on the market portfolio, $R_{m,t}$:

$$E_{t-1}[R_{i,t}] - R_{ft} = E_{t-1}[R_{m,t} - R_{f,t}]\beta_{i,t}, \qquad (3)$$

where

$$\beta_{i,t} = \frac{\text{cov}_{t-1}(R_{m,t},R_{i,t})}{\text{var}_{t-1}(R_{m,t})}$$

is the conditional 'beta' for asset i in period t, and the subscripts on expectations and covariances indicate conditional moments. Assuming that no dynamics exist in the conditional expectations, (3) reduces to the unconditional CAPM

$$E[R_{i,t}] - R_{f,t} = E[R_{m,t} - R_{f,t}]\beta_i. \qquad (4)$$

There is an extensive empirical literature on the unconditional CAPM, most of which has tested how well this model can explain stock returns, with important early work by Black, Jensen, and Scholes (1972) and Fama and MacBeth (1973).[4] However, the CAPM has been used as a model to explain the returns on other assets. For example Bryan (1985) uses it to perform asset pricing tests of art, while Gyourko and Nelling (1996) use it to analyse the performance of real estate investment trusts (REIT). In a similar fashion to these and other studies, we use the following empirical version of the unconditional CAPM:

$$r_t = \alpha + \beta r_{M,t} + e_t, \qquad (5)$$

where r_t is the excess return on the art index in period t (return on the art index minus the yield on a risk-free security), $r_{M,t}$ is the excess market return, e_t is a disturbance, and α and β are parameters. The CAPM suggests that β measures how much of the return to a particular asset (in our case art) is priced as systematic risk, or the portion of returns that are generated by the asset's correlation to that of the market. A simple t-test of the parameter will test if any portion of the asset's return is systematic, that is, if $\beta = 0$.

If there is some component of returns that is not due to market risk exposure as measured by β, but is persistent, it will appear in the intercept, α. If the CAPM is the true model describing returns, $\alpha = 0$, whereas a finding that $\alpha \neq 0$ would signal average returns that cannot be explained by market risk. A t-test of $\alpha = 0$ will test the CAPM's ability to explain the returns of a particular asset. One could also test for the significance of additional regressors in (5). For example, in analyses of stock returns, Banz (1981) includes market size and Fama and French (1992, 1993) consider a firm's book value to market value ratio as well as size.

---

[4] See Campbell, Lo, and MacKinlay (1997) for a more comprehensive discussion of empirical tests of the CAPM.

Alternative to the unconditional model, if we believe the dynamics in the conditional moments play an important role then our estimation and testing should allow for these moments to move over time. To do so we redefine the r_t (now bolded) as a vector that includes the excess return on the art index as its first element and the market portfolio as its second. We also define the conditional covariance matrix of $\mathbf{r}_t$ to be $\mathbf{H}_t$. This reformulation leads to the following return model for a single asset's return

$$E_{t-1}[r_{i,t}] = \varphi \frac{H_{i2,t}}{H_{22,t}}, \tag{6}$$

where φ is $E_{t-1}[r_{m,t}]$ and $H_{i2,t}$ corresponds to the off diagonal element of $\mathbf{H}_t$, or the conditional covariance of $r_{i,t}$ with $r_{m,t}$ or the market return.

Empirically, (6) can be written in the following manner:

$$\mathbf{r}_t = \boldsymbol{\alpha} + \frac{\varphi}{H_{22,t}} \mathbf{H}_{i,t} + \mathbf{e}_t \tag{7}$$

where $\boldsymbol{\alpha} = [\alpha \,|\, 0]$, $\mathbf{H}_{i,t}$ is a 2×1 vector with the covariance between asset i in the first element and the market variance in the second, and $\mathbf{e}_t$ is a vector of residuals. In order to arrive at a completely specified econometric model we must specify the form of our conditional covariance matrix $\mathbf{H}_t$ and our disturbance process $\{\mathbf{e}_t\}$. Perhaps the most popular parametric model of conditional covariances are of the generalized autoregressive conditional heteroscedasticity (GARCH) family. Models of this type were developed by Engle (1982) and Bollerslev (1987) with a vast literature of models and empirical applications. GARCH models of volatility have been shown to parsimoniously capture time-varying second moments. Our model draws heavily on that of Baba, Engle, Kraft, and Kroner (BEKK).[5] Our general model of conditional volatility will be the following modified version of the BEKK model:

$$\mathbf{H}_t = \mathbf{C}^T \mathbf{C} + \mathbf{A}^T \mathbf{e}_{t-1} \mathbf{e}_{t-1}^T \mathbf{A}, \tag{8}$$

where $\mathbf{C}$ and $\mathbf{A}$ are defined as

$$\mathbf{C} = \begin{bmatrix} c_{11} & 0 \\ c_{21} & c_{22} \end{bmatrix}$$

$$\mathbf{A} = \begin{bmatrix} a_{11} & 0 \\ a_{21} & a_{22} \end{bmatrix}$$

Hence, conditional covariances will have an unconditional component as measured by $\mathbf{C}$, and the dynamic component will allow last period's return

---

[5] Named after a working paper referenced by Engle and Kroner (1995).

shock, e_t, to influence the conditional covariance as measured by **A**. We call our version an ARCH model because we only allow last period's shock to influence covariance, while the more general GARCH models include an autoregressive term in the conditional covariances. Given our model defined above, our parameter vector to estimate will have eight elements: α, φ, c_{11}, c_{12}, c_{22}, a_{11}, a_{12}, and a_{22}. Last, we will assume the distribution of the conditional residuals to be multivariate normal for the purposes of estimation.

3.1. Data and estimation

We make use of the art price index developed in the previous section to generate a series of art returns. We construct a series of 65 returns by calculating percent changes in the semi-annual (July–December and January–June) index data and a series of 32 returns using the annual (July–June) data.[6] To construct excess returns we subtract from our art returns the yield of a maturity-matched Canadian government bond, where yields are obtained from the Bank of Canada. For the semi-annual data, we use the yield on six-month to maturity bonds at months ending June and December. We use the yield on bonds with maturities ranging from one to three years for the annual data.[7]

Our measure of market returns is taken from Morgan Stanley Capital International's (MSCI) Canadian equity index. This is a broad-based Canadian equity index that includes capital gains as well as dividends on over 85% of the country's market capitalization. We construct returns to the market portfolio, $R_{m,t}$, as the percent change in this index from 1 July to 31 December and 1 January to 30 June for the semi-annual data and 1 July to 30 June for the annual data. We are only able to obtain data on the market index starting January 1969, so our semi-annual sample includes 63 observations and the annual sample includes 31 observations.

Summary statistics for the art index returns, risk-free rates, and market returns are found in table 4 and a plot of the semi-annual data is shown in figure 1. Table 4 and figure 2 report the results for the annual data. In table 4 we provide results for nominal returns in panel A and real returns (returns adjusted by percent change in the CPI index) in panel B. In general, our results are similar to those of earlier studies. For example, Mei and Moses (2002) find that during the last 50 years the annual return to art based on New York auctions was 8.2% with a standard deviation of 21%, while our studies find Canadian art returning 7.6% annually with a standard deviation of 17.3%. We find that Canadian market equity index returned 14.2% annually, with a

---

6 Preliminary fitting of an AR(1) model to the returns suggested little autocorrelation in the semi-annual series, with parameter estimate and standard error of −0.066 and 0.121, respectively. The AR parameter estimate in the annual series was greater, at 0.305, but was not significant, since the standard error was 0.179. The respective R^2 were 0.005 and 0.093.

7 These maturities are not identical to the art index return horizons but were the closest yields associated with maturities greater than or equal to one year.

TABLE 4
Summary Statistics

Panel A: Nominal returns

	Mean	Std Dev.	Min	Max	Correlations Art	Market	Risk-free
Semi-annual							
art index (R_t)	0.036	0.158	−0.404	0.463	1	0.20	−0.01
Market ($R_{M,t}$)	0.065	0.137	−0.273	0.462		1	−0.21
Risk-free ($R_{f,t}$)	0.040	0.016	0.016	0.089			1
Annual							
R_t	0.076	0.174	−0.376	0.404	1	0.03	0.13
$R_{M,t}$	0.142	0.245	−0.394	0.848		1	−0.16
$R_{f,t}$	0.082	0.032	0.033	0.170			1

Panel B: Real returns

	Mean	Std Dev	Min	Max	Correlations Art	Market	Risk-free
Semi-annual							
R_t	0.011	0.158	−0.416	0.441	1	0.21	−0.06
$R_{M,t}$	0.039	0.138	−0.336	0.434		1	−0.07
$R_{f,t}$	0.014	0.016	−0.020	0.046			1
Annual							
R_t	0.023	0.164	−0.431	0.306	1	0.02	−0.19
$R_{M,t}$	0.090	0.251	−0.507	0.793		1	0.02
$R_{f,t}$	0.030	0.029	−0.038	0.084			1

NOTES: This table provides summary statistics on art index returns, market returns, and risk-free rates for semi-annual and annual horizons over the period July 1970 through June 2001 measured in percentage points. Art index returns are constructed from the hedonic regressions. Market returns are the return of the value-weighted composite from the MSCI Canadian equity index including dividends. Risk-free rates are yield-to-maturities of bond with either six-month for panel A or one-year horizons for panel B, and are obtained from the Bank of Canada.

standard deviation of 24.5%. Our correlations show that, on both a semi-annual and an annual basis, art did provide diversification benefit to a portfolio of Canadian equities. This result is similar to that of Mei and Moses (2002) in the relationship between U.S. equities and art, but is in sharp contrast to Goetzmann's (1993) finding based on London art auctions and the London Stock Exchange index returns.

Results from estimating the CAPM on our two data sets are found in table 5.[8] For the unconditional CAPM, whose results are found in panel A, we find

---

[8] We report our estimations of the CAPM using nominal returns. Estimations using real returns were similar to those reported and consequently were not reported.

TABLE 5
CAPM Estimations

Panel A: Unconditional CAPM

		α	β	R^2	J-B	GRS
Semi-annual	Est	−0.011	0.251	0.051	2.51	0.005
	SE	0.02	0.149		(0.28)	(0.94)
Annual	Est	−0.008	0.042	0.014	2.951	0.78
	SE	0.032	0.128		(0.22)	(0.38)

Panel B: Conditional CAPM

		a	ψ	c_1	c_2	c_3	a_1	a_2	a_3
Semi-Annual	Est	−0.003	0.029	0.150	0.025	0.137	−0.038	0.042	−0.010
	SE	0.019	0.018	0.013	0.018	0.012	0.048	0.055	0.053

NOTES: This table includes estimated coefficients (Est) and standard errors (SE) of coefficients from estimation of two different CAPMs using both semi-annual and annual Canadian art index returns. In panel A, an unconditional CAPM is estimated using the following model: $r_t = a + \beta r_{m,t} + u_t$, where r_t is the excess return on the art index and $r_{m,t}$ is the excess return on the MSCI Canadian equity index return. Standard errors in this panel are computed using Newey and West (1987) correction for the presence of heteroscedasticity and serial correlation. In this panel we also report the R^2, Jarque-Bera (J-B) normality test on the residual of the regression, and the Gibbons, Ross, and Shanken (1989) (GRS) market efficiency test statistic (p-value below in parenthesis). In panel B, we report the estimated coefficients and standard errors of the following conditional CAPM on the semi-annual data: $r_t = \alpha + (\psi/H_{22,t}) H_{1,t} + u_t$ with the following conditional variance parameterization: $H_t = C^T C + A^T u_{t-1} u_{t-1}^T A$. Standard errors in this panel are computed by taking the inverse of the Hessian.

that art has less systematic risk than the market, as evidenced by our estimates of β being less than one (0.042 for the annual data, and 0.251 for the semi-annual data). The β estimated on the semi-annual returns is statistically significantly different from zero at the 10% level, but the standard error on the annual β is too large to admit statistical significance. These results also are in contrast with findings of Goetzman (1993), who estimates that the β for the London art returns lies above 1 with strong statistical significance. Again, our results support the notion that portfolios of Canadian art pieces would have provided a strong diversification benefit to Canadian equity holders over the past 30 years given the low correlation between the two series and the similar average returns and risks of both art and equities. The small absolute values of the point estimates of α and their respective standard errors suggest that we fail to reject the unconditional CAPM. Caution again must be used in this interpretation of the coefficients and asymptotic t-tests, given the small data sets we use in our estimations. Consequently, we construct tests of market efficiency as found in Gibbons, Ross, and Shanken (1989) using the following formula:

$$\text{GRS} = (T-1)\left[1 + \frac{\hat{\mu}_M}{\hat{\sigma}_M^2}\right]^{-1} \frac{\hat{\alpha}^2}{\hat{\sigma}_u^2}.$$
$$\sim F_{1,T-2}.$$

This test of market efficiency has an exact finite sample distribution under the assumption of normality, and given that our sample sizes are small, this test may provide better market efficiency tests than asymptotic t-tests. Panel A provides Jarque-Bera normality tests of the residuals from the unconditional CAPM regressions and indicates that normality appears to be a reasonable assumption. In the final column of panel A, the Gibbons, Ross, and Shanken (1989) statistics, denoted GRS, and their associated p-values indicate that we cannot reject the notion that our art index return behaviour is described by an unconditional CAPM.

A finding of $\alpha = 0$ can have a number of possible interpretations. The one posited above is that returns to the art market are adequately captured by the CAPM, and that only systematic risk is important for returns in this market. A second possibility is that there are returns not related to systematic risk, but that they are offset by the costs associated with art ownership (costs referred to earlier but that we have not explicitly attempted to measure). Among the pecuniary and non-pecuniary returns associated with art ownership that we have also not attempted to measure are the fees that may be obtainable through loans to gallery or museum exhibitions or through reproduction rights and the direct utility afforded by a picture to its owner. Another way of looking at it is in considering that, under the maintained hypothesis that the CAPM holds, the unmeasured costs and benefits of holding art referred to here balance one another exactly (since under the CAPM, any such imbalance would result in a non-zero α, positive if costs outweigh benefits and negative otherwise).

Estimation of the conditional CAPM using the semi-annual data, found in panel B of table 5, yields similar conclusions. The estimated α is both economically and statistically insignificant, suggesting that the conditional CAPM cannot be rejected by the data. An estimated value of .029 for φ is consistent with an annual equity premium of 5.9%, which is roughly equivalent to U.S. equity premiums estimated using stock market data over the same horizon. We do find that allowing second moments to move over time in an ARCH model adds little to the model. Specifically, the coefficients in the C matrix, which represent the unconditional portion of conditional covariances, are statistically significant, while the coefficients in the A matrix, which represent the conditional or time-varying portion of conditional covariances, are not significant. The insignificance of the time-varying nature of the conditional covariances is partially caused by our small data set and partially driven by the length of our returns. Most ARCH and GARCH modelling uses data of a higher frequency (daily, weekly, or monthly), and most research finds that the higher the frequency the richer the dynamics of second moments. Using semi-annual data, a low frequency of returns may cloud our ability to capture the dynamics of second moments. We also intend to further investigate the ability of general asset pricing models (consumption CAPM, multivariate factor models) to explain the movement of art returns, given the conditional CAPM results as well as the low R^2 and marginal significance of systematic risk in the unconditional estimations.

4. Conclusions

Among the contributions of this study can be enumerated the facts that it is the first comprehensive econometric analysis of pricing and returns in the auction market for Canadian paintings, the first paper in the art pricing literature to adaptively estimate a hedonic regression (a fact that may also be of interest to econometricians working in the field of semi-parametric methods), and among the few to estimate a conditional capital asset pricing model for art returns. In estimating a hedonic regression for art prices over the period 1968–2001, we obtain estimated time series of prices and returns in the market, and a ranking of the top Canadian painters according to their individual market valuations. We feel that both sets of results may be of intrinsic interest to anyone interested in Canadian art.

In addition, we use the estimated returns to estimate and test unconditional and conditional versions of the capital asset pricing model. Our results here represent a contribution to the related literature that has the virtue of representing relatively 'independent' new evidence on these questions, since most previous work has been focused on European and American art. Our results are generally in line with the 'stylized facts' in the literature, viz. that art returns are generally lower than stock returns, although they are similarly variable, and that their betas with respect to the latter are small and positive. We find that extending the basic CAPM to a conditional model adds little to the analysis.

A number of extensions of this work are contemplated for future research. As mentioned above, considering returns at a more disaggregated level and possibly analysing individual artists are worth investigation, subject to sample size constraints. Also, an analysis of valuation as a function of an artist's age, along the lines of Galenson (2000) and as outlined in the text for the examples of Riopelle and Borduas, may be of interest.

Our analysis of returns has been carried out within the context of the simplest version of the CAPM and conditional CAPM models. It may also be of interest to consider more complicated multi-factor models, possibly including as factors measures of real economic activity and aggregate wealth (Macklem 1997), and perhaps more interestingly, measures of international art market movements. In particular, how closely do art price trends for Canadian art mimic those for American and European art? This line of analysis will also be subject to serious data constraints, however, since basic degrees-of-freedom considerations will limit the number of variables that can be included in any one model.

Appendix A: Bickel's (1982) adaptive estimator

The estimator is efficient under the assumption that the disturbances are independent and identically distributed (iid) with a density function $f(u)$ that is symmetric, so that $f(u) = f(-u)$. Using the OLS estimator $\widehat{\beta}$, compute the associated residuals $\widehat{u}_i = p_i - x_i'\widehat{\beta}$, $i = 1,\ldots,n$. For each residual $\widehat{u}_i$, $i = 1,\ldots,n$, one can use the remaining residuals to compute a kernel estimate of the level of the density f evaluated at $\widehat{u}_i$ as follows:

$$\widehat{f}_i(\widehat{u}_i) = \frac{1}{2(n-1)} \sum_{\substack{j=1, \\ j \neq i}}^{n} \left\{ K\left(\frac{\widehat{u}_i + \widehat{u}_j}{h_n}\right) + K\left(\frac{\widehat{u}_i - \widehat{u}_j}{h_n}\right) \right\},$$

where $K(\bullet)$ is a user-specified kernel weighting function and h_n is a user-specified bandwidth parameter that satisfies the asymptotic condition $h_n \to 0$ as $n \to \infty$.[9] We will also require the following estimate of the first derivative of f:

$$\widehat{f}_i'(\widehat{u}_i) = \frac{1}{h_n 2(n-1)} \sum_{\substack{j=1, \\ j \neq i}}^{n} \left\{ K'\left(\frac{\widehat{u}_i + \widehat{u}_j}{h_n}\right) + K'\left(\frac{\widehat{u}_i - \widehat{u}_j}{h_n}\right) \right\}.$$

We then have the estimated (negative of the) score of f, evaluated at $\widehat{u}_i$:

$$\widehat{\psi}_i(\widehat{u}_i) = \frac{\widehat{f}_i'(\widehat{u}_i)}{\widehat{f}_i(\widehat{u}_i)},$$

where some trimming conditions may need to be specified in the computation of $\widehat{\psi}_i$, depending on the kernel employed.[10]

The sample score vector and information matrix of the likelihood function can be approximated, respectively, by the following semiparametric estimators:

$$\widehat{S}_n = -n^{-1} \sum_{i=1}^{n} x_i \widehat{\psi}_i(\widehat{u}_i)$$

and

---

9 See Silverman (1986) for a good introduction to the topic of non-parametric density estimation.
10 We use a normal kernel with the rule-of-thumb bandwidth of Silverman (1986). Although trimming is theoretically required to calculate $\widehat{\psi}_i$, we elect not to trim, owing to the large size of our sample (Monte Carlo evidence prevented by Hsieh and Manski 1987 and Hodgson 1998, 1999 show that adaptive estimators with normal kernels behave well with very little trimming for sample sizes in the 100–200 range).

$$\widehat{\mathcal{I}}_n = \widehat{\Omega} n^{-1} \sum_{i=1}^{n} x_i x_i',$$

where $\widehat{\Omega} = n^{-1} \sum_{i=1}^{n} \widehat{\psi}_i(\widehat{u}_i)^2$. The adaptive estimator $\widetilde{\beta}$ is then computed using the following one-step Newton-style adjustment of the OLS estimator $\widehat{\beta}$:

$$\widetilde{\beta} = \widehat{\beta} + \widehat{\mathcal{I}}_n^{-1} \widehat{S}_n.$$

Under conditions specified by Bickel (1982), $\widetilde{\beta}$ will be consistent and asymptotically normal,

$$\sqrt{n}\left(\widetilde{\beta} - \beta\right) d \rightarrow^d N(0, \mathcal{I}^{-1}),$$

where the asymptotic covariance matrix $\mathcal{I}^{-1}$ is consistently estimated by $\widehat{\mathcal{I}}_n^{-1}$.

Appendix B: Painters

The following is a list of all 152 painters included in our study, in alphabetical order. The three numbers given in parentheses for each artist represent, respectively, the number of observations, the dummy parameter estimate for the painter, and the associated standard error:

William Armstrong (10, −2.5288, 0.1719); William E. Atkinson (10, −2.9040, 0.0669); Marcel Barbeau (28, −2.8138, 0.1058); Maxwell Bates (169, −1.9513, 0.0528); William Beatty (350, −1.5475, 0.0333); Henri Beau (84, −2.0644, 0.0625); Frederic Marlett Bell-Smith (237, −1.5492, 0.0396); Louis Belzile (21, minus;3.5003, 0.1202); Aleksandre Bercovitch (20, −3.2828, 0.1228); William Berczy (2, 1.2258, 0.3817); George Theodore Berthon (4, −2.3420, 0.2708); B.C. Binning (16, −1.0550, 0.1429); Ronald Bloore (7, −2.5194, 0.2093); Paul-Emile Borduas (56, 0.6804, 0.0748); Joseph Bouchette (3, −3.9160, 0.3130); Fritz Brandtner (41, −1.8293, 0.0874); Miller Brittain (4, −2.1444, 0.2835); Bertram Brooker (33, −1.9075, 0.0958); Archibald Browne (115, −3.1804, 0.0534); Franklin Brownell (102, −1.7625, 0.0570); William Blair Bruce (23, −1.9855, 0.1143); William Brymner (107, −1.5099, 0.0550); Dennis Burton (14, −3.2367, 0.1463); Jack Bush (35, −1.3777, 0.0937); Oscar Cahen (3, −1.5984, 0.3170); Frank Carmichael (68, 1.1390, 0.0676); Emily Carr (182, 0.7177, 0.0489); A.J. Casson (579, 0.0700, 0.0290); Jack Chambers (2, −0.9730, 0.3843); W.H. Clapp (43, −1.8069, 0.0844); Paraskeva Clark (34, −2.1551, 0.0945); Alex Colville (5, −0.0304, 0.2436); Charles Comfort (105, −1.5519, 0.0553); Stanley Cosgrove (709, −1.1038, 0.0275); Graham Coughtry (5, −3.1163, 0.2452); William Cresswell (25, −2.0739, 0.1097); Maurice Cullen (204, −0.1570, 0.0414); Jean Dallaire (54, −0.7721, 0.0760); Rodolphe de Repentigny (8, −1.0488, 0.1930); James Duncan (2, 0.9118, 0.3831); Wyatt Eaton (5, −1.7262, 0.2431); Allan Edson (70, −2.0339, 0.0674); Marcelle Ferron (63, −2.2649, 0.0731); Lemoine Fitzgerald (63, −0.7250, 0.0712); Tom Forrestall (15, −1.6062, 0.1973);

Daniel Fowler (1, −2.0596, 0.5422); Joseph Franchere (108, −2.1790, 0.0558); John A. Fraser (10, −1.6450, 0.1718); Louise Gadbois (117, −3.5359, 0.0600); Charles Gagnon (2, −0.9240, 0.3826); Clarence Gagnon (234, 0.0592, 0.0389); Pierre Gauvreau (15, −1.2929, 0.1418); Charles Gill (22, −2.8866, 0.1172); Eric Goldberg (36, −2.5217, 0.0922); Hortense Gordon (24, −2.7891, 0.1125); Richard Gorman (6, −3.1351, 0.2227); Theophile Hamel (11, −1.3427, 0.1647); Lawren P. Harris (5, −2.3675, 0.2421); Lawren S. Harris (364, 0.8866, 0.0329); Robert Harris (127, −1.7755, 0.0512); Prudence Heward (40, −2.0050, 0.0869); Randolph Hewton (123, −1.7887, 0.0590); William G.R. Hind (2, 0.0984, 0.3827); Tom Hodgson (11, −3.1535, 0.1664); Edwin Holgate (104, −0.2250, 0.0552); William R. Hope (4, −3.4231, 0.2705); Yvonne McKague Housser (86, −2.1649, 0.0613); Jack Humphrey (38, −1.7479, 0.0936); Charles Huot (44, −1.9976, 0.0843); Jacques Hurtubise (7, −2.1691, 0.2056); Gershon Iskowitz (17, −2.1881, 0.1335); A.Y. Jackson (1246, 0, 0); Otto Jacobi (102, −1.8244, 0.0565); C.W. Jeffreys (12, −1.5110, 0.1574); Jean-Paul Jerome (28, −3.4884, 0.1048); Frank Johnston (701, −0.8889, 0.0273); Paul Kane (7, 0.1248, 0.2053); Roy Kiyooka (1, −3.8628, 0.5407); Dorothy Knowles (43, −2.0714, 0.0861); Cornelius Krieghoff (472, 1.0400, 0.0311); Ludger Larose (24, −2.5270, 0.1129); Fernand Leduc (4, −1.1838, 0.2705); Ozias Leduc (41, −0.6804, 0.0866); Joseph Legare (8, −1.2237, 0.1919); Jean-Paul Lemieux (142, 0.1061, 0.0491); Ernst Lindner (8, −1.4078, 0.1924); Arthur Lismer (429, −0.3445, 0.0307); Kenneth Locchead (8, −1.9923, 0.1927); Alexandra Luke (2, −1.9796, 0.3824); John Lyman (77, −1.2186, 0.0641); J.E.H. MacDonald (406, 0.0672, 0.0326); Jock MacDonald (38, −1.0214, 0.0899); Thomas Mower Martin (264, −2.3458, 0.0382); Marmaduke Matthews (21, −2.4633, 0.1199); Jean McEwen (72, −2.3342, 0.0706); Isabel McLaughlin (11, −2.5150, 0.1639); Ray Mead (7, −2.4424, 0.2066); John Meredith (14, −2.2113, 0.1462); David Milne (98, 0.7502, 0.0579); Guido Molinari (6, −1.8016, 0.2254); James Wilson Morrice (191, 0.7704, 0.0427); Edmund Morris (40, −2.3422, 0.0874); Jean-Paul Mousseau (6, −2.7993, 0.2212); Louis Muhlstock (51, −2.7717, 0.0785); Kazuo Nakamura (27, −2.2942, 0.1059); H. Ivan Neilson (4, −3.2622, 0.2706); Lilias Torrance Newton (8, −2.7501, 0.1924); Jack Nichols (2, −3.0500, 0.3823); John O'Brien (3, −1.2969, 0.3121); Lucius R. O'Brien (24, −1.3425, 0.1122); Will Ogilvie (22, −2.7436, 0.1194); Paul Peel (78, −0.1055, 0.0645); Alfred Pellan (64, −0.9243, 0.0708); Sophie Pemberton (12, −2.5541, 0.1591); Antoine Plamondon (8, −1.8052, 0.1923); Christopher Pratt (3, 0.5187, 0.3120); William Raphael (80, −1.6400, 0.0631); Gordon Rayner (2, −4.3117, 0.3854); George Reid (90, −2.3449, 0.0603); Jean-Paul Riopelle (150, 0.3102, 0.0485); Goodridge Roberts (609, −0.6468, 0.0292); Sarah Robertson (37, −1.7654, 0.0912); William Ronald (38, −2.8152, 0.0924); Jean-Baptiste Roy-Audy (1, 0.3384, 0.5398); Joseph Saint-Charles (40, −2.9836, 0.0887); Henry Sandham (50, −2.2059, 0.0786); Carl Schaefer (27, −1.0083, 0.1056); Charles H. Scott (21, −2.7520, 0.1211); Marian Scott (18, −3.4891, 0.1292); Jack Shadbolt (67, −1.5123, 0.0712); Gordon A. Smith (75, −2.4670, 0.0687); Jori Smith (69, −2.7141, 0.0686); Michael Snow (1, −3.1115,

0.5407); Francoise Sullivan (1, −3.5141, 0.5400); Philip Surrey (97,−1.4724, 0.0580); Marc-Aurele de Foy Suzor-Cote (236, −0.4487, 0.0392); Tom Thomson (95, 1.7381, 0.0578); Robert Todd (3, −1.6705, 0.3123); Fernand Toupin (43, −3.0129, 0.0897); Harold Town (41, −2.2172, 0.0897); Tony Urquhart (10,−2.5434, 0.1719); Fred Varley (121, 0.2981, 0.0519); Frederick Arthur Verner (97,−0.3233, 0.0583); Adolph Vogt (8, −1.8144, 0.1922); Horatio Walker (79, −1.1572, 0.0633); Homer Watson (248, −1.2998, 0.0389); Gordon Webber (3, −3.0030, 0.3132); W.P. Weston (93, −1.1653, 0.0620); Robert Reginald Whale (39, −2.1395, 0.0897); Joyce Wieland (1, −2.6118, 0.5401); Curtis Williamson (36, −3.0842, 0.0920); Walter Yarwood (7, −2.4214, 0.2056)

References

Arnason, H.H. (1986) *History of Modern Art*, 3rd ed. (Englewood Cliffs, NJ: Prentice-Hall)

Banz, R. (1981) 'The relation between return and market value of common stocks,' *Journal of Financial Economics* 9, 3–18

Baumol, W.J. (1986) 'Unnatural value: or art investment as floating crap game,' *American Economic Review* 76, 10–14

Bryan, M. (1985) 'Beauty and the bulls: the investment characteristics of paintings,' *Economic Review of the Federal Reserve Bank of Cleveland* 1, 2–10

Campbell, H. (1973–75) *Canadian Art Auction Record 1971–1974*, vols 3–6 (Montreal: Bernard Amtmann)

Campbell, H., ed. (1980) *Canadian Art Auctions, Sales and Prices, 1976–1978* (Don Mills, ON: General)

Campbell, J., W. Lo, and A.C. MacKinlay (1997) *The Econometrics of Financial Markets* (Princeton, NJ: Princeton University Press)

Caves, R.E. (2000) *Creative Industries: Contracts between Art and Commerce*. (Cambridge, MA: Harvard University Press)

Chanel, O., L.A. Gérad-Varet, and V. Ginsburgh (1996) 'The relevance of hedonic price indexes: the case of paintings,' *Journal of Cultural Economics* 20, 1–24

Czujack, C. (1997) 'Picasso paintings at auction, 1963–1994,' *Journal of Cultural Economics* 21, 229–47

Engle, R. (1982) 'Autoregressive conditional heteroskedasticity with estimates of the variance of UK inflation,' *Econometrica* 50, 987–1008

Engle, R., and K. Kroner (1995) 'Multivariate simultaneous generalized ARCH,' *Econometric Theory* 11, 122–50

Fama, E., and K. French (1992) 'The cross-section of expected returns,' *Journal of Finance* 47, 427–65

Fama, E., and K. French (1993) 'Common risk factors in he returns on stocks and bonds,' *Journal of Financial Economics* 33, 3–56

Fama, E., and J. MacBeth (1973) 'Risk, return, and equilibrium: empirical tests,' *Journal of Political Economy* 71, 607–36

Flôres, R., V. Ginsburgh, and P. Jeanfils (1999) 'Long- and short-term portfolio choices of paintings,' *Journal of Cultural Economics* 23, 193–210

Galenson, D.W. (2000) 'The careers of modern artists: evidence from auctions of contemporary art,' *Journal of Cultural Economics* 24, 87–112

Gibbons, M., S. Ross, and J. Shanken (1989) 'A test of the efficiency of a given portfolio,' *Econometrica* 57, 1121–52

Goetzman, W.N. (1993) 'Accounting for taste: art and the financial markets over three centuries,' *American Economic Review* 83, 1370–76

Grampp, W.D. (1989) *Pricing the Priceless* (New York: Basic Books)

Gyourko, J., and E. Nelling (1996) 'Systematic risk and diversification in the equity REIT market,' *AREUEA Journal* 24, 493–515

Hodgson, D.J. (1998) 'Adaptive estimation of cointegrating regressions with ARMA errors,' *Journal of Econometrics* 85, 231–267

— (1999) 'Adaptive estimation of cointegrated models: Simulation evidence and an application to the forward exchange market,' *Journal of Applied Econometrics* 14, 627–50

Hsieh, D.A., and C.F. Manski (1987) 'Monte Carlo evidence on adaptive maximum likelihood estimation of a regression,' *Annals of Statistics* 15, 541–51

Jarque, C.M., and A.K. Bera (1980) 'Efficient tests for normality, homoskedasticity, and serial independence of regression residuals,' *Economics Letters* 6, 255–9

Lintner, J. (1965) 'The valuation of risky assets and the selection of risky investments in stock portfolios and capital budgets,' *Review of Economics and Statistics* 47, 13–37

Locatelli-Biey, M., and R. Zanola (2002) 'The sculpture market: an adjacent year regression index,' *Journal of Cultural Economics* 26, 65–78

Macklem, T. (1997) 'Aggregate wealth in Canada,' *Canadian Journal of Economics* 30, 152–68

Mei, M., and M. Moses (2002) 'Art as an investment and the underperformance of masterpieces,' *American Economic Review* 92, 1656–68

Newey, W., and K. West (1987) 'A simple positive semi-definite heteroscedasticity and autocorrelation consistent covariance matrix,' *Econometrica* 55, 703–8

Pesando, J.E. (1993) 'Art as an investment: the market for modern prints,' *American Economic Review* 83, 1075–89

Pesando, J.E., and P.M. Shum (1999) 'The returns to Picasso's prints and to traditional financial assets, 1977 to 1996,' *Journal of Cultural Economics* 23, 183–92

Reid, D. (1973) *A Concise History of Canadian Painting* (Toronto: Oxford University Press)

Reitlinger, G. (1961) *The Economics of Taste* (London: Barrie and Rockcliff)

Sharpe, W. (1964) 'Capital asset prices: a theory of market equilibrium under conditions of risk,' *Journal of Finance* 19, 425–442

Silverman, B. (1986) *Density Estimation for Statistics and Data Analysis* (London: Chapman and Hill)

Sotheby's (1975) *Canadian Art at Auction, 1968–1975* (Toronto: Sotheby's & Co. Canada)

— (1980) *Canadian Art at Auction, 1975–1980* (Toronto: Sotheby's Parke Bernet Canada)

Stein, J.P. (1977) 'The monetary appreciation of paintings,' *Journal of Political Economy* 85, 1021–35

Valsan, C. (2002) 'Canadian versus American art: what pays off and why,' *Journal of Cultural Economics* 26, 203–216

Westbridge, A.R. (1981–2002) *Canadian Art Sales Index, 1977–2001* (Vancouver: Westbridge)

Pre-sale Estimates, Risk Analysis, and the Investment Quality of Fine Art

Clare Mc Andrew
Kusin & Company

Rex Thompson
Southern Methodist University

September 2003

PRELIMINARY DRAFT

Abstract

This paper examines the importance of the inclusion of buy-in data in analyzing the risk of investment in works of art. Using the data set of French Impressionist paintings brought to auction from 1985 to 2001, we construct a theoretical lognormal distribution to include the value of works that are bought in-house, and use this to examine bias in the pre-sale estimates of auction experts. It turns out that experts are accurate and unbiased if we consider both how potential buyers value works, and the valuations of the seller or their reserve price. We also show how this distribution can be used by financiers to assess the risk of art portfolios.

(JEL G11, G14, G12, C160, Z10)

The annual volume of transactions in works of art constitutes a multi-billion dollar global market. In 2001, approximately 1.2 million transactions took place internationally, representing around $23.4 billion of fine and decorative art changing ownership. Approximately 92% of these art sales took place in the US and Europe with over 72% in the US and UK alone.[1] Consumers are the stereotypical high net-worth individuals who participate in organized financial markets around the world. As a result there is natural interest in drawing the markets for fine art and those for financial instruments onto what common footing exists across them. Investors need to be able to describe the art market and the market for financial instruments using similar language and methodology, and the process of assessing the financial risk of investments is a major component for developing consistent analysis across assets classes.

Several papers have inquired into the return history of investment in art and other collectibles (such as wine, stamps, and coins). Most of these studies concern the development of art indices to examine returns from investing in art and for comparisons with financial indices. The two most commonly used methods for constructing art indices have been using repeat-sales and the hedonic regression method. Each technique has its own merits and drawbacks and both have a number of flaws regarding their applicability to the real process of actually buying and selling art. These indices do however show that theoretically there are grounds for being able to set a plausible range of monetary returns for investment in art. Most of the returns reported are low and positive, and it is often implied that the "consumption yield" from art is a significant component of the total return necessary to compete with the returns from pure financial instruments.

In this paper we concentrate on some of the elements of the risk of returns on art that arise from fluctuations in the rate of price appreciation. While there is a variety of standard risk analytics that can be used across a range of assets, the

---

[1] Kusin &Company (2002)

daily operational functioning of the art market provides an additional, unique platform for risk analysis: pre-sale estimates provided by auctioneers, and the role of "expert opinion" in analyzing the decision to invest in art. This paper investigates how these features can be used to help assess risk and focuses particularly on the importance of including the critical risk that a particular work may not sell at all when brought to auction, or the phenomenon of "buy-ins". Buy-ins are works that are brought to auction, do not sell, and are "bought in-house" by the auctioneer on behalf of the seller. Despite the salience of this feature of art sales, buy-ins have been virtually ignored until now in research analyzing the investment in works of art.

1. Art Auctions and Price Formation

The market value of important art works is established primarily through a public auction process, either through an actual sale, or indirectly as a point of price reference.[2] The different set of issues revolving around the institutional details of art auction markets is explored by Ashenfelter (1989).[3] He notes that auction markets for wine and art have institutional arrangements that differ from those usually assumed in pure financial markets and the theory of auction markets. Moreover, these arrangements play an important role in the price formation and price reporting processes.

Ashenfelter (1989) describes the format of "English" or "ascending price" auctions in art auction houses such as Sotheby's, Christie's, and Phillips. Bidding starts low and rises as the auctioneer calls out higher and higher prices. When the bidding stops the item is "hammered down" at the final "hammer price." However, many items that go through the auction process are not actually sold but, rather, are "bought-in" by the auction house. These items are either sold at a later date, put up for sale elsewhere, or taken off the market. Ashenfelter (1989) estimates that about one-third of the data set of Impressionist paintings he examined did not find buyers. The data for French Impressionist paintings used in this paper reflects a sales rate with 28% of all lots offered being bought in-house. Thus buy-ins represent an important dimension of the auction process and of the price data retrieved from the auction experience. In this paper, we

---

[2] There are a small number of highly specialized niche art markets that conduct the majority of their trade outside the auction process. For example, the results of dealer interviews and polling conducted by Kusin & Company in 1999 indicted that around 85% of sales of Caneletto paintings are conducted exclusively through dealers.

[3] The literature surrounding "general" auction theory and empirics is voluminous with modern studies originating from Vickery's (1961) seminal paper approaching auctions and the bidding processes from game theoretic perspective. The collection of papers by Klemperer (2000) provides a comprehensive survey and useful guide to the literature on auction theory.

examine sales rates and the effect of buy-ins on risk assessment and investment in art. The inclusion of buy-in data in studies of art prices and returns has been almost exclusively ignored until now despite their importance in the auction price formation process.

"Reserves" are the selling prices below which the consignor will not allow the work to be sold, and as such indicate the seller's marginal valuation of the work or the marginal price at which they would be willing to sell the painting versus holding it and waiting for the next auction. As such reserve prices act as a form of clearing mechanism for parties coming together at auction: works of art can only be bought in rather than sold if they do not meet the reserve price. Reserves are typically set below the low estimate as it would be misleading to indicate that the seller's marginal valuation of the work is more than the range within which it is expected to sell. Once a work is brought to auction with a reserve price, and the bidding exceeds the reserve, the work cannot be withdrawn and must be sold to the highest bidder. In some cases, works are brought to auction without a reserve price. This is not common practice, but there have been significant auctions without reserves, such as the liquidation of well-known dealer stock or the auction of important estates that benefit charity.

In the presale catalogues, the auction houses publish a presale low and high estimate for each work of art. The auction house does not publish or indicate in any way what the sellers' reserve prices will be. Experts setting the auction estimates will indicate to the consignor the range of prices they believe the work will sell in, and then the auction house in conjunction with the seller will set the reserve. Ashenfelter and Graddy (2002) point out that there are common value components to investing in art, and this would lead one to question why the reserve is kept secret when it clearly represents information on each seller's valuation, which it would be optimal for them to reveal at auction. Secret reserves may remain in place at art auctions to prevent collusive buyer bidding rings the would depress bids and subsequent sales prices, or to prevent certain bidders being discouraged from coming to auction (Vincent, 1995).

Ashenfelter, Graddy and Stevens (2003) look at sales rates and reserve prices across a number of different art auctions and explore the market forces that drive the reserve setting process. They develop a model of optimal reserve prices in which the reserve price is a constant proportion of the estimated price and that this "natural sales rate" depends only on the variance of log prices and the seller's discount rate. They explain high reserve prices and the resulting high buy-in rates as optimal search in the face of stochastic demand (similar to the models used in labor economics of workers searching for employment where their optimal policy will be to set a reservation wage). They estimate the reserve price is generally set at around 70 to 80 % of the pre-sale low estimate, which fits with the market place reality reported by the major auction houses, where the unwritten rule is that reserve prices should on average be set at around 75% of the pre-sale low estimate. In this paper we use the estimated reserve price to show that in deriving presale estimates, auction houses take account of both buyer and sellers valuations, and when we account for both of these forces, estimates are generally accurate and unbiased.

The analysis of the role of expert opinions in economic decisions in the art market has developed as an important area in art auction research. The accuracy and bias in art experts' opinions, via their published presale high and low estimates, has been questioned in several papers with mixed results. Milgrom and Weber (1982) showed that, in most auction models, including the English variety, "honesty is the best policy" for sellers. Ashenfelter's (1989) study also reiterates these conclusions, showing that auction houses are generally truthful since presale high and low estimates are highly correlated with the price actually received. Beggs and Graddy's (1997) results show that while honesty may hold generally, there are systematic under and over predictions in certain circumstances and genres. In the contemporary art sector for example, they find more recent works were overvalued and larger paintings under-valued. Chanel et al (1996) show that estimates tend to undervalue most types of jewelry at auction in their study, while Bauwens and Ginsburgh (2000) find small but significant downward bias in their study of English silver.[4] They also find that the bias in estimates differs between auction houses: Christies systematically underestimates hammer prices, while Sotheby's overvalues less expensive pieces and undervalues expensive ones. Their study also shows that experts do not optimally process all publicly available information in reaching their decisions and that they could in fact improve their estimates by making better use of the information contained in sales catalogues.

Mei and Moses (2003) also investigate art auction price estimates, building on their earlier analysis of the "Masterpiece Effect" where investors tend to overpay for masterpieces when in reality this group of paintings (defined by their price) actually tend to under-perform the market.[5] They found that while, in general, estimates are highly correlated to prices paid, there was an apparent upward bias for very high price paintings, indicating that the actual price paid is often less than the average of the high and low estimates. They claim that this is because

---

[4] Both of these data sets of jewelry and silver are examples of collectibles and could even be viewed as having utilitarian value and are therefore have markedly different characteristics to works of art.
[5] Mei and Moses investigate the Masterpiece Effect in their earlier (2002) paper, finding that expensive paintings tend to under-perform their "art market index." Pesando (1993) studied the adjacent market for prints and reached a similar conclusion that there was no evidence of masterpieces outperforming the market and that most of the desirable characteristics of these works are capitalized into their prices, i.e. the market for prints is relatively efficient.

auction houses will try to maintain an overall unbiasedness in their estimates, but tilt their estimates upward for expensive paintings, since they can benefit the most from such bias if investors are credulous; and in doing so auctioneers receive higher commissions on these sales. They find that investors are significantly influenced by price estimates and they also tend to pay more when the spread of the estimates between high and low is larger.[6]

There is little compelling evidence or intuition that supports any purposeful manipulation of estimates for strategic purposes. The most likely explanations of bias lie in random error, inefficiency, or in some cases the underlying data chosen for analysis. Although a seller might prefer a higher pre-sale estimate, the reserve price is generally set at around 75% of the pre-sale low, and setting this too high may discourage prospective buyers. It could be suggested that auction houses might push for lower estimates in the hopes of attracting more buyers, or even in the hope that if works sell for higher than expected, this might attract more sellers to more successful auction houses that achieve record or unexpectedly high prices at auction. In the US and UK, the major auction houses have experts in-house setting estimates so it is conceivable that some internal pressure could be imposed. A balanced view would suggest however, that if estimates are too low, sellers will simply refuse to consign works, especially in the face of unpredictable markets. This paper is not concerned with the motivations of auction houses or experts, or the reasons for bias, but with its measurement and implications for the measurement of downside risk in investing in works of art.

Finally, Ashenfelter and Graddy (2002), in their survey of empirical studies of art auctions, review the effects of the auction institution on price formation. An extensive body of research is being built up around price dynamics in sequential auctions, such as the declining price anomaly or "afternoon affect" witnessed in auctions of wine, jewelry and other collectibles.[7] The attributed cause of the anomaly varies with explanations including buyer options, risk aversion, participation costs, absentee bidders, or the degree of heterogeneity between the items. Most of the items studied, however, were distinctly more homogenous and substitutable, albeit imperfectly, when compared with the works of art that are analyzed in this study.[8]

---

[6] The data set they use is restricted only to selected large auction sales in New York, and then only repeat sale transactions. Repeat sales regressions drastically reduce and skew the data available and, by nature, ignore buy-ins.

[7] See empirical work on this price anomaly in wine auctions by Mc Afee and Vincent (1993), Di Vittorio and Ginsburgh (1994) and Ashenfelter (1998); jewelry by Chanel et al (1996); ancient porcelain by Ginsburgh and Van Ours (2003); and prints by Pesando and Shum (1996).

[8] Two exceptions are notable: Beggs and Graddy (1997) study of Impressionist, modern and contemporary art auctions found that the final bid relative to the auctioneer's estimated price declines throughout the

2. Data description

The data set used in this analysis was compiled by Kusin & Company using art auction data from ArtNet and ArtFact.[9] The works sold are French Impressionist paintings, which, using the Kusin & Company Classification Code, comprised the complete set of 14 artists.[10] The data consists of 4,280 attempted auction sales from the 16-year period between January 1985 and December 2001 from a cohort of 130 international auction houses. Prior to an auction, a pre-sale catalogue is published with information on artist, title, date of sale, auction house/location of sale, size, medium, lot number, year, and a pre-sale low and high price estimate. The auction houses do not publish reserve prices, but commonly observe the custom of setting it at or below the low estimates, again about 75% of the pre-sale low estimate.[11] The 4065 complete transactions that are analyzed consist of all fully attributed paintings for which the following items of information are available: high and low pre-sale estimates, the date and location of the auction, the artist's name and lot number.[12] If the work was actually sold, the hammer price and/or the premium price are listed. If there are only premium (hammer) prices recorded, these were converted to hammers (premiums) using the buyers' premiums from Christie's, Sotheby's and an average of the other major auction houses. Changes in the buyers' premium over time are also taken into account in these calculations.

To overcome the common sample selection problem of only having data on lots actually sold, we also estimate a price for paintings that were bought-in. To estimate what the reserve price might be, we use a value of 75% of the pre-sale low estimate. Reserve setting policies do vary between different auction houses and sales. Christie's stated policy is that the reserve price must be set below the

---

course of an auction. Picci And Scorcu (2002) also look at Italian auctions of modern and contemporary art finding no evidence of the afternoon effect and slight evidence of the opposite or a "morning effect."

[9] Much of the data from both of these sources were incorrect and/or incomplete, for example missing a price or pre-sale estimates or outside the realms of marketplace reality, for example a Renoir with a $50 hammer price. Where possible therefore, Kusin and Company cleaned and corrected the data with reference to the original auction catalogues or correspondence with the relevant auction house. Auction data without an attributable hammer price or without presale estimates were omitted from the study.

[10] Work by these 14 artists represents the accepted scholarly canon of French Impressionist painters: Frederic Bazille, Gustave Caillebotte, Mary Cassatt, Paul Cezanne, Edgar Degas, Eva Gonzales, Paul Gauguin, Armand Guillaumin, Edouard Manet, Claude Monet, Berthe Morisot, Camille Pissarro, Auguste Renoir, and Alfred Sisley.

[11] This figure is based on correspondence with the major auction houses and Kusin & Company. Ashenfelter, Graddy and Stephens (2002) estimate the reserve price using a random effects probit model and come up with a similar result.

[12] A fully attributed painting is one for which there exists no controversy over the artist that created it. All works with attributions that include statements such as "in the style of", " in the school or circle of", or "attributed to" are not included in the data.

low estimate and advise that it is usually between 70 and 80% for paintings. The only stipulation in Sotheby's policy, on the other hand, is that the reserve be below the high estimate, and generally ranges between 50 to 100% of the low estimate depending on the value of the item, and sellers' preferences. The only definitive statement that can be made regarding the value of buy-ins (so far), is that, at a particular auction, buyers failed to bid beyond the final reserve. Using an estimate of the reserve price is likely therefore to contain an element of upward bias if used as a proxy for buy-in value since no works bought-in reached the reserve.

An alternative investigated by Beggs and Graddy (1997), is to use the final bid which also must exist for all works brought to auction even if they are unsold, even if the bid is fictitious and merely announced by the auctioneer on a seller's behalf to get the bids started. This is often called 'bidding off the chandelier' and can only continue until the reserve price has been met by a bona fide bidder. The auctioneer can also announce so-called "commissioned bids" which are placed on behalf of an anonymous potential buyer who wishes to bid for the work but not to be present or known at auction. Their paper analyzed sales from two auction houses only, but the 130 houses in our sample made obtaining final bid data impossible.

Data on final bids is not published by the auction houses directly, or even indirectly listed in art price data sets. The auction houses we approached, with the exception of Sotheby's, were unwilling to release this information. From the data set, we selected a random sample of 25 works bought-in from auctions at Sotheby's London from 1985-2001. From this sample, the final bid was on average around 50% of the presale low (ranging from 39 to 71 % with a standard deviation of 8%). A major problem with using the final bid data to estimate value is the necessity of being able to distinguish between at least 3 buy-in situations:

1. If the work was unsold against a "bid off the chandelier";
2. If the work was unsold after the last bid in the room was placed; and
3. If the work was unsold and there was in fact no bona fide bidding at all.

In situations such as number 3, the final bid is merely the bid at which the auctioneer chose to start the bidding and so will be an inaccurate measure of value, that possibly contains a significant downward bias. Unless there is a means to distinguish these contexts (and auction houses will not divulge this information publicly), data on the final bid may have little relevance to the evaluation of buy-in value.

Table 1 shows summary information about the paintings. In total, 2925 works were sold, representing $3, 015, 452, 272 in transactions. From the works with complete data, 1140 paintings, or 28% of those lots available were bought in. The Table gives two proxies for the potential value of the works bought in. Value 1 is the geometric mean of the presale high and low estimates for works bought-in and on this basis, these works represent 18% of the value of auction inventory. Value 2 gives an approximation of the reserve using the 75 % rule discussed above which gives a value at 16%. Of course we do not know what the bought in paintings would have sold for were they sold with no reserve. The two largest auction houses, Christie's and Sotheby's offered at total of 3432 works, or 85% of the auction market, with Sotheby's leading slightly with 45% of the total value of French Impressionist sales.

3. The impact of buy-ins

At this juncture, we are ready to consider the impact of buy-ins on the auction price information process. Were we to focus too sharply on the valuations of works actually sold, we would miss the risk that a work, once purchased, might not sell when offered at a later date. Thus the data on auction sales clearly contains a selection bias: in order to purchase a painting, buyers must pay more than the reserve. When the buyer ultimately wishes to sell a painting, there is no guarantee that the painting will exceed the same reserve percentage. Thus a time series of hammer or "sale" prices overstates the rate of return to expect from investing in art.

In this data set of French Impressionist paintings, the buy-in rate is 28 % of the sales volume but only 16% in terms of value.[13] A phenomenon in art auctions appears to be, that buy-in volume is a smaller percentage than buy-in value. In other words, the higher the value of the work, the higher the sales rate. The implication is that for high value works, there may be a lower risk of being bought-in. This result appears at first to be somewhat counterintuitive. If a work is expected to reach a higher price, the pre-sale low estimate should be higher, and hence also the reserve price. Normal auction logic would therefore imply that it would run a higher risk of not reaching above the reserve and hence being bought in house. In the art market, however, higher priced paintings are generally more likely to be those that are more well known or fashionable, with

---

[13] Buy-in data in a compilation of other species fine and decorative art data from Kusin & Company ranged between 19-43% of lots brought to auction and between 3-35% of the total value offered. The figure of 16% is based on the estimate of the reserve price, or the 75% rule. This does not affect the buy-in rate but is likely to overestimate the value. We see later that 16% is higher than the percentage value that we obtain when we estimate buy-in values from the lognormal distribution (which gives us a value of 13.5 % of total value).

well established provenance, such that they are nearly guaranteed to find buyers due to the defining market characteristic of limited market supply.

How buy-ins are treated also affects measures of price volatility and the accuracy of auction presale estimates of value. Table 2a shows additional summary statistics for the prices of works sold at auction. The table incorporates three pieces of information: the hammer price, the presale low estimate of value, and the presale high estimate. In this study, we measure the bias in estimates by constructing the hammer spread, defined as the ratio of the hammer prices achieved, to the geometric mean of the presale high and low estimates. The mean hammer spread is given in the lower section (part B) of the table. Volatility of the hammer price is taken as the standard deviation of the ratio of hammer price to the geometric mean of the presale high and low estimates. The first column shows raw ratios and the second shows the natural logs of the ratios. Also reported are the mean of the ratio and the mean of the log of the square root of the ratio. These appraisal spreads represent ex ante risk measures for the works.[14]

On the basis of Table 2a it would appear that auction experts are systematically low in their mean appraisal of raw values. The mean hammer spread, is 1.14 with a t-ratio from unity of 11.03.[15] This result does not appear to be driven by skewness in the data, since appraisals remain biased in log values. Table 2a shows the log of the mean appraisal to be a biased estimate of the log of the hammer price, with a mean difference 0.030 (t-ratio from zero of 3.9). Log transformations tend to compress larger values together and stretch out smaller ones, which can correct for skewness and create a more symmetrical distribution. Ratios can often produce skewed distributions as can data with a very wide range, and log functions can correct for these tendencies. The fact that appraisals remain biased when we take logs, suggests a more definite skewness in the nature of the data rather than a statistical artifact.

---

[14] Note that the term "appraisal" is used in this context to mean the estimates set by auction experts. The meaning of appraised value in certain legal settings may be different. In these instances it is used to define an independently determined valuation of a work and is generally a point estimate of value rather than a range.

[15] We use the geometric mean as the denominator for mean hammer spread which is always less than or equal to the arithmetic mean. The geometric mean is more appropriate with this data due to the skewed nature of the distribution. To ensure that the result of greater than unity (1.14) is not biased by the choice of mean, we also estimated the mean hammer spread using the arithmetic mean. The resulting mean hammer spread was 1.12 (with a t-ratio of 9.97), reinforcing the previous result that indicates experts tend towards underestimation of works actually sold.

Incorporating Buy-Ins in the Distribution

Impressions from Table 2 are based only on works successfully sold at auction. In order to process the complete auction experience, buy-ins must be incorporated. Since buy-ins are not successfully sold, they should impart a downward influence on the auction results, but, since no transaction occurred, we have to estimate an inferred high bid price. However it is clear from the data that there is no clean truncation of hammer spreads at, say, 50% of the mean appraisal. Some works are sold at less than this figure. Indeed, the minimum hammer spread in the sample is 0.02 and some 78 works sold for less than 50% of the mean appraisal (1.14).

Figure 1 shows the frequencies of all the works offered at auction that were actually hammered down on the one hand versus the theoretical frequencies based on the lognormal on the other. We divided the data into "bins" or groups of frequencies. The bin size and number are arbitrary, but we found it useful to use 5% increments with bins from 0.00 to 4.50 to cover the data adequately. Panel A of the chart shows the distribution of hammer spreads for the 2925 works successfully sold. Except for the lower tail, and a few extreme points in the upper tail, the distribution has a regular shape resembling a lognormal.[16] Panel B shows a fit of a lognormal with fit maximized by altering the mean and standard deviation of the lognormal. The lognormal is assumed to have 4065 observations, and the fit is maximized over the hammer spreads exceeding 0.80, the level around which we would expect the buy-ins to feature.

Over the range of spreads exceeding 0.80, the lognormal appears to fit the data rather closely . Lognormality cannot be rejected based on a Kolmogorov-Smirnov test .This is a test for distributional accuracy which in this case measures the "goodness of fit" of the data to the lognormal distribution. The Kolmogorov-Smirnov (d) statistic measures the maximum departure between the actual and predicted frequencies, which we want to be small if we infer that the theoretical

---

[16] An interesting observation in Figure 1 is the spikes in the distribution with a large frequency of transaction centered on the 0.90 and 0.95 bins and the possible inferences that may be drawn regarding buyer behavior. The concentration around the 90% level could indicate the predominance of so-called "trade buyers" in this market. These are buyers such as dealers or other agents that are at auction to purchase paintings to sell on in a secondary market or to buy directly on behalf of a client. They are generally very well informed, in the market frequently, and also often more price sensitive. They will frequently be willing to forgo a work if it has gone too far above its estimated value, or only bid within a certain range, since they attend auctions frequently, have established relationships with scholars and connoisseurs, and research sales themselves thoroughly. Individual private buyers, on the other hand, are more likely to be found in the upside tail of the distribution bidding at prices above estimated value. These buyers are often keenly focused on a single item at auction, are less price sensitive in their determination to win the particular lot, and are more prone to impulse bids and purchases.

and actual distributions are similar. (The d-statistic was 0.876 which is below the critical values at the 1, 5, and 10% significance levels).[17]

To infer the likely distribution of hammer spreads for the works bought-in, we integrate the left portion of the fitted distribution in excess of the actual distribution. Starting at a hammer spread of 1.00 and working backwards, the difference in distributions is integrated. Although it is somewhat subjective, we choose a hammer spread of 1.00 since we assume that we can say with certainty that there will be very few buy-ins greater than the mean of the estimates. This process leads to a difference of 889 works between the predicted and actual data, which is fairly close to the data indicating 925 works actually bought-in. We now want to establish the mean hammer spread for the 889 works missing from the actual distribution but reflected in the lognormal. To do this, we first take the difference between the frequencies of the predicted (lognormal) distribution and multiply these by the mean of the relevant bin. We then sum this product up to our cut-off point of 1.00. The next step is to divide this figure by the sum of the original difference above, which gives us the percentage of estimated buy-ins from the inferred distribution. In this case, the mean hammer spread of the works missing from the actual distribution but estimated in the lognormal is 0.53. As a percentage of the presale low, this would translate into about 0.61. In other words, using this distribution, the inferred value of the buy-ins is 61 % of the presale low (and 53% of the mean of the high/low estimate). It is interesting to note that this figure is closer to the result of 50% of the presale low, which was estimated from the final bids data at Sotheby's indicating that this might be an area to investigate further if the data becomes available. As we also predicted , using 75% of the presale low overstates the value of buy-ins, since many items will not get to the reserve price which this rule emulates.

Armed with the fitted distribution shown in Figure 1, the question of appraisal accuracy and investment risk can be revisited. Based on the expected hammer price for buy-ins corresponding to 53% of the mean appraisal value, the estimated mean hammer spread is 0.947. This figure is estimated by performing a transformation of the logged data back to "raw data." This process gives us a mean of 0.947 and standard deviation of 0.46 as the moments of the estimated distribution of what the raw data would be. Tests of significance reveal that the mean appraisal is actually quite conservative, and we reject the null hypothesis that the mean is not significantly different from 1. So while the data that do not include buy-ins (in Table 1) shows evidence of underestimation or conservative estimates (with a ratio of 1.14), the data including buy-ins generated from the

---

[17] See Appendix II for an explanation of the Kolmogorov-Smirnoff methodology.

lognormal distribution shows evidence of overestimating or aggressive estimates.

We know that the experts setting the estimates must try to take account of potential buyers' valuations when setting auction estimates, and that in doing so tend to overestimate or underestimate depending on whether they account for buy-ins or not. It may be also the case, however, that these experts not only account for buyers, but also take into consideration what they feel sellers would be willing to sell for (or not) or their marginal or reserve price. To investigate this, we return to the 75 % rule. In the calculation of the hammer spread, we replace the numerator of the ratio (price) with 0.75 of the presale low and it turns out that this generates a mean of almost exactly 1.00 (with a standard deviation of 0.616). In other words if we consider that experts take into account both buyer and seller valuations, their estimates are accurate and unbiased.

We can also reveal these differences in bias by returning to our calculations of mean hammer spread in the original data, as we did in Table 2a. In Table 2b we include buy-in values. For every work in the data set that was bought-in, instead of omitting a price, we include an estimated value of 53% of the mean of the estimates, as indicated by the theoretical distribution. The mean hammer spread is now 0.956 with a negative t-statistic of –4.44 which indicates, as predicted, overestimation.[18] In Table 2c, instead of the estimated buy-in value we include an estimated value of the reservation price for the works that were bought-in using 75% of the presale low. This again turns out a result of unbiased estimation with a nearly perfect ratio of 0.99 and a t-statistic dropping to –0.78.

Using our three price distributions of hammers, buy-ins, and reserves, we can run regressions to further investigate how the hammer spreads ex post relate to the appraisals ex ante. We regress the mean appraisal and spread of the appraisal on the hammer spread using the actual hammer price, the price including buy-ins from our distribution, and finally the estimated reserve price for works that were bought in.[19] In the initial regression runs, we detected heteroskedasticity, which was most likely caused by the presence of outliers in the data. These outliers are unusual or record high or low hammer prices and are an important part of the data set. Instead of omitting outliers therefore, we correct for

---

[18] The estimates from the transformation of the log data (0.947, 0.63) are viewed as the more accurate, although similar, to the estimates of mean and standard deviation of the distribution shown in Table 2b (0.956, 0.633).

[19] In these regressions we define the mean of the appraisals as the arithmetic mean i.e. the sum of the high and low estimates divided by 2. The appraisal spread is measured by the difference in the estimates (divided by the mean) and the hammer spread is hammer (or estimated) price divided by the arithmetic mean minus 1. We use the arithmetic mean because we assume appraisers will consider the actual distribution (rather than log) in setting their estimates.

heteroskedasticity using White-corrected standard errors or report the results of robust regressions.

In the first regression ignoring buy-ins, the appraisal spread is insignificant but the mean turns out to be significant with a tiny negative coefficient. (See Table 3 for regression results). This implies that the hammer spread is lower (tends towards overestimation) for works that have been appraised at a higher mean estimate value. This corroborates with the conclusions of Mei and Moses (2002) who found that price estimates tend to have an upward bias, or there is overestimation, for higher valued works. The subsequent regressions however show that the significance of the value of estimates only holds because buy-ins are ignored. The intercept is also significant and positive indicating possible bias, or that prices tend to be higher than estimated.

We ran the same regression but taking account of buy-ins in the hammer spread calculation by estimating the price or numerator component as 61% of the presale low estimate or 53% of the mean estimate. In this case, neither the mean nor the appraisal spread are significant using either definition of the Y-variable. In other words, when we account for buy-ins in the data the perceived riskiness or confidence in the investment measured by the mean appraisal and spread has no effect on the actual resultant hammer spread. The intercept term in this regression is significant and negative in both regressions, which indicates that prices tend to be lower than expected in the appraisals, or that experts are estimating higher than that on average.

Finally, when we run the regression using the reserve price estimate of 75% of the presale low we find that all of the variables on the right hand side of the regression equation are significant. In other words, the spread or the mean of the appraisals have nothing to do with how the price deviates from the mean. The intercept term representing the value of the hammer spread given that both of these X's are zero is also insignificant. These results strongly reinforce the result that appraisers tend to be unbiased and that deviations of the price from their estimates are not influenced by their appraisals when we consider the distribution using the reserve price.

We ran a series of diagnostic tests to ensure that the insignificance of the t-statistics is not caused by errors connected to omitting variables or correlation between the X's. We test that the model is correctly specified using the Ramsey regression specification error test (RESET) for omitted variables. We can reject specification error in all three cases at the 5% significance level. Very low t-statistics may be driven by high estimated standard errors caused by multicollinearity or a high correlation between the variables. A simple test of pair-wise correlation shows that the correlation between mean appraisal and appraisal spread is 0.035. We investigate this further using variance inflation factor (vif) tests. The "variable inflation factor" is equal to 1/(1-squared correlation between the X's) and hence will be inflated in the presence of multicollinearity. Multicollinearity between the X's is also not present on the basis of this test.

4. Assessing the Financial Risks of Art

Assessing the bias in presale estimates is an interesting exercise that generating this lognormal distribution allows. However the ability to assess the value of art works, including those without hammer prices, provides a basis for developing a number of tools and indicators that are more immediately important in a practical sense for the art investor. It is now possible to securitize art assets or make works of art into securities with claims against them such that the investor can separate individual wealth from their consumption on a flow basis.

One topic of interest to financiers is how to assess the risk of art portfolios as loan collateral. Lending policy using art as collateral requires an understanding of the downside risk associated with liquidating an individual work or entire collection. There are two central drivers behind the assessment of the risk associated with lending:

1. The probability of a loss : A bank might ask, "if we have lent, say, 50% of the appraised value of an art collection, what is our downside risk of default should the collection be repossessed in a default situation?" Alternatively, the question might be raised as to what percentage of a collection's appraised value should be lent without incurring a probability of loss in excess of , say, 5%, should liquidation be required.
2. The coverage in default: A bank will also want to know the extent of their expected loss in the event of default. If they lent out, say, $100,000 with a 5% risk of default, what percentage of that sum do they stand to lose in the event that default occurs.

These sorts of questions are easily addressed, given the distribution of hammer spreads estimated in Figure 1.

Table 4 shows some relationships between lending percentages or advance rates, numbers of works in a hypothetical portfolio, and a loan's downside risk. This table assumes that deviations between estimated values and hammer prices are independent across works, and that works are of equal value. To measure the downside risk, we integrate the left tail of the estimated distribution of hammer spreads from zero to the appropriate loan percentage. To obtain the probability of a loss with a loan amount of 50% of the value of the work or works, we use the original mean and standard deviation for our data and integrate the lognormal distribution from 0.5 through to the left tail. The results in Panel A, which correctly incorporates buy-ins, suggest a moderately conservative loan percentage for lending institutions. With only one work in a portfolio, the probability of loss with lending at 50% of the works value is 12.34%. However by adding four works to the portfolio, this probability drops to less than 1%, and by 10 plus works, the probability is close to zero.

The loan amount using one painting as collateral that keeps the risk of loss below 5% is nearly 40% of the mean estimated value. With 20 works in the portfolio, the loan amount rises to 71%. In comparison to loan percentages for other asset classes, the loan amount based on one painting is probably lower. Standard margin requirements for marketable securities allow loan amounts of 50% on single securities. Normal real estate loan percentages are 80% of transaction value at the time of purchase and 80% of appraised value at the time of refinancing. Loan practice on oil and gas properties is in the neighborhood of 50% of proven reserves. Thus, one can conclude that art works as an asset class reflect a slightly more risky venture for lending institutions than the more traditional assets with which these institutions have experience. However this risk is quickly dissipated as the number of independent works in the portfolio increases.

Some of the larger auction houses occasionally offer loans using art works as collateral. Sotheby's formally extends financial services to their consigners. Most items can be used by consigners as collateral for loans in advance of a sale of up to 40% of its low estimated auction value. It is Sotheby's general policy, subject to exceptions, that the minimum loan for such an advance is $50,000 in the US and £25,000 in the UK. They also allow borrowing against the value of collections of works of art. Using works of art as collateral, they can make term loans or establish lines of credit of, again, up to 40% of the low estimated auction value. The minimum loan of this type is generally $1,000,000 in the U.S. and £500,000 in the UK.[20] Christies also extends lines of credit and financial guarantees and uses a similar lending percentage, but their policy is more ad hoc and based on their own particular cost of capital.

Some banks also offer 'art services' although many are simply advisory services, and very little lending takes place. Citigroup Private Bank offers lending with art as collateral through its "Art Advisory Service." This service makes loans of

---

[20] Sothebys (2003)

up to 50% of the value of a collection or art work. They conduct valuation in-house, but base value on their best estimate of market value, which they report as around the mid-point of the presale high and low. Their clients tend to be affluent collectors with a minimum loan amount of $5 million, reflecting artworks used as collateral worth at least $10 million. They also stipulate that if a collection is offered, the unit value for each piece must be greater than $100,000.

The last column in Panel A also shows estimates of the expected loss should default occur or "coverage in default." What we consider here is, given that a loan is in default or has a portfolio value less than the loan amount, what percentage of the loan can be recovered if we sell the works without reserve? In order to get the answer, we again create the distribution with the correct mean and variance. We then integrate the left tail up to the loan amount or advanced funds level. This amounts to getting the probability of each possible loan value and multiplying the values by their probabilities, then summing all of these values. When this total is divided by the probability of being below the loan value, the expected value of the portfolio in default is defined. The expected loss is the loan amount minus the expected value of the portfolio. In other words, this figure shows that if $100, 000 is advanced against one work as collateral (and with the risk of default less than 5%), the expected loss if the loan defaults is 16.34% or $16,340. The expected loss on the loan drops significantly as the number of works in the portfolio increases. With 20 works, the expected loss in default has dropped to less than 5 % (or a loss of $4,740 on a $100,000 loan) which is less than a third of the loss with only one work. So, although all of these loans have the same risk of default (less than 5%), their actual net risk is different depending on the number of works, because of the difference in expected loss on default.

Percentages for expected loss can also be used to determine suitable rates for lending based risk level preferences. For example, from Table 4, the expected loss for a one work portfolio with 5% risk of default is 16.34%, or we can expect to lose 16.34% of the loan 5% of the time. The other 95% of the time, the expected loss is nil. An average of these two possibilities is a loss of 0.82%. Therefore a loan with the risk of default of 5% or 0.82%, requires an interest rate of 5.82% to cover expected loss .Table 6 shows these lending rates for correlated and uncorrelated works. Although the rates are below 1%, it is clear from the table that rates drop much more quickly when works are not correlated. The ability to determine rates for lending is a crucial part of the underwriting process and again shows the usefulness of this distribution in assisting in financial decision making.

Panel B of Table 4 shows the downside risk exposure that would be inferred if the data on auction sales excludes buy-ins. There is a significant difference in the risk measures in the Table which shows that ignoring buy-ins leads to significant underestimation of risk. The probability of loss with a 50% loan amount is reduced to 9.51 % with one work, and more than half of estimated risk of Panel A with 5 works or more at 0.29%. The loan amount with 5% risk of default is also somewhat higher. With only one work, nearly 42% could be lent out with the risk of default below 5%. A portfolio of twenty paintings could support an 83% loan amount with the same risk, which is 12% higher when buy-ins are included. The apparent downside risk is significantly altered and will be underestimated by ignoring the impact of buy-ins. This is reflected in the final column of the panel where the expected loss will be greater if buy-ins are ignored.

Table 4 assumes that the uncertainty concerning the value of the works is uncorrelated. The correlation between different art categories and genres is often very low. Even within a particular school, such as French Impressionists, there are negative correlations across different artists and price segments. In Table 5 we account for the possibility of correlation between the works that are added to the portfolio. We include correlation between works by changing the "risk factor." This is simply the portfolio risk or variance as a percentage of the variance of one work. For independent works, the risk factor is the inverse of the number of works. When the works are correlated, the expression becomes more complicated and increases substantially. Given n works, the risk factor is:

Risk Factor = $1/n * \{ 1+ (n-1) * r \}$ where r is the correlation across the works.

So for example in the 10 works case, if the paintings are uncorrelated then the risk factor is 1/10 or 0.10 as r=0. If there is, say, 50% correlation across the assets the risk factor becomes $1/10*\{1+(10-1)*0.5\}$ which equals 0.50, or an increase by a factor of 4 on the previous case.

We can now see that risk is not dissipated as much or as quickly as under assumptions of independence. The probability of loss on a 50% loan is only reduced to 7.14% rather than less than 1% with 5 works, and this only drops 1.2% in a larger portfolio of 20 to 5.94%. The amount that can be loaned out with less than 5% default risk is also significantly less than under assumptions of independence. In a portfolio of 20 works, we now would only lend 48.57% as opposed to the previous 82.81%.

5. Conclusions

This paper has examined how presale auction estimates can be used to help assess the risk of investment in works of art. Because of their virtual neglect in the literature on art investment and pricing until now, the phenomenon of buy-ins has been our particular focus. We examine the importance of the inclusion of buy-in data in analyzing the risk using the large data set of fully attributed French Impressionist paintings. From the moments of the hammer price distribution we constructed a theoretical lognormal distribution to include values for works that are bought-in. This distribution allowed us to examine bias in the pre-sale estimates of auction experts. It turns out that experts estimates follow a very logical format :

1. If we exclude any value for buy-ins and only look at hammer prices on works that sold at auction we find a tendency towards conservative estimates, or underestimation of the hammer price.

2. If we include the (implied) value for works bought in house, estimates are aggressive, or over-estimated on average.

3. If we use the reserve price estimate which represents each seller's valuation of the marginal price for selling the work to value buy-in sales in the data, the result is that the estimates are accurate and unbiased.

The inference that can be drawn is that experts are in fact unbiased and accurate, but they take both the valuations of potential buyers and those of the seller into account in their estimate setting process. If we exclude buy-ins from the data, it appears that experts underestimate. A very important corollary of this is that when buy-ins are excluded from consideration, returns on investment in art will be overstated, while financial risk is understated. Despite this glaring fact, buy-in data has been almost exclusively ignored in the growing volume of studies on art investment and pricing.

We also show how this distribution can be used by financiers to assess the risk of art portfolios as loan collateral. It turns out that while the loan amounts for art may be a little more conservative than for other financial assets, as soon as more independent works are added to the art portfolio, the risk becomes on par with other assets, or even less. Although the impact of this risk reduction decreases when high positive correlations between works are accounted for, this is still an important result since the correlations between art forms are often low or negative.

The more important result is that this paper has developed the means to use the distribution to provide a number of tools to assess risk, based on whatever the particular art portfolio context may be. By determining the correlations between works, we can also see which combinations of art works work best together in reducing financial risk. The uses of the distribution in the banking sector are numerous and of critical importance for this relatively untapped reservoir of wealth. With a few minor exceptions, the banking sector has traditionally steered clear of offering loans against non-traditional assets such as works of art. Art works were considered 'too risky' to lend against although this was never defined or estimated. Banks, without exception, have never underwritten loans for art. Any lending up to now has been based on opinion and guesswork and recourse to unrelated assets. The techniques introduced in this paper defines the risks and allows the financing and investing in artworks to be established and rigorously tested. The French Impressionist market is among the more well informed and liquid art markets. Buyers are sophisticated and well informed, and likewise, values are well established and known. There may be fewer risks and distortions in this market place, and further research is need to investigate how the same dynamics play out in the numerous other art genres as well as within sections of this market itself.

Bibliography

Ashenfelter, O. (1998) " How Auctions Work for Wine and Art." *Journal of Economic Perspectives*. Vol. 3, No. 3, pp.23-26.

Ashenfelter, O. and Graddy, K. (2002) " Art Auctions: A Survey of Empirical Studies." *NBER Working Papers. No. 8997*. National Bureau of Economic Research: Cambridge, Massachusetts.

Ashenfleter, O., Graddy, K., and Stevens, M. (2003) "A Study of Sales Rates and Prices in Impressionist and Contemporary Art Auctions."

Bauwens, L., and Ginsburgh, V. (2000) "Art Experts and Art Auctions. Are Pre-sale Estimates Fully Informative?. " *Louvain Economic Review*. Vol.66 (1), pp.131-144.

Beggs, A. and Graddy, K. (1997) "Declining Values and the Afternoon Effect: Evidence from Art Auctions." *Rand Journal of Economics*. Vol. 28, Autumn, pp.544-565.

Chanel, O., Gerard-Valet, L., and Vincent, S. (1996)"Auction Theory and Practice: Evidence from the Market for Jewelry." In Ginsburgh, V. and Menger, P.(eds) *Economics of the Arts: Selected Essays*. Amsterdam:Elseiver.

Di Vittorio, A. and Ginsburgh, V. (1994) Pricing Red Wines of the Medoc Vintages from 1949 to 1989 at Christies Auctions." *Mimeo*. Universite Libre de Bruxelles.

Ginsburgh, V. and Van Ours, J. (2003) " How to Organize Sequential Auctions Results of a Natural Experiment." *Center Discussion Paper No. 2003-25*. Tilburg University.

Klemperer, P.D. (ed.) (2000) The Economic Theory of Auctions. UK: Edward Elgar.

Kusin & Company (2002) *The European Art Market in 2002: A Survey*. Helvorit: TEFAF.

Mc Afee, R. and Vincent, D. (1993) "The Declining Price Anomaly." *Journal of Economic Theory*. Vol. 60, pp.191-212.

Mei, J. and Moses, M. (2002) " Art as an Investment and the Underperformance of Masterpieces." *American Economic Review*. Vol. 92, No. 5, pp 1656-1668.

Mei, J. and Moses, M. (2003) " Are Investors Credulous? Some Preliminary Evidence from Art Auctions." ???

Pesando, J. (1993) " Art as Investment : The Market for Modern Prints." *American Economic Review*. Vol.83, No. 5, pp.25-32.

Pesando, J. and Shum, P. (1998) " The Returns to Picassos Prints and to Traditional Financial Assets 1997 to 1996." *Mimeo*, University of Toronto.

Picci, L. and Scorcu, A. (2002) "Price Dynamics in Sequential Auctions. New Evidence using Art Auction Data." *Economia Working Papers 352*. Universita degli Studi di Bologna.

Sotheby's (2003) " Sotheby's Financial Services. " Taken from http://search.sothebys.com/services/financial/

Vickery, W. (1961) " Counter Speculations, Auctions and Competitive Sealed Tenders." Journal of Finance. Vol. 16, No.1, pp. 8-37.

Vincent, D. (1995) " Bidding Off the Wall : Why Reserve Prices Might be Kept Secret." Journal of Economic Theory. Vol.62, No.2, pp.575-584.

APPENDIX I: TABLES

Table 1. Auction Statistics on French Impressionists for the period 1/1985- 12/2001

	Number	Average Buyer's Premium
Works with complete data	4065	12.54%
Works with incomplete data	215	

Summary of works with complete data:

	Number	Value 1*	Value 2**
Works sold	2925	$3,015,452,272	$3,015,452,272
Buy-ins	1140	$679,819,373	$574,825,226
Works at auction	4065	$3,695,271,646	$3,590,277,498
Percentage of Buy-ins	0.28	0.184	0.160

* In Value 1: the geometric mean of the high and low presale estimates is used as to estimate the value for 'buy-ins' and the subsequent total for 'works at auction'. 'Works sold' in both Value 1 and 2 is the real sum of the hammer prices.

** In Value 2: the buy-in value (and subsequent total at auction) is estimated using the approximation for the reserve price i.e. 75% of the presale estimate.

Table 2a. Auction Price Statistics
French Impressionists over the period 1/1985-6/2001

Total value of works sold	$3,015,452,272
Number of works sold	2925

	raw data	natural log
Mean hammer price	$1,030,924	12.447
Geometric mean of presale high and low	$959,015	12.417
Mean hammer spread	1.139	0.03
Standard deviation of hammer spread	0.68	0.426
t-ratio of mean hammer spread	11.03	3.866
Square root of appraisal spread	1.165	0.539

Based on works with complete data
Hammer spread is defined as the ratio of hammer price to the geometric mean of the presale high and low value estimates.
For raw data, t-ratio is for the mean minus unity

Table 2b. Auction Price Statistics including Estimated Buy-ins
French Impressionists over the period 1/1985-6/2001

Total value of works $3,487,233,840
Number of works   4174

	raw data	natural log
Mean estimated price	$835,446	12.196
Geometric mean of presale high and low	$885,307	12.365
Mean hammer spread	0.956	-0.169
Standard deviation of hammer spread	0.633	0.469
t-ratio of mean hammer spread	-4.44	-23.234
Square root of appraisal spread	1.163	0.535

Table 2c. Auction Price Statistics using Estimated Reserve Price
French Impressionists over the period 1/1985-6/2001

Total value of works $3,590,277,498
Number of works   4174.00

	raw data	natural log
Mean estimated price	$860,153	12.256
Geometric mean of presale high and low	$885,307	12.422
Mean hammer spread	0.993	-0.180
Standard deviation of hammer spread	0.611	0.562
t-ratio of mean hammer spread	-0.78	-20.626
Square root of appraisal spread	1.163	0.535

Table 3. Robust Regression Results and Diagnostic Tests

Variables/test statistics	1. No Buy-ins	2a. Buy-ins at 61% of PSL	2b. Buy-ins at 53% of Mean	3. Reservation Price
Mean appraisal*	-0.000 (-2.60)	-0.000 (-0.57)	-0.000 (-0.71)	-0.000 (-1.16)
Appraisal Spread*	0.057 (0.38)	0.089 (0.98)	0.170 (1.45)	0.045 (0.37)
Intercept*	0.116 (2.64)	-0.028 (-2.26)	-0.102 (-2.98)	-0.030 (-0.87)
Specification Error (RESET)	F= 2.96	F= 3.24	F= 3.87	F = 1.56
Multicollinearity (VIF test)	1.00	1.00	1.00	1.00

*coefficient (t-statistic)

Table 4. Downside Risk for Loan Percentages of Art Portfolios
Assuming the uncertainty surrounding the value of works is uncorrelated

Panel A. Distributional assumptions incorporating buy-ins

		raw mean	0.947	log mean	0.16
		raw sigma	0.46	log sigma	0.46
			Probability of loss with loan amount equal to 50%	Loan amount with less than 5% risk of default	Expected Loss % if loan defaults
Number of works		Risk factor			
1		1.00	12.34%	39.97%	16.34%
5		0.20	0.65%	59.86%	8.13%
10		0.10	0.02%	66.29%	6.41%
15		0.07	0.00%	69.39%	5.47%
20		0.05	0.00%	71.31%	4.74%

Risk factor is the portfolio's risk as a percentage of the risk of one work.

Panel B. Distributional assumptions ignoring buy-ins

	raw mean	1.139	log mean	0.03
	raw sigma	0.68	log sigma	0.426
		Probability of loss with loan amount equal to 50%	Loan amount with less than 5% risk of default	Expected Loss % if the loan defaults
Number of works in portfolio				
1		9.51%	41.55%	18.31%
5		0.29%	66.92%	9.91%
10		0.01%	75.74%	7.05%
15		0.00%	80.09%	6.16%
20		0.00%	82.81%	5.12%

Table 5. Downside Risk for Loan Percentages of Art Portfolios
Assuming the uncertainty surrounding the value of works has correlation = 0.5

Panel A. Distributional assumptions incorporating buy-ins

		raw mean	0.947	log mean	0.16
		raw sigma	0.46	log sigma	0.46
			Probability of loss with loan amount equal to 50%	Loan amount with less than 5% risk of default	Expected Loss % if loan defaults
Number of works	Risk factor				
1	1.00		12.34%	39.97%	16.34%
5	0.60		7.14%	46.84%	13.43%
10	0.55		6.35%	47.97%	12.86%
15	0.53		6.07%	48.37%	12.76%
20	0.53		5.94%	48.57%	12.62%

Risk factor is the portfolio's risk as a percentage of the risk of one work.

Panel B. Distributional assumptions ignoring buy-ins

		raw mean	1.139	log mean	0.03
		raw sigma	0.68	log sigma	0.426
			Probability of loss with loan amount equal to 50%	Loan amount with less than 5% risk of default	Expected loss % if the loan defaults
Number of works	Risk factor				
1	1.00		9.51%	41.55%	19.01%
5	0.60		5.02%	49.95%	15.70%
10	0.55		4.37%	51.38%	15.22%
15	0.53		4.15%	51.88%	15.03%
20	0.53		4.04%	52.14%	14.88%

Table 6. Lending Rates for loans with 5% risk of default

Number of Works	0.0 correlation	0.5 correlation
1	0.817%	0.817%
5	0.407%	0.672%
10	0.321%	0.643%
15	0.274%	0.638%
20	0.237%	0.631%

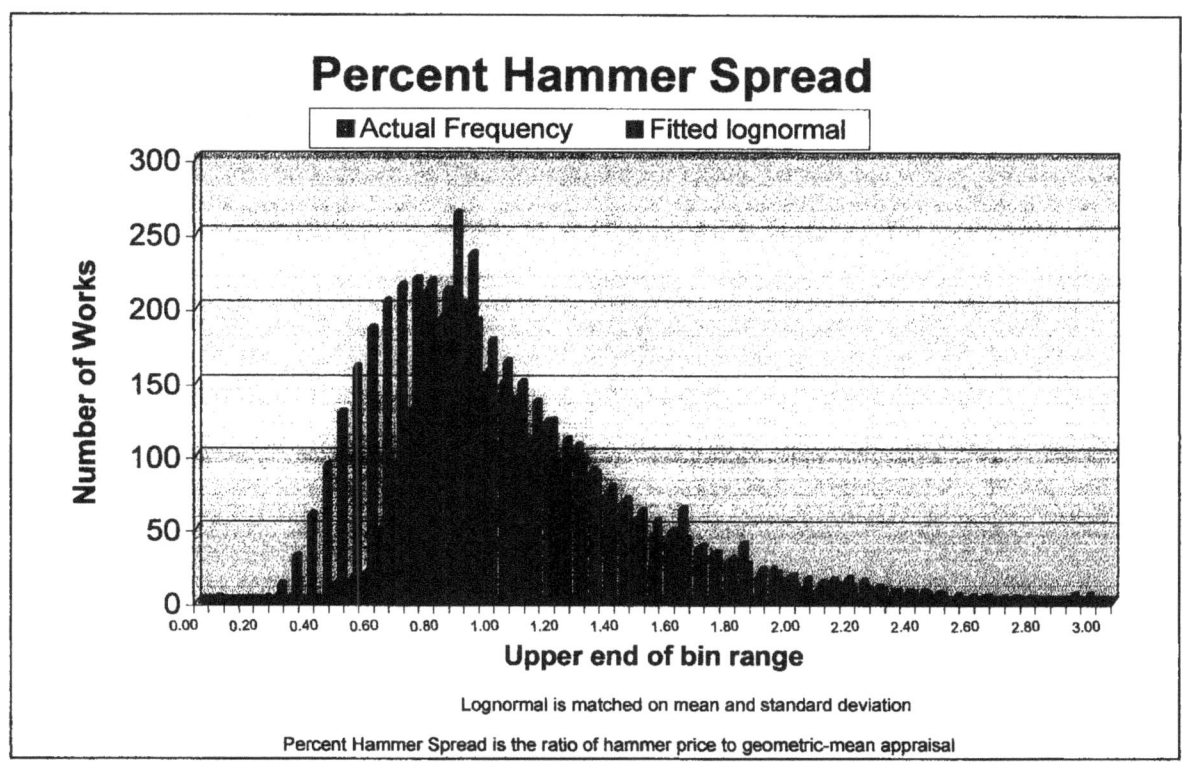

Figure 1. Hammer Spread Distribution and Fitted Lognormal.

Appendix II. The Kolmogorov-Smirnov Goodness-of-Fit Test

The Kolmogorov –Smirnov Test (KS-Test) is used to describe whether a given sample of data comes from a population with a specific distribution such as normal or lognormal. The test was developed in the 1930's and is intended for use with a continuous, fully specified distribution.
The KS-Test is defined by the following:

Ho: The data follow a specifies distribution (in this case a lognormal distribution)

Ha: The data do not follow the specifies distribution

Test Statistic: The KS-test statistic is defined as :

$$D = \max |F(Y_i) - i/N|$$

Where F is the theoretical distribution (lognormal) being tested of N ordered data points $Y_1, Y_2 \ldots Y_n$. The hypothesis regarding the distributional form is rejected if the test statistic , D, is grater than the critical value given in a KS-table. In this study , the D statistic represents the maximum departure between the actual frequencies and the predicted. If the D is greater than the critical value we reject Ho indicating that there is a large difference between the actual and the predicted values.

It turns out that the D statistic is 0.876 for this data set which is small and indicates a good fit or a small difference between actual and predicted such that we accept the Ho that the data follow a lognormals distribution. (The relevant critical values of 1.22, 1.36, and 1.63 for the 1, 5 and 10 % significance levels respectively).

Note: To derive the D-statistic, we firstly maximized the differences between actual and predicted frequencies over a certain range. We want to maximize from the point where the buy-ins come into play in the distribution so we tired various iterations of this, all of which gave similar results, for example :

- Using 1.00 (or 1000%) where P= GM gave a d-statistic of 0.310;
- Using 0.70 (or 70%) where P < GM gave a d-statistic of 0.907;
- Or using 0.80- which gave 0.876.

We then find the maximize from this point to the end of the distribution and then using this as the 'target' solve the problem of minimizing the D-statistic by altering the possible means and standard deviation of the distribution which provide us with the KS or D-statistic to compare in the statistical tables.

The KS-test has the advantage of being making no assumptions about the data, or is and is non-parametric and distribution free. As such it is independent of arbitrarily computational choices such as the distribution's width, so that data are assessed at all data points, avoiding such problems as determining the number of bands to split the data into.

It does have a number of limitations also:

- It only applies to continuous distributions (not discrete distributions such as binomial or Poisson);
- The distribution must be fully specified in that parameters such as location, scale and shape cannot be estimated from the data;
- It tends to be more sensitive near the center of the distribution rather than the tails. The drawback of this test is that its value is only determined by the one largest discrepancy or difference and it takes no account of the lack of fit across the rest of the distribution. In other words it would give a worse fit to a distribution with one large discrepancy than it would to a distribution that has a poor fit in general across the entire range.

Art as an Investment: The Market for Modern Prints
Author(s): James E. Pesando
Source: *The American Economic Review*, Vol. 83, No. 5 (Dec., 1993), pp. 1075-1089
Published by: American Economic Association
Stable URL: http://www.jstor.org/stable/2117549
Accessed: 05/02/2014 12:43

Art as an Investment: The Market for Modern Prints

By James E. Pesando*

Repeat sales of modern prints at auction are used to estimate a semiannual index of prices for the period 1977–1992. As in other studies of art as an investment, prints do not compare favorably to traditional financial assets. There is substantial noise in auction prices, but little or no support for the proposition that some artists command higher prices in certain countries or that masterpieces outperform the market. One puzzle is the continuing tendency for prices realized at certain auction houses to exceed those realized at others: notably, at Sotheby's relative to Christie's in New York. (JEL G14, Z10)

Amy Page (Editor, *Art & Auction*): *Is there an "efficient" art market?*
Jeffrey Deitch (art dealer): *Definitely not. That's one of the things that makes the market so interesting.*
[*Art & Auction*, April 1990, p. 163]

In a well-functioning capital market (and ignoring taxes), the risk-adjusted rates of return on all assets will be forced to equality. The equilibrium return on art, net of insurance and storage costs and any flow of consumption services, will equal the equilibrium return on competing assets with identical risk. If this is not the case, then art is an investment which compares "favorably" (or "unfavorably") with traditional financial assets. If the art market is efficient, then—as in all such markets—one should not be able to earn excess returns on the basis of known information.

A major obstacle to testing the economic efficiency of the art market is the difficulty in tracking the prices of individual works of art over time. Since multiple sales of unique art objects occur infrequently, it is difficult to construct data on returns to art that are readily aligned with data on the periodic returns to traditional financial assets.

The present paper circumvents this problem by focusing on the auction market for modern prints. Because prints are multiples, often published in editions of 50–100 or more, several impressions of the same print may be offered for sale at auction in a single season. As a result, the increase in the number of repeat sales is quite dramatic. William J. Baumol (1986) uses the data recorded by Gerald Reitlinger (1961) to study the returns on paintings which sold two or more times, at least 20 years apart, during the period 1652–1961. His data set, which spans three centuries, contains 640 multiple sales. For the 28 artists included in the present study, there are 27,961 repeat sales of modern prints during the 16-year period from 1977 to 1992.

I use the data on modern prints to estimate a semiannual price index, in U.S. dollars, for the period 1977–1992. The price index is then used to address the question of whether the risk–return characteristics of prints compare favorably to those of traditional financial assets, such as common stocks and fixed-income securities.

Economists may be predisposed to assume that the auction market for art is efficient, like the market for traditional financial assets. In sharp contrast, the folklore of the art trade suggests that this market is decidedly inefficient.

---

*Department of Economics and Institute for Policy Analysis, University of Toronto, Toronto, ON M5S 1A1. I am indebted to Pauline Shum, Jin Park, Mark Flanagan, and Corrine Sellars for research assistance, and to Martin Gordon, Chris Leowski, and Clarence Kwan for helpful suggestions.

The data on print prices permit tests of two propositions frequently advanced by art dealers and other specialists. Art dealers traditionally advise clients to buy only the top works of the most established artists and to eschew middle-market works of art. I evaluate this strategy by estimating separate price indexes for top-end, middle-level, and low-end prints, and then examining the risk–return characteristics of these alternative portfolios. The trade also maintains that the works of at least some artists command systematically higher prices in certain geographic markets than in others. If the art market is efficient, and if the prints of an artist are actively traded in two or more markets, the "law of one price" should prevail. I examine this proposition directly by observing whether systematic price differences exist for prints sold in different markets within a specified time window.

The paper is organized as follows. In the first section, I discuss the data on prices realized at auction and review the regression procedure used to estimate the indexes of print prices. In Section II, I present estimates of semiannual print price indexes for the period 1977–1992. In Section III, I calculate the real returns to portfolios of prints, and compare these returns to those on traditional financial assets. I also identify the systematic risk of a portfolio of modern prints and examine the serial dependence in excess returns. In Section IV, I determine whether masterpieces do, in fact, outperform the market. In Section V, I examine whether the print market satisfies the law of one price. A summary and conclusion section completes the paper.

I. The Data and the Method for Estimating Print Price Indexes

Gordon's Print Price Annual, published each year since 1978, contains a complete record of the prints sold at the world's major auction houses (Sotheby's, Christie's, Hotel Druout, Hauswedell & Nolte, Kornfeld, etc.) during the previous year. The *Annuals*, compiled from the catalogues prepared in advance of the sales and the price lists released thereafter, currently contain over 35,000 entries. Each print is identified by artist, title, and its number in the standard reference catalogue (catalogue raisonné) of the artist's work. Information is also provided on the price, location, and date of sale. Price is inclusive of the buyer's premium and is recorded in the currency of the nation in which the auction is conducted. If the auction did not take place in the United States, the price is translated into U.S. dollars using *The Wall Street Journal*'s daily conversion rates. The *Annuals* also indicate whether the print is signed by the artist. An unsigned impression will typically sell at a substantial discount relative to the price of a signed impression of the same print. No information is provided on the physical condition of the print or the quality of the impression, both of which can influence price.

Prints sold at auction are classified into three groups: modern, old masters, and contemporary. Old-master prints (Rembrandt, Durer, etc.) vary sharply in both condition and quality. Contemporary prints (Johns, Hockney, Stella, etc.), although likely to be in good condition and of uniform quality, are less likely to have a history of sale at auction. For these reasons, I focus on the market for modern prints (Picasso, Chagall, Miro, etc.). Here, price differences due to "nonobserved" variations in condition and quality are less important, and there is an established history of sale at auction.

In order to quantify the risk–return characteristics of modern prints, I first estimate an index of print prices. To do so, I employ the repeat-sale regression (RSR) method first advanced by Martin J. Bailey et al. (1963).[1] The RSR method yields an estimate, as well as the standard error, of each value of a log-price index.

A repeat sale occurs whenever the "identical" print (i.e., same artist and catalogue

---

[1]The RSR method has been extensively used to estimate indexes of real-estate prices (e.g., Karl E. Case and Robert J. Shiller, 1989; Arthur J. Hosios and Pesando, 1991) and has also been used to estimate indexes of art prices (Robert C. Anderson, 1974; William N. Goetzmann, 1993).

raisonné number, and signed or not) is sold on two different occasions. For each pair of sales, the log-price relative is calculated: the log of the price on the later sales date less the log of the price on the earlier date. The log-price relatives are then regressed on a set of dummy variables, one for each observation of the log-price index. For each observation of the dependent variable, the dummy is set equal to $+1$ at the time of the second sale, -1 at the time of the initial sale, and 0 at all other times.[2] If the initial sale is in the first time period, there is no dummy variable corresponding to the initial sale. Econometrically, this procedure is equivalent to regressing the price of each repeat sale on a corresponding time-period dummy, whose coefficient is the estimated value of the index, and an individual "print" dummy.

Auction sales are concentrated during May–June and November–December, and it is natural to work with semiannual observations. To calculate returns from the estimated price indexes, I adopt the simplifying assumption that all sales occur at the end of each observation period. Although not strictly true, it is not a great injustice to the facts.[3] If a particular print is sold more than once in an observation period, its average price is used in the construction of each matched pair of sales.

[2] The regression is:

$$r_{itt'} = \sum_{j=1}^{T} b_j x_j + u_{itt'}$$

where $r_{itt'}$ is the log-price relative of print i, with initial sale at time t and final sale at time t'; x_j is a dummy variable which equals $+1$ at the time of the final sale, -1 at the time of the initial sale, and 0 otherwise; b_j is the value of the log-price index in period j (to be estimated); and $u_{itt'}$ is a disturbance term. The log of the initial value of the index (b_0) is normalized at zero, and the T subsequent values of the log-price index are estimated by the regression.

[3] The major spring sales at Sotheby's and Christie's in London take place at the end of June. In some years, the sales at Christie's actually take place in the first week in July. Prints sold in these sales are included in the first half of the year for the purpose of estimating the print price indexes.

II. The Estimated Print Price Indexes

The aggregate price index for modern prints, based on semiannual observations for the period 1977:1–1992:2, is presented in Table 1 and depicted in Figure 1.[4] In Figure 1, I also present the corresponding *real* price index, which equals the nominal index deflated by the U.S. consumer price index. In addition to estimating an aggregate index, I also estimate a price index for the prints of Picasso. Picasso is the artist whose prints are the most frequently sold at auction, and it is instructive to determine how well the prices of Picasso prints mirror movements in the market as a whole. The nominal price index (only) for Picasso prints is also shown in Figure 1.

For the aggregate index, there are 27,961 repeat sales; for the Picasso index, 6,010. The R^2 for the aggregate index is 0.239; for the Picasso index, 0.390. This fact indicates that the prices of Picasso prints tend to move more closely together (and thus are better approximated by a single index) than do the prices of the more diverse set of artists whose prints are included in the aggregate index. The relatively low R^2's are due, in part, to the substantial "noise" in auction prices. As discussed in Section V, prices of "identical" prints that are sold within relatively narrow windows often vary substantially.

There is a sharp spike in both nominal and real print prices in 1990 (Fig. 1). After falling during the recession of 1981–1982, nominal print prices rose steadily throughout the 1980's, and at an accelerated pace after 1985. The boom in the art market in the late 1980's is, of course, well documented. The print price indexes, however, allow one to identify the precise time that

[4] The 28 artists included in the index are Picasso, Chagall, Miro, Matisse, Whistler, Nolde, Heckel, Schmidt-Rottluf, Kirchner, Kandinsky, Klee, Mueller, Bellows, Benton, Hopper, Munch, Renoir, Sloan, Vuillard, Braque, Bonnard, Cassatt, Kollwitz, Laurencin, Leger, Rouault, Toulouse-Lautrec, and Villon.

TABLE 1—THE PRINT PRICE INDEX: SEMIANNUAL, 1977–1992

Year	b = log index	SE(b)	$b - b_{-1}$	SE($b - b_{-1}$)
1977:1	0.000	0.000	—	—
1977:2	−0.025	0.027	−0.025	0.027
1978:1	0.178	0.024	0.203	0.024
1978:2	0.028	0.152	0.022	0.022
1979:1	0.421	0.025	0.090	0.022
1979:2	0.529	0.026	0.108	0.019
1980:1	0.597	0.024	0.067	0.018
1980:2	0.666	0.026	0.068	0.017
1981:1	0.628	0.024	−0.038	0.017
1981:2	0.576	0.026	−0.052	0.017
1982:1	0.497	0.025	−0.078	0.018
1982:2	0.443	0.028	−0.054	0.020
1983:1	0.496	0.026	0.053	0.021
1983:2	0.472	0.027	−0.023	0.019
1984:1	0.548	0.026	0.075	0.018
1984:2	0.541	0.027	−0.006	0.017
1985:1	0.619	0.026	0.078	0.018
1985:2	0.645	0.028	0.025	0.019
1986:1	0.839	0.026	0.194	0.019
1986:2	0.872	0.028	0.033	0.019
1987:1	1.092	0.026	0.220	0.019
1987:2	1.117	0.028	0.024	0.019
1988:1	1.258	0.026	0.141	0.019
1988:2	1.367	0.027	0.108	0.017
1989:1	1.456	0.026	0.089	0.016
1989:2	1.553	0.027	0.097	0.015
1990:1	1.577	0.027	0.023	0.015
1990:2	1.459	0.028	−0.118	0.017
1991:1	1.257	0.029	−0.201	0.019
1991:2	1.228	0.031	−0.029	0.021
1992:1	1.213	0.030	0.014	0.022
1992:2	1.088	0.033	−0.124	0.024

Notes: See text for description of regression method employed to estimate the log-price index (b). SE(b) is the standard error of the estimated log-price index, and $b - b_{-1}$ is the first difference in the index.

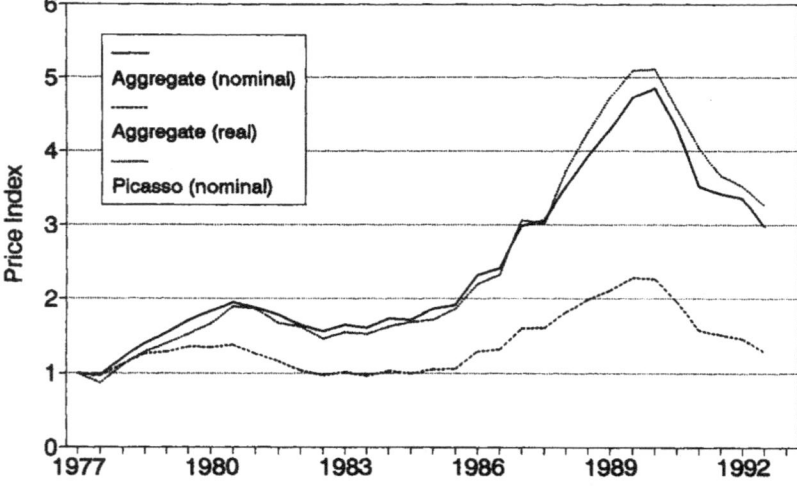

FIGURE 1. NOMINAL AND REAL PRINT PRICES: SEMIANNUAL, 1977–1992

this segment of the art market peaked: the spring of 1990. Prices then fell sharply. At the end of 1992, nominal prices were 38.6 percent beneath their previous highs; real prices, 44.2 percent. Movements in the prices of the prints of Picasso mirror those of the market as a whole. For both nominal indexes, the sharp run-up in prices and subsequent decline is suggestive of bubble-like behavior. I return to this issue later in the paper.

The first difference in the log-price index measures the semiannual return on the print portfolio. It is natural to ask how well these semiannual returns are measured. Case and Shiller (1989) suggest that the ratio of the standard deviation of a variable to the average standard error of that variable is a useful summary statistic. The standard deviation of the first difference in the aggregate index equals 0.099, and the average standard error of the estimates of these first differences equals 0.019. This ratio thus equals 5.21, which indicates that returns are accurately measured. For the first difference in the Picasso index, this ratio equals 3.59. This indicates that the semiannual returns for the Picasso portfolio are less accurately measured than those for the aggregate portfolio.[5]

The estimated price indexes do not reflect the fact that the "buy-in" rate, the fraction of lots not sold, varies over time. For this reason, the estimated price index may underestimate the true volatility of bid prices. During most of the sample period, the buy-in rate for prints was relatively small, although the buy-in rate approached 30 percent in some of the major sales during the recent period of market weakness.

III. Real Returns to Modern Prints

For each six-month period, the real return (in U.S. dollars) to investing in prints is readily calculated from the index of real print prices. The (annualized) real returns, for the aggregate and for the Picasso portfolios, are summarized in Table 2. The table also shows the corresponding real returns to U.S. stocks (as measured by the Standard & Poor's 500 Stock Index), U.S. government bonds, and 180-day U.S. Treasury bills.[6]

The mean real return on the aggregate print portfolio equals 1.51 percent; on the Picasso portfolio, 2.10 percent. Both are beneath the mean real returns on Treasury bills (2.23 percent) and long-term bonds (2.54 percent), and far beneath the mean real return on stocks (8.14 percent). The standard deviation of the real returns to the aggregate print portfolio is 19.94 percent; to the Picasso portfolio, 23.38 percent. By this measure, both print portfolios have a degree of risk that is (roughly) comparable to the risk of stocks and long-term bonds. Treasury bills are, of course, far less risky.

Prints could still provide an attractive investment if their inclusion in a portfolio of traditional financial assets would serve to reduce its risk. Based on the real returns summarized above and the correlations presented in Table 2, prints do have some capacity to promote efficient diversification in the framework advanced by Harry Markowitz (1959). In the absence of short-selling, only prints and Treasury bills are

---

[5]Case and Shiller (1989), in constructing their index of house prices, argue that the variance of $u_{itt'}$ in footnote 2 is likely to increase with the length of time between house sales, reflecting drift due to features such as change in neighborhood quality. Case and Shiller propose a three-stage procedure, to lessen the weight assigned to repeat sales that are widely separated in time. First, the index is estimated by ordinary least squares (OLS). Second, the squared residuals are regressed on a constant term and the time between sales. Third, the index is reestimated by generalized least squares (GLS) with each observation divided by the square root of the fitted value in the second stage. For the aggregate print price index, the slope coefficient in stage 2 is positive with a t statistic equal to 14.77. Yet the returns calculated from the index estimated by GLS are very similar to those calculated from the index estimated by OLS. The correlation coefficient between the two sets of returns equals 0.9994. In the text, I use the returns calculated from the OLS estimates of the print indexes.

[6]All data are drawn from the Bank of Canada Review, as accessed through the CANSIM (Canadian Socio-Economic Information Management Systems) tape. The nominal returns on long-term bonds are calculated from the interest-rate data using the linearized expression for the holding-period return derived by Shiller (1979).

TABLE 2—REAL RETURNS ON MODERN PRINTS AND TRADITIONAL FINANCIAL ASSETS, 1977:1–1992:2

A. *Real Returns (U.S. Dollars):*

Portfolio	Mean	Standard deviation	Range
Prints			
Aggregate	1.51	19.94	−35.34–47.18
Picasso	2.10	23.38	−28.58–65.50
Stocks	8.14	22.47	−35.89–66.90
U.S. government bonds	2.54	21.83	−38.35–76.09
180-day Treasury bills	2.23	3.43	−4.11–11.32

B. *Correlations:*

	Portfolio				
Portfolio	Picasso prints	Stocks	Bonds	T-Bills	Inflation
Prints					
Aggregate	0.91**	0.30	−0.10	−0.21	0.03
Picasso		0.34	−0.17	−0.27	0.08
Stocks			0.46**	0.27	−0.31
U.S. government bonds				0.73**	−0.56**
180-day Treasury bills					−0.73**

Notes: Semiannual returns are expressed at annual rates. Returns to stocks are based on the Standard & Poor's 500 Stock Index.
**Statistically significant at the 1-percent level.

included in low-risk portfolios. The minimum-variance portfolio, with a real return of 2.19 percent and a standard deviation of 3.19 percent, is composed 94 percent of Treasury bills and 6 percent of modern prints. The negative correlation between the real returns to prints and Treasury bills underlies this result. For mean-variance-efficient portfolios with an expected real return of 3 percent or more, however, prints are not included. It is useful to note that the real returns to prints are positively correlated with inflation, unlike the real returns to traditional financial assets. However, the simple correlation coefficients are low (0.03 for the aggregate portfolio and 0.08 for Picasso) and not statistically significant.

The returns calculated from the estimated print price indexes, as well as the returns on traditional financial assets, are gross of transaction costs. Although this is the usual practice in such comparisons, one should note that the transaction costs associated with buying and selling prints are likely to exceed those associated with the purchase and sale of traditional financial assets. During the period 1977–1992, for example, Christie's and Sotheby's in the United States charged the seller a commission of 6 percent if the seller was a dealer, and 10 percent otherwise. In addition, the buyer paid a commission of 10 percent. For short holding periods such as six months, the amortized value of these trading costs is considerable.

There have been no detailed studies by economists of the investment performance of the print market. Economists have examined the real returns to paintings, but over much longer horizons than that considered in the present paper. The investment performance of prints during the period 1977–1992 is consistent with the findings of these studies, in that art does not compare favorably to traditional financial assets. Baumol (1986) and Bruno S. Frey and Werner W. Pommerehne (1989) conclude that the real return on investment in art is low relative to the real returns provided by long-term bonds. Baumol calculates the average compound real return for the 640 multiple sales of paintings that occur during the period 1652–1961. This figure equals 0.55 percent, which is considerably less than the average real interest rate of 2.5 percent provided by

British government bonds during this period. Frey and Pommerehne calculate an average annual real return (net of transactions costs) of 1.5 percent for their sample of 2,396 multiple sales of paintings during the period 1635–1987. Goetzmann (1993) uses the repeat-sales regression method to estimate the decade-average returns to paintings, using data from the period 1715–1986. He finds that the return to paintings falls short of the return to long-term bonds during the full sample, but this result is reversed for the period since 1850. In this latter period, paintings have a higher return and a much higher standard deviation than do either stocks or long-term bonds. This finding contrasts sharply with the performance of the print market during the period 1977–1992. In part, the high returns to art estimated by Goetzmann reflect the fact that his sample period ends in 1986, prior to the recent collapse in prices.

In Table 3, I present estimates of the capital-asset-pricing model (CAPM) for the aggregate print and Picasso portfolios, when the Standard and Poor's 500 Stock Index serves as the proxy for the market portfolio. The print portfolios have low systematic risk, with β coefficients of 0.315 (aggregate) and 0.430 (Picasso). Risk-adjusted excess returns are negative, but not significant.

In an efficient market, it is not possible to earn excess returns on the basis of known information. This proposition is widely tested in the finance literature, where evidence seems to support the efficient-market paradigm. Recently, economists (e.g., David M. Cutler et al., 1990) have revisited the question of serial correlation in excess returns. For this reason, I examine the extent to which excess returns to prints are predictable on the basis of their prior values. For simplicity, I define the excess return to prints as the difference between the nominal return on prints and the interest rate on 180-day Treasury bills.[7] Because I work with an *estimate* of the true price index, there exists the possibility of spurious serial correlation in the returns so calculated. This spurious correlation would contaminate tests of the forecastability of future changes in an estimated index based on prior changes in this *same* index. Like Case and Shiller (1989), I use the simple expedient of dividing the sample in half and estimating two separate indexes. I then regress the current change in one index on prior changes in the other.

The coefficients of the lagged values confirm a familiar pattern: excess returns are positively correlated at short horizons and negatively correlated at long horizons. This finding is consistent with the "stylized fact" documented by Cutler et al. (1990) in their review of international evidence in the markets for stocks, bonds, foreign exchange, and various real assets. For both print portfolios, only the coefficients of the second lagged value of excess returns are statistically significant. Nonetheless, the impact of the serial correlation is quantitatively important. For the aggregate portfolio, 28.6 percent of the current excess return persists to the next six-month period; 53.5 percent, to the following six-month period. In the ensuing 12 months, excess returns then *fall* by a total of 27.9 percent of the current excess return.

The dramatic rise in print prices (and in the prices of unique works of art) in the late 1980's suggests the possible presence of a rational bubble. Art investors, like those who invest in common stocks, may believe that prices have surged ahead to unsustainable levels but continue to buy in the belief that short-run prospects for continued gains are sufficient to compensate for the risk that the price bubble might burst. The pattern of serial dependence in the excess returns to modern prints, with strong positive correlation at short horizons and negative correlation at longer horizons, is consistent with bubble-like behavior. In light of the relatively short sample period, however, this result can only be viewed as suggestive.

IV. Do Masterpieces Outperform the Market?

Art dealers traditionally advise clients to buy the most expensive artworks they can

---

[7]This is the definition used in the results summarized by Cutler et al. (1990). When I use the estimated value of β from Table 3 to define the excess return, the pattern of estimated coefficients remains the same.

TABLE 3—SYSTEMATIC RISK AND THE PREDICTABILITY OF EXCESS RETURNS, 1977–1992

A. *Estimates of CAPM:*

$$R_t^P - r_{f,t} = \alpha + \beta(R_{m,t} - r_{f,t}) + u_t$$

Portfolio	α	β	R^2
Aggregate prints	−0.015 (0.36)	0.315 (1.84)	0.105
Picasso prints	−0.012 (0.26)	0.430 (2.19)	0.141

B. *Predictability of Excess Returns:*

$$\text{ER}_t^P = b_0 + b_1 \text{ER}_{t-1}^P + b_2 \text{ER}_{t-2}^P + b_3 \text{ER}_{t-3}^P + b_4 \text{ER}_{t-4}^P + e_t$$

Portfolio	Regression	b_0	b_1	b_2	b_3	b_4	R^2
Aggregate prints	(1)	0.011 (0.27)	0.324 (1.82)				0.106
	(2)	−0.014 (0.41)	0.225 (1.46)	0.425* (2.74)			0.334
	(3)	−0.017 (0.51)	0.258 (1.44)	0.483* (3.10)	−0.202 (1.18)		0.376
	(4)	−0.011 (0.31)	0.286 (1.43)	0.535* (2.81)	−0.226 (1.19)	−0.053 (0.27)	0.376
Picasso prints	(1)	0.014 (0.30)	0.280 (1.64)				0.088
	(2)	−0.016 (0.41)	0.221 (1.51)	0.455* (3.12)			0.351
	(3)	−0.028 (0.76)	0.188 (1.12)	0.489* (3.50)	−0.049 (0.29)		0.394
	(4)	−0.010 (0.26)	0.188 (1.17)	0.666* (4.07)	−0.058 (0.36)	−0.299 (1.77)	0.482

Notes: R_t^P denotes the return on the indicated print portfolio; $R_{m,t}$ denotes the return on the market portfolio, as measured by the S&P 500 stock index; $r_{f,t}$ denotes the risk-free rate, as measured by the interest rate on 180-day Treasury bills; and ER_t^P equals R_t^P minus $r_{f,t}$. Numbers in parentheses are t statistics.
*Statistically significant at the 5-percent level.

afford, on the presumption that the top works of the most established artists will outperform the market. The proposition appears to be that the cumulative return on a masterpiece portfolio will exceed that on the market as a whole, for an unspecified holding period. It is frequently noted, as well, that masterpieces are less susceptible to market downturns. If so, a masterpiece portfolio might have a higher expected return, for a given level of risk, than middle-level and lower-level works of art. This cannot be true if the art market is efficient, since the desirable characteristics of masterpieces will simply be capitalized into their prices. While this result may seem self-

TABLE 4—THE PERFORMANCE OF "MASTERPIECES" RELATIVE TO THE MARKET

Portfolio	n	Log-price index				
		1984:2	1986:2	1988:2	1990:2	1992:2
A. *Selection Period 1977–1979; Estimation Period 1980–1992:*						
Masterpiece: top 10 percent	1,312	−0.1475	0.3665	0.9238	1.0001	0.2561
Middle market: middle 80 percent	10,437	−0.1023	0.2100	0.6878	0.8085	0.4302
Inexpensive: bottom 10 percent	1,104	−0.2285	0.1652	0.4328	0.4864	0.6626
Masterpiece: top 20 percent	2,768	−0.0204	0.3089	0.8757	0.9969	0.3888
Middle market: middle 60 percent	7,820	−0.0640	0.3237	0.7781	0.8911	0.5042
Inexpensive: bottom 20 percent	2,232	−0.2114	0.0600	0.4781	0.5067	0.5641
B. *Selection Period 1980–1982; Estimation Period 1983–1992:*						
Masterpiece: top 10 percent	398	−0.1736	−0.0527	0.6975	0.9108	0.3810
Middle market: middle 80 percent	6,267	0.0696	0.3979	0.9032	0.9589	0.5925
Inexpensive: bottom 10 percent	293	−0.0691	0.5838	0.9562	1.0868	0.9010
Masterpiece: top 20 percent	1,167	0.0160	0.2578	0.8338	0.9068	0.3333
Middle market: middle 60 percent	4,030	0.0287	0.3839	0.8961	0.9296	0.5938
Inexpensive: bottom 20 percent	656	0.1478	0.5634	0.9831	1.0377	0.9400

Note: n is the number of observations in the repeat-sales regression.

evident to economists, it is clearly unfamiliar to those in the art trade.

In a bold—but not atypical—expression of the trade view, art dealer Edward Merrin observes that "...it's always better to buy one $10,000 object than ten $1,000 objects, or one $100,000 object—if that is what you can afford—than ten $10,000 ones" (quoted in *Art & Auction* ["Antiques"], September 1988, p. 131).

I follow the implied suggestion and allow the market to identify the masterpiece portfolio. I proxy the masterpiece portfolio by the top 10 percent or the top 20 percent of prints by price. In the first experiment, I use prices realized in each of the years 1977, 1978, and 1979 and estimate price indexes for the period 1980–1992. To be precise, I first identify the top 10 percent (by price) of prints sold in 1977:1 and assign these to the masterpiece portfolio. The remainder are assigned, in a similar manner, to the middle market and to the inexpensive portfolios. For all prints sold in 1977:2 that were not sold in 1977:1, I repeat this procedure; and so on. In the second experiment, I use prices realized in 1980, 1981, and 1982 and estimate price indexes for the period 1983–1992. Price indexes are estimated for each masterpiece portfolio and two alternatives: a middle-market portfolio which excludes the top 10 (20) percent and bottom 10 (20) percent of prints by price; and an inexpensive portfolio comprising of the bottom 10 (20) percent of prints by price. The sample periods in which the indexes are estimated do not overlap with the sample periods used to assign prints to the three portfolios.

If the trade view is correct, the estimated price indexes for the masterpiece portfolios must lie uniformly above the estimated price indexes for the alternatives. This is a necessary, but not sufficient, condition for the cumulative return on masterpieces to exceed the cumulative return on mid-market and inexpensive prints for all possible investment horizons.

There are 12 estimated price indexes, six for each experiment. To conserve space, I present in Table 4 the estimated values of the several indexes for (only) year-end 1984, 1986, 1988, 1990, and 1992. The results provide no support for the view that masterpieces outperform the market. In the first experiment, the estimated price index for masterpieces (top 10 percent) is beneath the mid-market portfolio in 1984, remains above the mid-market and the inexpensive portfolios until 1990, and then falls beneath both in 1992. Thus, for the full 1980–1992 period, masterpieces provide the *lowest* cumulative return. The latter result also occurs when masterpieces are defined as the top 20 percent of prints by price. In the second experiment, the results provide a more dramatic rejection of the trade proposition. The estimated values of the price index, and hence the cumulative returns from 1983 to each of the indicated dates, are uniformly lower for the masterpiece than for the alternative portfolios. This is true regardless of whether masterpieces are defined as the top 10 percent or top 20 percent of prints by price.

V. Does the Print Market Satisfy the "Law of One Price"?

The print prices used in this study are inclusive of the buyer's premium and thus reflect the final prices paid by purchasers. If an artist's prints are actively sold in two or more geographically distinct markets, the "law of one price" dictates that no significant price differences persist, in the absence of transactions costs. If systematic price differences exist, buyers would face an obvious incentive to undo them. In spite of this fact, the trade maintains that such systematic price differences do exist, at least for some artists (Theodore B. Donson, 1977 p. 233).

Ideally, one would like to compare the prices of identical prints that are sold in different markets at the same moment in time. Unfortunately, this is not possible, since the major auctions are staggered in order to facilitate participation by potential buyers. The major fall sales at Christie's and Sotheby's in New York, for example, take place in mid-November, while the London sales take place at the beginning of December.

To compare prices realized in different markets, one must specify a window within which sales are deemed to be contemporaneous. There is an obvious trade-off. The wider the window, the greater will be the number of sales of identical prints in the sample; yet the more suspect will be the assumption that the sales are contemporaneous. For the period 1977–1992, I choose to focus on a 30-day window, that is, on the sale of identical prints in different markets which occur within 30 days of each other.

The program identifies the first sale of a particular print and then compares its price with the price of all sales in the "other" market within the next 29 days. If there are no such sales, the program identifies the second sale of the print and repeats the procedure. After a comparison has been made, the program identifies the first sale after this window has elapsed and then continues. If there are two or more sales of the print in the same market within the "window," the average price is used in the price comparison.

Price comparisons for the German Expressionists, the School of Paris, and American artists, as well as for Picasso, Chagall, and Miro, are summarized in Table 5. Prices realized in the United States are compared to prices realized in London and in Europe. To provide an additional benchmark, prices are compared across these three markets for all artists contained in the aggregate portfolio.

One is immediately struck by the substantial price variation that occurs in the contemporaneous sales of the same print. This price variation is seen in the ratio of the mean absolute price difference to the mean price in each comparison. For Picasso prints sold in the United States and in Europe, for example, this ratio equals 30 percent. In the full set of comparisons, this ratio ranges from 18 percent to 59 percent.

In part, price differences reflect unobserved variation in the quality and in the condition of prints. Nonetheless, much of the price variation is simply due to "noise" in the realization of prices at auction. This is readily apparent in an extreme example. An impression from the edition of 250 of *Le Repas Frugal*, Picasso's first published print, sold for $374,000 at Christie's, New York on November 19, 1990, against an estimate of $160,000–$200,000. Two weeks later, at Christie's in London, an impression of this print sold for $189,980. The descriptions of the quality and the condition of these impressions in the respective auction

Table 5—The Print Market and the "Law of One Price": 30-Day Window, 1977–1992

Artist(s)	Market (1)	Market (2)	Number of pairs	Percent positive	Price difference, (1)−(2)		Significance of mean difference (t)	Mean difference in sales dates
					Mean difference ÷ mean price	Mean absolute difference ÷ mean price		
German Expressionists[a]	U.S.	Europe[b]	56	60	0.06	0.21	1.12	−12
	U.S.	W. Germany	42	64	0.14	0.25	1.63	−12
School of Paris[c]	U.S.	London	518	51	0.07	0.33	1.61	−11
	U.S.	Europe	502	52	0.13	0.45	2.61	−8
American[d]	U.S.	Europe	63	68	0.30	0.59	2.51	−2
Picasso	U.S.	London	179	48	0.05	0.33	0.52	−12
	U.S.	Europe	139	58	0.11	0.30	2.58	−9
Chagall	U.S.	London	83	39	−0.04	0.18	1.29	−11
	U.S.	Europe	142	41	−0.01	0.25	0.15	−7
Miro	U.S.	London	71	54	0.06	0.30	1.06	−9
	U.S.	Europe	76	46	0.20	0.55	1.45	−10
All artists	U.S.	London	661	54	0.07	0.36	1.50	−10
	U.S.	Europe	685	55	0.10	0.43	2.46	−8
	London	Europe	496	48	0.00	0.38	0.03	8

Notes: Price comparisons are for sales of the identical print (artist, catalogue raisonné, signed or unsigned) that occur in the two markets within 30 days of each other. The "significance of the mean price difference" column reports the t statistic for the null hypothesis of no price difference. For the "mean difference in sales dates" column, a negative number indicates that, on average, the sales in market 1 precede those in market 2.

[a] Nolde, Heckel, Schmidt-Rottluf, Kirchner, Kandinsky, Klee, and Mueller.
[b] In this comparison, London is included in Europe.
[c] Picasso, Chagall, Miro, Matisse, Braque, Leger, Rouault, Toulouse-Lautrec, and Villon.
[d] Whistler, Bellows, Benton, Hopper, Sloan, and Cassatt; in this comparison, London is included in Europe.

catalogues are virtually identical. There is no apparent justification for this dramatic price discrepancy.

The results summarized in Table 5 indicate that, on average, prices during the period 1977–1992 are higher in the United States than in either London or Europe. (This is *not*, one should note, the essence of the trade proposition.) For all artists, the mean price of prints sold in the United States exceeds the mean price in London by 7 percent, and the mean price in Europe by 10 percent. The latter spread is statistically significant at the 5-percent level. The mean price difference is, of course, sensitive to extreme observations.[8] For this reason, it is also instructive to calculate the number of times that prints realize higher prices in one market than in the other. For all artists, realized prices for identical prints were higher in the United States than in London for 54 percent of the 661 matched sales, and higher in the United States than in Europe for 55 percent of the 685 matched sales.

The above result, however, is somewhat misleading. In an earlier version of this paper, I had access only to data for the period 1977–1988. In this shorter sample period,

---

[8] If the dramatic price discrepancy noted previously were omitted, the mean price for Picasso prints in the United States would be 4 percent less than in London, not 5 percent more. Note also, in this regard, that only 48 percent of prices realized for Picasso prints in the United States were higher than their comparable sales in London.

there is no tendency for auction prices in the United States to exceed prices realized in London or Europe. Additional tests for the subperiod 1989–1992 confirm that the reported excess of prices in the United States is confined to this later period. For all artists, the mean price realized in the United States exceeds the mean price realized in London by 11 percent during the period 1989–1992, compared to only 3 percent in the period 1977–1988. Similarly, the mean price realized in the United States exceeds the mean price in Europe by 17 percent during the period 1989–1992, compared to only 2 percent in the period 1977–1988. The U.S.–Europe spread (but not the U.S.–London spread) is statistically significant during the period 1989–1992. The fact that the mean U.S.–London spread of 11 percent is not significant signals, again, the substantial noise that characterizes auction outcomes.

There is no ready explanation for this rather anomalous finding. In general, one would expect any price differences that did exist to become attenuated with the passage of time, as dealers and collectors respond to the evident incentives. A trade explanation is likely to focus on the very active buying by Japanese dealers that occurred during 1989 and 1990, primarily in New York.

There are a number of other results that merit note. The mean price for German Expressionist prints is 14-percent higher in the United States than in West Germany. This finding is contrary to the trade suggestion (Donson, 1977 p. 233) that prices for these prints are systematically higher in German-speaking countries. For the American artists, however, prices are 30-percent higher in the United States than in Europe and London (combined). This difference is statistically significant. The results for the American artists are interesting on another account. There were no matched sales for three of the six American artists (Bellows, Hopper, and Sloan), one matched sale for Benton, and six for Cassatt. In fact, only 3 of the 154 sales of prints by Hopper occurred outside the United States; 8 of the 1,454 sales of Benton; 7 of the 619 sales of Bellows; and 2 of the 784 sales of Sloan. The only American artist whose prints are actively sold in Europe/London as well as in the United States is Whistler. For his prints, alone, there is a tendency for prices to be higher in the United States. For the others, there is *only* the U.S. market. This is, of course, consistent with the prediction of the "law of one price": if certain prints are likely to command higher prices in the United States, then sales should occur only in the United States.

There is also evidence that prices are systematically higher at certain auction houses than at others (Table 6). For the 447 matched sales at Sotheby's and Christie's in New York, prices average 14 percent higher at Sotheby's, and this difference is statistically significant. Dividing the full sample into the 1977–1984 and 1985–1992 subperiods, there is no evidence that this spread is declining over time. In London, by contrast, there is essentially no difference in the prices realized at the two major auction houses. Kornfeld and Klipstein (now, Kornfeld) in Switzerland obtains higher prices than do other auction houses, as suggested by the trade (Donson, 1977). In two-thirds of the cases, realized prices are higher at Kornfeld than at the alternative auction house. The average premium at Kornfeld has risen from 20 percent (1977–1984) to 23 percent (1985–1992). The former spread is significant at the 1-percent level; the latter, at the 5-percent level.[9]

---

[9]These comparisons use all of the observations in the print data bank. As noted, there is no information recorded on the condition or the quality of the print. Undoubtedly, there are instances (for example) when a damaged print realizes a very low price that reflects its substandard condition. This problem is particularly important when one is comparing prices realized for an "identical" print in two markets at a given point in time. If a simple filter is applied to eliminate observations when either print sold for more than five times the price of the other, the mean spread in prices realized at Kornfeld versus the other auction houses declines to 17 percent in the period 1977–1984, and to 14 percent in the period 1985–1992. The former spread is significant at the 1-percent level; the latter, at the 10-percent level. The (proportionate) number of observations eliminated by applying this filter—as well as its impact—is greatest for the comparison of Kornfeld with the other auction houses. This may reflect the reluctance of Kornfeld to accept damaged or inferior impressions for sale.

The results for the New York salesrooms of Sotheby's and Christie's are the most puzzling. Unlike price discrepancies that might emerge between the United States and either London or Europe, there is no geographical barrier to arbitrage. Since the buyer's commission at both houses was 10 percent and the seller's commission (for dealers) was 6 percent, the 14-percent spread between Sotheby's and Christie's in New York is not sufficient to allow a dealer to buy profitably at Christie's and sell at Sotheby's. A dealer would have to inventory such prints, while waiting (at the earliest) for the next major sale at Sotheby's. Further, as evidenced by the substantial price variation in the sale of identical prints, such arbitrage would not be risk-free. The obvious incentive for buyers to purchase at Christie's, until average prices are equalized, remains a puzzle.

During the sample period, the number of lots sold at Sotheby's was more than twice the number sold at Christie's. In the trade, the belief is that the larger number of lots in a typical sale at Sotheby's attracts a larger audience of out-of-town and foreign dealers who bid more aggressively in person than when leaving order bids. The larger audience, in turn, is due to the greater likelihood of acquiring inventory, in light of the larger number of prints for sale. From the economic analysis of auctions, it is known that increasing the number of bidders serves to increase the average price if bidders have independent private values (R. Preston McAfee and John McMillan, 1987). In common-value auctions, where bidders lack complete information about the item's true value, the auction price converges to the true price if the number of bidders is sufficiently large. If the audience were composed exclusively of dealers buying for resale, the common-value assumption might be more appropriate. If so, the greater number of bidders is less likely to explain the higher prices realized at Sotheby's, so long as the number of bidders at Christie's is sufficiently large. At both auction houses, however, there will be some collectors buying for their own use rather than for resale, and hence the private-value assumption may also be relevant. As noted previously, this could help explain the higher prices realized at Sotheby's. The puzzle, however, is just drawn back one step: why do private collectors not eschew Sotheby's in favor of Christie's?[10]

VI. Summary and Conclusion

Using information on the repeat sales of identical prints, I estimate a semiannual index of prices for the period 1977–1992. From this index, the mean and standard deviation of the (semiannual) returns to modern prints are readily derived. The mean real return (annual rate) on the aggregate print portfolio is only 1.51 percent, well beneath the real returns on stocks, U.S. government bonds, and even U.S. Treasury bills. Further, the risk (as measured by the standard deviation of real returns) of investing in prints is comparable to the risk of investing in stocks or long-term bonds. One must conclude, based on the risk–return criterion, that investment in this segment of the art market compares unfavorably to an investment in traditional financial assets.[11]

By positing a positive flow of consumption services, one might reconcile the low monetary return noted above with the proposition that the risk-adjusted rates of return on all assets would be forced to equality in an efficient market. On other requirements of market efficiency, however, the evidence is mixed. The most important results are as follows:

(i) Excess returns on prints, defined (simply) as the actual return less the corre-

---

[10]See Orley Ashenfelter (1989) for a discussion of puzzling results observed at auction, including the tendency for identical lots of wine to sell at lower prices if sold later in the same auction. For additional evidence regarding this price-decline anomaly, see Orley Ashenfelter and David Genesove (1992).

[11]One caveat to this finding is that, given the relatively short sample period, conclusions regarding the risk and return of investing in prints may prove sensitive to changes in the sample period. For example, an earlier version of this paper used data for the period 1977–1988 and drew a much more favorable conclusion regarding the attractiveness of prints as an investment.

TABLE 6—THE IMPACT OF AUCTION HOUSES ON SALES PRICES: ALL ARTISTS, 30-DAY WINDOW

Period	Market (1)	Market (2)	Number of pairs	Percent positive	Price difference, (1)−(2)			Mean difference in sales dates
					Mean difference ÷ mean price	Mean absolute difference ÷ mean price	Significance of mean difference (t)	
1977–1992	Sotheby's (New York)	Christie's (New York)	447	63	0.14	0.28	4.43	−1
1977–1992	Sotheby's (London)	Christie's (London)	105	54	−0.01	0.22	0.26	0
1977–1992	Kornfeld & Klipstein	All other	395	67	0.22	0.40	3.05	6
1977–1984	Sotheby's (New York)	Christie's (New York)	169	65	0.13	0.33	1.92	−1
1985–1992	Sotheby's (New York)	Christie's (New York)	278	62	0.14	0.28	4.05	0
1977–1984	Kornfeld & Klipstein	All other	176	66	0.20	0.35	4.01	7
1985–1992	Kornfeld & Klipstein	All other	219	68	0.23	0.42	2.50	5

Notes: Price comparisons are for sales of the identical print (artist, catalogue raisonné, signed or unsigned) that occur in the two markets within 30 days of each other. The "significance of the mean price difference" column reports the t statistic for the null hypothesis of no price difference. For the "mean difference in sales dates" column, a negative number indicates that, on average, the sales in market 1 precede those in market 2.

sponding yield on U.S. Treasury bills, exhibit a pattern common to many other markets: positive correlation at short horizons and negative correlation at longer horizons. Further, the short-run persistence in excess returns (and hence print prices) is quantitatively important.

(ii) There is no evidence that a masterpiece portfolio of higher-priced prints will outperform the market as a whole. Economists may view as self-evident the proposition that any desirable characteristics of masterpieces will be capitalized into their prices. To the art trade, however, this proposition is unfamiliar.

(iii) There is substantial price variation in the contemporaneous sale of identical prints. For identical prints sold within 30 days of each other, the mean absolute price difference divided by mean price is on the order of 30 percent. Although unobserved variation in quality and condition contribute to this result, there is undoubtedly a lot of "noise" in auction outcomes.

(iv) During the subperiod 1989–1992, prices realized at auction for "identical" prints were on average higher in the United States than in London or Europe. This was not the case during the period 1977–1988. Contrary to the trade view, there is no evidence that the German Expressionists command higher prices in Europe or West Germany than in the United States. There is evidence that the prints of American artists, chiefly Whistler, realize higher prices in the United States.

(v) There is evidence that prices paid by buyers are systematically higher at certain auction houses. The prices of prints sold at Sotheby's in New York average 14 percent higher than the prices of identical prints sold at Christie's in New York. As is widely known in the trade, prices realized at Kornfeld in Switzerland are well above those realized in the rest of Europe, London, or the United States. There is no ready answer to the puzzle posed by the disparity in prices realized at the New York auction houses. The substantial price variation in the contemporaneous sale of identical prints, together with the commission structure, would appear to preclude simple arbitrage. Yet, especially within the same city, it seems surprising that buyers do not "undo" the price spreads, by shifting their activity (at least in part) from Sotheby's to Christie's.

REFERENCES

Anderson, Robert C., "Paintings as Investment," *Economic Inquiry*, January 1974, *12*, 13–26.

Ashenfelter, Orley, "How Auctions Work for Wine and Art," *Journal of Economic Perspectives*, Summer 1989, *3*, 23–36.

_____ and Genesove, David, "Testing for Price Anomolies in Real-Estate Auctions," *American Economic Review*, May 1992 (*Papers and Proceedings*), *82*, 501–5.

Bailey, Martin J., Muth, Richard F. and Nourse, Hugh O., "A Regression Method for Real Estate Price Index Construction," *Journal of the American Statistical Association*, December 1963, *58*, 933–42.

Baumol, William J., "Unnatural Value: Or Art Investment as Floating Crap Game," *American Economic Review*, May 1986 (*Papers and Proceedings*), *76*, 10–14.

Case, Karl E. and Shiller, Robert J., "The Efficiency of the Market for Single-Family Homes," *American Economic Review*, March 1989, *79*, 125–37.

Cutler, David M., Poterba, James M. and Summers, Lawrence H., "Speculative Dynamics and the Role of Feedback Traders," *American Economic Review*, May 1990 (*Papers and Proceedings*), *80*, 63–8.

Donson, Theodore B., *Prints and the Print Market*, New York: T. Crowell, 1977.

Frey, Bruno S. and Pommerehne, Werner W., *Muses and Markets: Explorations in the Economics of the Arts*, Oxford: Blackwell, 1989.

Goetzmann, William N., "Accounting for Taste: Art and the Financial Markets over Three Centuries," *American Economic Review*, December 1993, *83*, 1370–6.

Hosios, Arthur J. and Pesando, James E., "Measuring Prices in Resale Housing Markets in Canada: Evidence and Implications," *Journal of Housing Economics*, December 1991, *1*, 303–17.

Markowitz, Harry M., *Portfolio Selection: Efficient Diversification of Investments*, New York: Wiley, 1959.

McAfee, R. Preston and McMillan, John, "Auctions and Bidding," *Journal of Economic Literature*, June 1987, *25*, 699–738.

Reitlinger, Gerald, *The Economics of Taste: The Rise and Fall of the Picture Market, 1760–1960*, New York: Holt, Reinhart and Winston, 1961.

Shiller, Robert J., "The Volatility of Long-Term Interest Rates and the Expectations Models of the Term Structure," *Journal of Political Economy*, December 1979, *87*, 1190–1219.

American Economic Association

Accounting for Taste: Art and the Financial Markets Over Three Centuries
Author(s): William N. Goetzmann
Source: *The American Economic Review*, Vol. 83, No. 5 (Dec., 1993), pp. 1370-1376
Published by: American Economic Association
Stable URL: http://www.jstor.org/stable/2117568
Accessed: 05/02/2014 12:54

Your use of the JSTOR archive indicates your acceptance of the Terms & Conditions of Use, available at
http://www.jstor.org/page/info/about/policies/terms.jsp

JSTOR is a not-for-profit service that helps scholars, researchers, and students discover, use, and build upon a wide range of
content in a trusted digital archive. We use information technology and tools to increase productivity and facilitate new forms
of scholarship. For more information about JSTOR, please contact support@jstor.org.

American Economic Association is collaborating with JSTOR to digitize, preserve and extend access to *The American Economic Review.*

Accounting For Taste:
Art and the Financial Markets Over Three Centuries

By WILLIAM N. GOETZMANN*

In this paper, transaction prices of paintings brought to market at least twice over the period 1715–1986 are used to construct an art return index. The index allows a comparison of painting price movements to stock-market fluctuations, and also an evaluation of the risk and return characteristics of art investment. I find evidence of a strong relationship between the demand for art and aggregate financial wealth over the very long term, manifested by the fact that the art index and an index of London Stock Exchange shares over the same period are highly correlated. I interpret this as evidence that the demand for art increases with the wealth of art collectors.

This relationship between art prices and wealth has further implications for art as an investment vehicle. While an art buyer might expect that holding a "collectable" asset provides a hedge against the fluctuations of the stock market, the opposite appears to be the case. Consequently, the risk and return characteristics of a painting portfolio suggest that a risk-averse agent would typically not find art to be an attractive purchase for investment purposes alone. While returns to art investment have exceeded inflation for long periods, and returns in the second half of the 20th century have rivaled the stock market, they are no higher than would be justified by the extraordinary risks they represent. My results tend to support the analysis of others who have found a positive relationship between art and the stock market over shorter time periods (see John Picard Stein, 1973, 1977; Michael F. Bryan, 1985; Olivier Chanel et al., 1990a,b; Leslie Singer, 1990) and to confirm the finding by William Baumol (1986) that art may be dominated as an investment vehicle. It differs from previous research (e.g., Singer, 1978, 1990; Bruno Frey and Werner W. Pommerehne, 1989a,b) in that it focuses on the time-series behavior of art and the stock and bond markets over very long periods.

I. Painting Data: Sources and Biases

Following Robert C. Anderson (1974) and Baumol (1986), I obtain repeat-sale transactions from Gerald Reitlinger (1961, 1963, 1971), and I extend the Reitlinger data with information from Enrique Mayer (various years: 1971–1987). In both sources, I identify purchase prices, sale prices, purchase dates, and sales dates of paintings that sold more than once.[1] The auction prices are not always transaction prices. "Bought in" paintings—those that failed to make the seller's reserve—may be recorded as sales at the reserve price. Prices are converted to British currency using end-of-year conversion ratios from R. L. Bidwell (1970), Michael Collins (1986), and the *International Statistics Yearbook*. The combined sample consists of 3,329 price pairs of 2,809

---

*Columbia Business School, 408 Uris Hall, Columbia University, New York, NY 10027. I thank Stephen Ross, John Hartigan, Roger Ibbotson, Jonathan Ingersoll, Jr., Martin Shubik, William H. Goetzmann, Douglas Diamond, Michael Montius, Robert Shiller, Ann Marie Logan, Burton Fredrickson, two anonymous referees, and the participants in the 1991 CRSP conference for their helpful conversations and comments on this research. Vanessa Brown, Christopher Musto, and Kate Ross have provided invaluable assistance with data collection.

[1] Reitlinger lists works by artist, so that painting titles and often dimensions may be matched. Mayer is an annual auction record. Paintings for which there exists previous sales information are noted, and earlier sales dates and prices are recorded.

different paintings over the period 1715–1986.

The selection bias in the data set is an important issue that bears on the interpretation of the index to be estimated. Most of the purchase prices and virtually all of the sales prices are drawn from auction records. Reitlinger explains that his criterion for inclusion was subjective: whether the artist was at one time fashionable, or recognized as classical. Mayer does not explain where earlier sales records are obtained, although one may presume that they are provided by the seller, along with other provenance information. These selection procedures tend to truncate both the high and the low end of the return distribution. Paintings that became worthless after their first auction sale do not appear in my sample, and by the same token, masterpieces that ended up in museums through donation rather than auction sales are likewise excluded from the sample.

Because of the selection bias, auction transactions may not adequately reflect one of the most important elements of risk for the art investor: stylistic risk. For paintings regarded as investment goods, the future sales price will depend upon both the number of people who wish to buy the work of art when it is put up for sale and the wealth of the individuals or institutions who desire it at that time. Since the repeat-sales data principally reflect auction transactions, they necessarily focus upon art works that satisfy the first criterion, that is, paintings in broad enough demand to attract a number of competitive bidders. Auction houses have little incentive to hold sales for art with insufficient public interest. While there is a market for works with few prospective buyers, it is the dealer market, in which there are large rewards for matching specialized artworks to particular collectors. Thus, the repeat-sales records—indeed most auction records—will fail to capture the price fluctuations of paintings that are not broadly in demand.

There are other selection biases as well. For instance, the decision by an owner to sell a work of art (and consequently the occurrence of a repeat sale in the sample) itself may be conditional upon whether or not the value increased. This would also tend to bias the estimated return upward. In addition, the proportion of paintings brought-in, rather than sold, in the sample is unknown. Not only would they likewise bias the estimated return to art investment upward, but one might also expect that the effect will differ in importance through time: in periods of rising prices, fewer paintings might be expected to be bought in. Because of these biases, the mean annual return to art investment provided by repeat-sale data must be regarded as approximate, and quite possibly as an upper bound on the average return obtained by investors over the period, particularly since it does not incorporate transactions costs.

II. Methodology

The repeat-sales regression (RSR) uses the purchase and sale price of individual properties to estimate the fluctuations in value of an average or representative asset over a particular time period. The RSR has most frequently been applied to estimating an index of real-estate returns (see e.g., Martin J. Bailey et al., 1963; Karl E. Case and Robert J. Shiller, 1987; Goetzmann, 1992). Anderson (1974) and Goetzmann (1991) apply it to the art market, using the Reitlinger data set and available years of the Mayer data. The benefit of using the RSR is that the resulting index is based upon gross investor returns and is invariant to different specifications of a hedonic model. Since returns are price relatives of the same painting, the methodology controls for the differing quality of assets. The drawback is that the index is constructed from a subset of the available transactions.

To apply the RSR, I assume that the log of 1 plus the return for a certain asset i in period t, $(r_{i,t})$ may be represented by μ_t, the log of 1 plus the return of an index of properties, and an error term:

$$(1) \qquad r_{i,t} = \mu_t + \varepsilon_{i,t}$$

where μ_t may be thought of as the average return in period t of properties in the portfolio. I wish to use sales data about individual properties to estimate the index μ over some interval $t = 1 \ldots T$. In this notation, μ is a T-dimensional vector whose individual elements are μ_t. The observed data consist of purchase and sales price pairs, $P_{i,b}$ and $P_{i,s}$ of the individual properties comprising the index, as well as the dates of purchase and sale, which I will designate with b_i and s_i. Thus, the logged price relative for asset i, held between its purchase date b_i and its sales date, s_i may be expressed as

$$(2) \quad r_i = \ln\left(\frac{P_{i,s}}{P_{i,b}}\right) = \sum_{t=b_i+1}^{s_i} r_{i,t}$$

$$= \sum_{t=b_i+1}^{s_i} \mu_t + \sum_{t=b_i+1}^{s_i} \varepsilon_{i,t}.$$

Let $\mathbf{r}$ represent the N-dimensional vector of logged price relatives for N repeated sales observations. Goetzmann (1992) shows that a generalized least-squares regression of the form

$$(3) \quad \hat{\mu} = (\mathbf{X}'\Omega^{-1}\mathbf{X})^{-1}\mathbf{X}'\Omega^{-1}\mathbf{r}$$

provides the maximum-likelihood estimate of μ, where $\mathbf{X}$ is an $N \times T$ matrix which has a row of dummy variables for each asset in the sample and a column for each holding interval. When asset i is purchased in period b_i and sold in period s_i, $X_{i,j}$ takes on the value 1 for $b_i < j \leq s_i$, and zero otherwise. Under the assumption that $\varepsilon_{i,t}$ are independent in time, the weights in Ω are the times between sales.[2]

The RSR is known to introduce certain biases in the estimated series. The most serious of these are a spurious negative autocorrelation in the estimated return series and an overestimate of the variance of the series. Goetzmann (1992) shows that these biases are potentially severe when the number of assets in the portfolio is low, and they are strongest at the beginning of the estimated series, when the portfolio is small and poorly diversified. The effect of these problems on the early part of the series may be reduced through shrinkage techniques.[3] Despite incremental improvements, however, later periods in the sample are estimated with more data and are more reliable.

III. Art in the Investment Portfolio

Table 1 reports the regression results and the decade-by-decade annualized capital appreciation returns over the period 1720–1990.[4] The t statistics suggest that the returns before 1850 are poorly estimated, while those in the late 20th century are relatively reliable. The R^2 indicates that there exists a common component to the

---

[2] Case and Shiller (1987) propose a three-stage estimation procedure. In the first step, they set Ω equal to the identity matrix. Then they estimate the elements of Ω in the second stage of the procedure by regressing the squared errors from the ordinary least-squares regression on an intercept and the time between sales:

$$\hat{e}_i^2 = \alpha + \beta(s_i - b_i) + \varepsilon_i.$$

The slope from the regression captures the effect of error variance compounding linearly through time, which they interpret as the residual risk per period.

[3] Goetzmann (1992) shows that a Bayes formulation of the regression mitigates the negative autocorrelation of the series over the early periods. The Bayes formulation imposes an additional restriction on the estimation procedure. This restriction is that the return series μ_τ is distributed normally and is independently and identically distributed. The form of the Bayes estimator is

$$\mu_{\text{Bayes}} = \left[(\mathbf{X}'\Omega^{-1}\mathbf{X}) + \kappa\left(\mathbf{I} - \frac{1}{T}\mathbf{J}\right)\right]^{-1} \mathbf{X}'\Omega^{-1}\mathbf{r}$$

where $\mathbf{J}$ is a matrix of 1's and κ is a constant:

$$\kappa = \frac{\sigma^2}{\sigma_\mu^2}.$$

In practice the constant κ is chosen to satisfy the restriction. The effect on the estimate is dramatic for the early period in which data are scarce, and minimal for the period in which data are plentiful.

[4] The first and last decade estimates are based upon incomplete data, since the first purchase dates from 1715 and the last sale is in 1986.

TABLE 1—ANNUALIZED RETURNS TO ART INVESTMENT, 1720–1990

Decade	OLS estimator			GLS estimator			Bayes estimator		
	Coefficient	t	Annual return	Coefficient	t	Annual Return	Coefficient	t	Annual
1720[a]	−10.80	−1.18	−0.66	−10.73	−1.04	−0.65	−2.86	−0.56	−0.25
1730	−1.62	−0.32	−0.15	−1.11	−0.19	−0.11	−0.80	−0.23	−0.08
1740	3.69	0.73	0.45	3.59	0.56	0.43	1.60	0.43	0.17
1750	−2.01	−0.53	−0.18	−2.66	−0.70	−0.23	−1.37	−0.50	−0.13
1760	0.98	0.28	0.10	1.84	0.49	0.20	1.03	0.35	0.11
1770	0.94	0.59	0.10	0.56	0.30	0.06	0.82	0.52	0.08
1780	−0.01	−0.01	0.00	−0.02	−0.02	−0.00	−0.06	−0.07	−0.01
1790	0.00	−0.01	0.00	0.04	0.05	0.00	0.04	0.05	0.00
1800	0.89	1.49	0.09	0.61	1.09	0.06	0.59	1.07	0.06
1810	0.02	0.04	0.00	0.28	0.76	0.03	0.30	0.08	0.03
1820	0.50	0.94	0.05	0.04	0.10	0.00	0.04	0.08	0.00
1830	−0.74	−1.39	−0.07	−0.09	−0.20	−0.10	−0.09	−0.21	−0.01
1840	−0.09	−0.20	−0.01	−0.39	−1.07	−0.04	−0.39	1.03	−0.04
1850	0.41	1.08	0.04	0.46	−0.42	0.05	0.46	1.43	0.05
1860	0.61	1.88	0.06	0.66	2.38	0.07	0.66	2.40	0.07
1870	1.21	3.79	0.13	1.01	3.74	0.11	1.01	3.76	0.11
1880	−0.71	−2.44	−0.07	−0.53	−2.12	−0.05	−0.51	−2.12	−0.05
1890	0.41	1.77	0.04	0.29	1.50	0.03	0.29	1.51	0.03
1900	−0.10	−0.43	−0.01	−0.06	−0.32	−0.01	−0.06	−0.32	−0.01
1910	0.44	2.02	0.05	0.49	2.65	·0.05	0.49	2.66	0.05
1920	0.06	0.28	0.01	0.03	0.19	0.00	0.03	0.19	0.00
1930	0.15	0.68	0.02	−0.13	−0.73	−0.01	−0.13	−0.73	−0.01
1940	−1.05	−4.87	−0.10	−0.56	−3.10	−0.05	−0.56	−3.12	−0.05
1950	1.31	5.70	0.14	0.86	4.49	0.09	0.86	4.52	0.09
1960	1.06	5.26	0.11	1.45	9.04	0.15	1.45	9.08	0.15
1970	1.02	6.32	0.11	1.70	14.30	0.18	1.70	14.36	0.19
1980	0.70	5.49	0.07	0.89	9.54	0.09	0.89	9.59	0.09
1990[a]	1.74	9.16	0.19	2.76	14.42	0.23	2.08	14.47	0.23

Notes: Regression statistics for the ordinary least-squares (OLS) RSR estimator: $R^2 = 0.59$, F value = 167.19, with 28 and 3,301 degrees of freedom. Regression statistics for the generalized least-squares (GLS) RSR estimator: $R^2 = 0.70$, F value = 278.31 with 28, and 3,301 degrees of freedom. Annualized returns are calculated as $\exp(\mu_t + \sigma^2/2)^{0.1} - 1$, where σ^2 is estimated in the second stage of the RSR as described by Case and Shiller (1987). The Bayes estimator shrinks the returns in the early years toward values consistent with the assumption that μ_t is a random walk. Its formulation is described in Goetzmann (1992).
[a] Estimate based on incomplete data for the decade.

capital appreciation of paintings: a significant percentage of the variation in the logged change in painting prices is explained by the estimated index. The shrinkage estimate reduces the wide swings of the series induced by the RSR due to lack of data over the early decades, while leaving the coefficients for the later periods practically unchanged.

The table provides an interesting perspective on long-term trends in the art market. There are three apparent bull markets in art: 1780–1820, 1840–1870, and finally the post-Depression era, 1940–1986. The most recent bull market is the longest and strongest of the three. The 18th- and 20th-century bull markets coincided with rising consumer price levels, while the 19th-century increase in art values strayed significantly from the prevailing deflationary trend. There were three bear markets in art: 1830–1840, 1880–1900, and 1930–1940. These also correspond to broad economic recessionary periods in Britain and the United States. The period since 1940 shows the most dramatic increase in art prices and is the most reliably estimated. In fact, this bull market in painting prices is unprecedented and suggests a fundamental change in the demand for works of art.

Table 2 compares the annualized estimates of the mean and standard deviation for the art index to the capital appreciation of stocks, the total returns to bonds, and

TABLE 2—ANNUAL MEAN, STANDARD DEVIATION, AND CORRELATION
FOR ART AND OTHER INVESTMENTS

Return	Mean	Standard deviation	Correlations			
			INF	BofE	CON	LSE
1716–1986 (decade returns):						
Inflation (INF)	0.012	0.183	1.00			
Bank of England rate (BofE)	0.045	0.093	0.53	1.00		
Consol bond returns (CON)	0.043	0.169	0.26	0.59	1.00	
London Stock Exchange (LSE)	0.015	0.196	0.11	0.13	0.38	1.00
Art	0.032	0.565	0.28	0.42	0.29	0.67
1850–1986 (decade returns):						
Inflation	0.024	0.242	1.00			
Bank of England rate	0.042	0.130	0.60	1.00		
Consol bond returns	0.041	0.215	0.35	0.68	1.00	
London Stock Exchange	0.026	0.260	0.00	0.17	0.41	1.00
Art	0.062	0.650	0.25	0.53	0.53	0.79
1900–1986 (annual returns):						
Inflation	0.042	0.088	1.00			
Bank of England rate	0.047	0.036	0.58	1.00		
Consol bond returns	0.048	0.106	0.32	0.67	1.00	
London Stock Exchange	0.049	0.219	−0.09	0.14	0.39	1.00
Art	0.175	0.528	0.18	0.52	0.54	0.78

Notes: Means for decade returns are annualized values based upon the Bayes RSR coefficients. Means for annual returns are based upon annual RSR coefficients. Standard deviations for decade returns are annualized estimates based on the assumption that the 10-year series variance is equal to 10 times the annual variance. Standard deviations for annual returns may be overstated due to bias in the RSR procedure. All correlations are based upon decade returns.

inflation.[5] Notice that over the entire period, bond returns exceeded the return to art investment. This is due to the strong negative art returns over the first five decades of the sample period. When attention is restricted to the period since 1850, over which the index is well estimated, one finds that art returns exceeded the capital appreciation of stocks and the returns to bonds. Painting prices grew at a rate of 6.2 percent, while stock prices grew at a rate of 2.6 percent. While impressive, this growth in art prices was accompanied by high volatility, and there was strong positive correlation to other assets, especially stocks. Thus, although art returns were high, it is unlikely that art was a superior investment.

Equity-dividend yield information is unavailable until the second half of the 20th century, and then only for U.S. stocks (see Alfred Cowles, 1938). However, when a conservative estimate of yields (3–5 percent) is added to the capital-appreciation return to the stock market, it makes art and stock returns about equal over the period 1850–1986. Even if art returns exceeded stock returns over the very long term, as they appear to have done since 1900, art would not be attractive to an investor who allocated a major proportion of his or her portfolio to bonds. Art only appears attractive to the nearly risk-neutral investor, and then only if the expected returns to art exceed the expected returns to stocks. The high correlation between the art and the stock and bond markets clearly makes art a

---

[5] All long-term financial series are based on investments in the United Kingdom over the period 1716–1986. The capital appreciation index for the London Stock Exchange is spliced from seven different sources and is described in detail in Goetzmann (1993). The bond returns are reported in Sidney Homer (1977), and the inflation series is from E. H. Phelps-Brown and Sheila Hopkins (1956) and the *International Statistics Yearbook*.

poor vehicle for the purposes of diversification.

It is difficult to imagine two assets whose dividend streams differ as much as do the dividends of a share of stock and the dividends of a work of art. The share of stock represents the claim to monetary returns from productive economic assets, while the painting provides aesthetic pleasure and social status to its owner. Why then should the prices of the two move together?[6] To answer this, I examined the lagged relation between art and changes in investor wealth, as defined by growth of share prices on the London Stock Exchange. A Granger test performed on annual data over the period 1900–1986 indicates strong evidence of a causal relation from the stock market to the art market.[7] Art prices tended to follow stock-market trends, at least in this century. The clear implication is that demand for paintings increased when investor wealth grew.

IV. Conclusion

The subjective nature of aesthetic valuation would suggest that the only constraint limiting the price of a work of art is the wealth of the collectors who desire it. In this paper, I construct an index that may be an upwardly biased measure of the capital appreciation of paintings. It demonstrates that the last 50 years have seen an unprecedented growth in art prices. Despite this growth, however, there is little evidence that art is an attractive investment for a risk-averse investor. Art, absent its aesthetic dividend flow, is only potentially attractive to an agent who would otherwise choose a relatively volatile portfolio. This helps explain why the art market is correlated to stocks. If wealth is the major constraint to price appreciation for paintings, then a rise in the stock market may relax this constraint. A Granger tests provides evidence to support this hypothesis.

The results of investigating the relationship between the art market and the financial markets have implications for institutions as well as for individuals. For institutions constrained to hold a significant proportion of their assets in paintings, the analysis of the behavior of a portfolio of paintings offers some guidance for reducing the volatility of the investment portfolio by holding assets other than stocks. My estimate of the risk of art investment suggests that the total value of a museum's collection is likely to fluctuate dramatically—even when that collection is diversified broadly across different styles.

My investigation into the transaction prices for paintings over 271 years reveals something about the role of art in culture that most students of art history have long suspected—that there is a basic connection between art and money. It may not be a coincidence that extraordinary prices obtained at auction for paintings such as Van Gogh's *Sunflowers* occurred during an unprecedented decade for global stock investment. Wealth, however, is not the sole ingredient in the demand for art; another is taste. It is tempting to interpret the growth in painting prices since World War II as evidence of the globalization of aesthetic values. The demand for French Impressionist paintings, for instance, has expanded from a nationalistic phenomenon (see Nicholas Green, 1987) to an intercontinental passion including American, Australian, and Japanese collectors and institutions. In fact, a large number of the works comprising the Reitlinger and Mayer data sets are French Impressionist paintings. This expanding uniformity of taste may have contributed to the increase in painting prices and the difficulty that museums encounter in their attempts to purchase works they consider important.

---

[6] Comovement of the art series and the stock-market series is equally significant in real terms. In fact, regressions of art returns on stock returns, expressed in real terms or as premia over the riskless rate, suggest that the β of art is significant and greater than 1 see Goetzmann (1991).

[7] Following Clive W. J. Granger (1969) two lag-5 vector autoregressions for annual art returns were specified, one with and one without lagged values of the stock market. The chi-square test rejected the null hypothesis of no causality from the stock market to the art market at the 0.5-percent level $X^2_{[5]} = 10.23$). The coefficients for the London Stock Exchange were significant for lags 2–4.

REFERENCES

Anderson, Robert C., "Paintings as Investment," *Economic Inquiry*, March 1974, *12*, 13–26.

Bailey, Martin J., Muth, Richard F. and Nourse, Hugh O., "A Regression Method for Real Estate Price Index Construction," *Journal of the American Statistical Association*, December 1963, *58*, 933–42.

Baumol, William, "Unnatural Value: or Art Investment as a Floating Crap Game," *American Economic Review*, May 1986 (*Papers and Proceedings*), *76*, 10–14.

Bidwell, R. L., *Currency Conversion Tables; A Hundred Years of Change*, London: Rex Collins, 1970.

Bryan, Michael F., "Beauty and the Bulls: The Investment Characteristics of Paintings," *Economic Review of the Federal Reserve Bank of Cleveland*, First Quarter 1985, pp. 2–10.

Case, Karl E. and Shiller, Robert J., "Prices of Single-Family Homes Since 1970: New Indexes for Four Cities," *New England Economic Review*, September–October 1987, 45–56.

Chanel, Olivier, Gerard-Varet, Louis-André and Ginsburgh, Victor, (1990a), "Is Art Such a Bad Investment? working paper, École des Hautes Études en Sciences Sociales, Marseilles, 1990.

_____, _____ and _____, (1990b) *Formation des Prix des Peintures Modernes et Contemporaines et Rentabilité des Placements sur le Marché de L'Art*, Marseilles: Groupe de Recherche en Economie Quantitative et Econometrie, December 1990.

Collins, Michael, "Sterling Exchange Rates, 1847–80," *Journal of European Economic History*, September 1986, *15*, 511–33.

Cowles, Alfred, 3rd., *Common Stock Indices, 1871–1937*, Cowles Commission for Research in Economics Monograph No. 3, Bloomington, IN: Principia, 1938.

Frey, Bruno and Pommerehne, Werner W., (1989a) *Muses and Markets: Explorations in the Economics of the Arts*, London: Blackwell, 1989.

_____ and _____, (1989b) "Art Investment: An Empirical Inquiry," *Southern Economic Journal*, October 1989, *56*, 396–407.

Goetzmann, William N., "Accounting For Taste: An Analysis of Art Returns Over Three Centuries, First Boston Working Paper, Columbia University, 1991.

_____, "The Accuracy of Real Estate Indices: Repeat Sale Estimators," *Journal of Real Estate Finance and Economics*, March 1992, *5*, 5–53.

_____, "Patterns in Three Centuries of Stock Market Prices," *Journal of Business*, April 1993.

Granger, Clive W. J., "Investigating Causal Relations by Econometric Models and Cross-Spectral Models," *Econometrica*, July 1969, *37*, 424–38.

Green, Nicholas, "Dealing in Temperments: Economic Transformation of the Artistic Field in France During the Second Half of the Nineteenth Century," *Art History*, March 1987, *10*, 59–78.

Homer, Sidney, *A History of Interest Rates*, New Brunswick, NJ: Rutgers University Press, 1977.

Keene, Geraldine, *Money and Art: A Study Based on the Times-Southeby Index*, New York: Putnam, 1971.

Mayer, Enrique, *International Auction Records*, New York: Mayer & Archer Fields, various years.

Phelps-Brown, E. H. and Hopkins, Sheila, "Seven Centuries of the Price of Consumables, Compared with Builders' Wage-Rates," *Economica*, November 1956, *23*, 296–314.

Reitlinger, Gerald, *The Economics of Taste*, Vol. 1, London: Barrie and Rockcliff, 1961; Vol. 2, 1963; Vol. 3, 1971.

Singer, Leslie, "Microeconomics of the Art Market," *Journal of Cultural Economics*, June 1978, *2*, 21–40.

_____, "The Utility of Art versus Fair Bets in the Investment Market," *Journal of Cultural Economics*, December 1990, *14*, 1–13.

Stein, John Picard, "The Appreciation of Paintings," Ph.D. dissertation, University of Chicago, 1973.

_____, "The Monetary Appreciation of Paintings," *Journal of Political Economy*, October 1977, *85*, 1021–35.

International Statistics Yearbook, Washington, DC: International Monetary Fund, annual.

Rate of Return to Investment in American Antique Furniture
Author(s): Paul Graeser
Source: *Southern Economic Journal*, Vol. 59, No. 4 (Apr., 1993), pp. 817-821
Published by: Southern Economic Association
Stable URL: http://www.jstor.org/stable/1059743
Accessed: 05/02/2014 12:55

Rate of Return to Investment in American Antique Furniture*

I. Introduction

Most research on the market for "collectibles" has focused on their potential for long term price appreciation. Formal and informal estimates of the rate of return on visual art, especially paintings, are common [1; 2; 4; 6; 10]. An interesting exchange on bottled wine as an investment is provided by Krasker [8] and Jaeger [5]. Recently, Ross and Zondervan [9] analyzed the investment market for Stradivarius violins.

The research strongly suggests that paintings *as a group* are a poor long-term investment. Ross and Zondervan [9, 539] conclude the Stradivarii ". . . may give a return in excess of the long-term real rate of interest of 2.5 per cent if taxes are absent and the user benefits are significant," but they are unable to establish a clear indication of user benefits. A possible exception to these negative assessments is bottled wine. Jaeger [5, 590] shows that correcting Krasker's [8] storage cost estimate and taking a time period that bridges recessions (to which all wine prices are very sensitive) yields a substantial premium rate of return on fine wines over the T-bill rate. Her explanation [5, 584] is that bottled wines improve in quality up to an (uncertain) peak year, which can range from ". . . 20–40 years in the case of some reds, while a few refuse to retire at 65," after which their market value drops sharply; we see here an apparent influence on the wine market of user benefit.[1]

This paper will extend the above research by estimating rates of return on American antique furniture (hereafter, "antiques").

II. Antique Furniture Prices

Data

By far, the most extensive data base of antique prices is provided by Ralph and Terry Kovel [7]. Their mail surveys and personal research yield almost a thousand antique furniture price quotes yearly. In the Kovel's data base, "Prices are the actual asking price, although the buyer may have negotiated to a lower figure . . . each price is one you could have paid for the object" [7 (1987), p. v.]. In other words, these are raw data, directly from the showroom. But the Kovels also omit items of no interest to collectors, such as "used" furniture and old furniture in bad condition. They omit survey responses with ambiguous, incomplete or inconsistent data. And they omit outliers—extremely high prices due, in their opinion, to " 'auction fever' " [7 (1990), iii–v]. For the Kovels, the behavior of typical American collectors defines "antique" furniture.

---

*For their assistance, I thank Sarah Cohen, Dunning's Auction Service, Terry Kovel, Susan Porter-Hudak, Sasipen Phuangsaichi and William Sjostrom. Remaining errors and omissions are mine.
1. The benefit from *consuming* a great vintage wine is a user benefit. The wine's value as a *collectible* inheres in its age and vineyard, which are aesthetic qualities.

COMMUNICATIONS

Regarding opportunity costs, we follow precedent. We compare the investment "yield" implicit in the behavior of antique prices with the yield on U.S. Treasury 90-day bills [3].

Data Management

Generally, unlike Stradivarius violins, bottled wines, etc., one cannot trace the market value of a given piece of antique furniture over time. The exceptions are those very rare, expensive items whose auction prices are unrepresentative of the rest of the market. Moreover, even if one could tag a piece of furniture and follow its market history, the result (as we infer below) would be an unreliable estimate of the huge market for antiques in general. Antiques' heterogeneity, as to place of sale (they are expensive to ship) and individual physical characteristics (requiring personal inspection) causes substantial and unpredictable variations in price. An antiques 'investor' who concentrates on a narrow genre and type is accepting above average risks; such dealing is really speculation. The wide diversity of items carried by the typical retail dealer is partly an effort to minimize these risks.

Fortunately, similar or identical furniture appear at estate auctions, in dealers' showrooms and in advertisements year after year. We may gain insight into antiques' investment potential by constructing 'portfolios' of various general types of antiques. These portfolios can be assembled from the Kovels' [7] antiques data base. It is only necessary to construct a price index for certain broad categories.

In this study, we construct indices of the price history of the living room chair; the dining room chair, table, buffet, cabinet; bedroom dresser (or vanity), chest of drawers, and bedstead. These eight general furniture types are each filled from the very similar sub-types identified among the Kovels' [7] price data. The actual procedure mimics that for any price index. First, we determine the mean price, in a given year, of a particular kind of furniture, e.g., "candlestands" as a sub-type within the general type of living room tables:

$$\overline{P}_{ijt} = (\sum_{k=1}^{k=K} P_{ijtk})/K_{ijt}. \qquad (1)$$

This is the mean price, $\overline{P}$, of the ith sub-type (e.g., candlestands), within the jth general type (e.g., Living Room tables, here) for which we find in Kovel [7] K price quotes[2] in the year t. These mean prices are then fixed-weighted using the *aggregate* of the K values of the given (or ith) sub-type as reported by the Kovels [7] over the full 20 year period:

$$N_{ij} = \sum_{t=1}^{t=20} K_{ijt}. \qquad (2)$$

Using the resulting values of $\overline{P}$ and N, it is a simple matter to combine the n sub-type values ($i = 1, \ldots, n$) common to a given jth general type, into a fixed-weighted index (or average) of the general type,

$$P_{jt} = \sum_{i=1}^{i=n_{jt}} \overline{P}_{ijt} N_{ij} / \sum_{i=1}^{i=n_{jt}} N_{ij}, \qquad (3)$$

from which we have the index price, P_{jt}, of general type j furniture ($j = 1, \ldots, 8$) in period t ($t = 1, \ldots, 20$).

---

2. In six per cent of the sub-type cells, $K_{ijt} = 0$. The fortran program written for data management deals with these empty cells, thus avoiding the obvious bias. (I am indebted to Susan Porter-Hudak for this useful program.)

Table I Rates of Return (%) on Antique Furniture,[a] 90-day T-bill[b]

Periods	All Types[c] (1)	LIVING ROOM Tables (2)	DINING ROOM			BEDROOM			90-day T-bills (10)
			Tables (3)	Chairs (4)	Buffets (5)	Cabinets (6)	Beds (7)	Vanities (8)	Chest of Drawers (9)	
1. 1967–1986	6.97	8.0	3.5	6.1	5.1	6.6	11.9	8.8	5.8	7.31
2. 1967–1976	8.24	9.4	3.8	7.1	8.0	5.9	15.3	9.7	6.7	5.66
3. 1977–1986	5.71	6.7	3.2	5.1	2.3	7.3	8.5	7.7	4.9	8.99

a. Antiques' rates of return are compounded continuously, between period endpoints (see text, Part III).
b. T-bill rates of return are compounded annually, between actual end years.
c. The "All Types" rate of return is the unweighted arithmetic mean of rates of return in columns (2) through (9).

After aggregating and fixed-weighting, we have a portfolio based on a specific product mix defined for the entire 20 years by the fixed-weights.[3] From these weighted means, each year we have 8 antique index prices, with a total of $8 \times 20 = 160$ such prices over the 20 years. These prices are the expected prices available to antiques investors, although much of the risk-generating price variance has been suppressed.

III. Rates of Return

Following [9], we estimate the capital gains rate of return on a general type of antique furniture from

$$P_t = P_0 e^{rt}.$$

We define P_t and P_0 as period 'endpoint' prices, using the mean prices of the first three and last three years of the 20 year span, yielding a time-base of 18 years. The mean price of the four middle years is used as an end 'year' when calculating beginning and ending 9 year estimations. Using these end points, r is a continuous compound-interest statistic.

The results of these calculations are shown in Table I. We first observe that the yields vary across types. For example, for the full 20 years (row 1) the highest rate of return (row 1, column 7) was 11.9 per cent while the least return (row 1, column 3) was 3.5 per cent. Despite our fixed-weight aggregation of sub-types into more diversified portfolios, the remaining influence of antiques price variance is substantial.

The price variance would be of little interest if rates of return exceeded opportunity cost. The estimated annual rate of return on all antique types, collectively, for 1967–1986 is shown in Table 1 (row 1, column 1) as 6.97 per cent. The corresponding 90-day T-bill yield [3] (row 1, column 10) is 7.31 per cent. Even if retail and wholesale antique prices were alike, the net return from buying and holding a broadly inclusive portfolio of antiques for the 20 years would have been *minus* 0.34 per cent.

---

3. The method is similar to computing the well known Consumer Price Index. One difference is that the antiques index uses the entire 20 year period to determine the weights, instead of the less reliable Laspeyre's single base-year weights. Also, the antique "product" itself does not depreciate. Indeed, the antiques market is essentially a circulating stock: vendor offerings of antiques, unlike offerings of typical consumer goods, collectively change little or none over time.

The time period makes a difference. In the decade from 1967 through 1976, the inclusive antique portfolio earned 8.24 per cent while T-bills' yield was only 5.66 per cent (row 2, columns 1 and 10), for a 2.58 per cent premium. As with many collectibles, however, the wholesale discount is significant; for antiques, from 20 to 50 per cent [7 (1987), v]. The 2.58 per cent premium is offset or more than offset by the wholesale discount.

As noted above, the more specialized the portfolio, the greater the price variance over time and the greater the opportunity for gain or loss. By choosing the right antique type, instead of a more diverse portfolio, one could have done better. For example, a portfolio of beds bought and held during 1967–1977 yielded 15.3 per cent (row 2, column 7) when T-bills were yielding 5.66 per cent. The largest wholesale discount of 50 per cent would still have yielded almost 3 per cent net. But, as with all relatively specialized portfolios, *ab initio* a sub-set like this would have been riskier, especially relative to financial instruments.

During the second half of the two decade span, opportunities for gainful investment in antiques deteriorated substantially. The antiques' overall rate of return fell from 8.24 per cent in the first decade to only 5.71 per cent in the second decade (rows 2 and 3, column 1), while T-bill rates were soaring (rows 2 and 3, column 10) from 5.66 to 8.99 per cent. Every portfolio depicted in the table, even beds, would have yielded a clear loss.

IV. Conclusion

The results in Table I are generally consistent with those of previous research. Studies of the monetary rate of return on investments in collectibles, through long-term price appreciation, typically conclude they are a poor investment relative to financial instruments.

Since collectibles, in fact, are more than mere financial instruments to their owners (who otherwise presumably would be collecting financial instruments, instead), one suspects we are measuring collectibles' rates of return against the wrong criteria. Along with pecuniary gains, we ought to be including nonpecuniary user benefits. Only in one case, that of bottled wine, does the pecuniary yield appear to reflect the natural *increase* in user benefit at the final imbibing.

The problem is that user benefits, from daily association with an aesthetic object, are not readily disentangled from the object's financial yield. If use and ownership were separate, the user paying a rent to the owner for exclusive daily association with the collectible and the owner getting, in addition to the rent, the financial yield from any price appreciation, then the market would reflect the *total* return—rent plus capital gain—from the collectible. One suspects the mean value of this total return would easily stand comparison with yields on financial instruments.

Such rental arrangements seem very rare. At least, we have no public data base of the kind. There is the problem of agency. The principal hindrance to such a market may be the lack of motivation in the renter to preserve and protect the aesthetic object as would an owner-in-possession. Buying collectibles to rent out, therefore, may simply be unprofitable.

Paul Graeser
Northern Illinois University
DeKalb, Illinois

References

1. Anderson, Robert C., "Paintings as an Investment." *Economic Inquiry*, March 1974, 13–26.
2. Baumol, William J., "Unnatural Value: or Art Investment as a Floating Crap Game." *American Economic Review*, May 1986, 10–14.
3. *Federal Reserve Bulletin*, 1970–1988. Washington, D.C.: Board of Governors of the Federal Reserve System.
4. Frey, Bruno S. and Werner W. Pommerehne, "Is Art Such a Good Investment?" *The Public Interest*, Spring 1988, 79–86.
5. Jaeger, Elizabeth, "To Save or Savor: The Rate of Return to Storing Wine." *Journal of Political Economy*, No. 3, 1981, 584–92.
6. Keen, Geraldine. *Money and Art: A Study Based on the Times-Sotheby Index*. New York: G.P. Putnam's Sons, 1971.
7. Kovel, Ralph and Terry Kovel. *Kovels' Antiques and Collectibles Price List*. New York: Crown Publishers, annually 1968–1987.
8. Krasker, William S., "The Rate of Return to Storing Wines." *Journal of Political Economy*, No. 6, 1979, 1363–67.
9. Ross, Myron H. and Scott Zondervan, "Capital Gains and the Rate of Return on a Stradivarius." *Economic Inquiry*, July 1989, 529–40.
10. Stein, John P., "The Monetary Appreciation of Paintings." *Journal of Political Economy*, October 1977, 1021–35.

The Smithsonian Institution

Art as a Commodity? Aspects of a Current Issue
Author(s): Lisa Koenigsberg
Source: *Archives of American Art Journal*, Vol. 29, No. 3/4 (1989), pp. 23-35
Published by: The Smithsonian Institution
Stable URL: http://www.jstor.org/stable/1557730
Accessed: 05/02/2014 12:56

Your use of the JSTOR archive indicates your acceptance of the Terms & Conditions of Use, available at
http://www.jstor.org/page/info/about/policies/terms.jsp

JSTOR is a not-for-profit service that helps scholars, researchers, and students discover, use, and build upon a wide range of content in a trusted digital archive. We use information technology and tools to increase productivity and facilitate new forms of scholarship. For more information about JSTOR, please contact support@jstor.org.

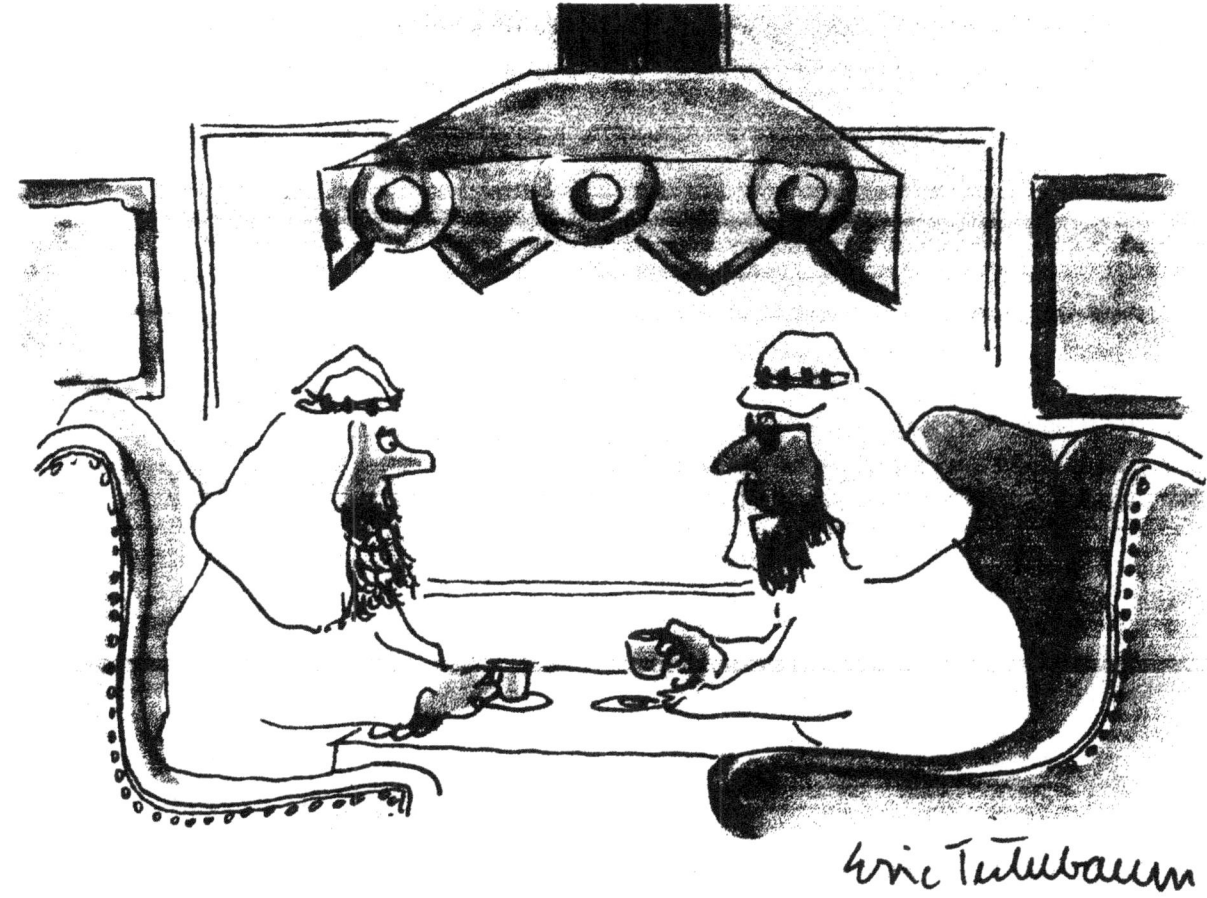

"Through it all we're still heavily invested in oil—primarily Picasso and Rembrandt."
Drawing, Eric Teitelbaum, © 1990 The New Yorker Magazine, Inc. Reprinted by special permission, all rights reserved.

art as a commodity?
aspects of a current issue

LISA KOENIGSBERG

THIS PAPER CONSTITUTES A PRELIMINARY DISCUSSION of the trend that has been loosely called the rise of art as a commodity and the possible relationship of that process to the writing of American art history. Three issues will be examined in this essay. First, cultures that collect and value art have been characterized by behavioral, institutional, and economic factors that have been articulated by Joseph Alsop in *The Rare Art Traditions: The History of Collecting and Its Linked Phenomena*; examination of these

---

This is the text of a paper given at the National Museum of American Art's symposium "Hindsights and Insights: Scholarship in American Art, 1970-1990," on April 20, 1990.

I would like to thank Lois Fink, Marcus Edward, Ronald G. Pisano, Garnett McCoy, and Darcy Tell for their kind help in preparing this article.

---

factors provides insights helpful to our understanding of elevated price levels and, hence, how art has come to serve as a financial investment. Second, the view that art, in our own time, is seen by many as a financial investment will be discussed. Finally, aspects of the substantive relationship between elevated prices and American art historical scholarship and institutions will be considered.

The *Penguin Dictionary of Economics* defines a commodity: "in economic theory, a tangible good or service resulting from the process of production." In common usage, commodity has come to mean "a primary product such as coffee, copper, cotton, wool, rubber, and tin," samples of which can be tested and which can be traded in bulk and standardized.[1] In this sense, art—with the possible exception of graphics or multiples—is not a commodity. Perceived as scarce, works are characterized by their uniqueness and are evaluated for their standing on a hierarchy of technical, intellectual, and thematic values. As such, art is the opposite of a basic substance or product which can be priced in bulk, despite the implications to the contrary suggested by the chart of a representative basket of nineteenth and early twentieth-century American paintings that was recently featured in the *New York Observer*.[2]

Having said that, it is also clear that, for some people, art has become an investment as the term is commonly defined: expenditure to acquire financial or real assets.[3] It might be said that art produces an aesthetic dividend and can later be sold for an appreciated price. Roughly, within the past two or three decades the traditional collector, who collects primarily out of aesthetic feeling and views increases in value as fortuitous by-products of the activity, has been joined by a new breed of collector who is essentially interested in the financial return on his investment in art.

The recent headlines announcing astounding prices for art affirm the notion that—for good or ill—art has become an investment, as is suggested by a graph comparing investment alternatives that appeared in the *New York Times* in February 1990.[4] A cursory examination shows that an explosion in prices is evident in almost every category, including those of particular concern to us as so-called Americanists: American paintings, sculpture, decorative arts, and contemporary paintings. For example, in 1979, the Texas financier Lamar Hunt bought Frederic Edwin Church's *Icebergs* for $2.5 million.[5] The 1982 private sale of Samuel F. B. Morse's *Exhibition Gallery of the Louvre* by Syracuse University to Daniel Terra yielded $3.5 million.[6] In 1987, George Caleb Bingham's *Jolly Flatboatmen* fetched $6 million, and in November 1988, Jasper Johns's *False Start* sold for over $17 million. In June 1989, a Newport six-shell secretary attributed to John Goddard sold for $12.1 million at Christie's. In January 1990, a Philadelphia pier table carved by Thomas Tufft in 1775-1776 brought $4.6 million and thus became "the most expensive table in the world."[7] And the list of superprices goes on and on.

Despite such breathtaking price tags, American art is still seen as a good buy. In December 1987, J. Brian Cole, senior vice president of Christie's, stated that American art, which had attracted relatively little foreign buying, was thus "one area not affected by the cheaper dollar."[8] The following year, *Business Week* author Judith Dobrzynski, who noted some foreign buying for artists such as Mary Cassatt and Winslow Homer, reported that American art ("art completed up until about the end of World War II and works by traditional artists since then") was still "an under-valued category," which might receive more attention by virtue of exhibitions abroad.[9] Recently, James L. Reinish, senior vice president of Hirschl & Adler, concurred with this assessment, noting that despite rising prices American art continues to be undervalued and that decorative arts, sculpture, painting (including portraiture and works by women), and works on paper remain promising areas for the collector.[10]

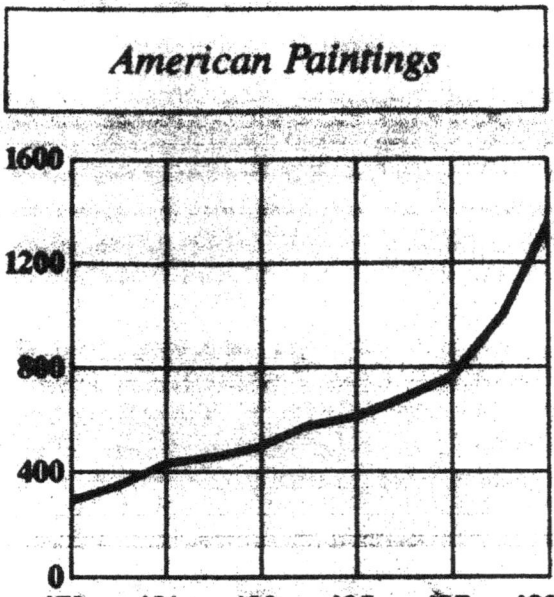

A graph plotting the market value of a "representative 'basket' of American paintings, *The New York Observer* (source: Sotheby's; *The New York Observer*).

Although it is not an American canvas, the work that is most emblematic of the art market's explosion and the attendant discussion of art as an investment is Vincent Van Gogh's *Irises*. Purchased in 1947 by Joan Whitney Payson for $84,000, one month after the so-called stock market crash in October 1987, the work sold for $53.9 million at Sotheby's.[11] This event has been, according to *New York Times* critic Rita Reif, the "bench mark most often cited as proof that art was a commodity that had weathered the economic crisis."[12] For this reason, aspects of the sale will be discussed briefly.

After the sale was announced, Sotheby's exhibited the work in the host countries of likely purchasers. After the auction, *Irises* vanished from view for two months until Alan Bond, the "Australian billionaire" who has since encountered enormous financial difficulties, announced that he was the new owner of the work, which he described as "the most important painting in the world."[13] In October 1989, it was disclosed that Sotheby's had lent Mr. Bond about half the purchase price, in financing that was negotiated prior to the sale, and that the firm would retain control of the work, which had served as collateral for the loan and was then being stored in an unidentified location, until Mr. Bond completed payment.[14] Although Bond sold a Manet in November 1989 to repay part of the loan, a remainder was still outstanding, and the painting was once again up for sale. It was recently disclosed that the Getty Museum has purchased the work for an amount that is not to be divulged; thus, as Michael Kimmelman has observed, collectors, dealers, and others cannot use the painting's price as a yardstick of the current state of the market.[15]

Because all value is socially determined and negotiated, logically it follows that before art can be viewed as an investment, a complex network of phenomena must be in place to maintain elevated price levels. Thus, astonishing in and of themselves, superprices are worthy of even closer scrutiny because they indicate that a social agreement on the value of art, not to mention on the value of a work, has been reached.

In *The Rare Art Traditions: The History of Collecting and Its Linked Phenomena*, Joseph Alsop considered factors characteristic of cultures that collect and value art; study of his analysis deepens our understanding of elevated price levels and hence the process by which art has come to serve as a financial investment. For Alsop, art collecting is the assembling of objects belonging to a particular artistic category favored and focused upon by a collector. As such, collectors define their own collections and have a hand in creating their own rarities. Once becoming part of a collection, objects which may have had social or functional uses are viewed as essentially aesthetic objects, what Alsop terms "art-as-an-end-in-itself." As objects are absorbed into collections (be they public or private), those that remain on the market are increasingly in demand and bring higher prices. Moreover, all objects in a given desirable category tend to increase in value.

Alsop sees art history as a pivotal element in the activity of collecting. Whenever collecting exists, the history of objects—in this case art—is written by experts, such as Bernard Berenson, because authentication, qualitative assessment, and documentation of heavily sought-after and costly objects is essential to the market's development. Moreover, in order to define and refine a collection, a collector requires extensive knowledge and will often consult an expert whose services are key. In *Pricing the Priceless*, the economist William D. Grampp has contended that "the opinion of experts is the principal determinant of price."[16] It might be said that when a work of art enters a collection, its social use and functional context is subsumed and replaced by the artistic analysis and documentation provided by traditional art history. Yet another important aspect of art history is the bringing to light of heretofore unappreciated works; this widens the boundaries of aesthetic pleasure and understanding.

An interactive relationship exists between art history and the marketplace, which dealers such as Joseph Duveen did much to promote. From Alsop's point of view, art collecting automatically engenders an art market which supplies collectors. At its most basic, the art market is the marketplace which brings together, in a specialized and intricate system, those who create or own art and those who want to own it. The market includes collectors and their advisers, dealers who often possess expertise, and auction houses which have become retail, full-service, global operations handling the best objects and publish-

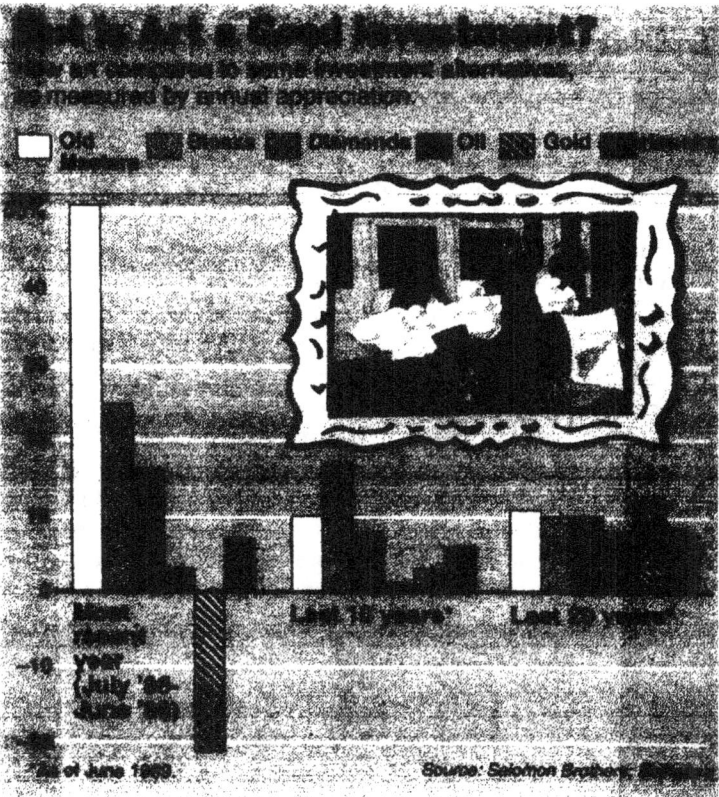

Steve Hart, "But is Art a Good Investment?" © 1990 The New York Times Company, reprinted by special permission.

ing catalogues written by their own experts. The art magazines and critics who fan opinion also participate in this market. The end result has been defined as a bargaining relationship entered into by the buyer and the seller in which the price—influenced by such factors as authenticity, provenance, and quality—"will be no less than what the seller will accept and no more than what the buyer will pay."[17]

Alsop also describes "secondary by-products" related to art collecting: these include museums, the creation of fakes, revaluation, collecting antiques, and the rise of superprices. Foremost are museums: permanently established nonprofit collections of works to which the public has access. Museums make visual heritages and aesthetic experience available to the many. When a work is taken off the market and placed in a "temple of art," the price of similar objects is likely to rise because inclusion in a museum collection serves as certification of quality and worth that is recognized by the market.[18]

The creation of fakes occurs whenever a competitive market serving competitive collectors exists. Faking creates another compelling raison d'être for art history, which by systematic analysis provides for detection of fraudulent works, authentication of original objects, and their qualitative assessment.

Revaluation, a corollary aspect of Alsop's network, has produced "a stock market of taste, on which works of all sorts go up and down in estimation all over the world."[19] As the works of some periods and artists soar in price, collectors may seek works that are less costly or easier to come by. Similarly, taste may shift and new fashions may come into vogue.

The rise of superprices resulting from the competition among collectors for objects deemed authentic and aesthetically desirable by art historians (who also ensure the inclusion of prime examples in museum collections) is the final factor for Alsop. Regulated by the art market, which is fueled by collectors who compete for the best examples of their chosen categories, superprices are seen by some as confirmation of the value inherent in the work.

The factors explicated by Alsop, which characterize our own time and place, define an active art world and create the climate (in fact, serve as the precondition) in which collectors are tempted to become investors and speculators. In America, the current art market includes both investors and speculators who believe that art is at least a component of an investment portfolio. But the idea that art is an investment is more widely held than this last statement might suggest. In a recent article in the *New York Times*, Peter Passell discussed what "economists believe is the most fundamental change in the market in recent years: the transformation of art into a practical vehicle for investment."[20]

The seriousness with which some, in our own time, hold the view that art is indeed a financial investment is indicated by the coverage it receives in the financial press. In addition to being routinely covered in such general-interest periodicals as *New York* and *Vogue* and in periodicals aimed at collectors, such as *Connoisseur*, *Art & Antiques*, and *Art & Auction*, financial publications such as *Forbes*, *Fortune*, *Business Week*, and *Manhattan, inc.* feature articles on art, art as investment, and profiles of dealers and collectors. *Asian Finance* and the *Far Eastern Economic Review* have also published articles on art as an investment.[21] The *Wall Street Transcript* runs a column entitled "Connoisseur's Corner," written by Richard Duveen, which usually includes descriptions of lots at auction accompanied by photographs of particularly important items.[22] Geraldine Norman, an art-market correspondent for the *Independent*, a British daily, until recently wrote a column for *Barron's* focusing on auctions in New York and London entitled "The Auction Action," and the magazine continues to publish articles on auctions and the art market.[23]

Some dealers have confirmed this perception of art's new function as an investment. David Tunick, who specializes in Old Master prints and drawings, has stated that "the art market has become so monetized ... people have begun to think of art as a legitimate form of investment."[24] And the New York dealer Richard L. Feigen has observed that works of art have become quasi-financial instruments due to changes in the art market which has itself become more of a financial market.[25]

The financial press has echoed this view. James Bartholomew, writing in the *Far Eastern Economic Review*, noted that: "art can be taken seriously as an investment medium ... you may do as well or better than with equities."[26] Dallas sculpture collector Raymond Nasher certainly shares the view that art is an investment: "I look at buying art as a transfer of assets within my portfolio. Quality art is as good an investment as anyone can have."[27] The Pritzker family of financiers in Chicago makes business investments in the art field, which are handled by Michael Botwinick, formerly director of the Brooklyn Museum and then of the Corcoran.[28]

The very rich are not alone in transforming their outlook about art, with some seeing their collections as investments and as desirable components of diversified portfolios. According to art consultant Lynda Deppe, there is a second-tier art market filled with young professionals looking for "investments with more status than stocks," including paintings and sculpture in the $10,000-$35,000 range and prints by artists such as Andy Warhol and James Rosenquist.[29]

Commenting on the market for contemporary paintings, the author of a recent article in the *Economist* observes that a new breed of buyer is appearing. These new players are "plain speculators who buy, wait for prices to jump, then sell. Some form groups to buy scores of pictures, which they may not even bother to pick up from the galleries or auction houses."[30]

Pension funds also invest in art. Between 1974 and 1981, as a hedge against inflation, the British Rail Pension Fund acquired over $70 million in paintings, drawings, furniture, and other first-class works to supplement more traditional investments. In 1986, a new management team decided to stop acquiring and start selling.[31] The Fund's profitability may serve as incentive to others contemplating the inclusion of art in pension funds.[32]

Art mutual funds have also been discussed and formed. According to a 1989 article in *Barron's*, Russell Blumenthal, managing director of Chase Art Investors, was the motive force behind the Chase Art Fund, an attempt to raise $300 million from pension funds by convincing them that there are impressive returns in museum-quality paintings and sculpture in the $1-10 million range, and although the idea has been put on hold, in part because of the high cost of expertise necessary for making the acquisitions, it may be pursued in the future.[33] An October 1989 *Art & Antiques* article mentions Fred Kline, a young Santa Fe dealer trying to raise $10 million for an art investment fund that he expected to increase in value by forty to fifty percent a year.[34]

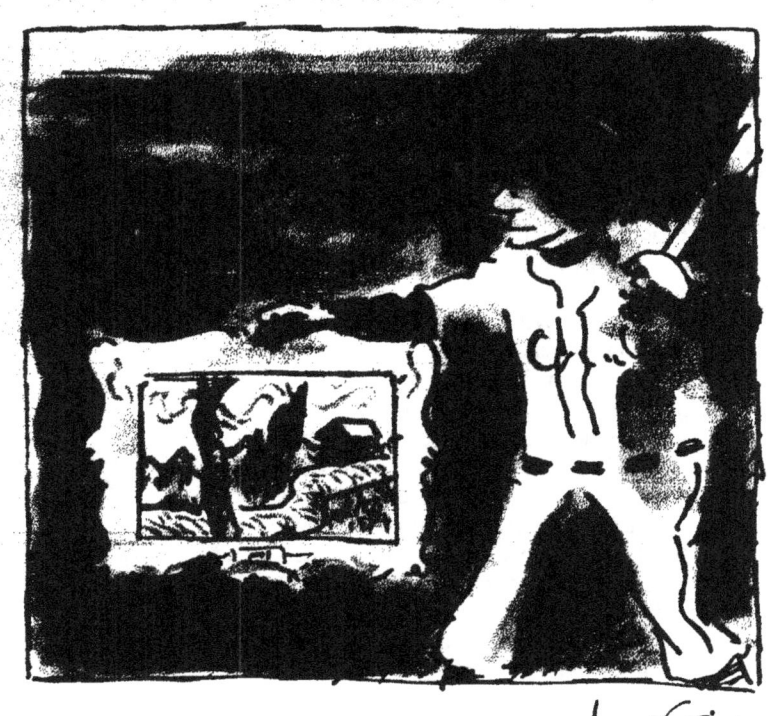

Lefty Duke Signs for a van Gogh Painting

Hard-hitting outfielder K.T. (Lefty) Duke signed a four-year contract with the Baltimore Orioles for which he will receive van Gogh's painting "The Crooked Road."

This contract exceeds that of Bananas Rohak, who signed yesterday for three years. Rohak will receive an early-nineteenth-century Regency desk. If he hits over .290, he will get the matching chair.

Duke hit .287 last season. Van Gogh painted "The Crooked Road" in 1884, and was unable to sell it in his lifetime. It was most recently owned by a private collector in Caracas.

Drawing by S. Harris, © 1990 The New Yorker Magazine, Inc. Reprinted by special permission, all rights reserved.

The merchandising by such retail chains as Martin Blinder's Martin Lawrence Limited Editions of lithographs and other graphics by "hot artists with catchy styles," is related to the perception of art as an investment, despite Blinder's statement that "we are selling art, as opposed to investment." Martin Lawrence and the two other publicly traded chains—the Circle Fine Arts and Dyansen Corporations, the latter founded by ex-investment banker Harris Shapiro—operate about sixty branch galleries; most have monthly payment plans or one-year trade-in policies.[35]

The use of analogies between art and financial instruments in writing on this topic also suggests that art is increasingly viewed as an investment in some quarters. In "The Art Boom and the Disease of Acquisition," Anthony Sampson observed that Sotheby's and Christie's persuaded collectors that "Old Masters were a currency in their own right, more reliable than pounds, dollars or even yen."[36] Susan Lee has written that investors in art have available to them a "diversity of instruments" because "dozens of categories [are] now considered collectible art."[37] In an analogy between stock and art, auction houses serve as the "exchanges" for this artistic equity. In "Clapping for Money at Auctions," John Russell stated that "auction prices are the Dow Jones of the art market."[38]

Dealers in works by living artists have also been compared to underwriters of new equity issues, and early sales of a living artist's work have been likened to initial public offerings of stock. It has been further observed that dealers, like stock underwriters, court their client base to keep it receptive to their offerings. Carrying the analogy farther, it has been argued that although the initial price is set by underwriters—in other words dealers—the eventual price is established in the auction houses, in other words, in the secondary markets.[39]

The author of a recent *Manhattan, inc.* profile of Richard Feigen noted that the dealer's inventory, which spans five hundred years, constitutes "a diversified portfolio," which "makes good business sense." Termed the preferred dealer to "today's ascendant class," as Duveen was in his day, Feigen has also been compared to the former "junk-bond king" Michael Milken, because both took gambles with "high risk investments that could conceivably yield astronomically high returns."[40]

The investment value in art has been perceived before. The eighth duke of Marlborough is, in some ways, related to today's collectors-investors, although he did not purchase the works in his collection himself. In the late nineteenth century, the duke saw the enormous unmined economic resources in the art collections accumulated by his family, which included such treasures as Van Dyck's *Equestrian Portrait of Charles I* and which, bound over under entail, passed from generation to generation. Savvy enough to see the potential in this dormant capital, the duke actively championed the 1882 Settled Land Act, which empowered a so-called tenant for life to sell, lease or otherwise dispose of any part of the settled land or even the whole of it, except the manor house and park, without the participation or agreement of the trustees. The timing of the duke's sales, which began in 1884, suggests that the Settled Land Act may have freed him from legal encumbrance; following the 1884 sale of the Van Dyck and Raphael's *Ansidei Madonna* to the National Gallery, in 1885 he sold some choice paintings in private sales, and in 1886 the duke auctioned large portions of the family's collections at Christie's. The proceeds from his sales were used for improvements at Blenheim and were invested in scientific agriculture and in urban land.[41]

The current phenomenon of viewing art as an investment has really taken off within the past twenty to thirty years. For the dealer Robert Miller, the evolution began in the 1960s when many large American corporations began hanging paintings and placing sculptures in lobbies and boardrooms.[42] Still others see the art market as having been "electrified" by the 1973 sale of Robert Scull's collection of American Abstract Expressionist and Pop Art works.[43] For many observers, including Jeffrey Deitch, now an independent art consultant and a cofounder and former vice president of Citibank's Art Advisory Service (a comprehensive art service for its wealthiest private banking customers), the trend was galvanized by the 1983 purchase of Sotheby's by A. Alfred Taubman and the subsequent transformation of the "staid" image of the auction house in order to attract retail customers, traditionally the province of the standard art gallery.[44]

What accounts for the widely held perception of art as investment? Prominent among causes are the growth in the size and scope of the auction houses and the globalization of the art market. Grace Glueck, an art writer for the *New York Times*, has cited the growing audience for art, the desirability of art as a status symbol, the scarcity of top-quality art, which fuels competition and rising prices, and the greater amounts of disposable income in America, Europe, and Japan.[45] Art has also been seen as an excellent hedge against inflation, as well as a currency hedge.[46] Recent trouble in the equity/stock market has been an additional factor: works of art appeared to be relatively safe repositories.[47] Other factors cited include the effect of new American tax laws on real estate, the poor showing of "so-called stores of value" such as gold and precious stones, and the 1986 Tax Reform Act.[48]

An additional cause (and effect) of art used as an investment has surely been the financing that is now available. Credit traditionally extended by dealers to clients has generally been interest free; now, financing of various types—some resembling that available for financial instruments—exists for art. Richard Feigen stated that the financing offered to Alan Bond by Sotheby's prior to his purchase of *Irises* "is exactly like buying on margin . . . by extending credit [prior to purchase] you are further inflating prices which are rapidly getting out of control."[49]

The auction houses have pursued financing as aggressively as the climate will permit. Diana D. Brooks, the president of Sotheby's North America and a former Citibanker, has stated that she has arranged financing for clients since shortly after she joined the firm in 1979. In 1984, Sotheby's Holdings—parent of the auction house—

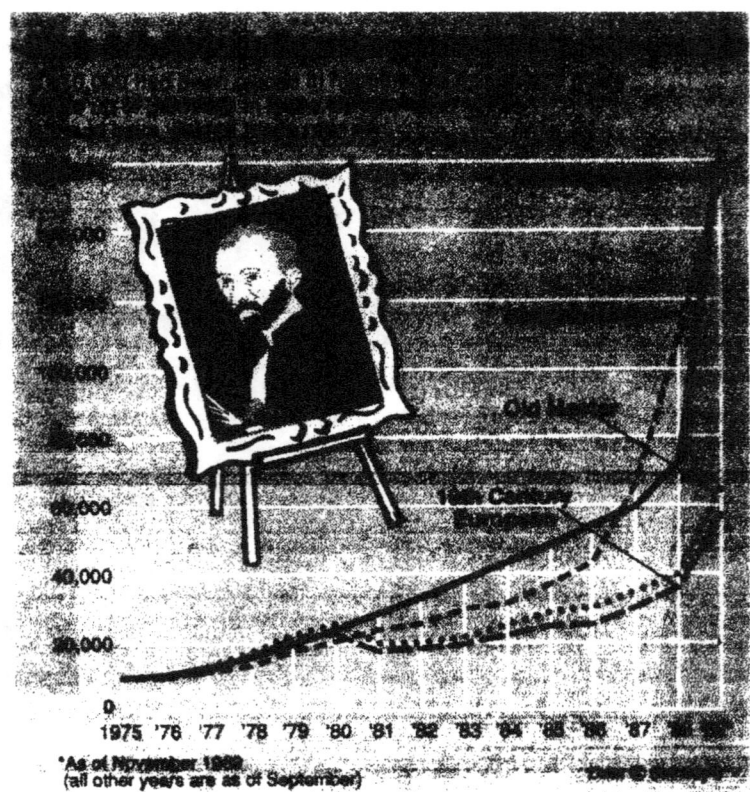

Steve Hart, "Not All Art Is Equal," © 1990 The New York Times Company, reprinted by special permission.

began to make loans secured on works of art.[50] In 1988, the firm extended its financing of art in a program operated by Sotheby's Financial Services; about that time, the house experimented with letting a buyer make a down payment of thirty percent, paying out the rest, principal and interest, in installments for a term of up to two years. Sotheby's will assist banks in making loans against art by making appraisals, will make the loan jointly, or make a loan itself.[51] Christie's the rival premier auction house, will assist clients who wish to seek financing.[52] Both Sotheby's and Christie's (despite previous protests registered by the latter) offer guarantees under which the seller and the auction house set a minimum price, for one lot or an entire collection, and the house is obligated to pay the seller at least that much, whether or not the art is sold.[53]

Major banks offer financing by lending against art that collectors already own. At Citibank and Chase Manhattan it has been possible to borrow to finance purchases and to use works as sources of financial leverage.[54] Other types of financing exist or have been contemplated. For example, Stephen R. Field of the legal firm Summit Rovins and Feldsman's tax department, noted two techniques, lines of credit and investment pools or partnership vehicles for about ten to fifteen individuals, each of whom invests $100,000 to $200,000.[55] Barry Ross Weiner's Vestpro Corporation even conceived an ArtMaster credit card which would have a credit line for art purchases.[56]

Financing has been provided to some art dealers by

financial houses. For example, in November 1988 when prices for antiquities had begun to soar and collectors squeezed out of the French Impressionist market were looking elsewhere to invest, Edward Merrin cemented a partnership agreement with Capital Corporation, which is controlled by Asher B. Edelman, "a free-wheeling corporate raider." According to *New York Times* writer William Grimes, through a new subsidiary called Canal Arts, Edelman would funnel $10 million into the Merrin Gallery in 1989 and share in the profits from any sales; it was at this time that Merrin electrified the art world by successfully bidding over $2 million on a Cycladic head.[57]

As has been examined, because participants in the art markets, like those in any other market, seek information about what they collect, an interactive relationship exists between scholarship, collecting, and the marketplace. Therefore, my contention that traditional approaches to American art will continue to flourish in the current climate should come as no surprise.

American art is riding high as the flurry of activity regarding the sale of Thomas Eakins's *Swimming Hole* of 1883-1885 demonstrates. An early announcement that the painting would be auctioned at Sotheby's on May 24, 1990, with a $10-$15 million estimate, the highest ever for an American painting, was followed by the painting's withdrawal from the sale, although it will still be deaccessioned.[58] The owner, the Modern Art Museum of Fort Worth, could benefit from the delay. It was reported that Stuart Feld, president of Hirschl & Adler, had previously valued the painting at over $20 million, a higher estimate than that placed on the work by Sotheby's and one that might very well be warranted if the conjecture that many pictures bringing the highest prices are "archetypes in their own categories . . . the instantly identifiable image" holds true.[59]

Alsop's and Grampp's view that art history in general authenticates and documents, evaluates and revalues is echoed by Wanda Corn's assessment of the majority of published scholarship in American art. In "Coming of Age: Historical Scholarship in American Art," she states that the work of Americanists "has always been dominated by a documentary tradition, usually focused upon the life and work of a single artist, a school of art, or a genre of art."[60] She ascribes this, in part, to the youth of the field and the concomitant need for basic foundation literature, including biographic and stylistic studies, *catalogues raisonnés*, and catalogues of museum holdings and private collections.

More importantly, Professor Corn cites another reason for the dominance of the documentary monograph: the close connection between American art scholarship, the museum, and the marketplace. The interests of the museum and the marketplace in some senses coalesce, for both are motivated by the collecting impulse. In a report on the brisk trade in nineteenth- and twentieth-century American art in the 1980s, Roger Howlett of Boston's Childs Gallery observed this interaction, remarking that museums and the market "feed on each other"; in other words, museum attention triggers the interest of the marketplace, which in turn prompts the writing of scholarly monographs.[61]

Professor Corn observes that the museum has traditionally been the principal sponsor of scholarly enterprise in American art and the main source of employment for Americanists. Not surprisingly then, in her view, the approach that has characterized museum scholarship, that of "cataloguing, describing and venerating the artist and the work, has dominated American art studies," although in the past decade scholars of American art have begun to work with literary and critical theories and interdisciplinary approaches.[62]

As Professor Corn has noted, while prices for American works are soaring, the commercial world is becoming a prime sponsor of scholarship. Although galleries and dealers are certainly motivated by good intentions, the publication of information about American art also benefits the marketplace because of the validation that expert opinion provides to collectors (private or institutional). Galleries and auction houses seek the benefits of what might be termed "the hype" that a publication and exhibition can provide and which often translates into increased profits for their operations. Scholarship also assists in locating works that might eventually come to the gallery or auction house for sale.

To this end, galleries and auction houses now supplement the activities of their staffs and hire scholars to do research, to mount exhibitions often accompanied by catalogues, and to produce *catalogues raisonnés*. Here again I turn to Wanda Corn who cites the preparation by Salander-O'Reilly of *catalogues raisonnés* of Marsden Hartley and Stuart Davis, Coe Kerr's catalogue of John Singer Sargent, Hirschl & Adler's Childe Hassam project; and the Spanierman Gallery's catalogue of John Henry Twachtman. The Spanierman Gallery, in association with Sona Johnson, has also recently announced its involvement in a Theodore Robinson catalogue. It is important to note that the preparation of *catalogues raisonnés* is expensive and time-consuming; therefore, galleries may be in a better position to foot the bill for such activities, which certainly benefit the scholarly community. However, caution may be warranted, since the gallery could have a vested interest in some of the judgments that are reached about some works.

The following vignette demonstrates aspects of the interrelationship between scholarship and the marketplace: the opening of the new Berry-Hill Galleries on East Seventieth Street in New York was accompanied by an exhibition of *trompe l'oeil* paintings of currency entitled Old Money, curated by Bruce Chambers, then the firm's resident art historian and the catalogue's author.[63] According to an article published in the business section of the *New York Times*, the gallery's owners indicated that they hoped the exhibition would enhance the painters' intellectual standing and the monetary worth of their works. For one artist in particular, Otis Kaye, the Gallery was searching for a price "floor" for Kaye's works. Clearly, prices would be bolstered and justified by the prominence of the artist's works in the exhibition and publication. Despite such commercial realities, a good exhibition and catalogue compensate for possible drawbacks to the writing of scholarship in the profit-making sector. Such writing is increasingly a feature of the American art field, particularly since galleries and auction houses can afford to hire the best scholars to write for their catalogues, research *catalogues raisonnés*, and curate exhibitions. But again, are these activities separable from the commercial process that is ultimately the raison d'être of the gallery or auction house?

Given that monographs often aid in the location of lost pictures and that the sale of works increases the monetary value of the entire corpus of an artist's work, it is not surprising that the auction house and the art dealer anticipate monographs devoted to an artist and revaluations of an artist's life and work as eagerly as does the scholarly community.

Still other scholarly approaches flourish in this investment-oriented climate, one of which I will term the "revealed master" approach to American art, borrowing a phrase from William H. Gerdts who in 1974 curated an exhibition with this same title. That show, which had as its express purpose the bringing to light of many nineteenth-century artists "who were regularly shown in the important exhibitions of the time [and] are now relatively unknown and are being rediscovered and reevaluated," included works by John White Alexander, George de Forest Brush, and S. S. David, all of whom are now sought after by collectors.[64]

What Alsop termed revaluation, in some senses synonymous with the "revealed masters" approach because it involves the reassessment of works of art and entire movements, is evident in Gerdts's continuing work on the American Impressionists, which began prior to 1974. In discussing the renewed popularity of the American Impressionists in his 1980 catalogue *American Impressionism*, Gerdts cited the "very beauty of the finest examples of this art movement," and noted the "frankly commercial aspect of the rise of interest in American Impressionism ... [as] prices for masterworks of [French Impressionism] moved into realms so astronomical" that alternatives had to be found.[65] Gerdts's 1980 catalogue was followed in 1984 by a substantive book on the topic and by an introductory essay for a 1985 catalogue entitled *The Hoosier Group: Five American Painters*. Meanwhile, the market for American Impressionists surges, with foreign buyers participating and galleries producing *catalogues raisonnés* of the work of the movement's principal proponents; perhaps responding to this popular enthusiasm, the National Gallery has mounted exhibitions of three of the movement's major figures.

This revaluation approach is closely related to the discovery of works that have heretofore not been widely appreciated, exemplified by the current focus on the Arts and Crafts movement, brought to our attention in the 1972 Princeton exhibition curated by Robert Judson Clark and documented in his catalogue *The Arts and Crafts Movement in America, 1876-1916*. Sharon Darling's impressive works on *Chicago Metalsmiths*, *Chicago Ceramics and Glass*, and *Chicago Furniture* added to our understanding of Chicago's culture, extended our previously limited concept of the Arts and Crafts movement, and familiarized readers with previously unknown craftsmen and firms. These and other regional studies were placed into a broader national and international context in *The Art That Is Life: The Arts and Crafts Movement in America, 1875-1920* organized by Wendy Kaplan for the Museum of Fine Arts, Boston, which brought together many of the recent discoveries in the field. That interest in the movement existed beyond the scholarly commuity—in the most established realm of the marketplace—is evidenced by the 1989 Hirschl & Adler exhibition and catalogue *From Architecture to Object* (with a preface by the distinguished scholar Richard Guy Wilson), which hinted at the regionalism and richness that characterize the movement, while documenting works being purveyed at impressive prices.[66]

As the above suggests, much exciting work in the field of American art now includes or focuses on the decorative arts, an area of surging price levels and collectors hungry for information. Important areas of scholarship that are likely to continue to flourish as a result of an active marketplace include the study of documented pieces to identify related, unattributed pieces.[67] In his 1982 exhibition and catalogue *The Work of Many Hands: Card Tables in Federal America, 1790–1820*, Benjamin Hewitt matched the characteristics of undocumented card tables with documented examples to create significant regional groups whose characteristics could then serve as the basis for interregional comparisons and the attribution of undocumented works. Thus his study exemplifies one approach with positive ramifications for both the market and the academy.[68]

Scholarship that employs sophisticated technology to aid in identification and authentication is also likely to thrive. Continuing in importance are studies that build on the micro-analysis of woods. Charles Montgomery, in his 1966 *American Furniture: The Federal Period*, observed that analysis of secondary woods provides a valuable tool for identifying the origin of furniture, including evidence for differentiating between American and European pieces, since most American east coast woods can be distinguished from those that grew in Europe. The continuing utility of micro-analysis was revealed when Morrison Heckscher, curator of American decorative arts at the Metropolitan Museum of Art, stated that prior to the museum's purchase of the splendid Philadelphia Rococo mirror (circa 1775) for $242,000, conservators analyzed the wood, which was identified as Northeastern white pine, used in Philadelphia, New York, and New England, rather than spruce or Scotch pine which would have indicated an English origin and suggested a lower price.[69]

The application of technology has been equally important for works on painting. Elizabeth Broun's important recent monograph on *Albert Pinkham Ryder* is enriched by an analysis of Ryder's technique and materials undertaken for the project by the Smithsonian's Conservation Analytical Laboratory because of the de-

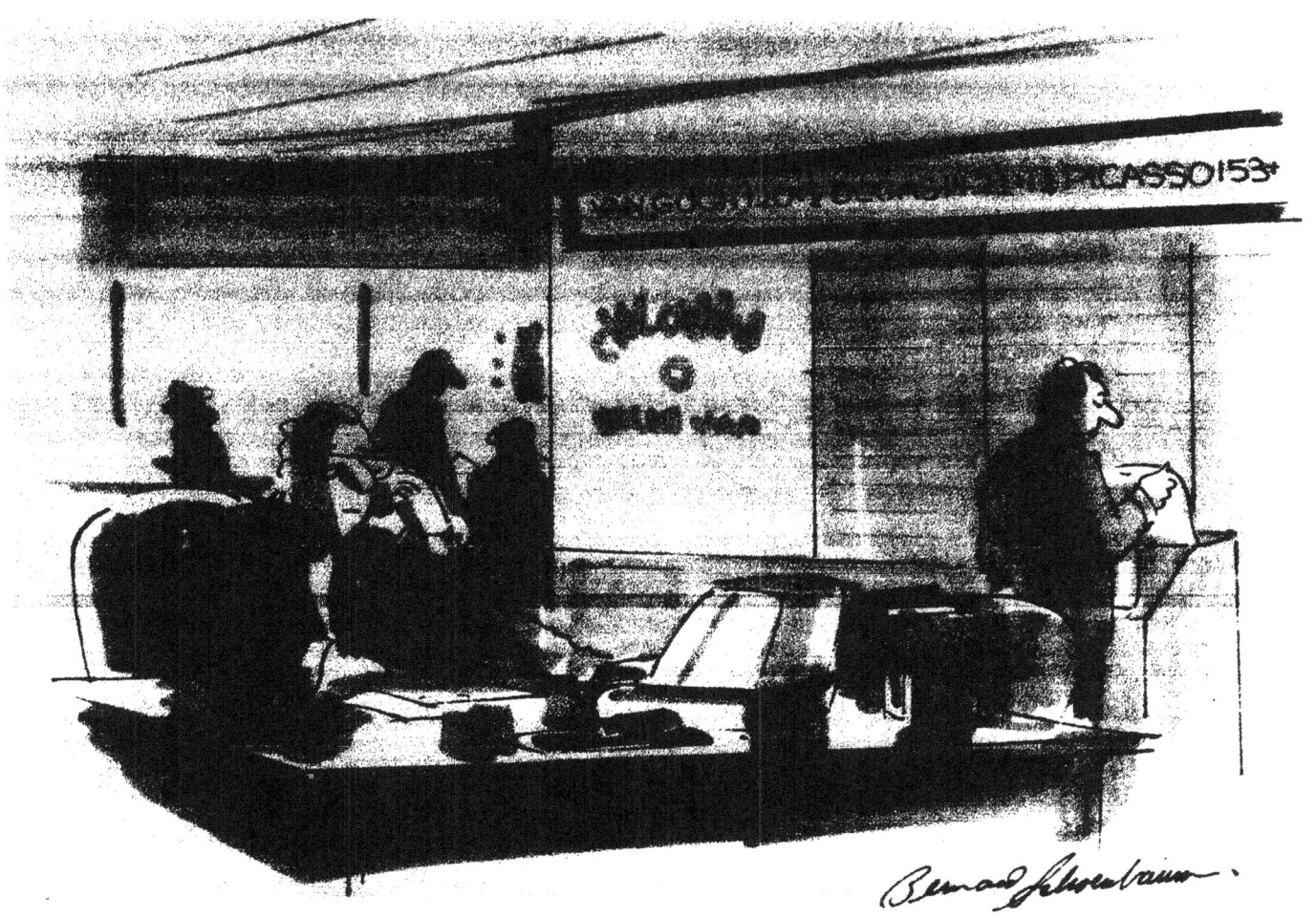

Drawing by Bernard Schoenbaum, © 1989 The New Yorker Magazine, Inc. Reprinted by special permission, all rights reserved.

terioration of many of the artist's works, the attendant restoration problems, and the existence of many forgeries.[70]

The publication of museum and private collection catalogues continues to be an important enterprise enabling collectors, galleries, and scholars to study examples deemed worthy of inclusion in a collection, and as such they have become an important market tool as well. Appearing just at the time that nineteenth-century objects were beginning to be widely collected, the High Museum's 1983 publication of the *Virginia Carroll Crawford Collection: American Decorative Arts, 1825–1917* documents the museum's trailblazing, systematic attempt to collect nineteenth-century decorative arts.[71] The recent exhibition of the Manoogian collection of American paintings at the Metropolitan Museum of Art, accompanied by a catalogue with several authors, exemplifies the merits of making a fine private collection available to the public.

As tantalizing as the visual realm is, other kinds of scholarship are also likely to grow as a result of the explosion in prices and the notion of art as an investment, such as what has recently been termed "a cottage industry . . . among economists interested in putting the notion of art-as-an-investment to the test."[72] Scholars in this area include Gerald Reitlinger whose *Economics of Taste* was an early study of economics, collecting, and the visual arts. William Grampp, who stated "art is a lackluster investment and as a speculation is not attractive except to people who relish risks," cites five recent works, four of which conclude that buying art with the sole intent of reselling at a higher price is not likely to be profitable.[73] Commenting on such broad inquiries, Jeffrey Deitch recently observed that "most of the economic studies tend to homogenize the art market too much . . . the real collector, the sophisticated dealer . . . are very specific about the kind of pictures they buy . . . it's all based on judgments of quality. If one can make those judgments, one can be a very successful collector/investor."[74] In response to comments such as Deitch's, studies of the price fluctuations over time within particular categories, as hinted at in the graph that accompanies Peter Passell's *New York Times* article "Vincent Van Gogh Meet Adam Smith," will doubtless be undertaken. Yet, these too pose problems because, even within narrowly focused categories, works of art, which are relatively scarce to begin with, can vary so greatly in quality and importance.

Related areas likely to flourish include study of the processes by which art is sold, exemplified by Charles W. Smith's 1989 consideration of art and antique auctions in his *Auctions: The Social Construction of Value*.[75] Similarly books on experts and dealers who assisted institutional and individual collectors with acquisitions and expertise are likely to proliferate; this category also encompasses histories of individual and institutional collecting.[76]

Big money and the escalation of prices also require creative and ambitious work in the legal field. For example, legal issues of particular import face those scholars involved in preparing *catalogues raisonnés*. It is even conceivable that scholars engaged in preparing such catalogues could need malpractice insurance as protection from angered collectors or owners, and some already request that clients sign a release prior to examining a work.[77]

The prosecution of those selling fraudulent works is also mandating serious attention from legal scholars. In *Arts Magazine*, Timothy Cone discusses a New York State appellate court's current review of the criminal convictions of two dealers who, having advertised Dali prints for their investment potential, were found to have sold counterfeits. The issue the court must decide is whether art can be considered a security; if it is not, laws might be drafted to ensure that the art market operates fairly, perhaps by requiring dealers to guarantee the authenticity of the work they offer. Such laws might be modeled on securities law and tailored to reflect the dynamics of the art market.[78]

The deep and fundamental impact on museums of the rise in the price of art and the notion of art as an investment must be examined, since museums have been the major employers of Americanists and much important scholarship takes the form of exhibitions and catalogues. The first dilemma is the most obvious: sky-rocketing prices have meant that few museums can participate seriously in the acquisitions market. The one institution that can regularly compete for high-priced objects of major importance is the Getty Museum, which, according to a 1988 estimate, has an annual acquisitions budget of roughly $50 million (about twenty-five times that of the Metropolitan Museum of Art), clearly a figure which recent purchases of a Pontormo portrait and *Irises* suggest can be exceeded.[79] Additionally, some curators may not have a sense of the current market and hence may not be getting the best deals for their institutions. As a result of their inadequate acquisitions budgets, institutions may also be more likely to mount exhibitions of private collections that they may hope to receive as gifts.

The rise in the value of works of art coupled with the Tax Reform Act of 1986 has made it less attractive financially to make over gifts of appreciated property (either works of art or securities) because, in general, deductions against taxable income for such gifts are now based on purchase price, rather than on current market worth, as they once were.[80] Instead, many of these works are being put up for sale at auction, where—as we have seen—few museums can seriously compete. Rising prices of art have also influenced the number of art thefts and the escalating price of insurance, which has also made it harder for museums to borrow objects and to organize major exhibitions, including so-called "blockbusters."[81]

The image that has emerged thus far from this inquiry is of a thriving traditional scholarship related to market and collecting concerns, and of institutional problems that are exacerbated by swelling prices and the notion of art as an investment. Yet creative solutions have resulted from these challenges. For example, in response to the difficulties of large-scale loan exhibitions presented by sky-rocketing insurance costs, museums have successfully pursued smaller-scale exhibitions focusing on single paintings or several canvases, such as the recent National Gallery of Art exhibition focusing on the *Feast of the Gods* and the 1984 exhibition and catalogue by David Park Curry centered on Winslow Homer's five oil paintings of croquet players, shown at Yale and other institutions.[82]

Although museums have tended to promote conservative scholarship that is in line with their collecting impulses, it is also true that museums have recently undertaken what Elizabeth Johns, in "Histories of Art: the Changing Quest," has called one of the most "salient" approaches in the field today: the coupling of discussions of painting and sculpture with considerations of decorative arts and architecture, as well as social and cultural history, as evidenced by the *American Renaissance, 1876–1917*.[83] The Museum of Fine Arts' book *New England Begins: The Seventeenth Century* examined the arts of the early Colonial period and integrated them into considerations of migration and settlement, mentality and environment, and style; in the exhibition and catalogue *The Great River: Art & Society in the Connecticut River Valley, 1635–1820*, discussions of culture and artifacts were combined with considerations of the broader environmental, cultural, and intellectual climate.[84] The Metropolitan Museum of Art's comprehensive recent catalogue *In Pursuit of Beauty*, which accompanied an important exhibition of the same name, included essays on furniture, surface coverings, paintings and sculpture, stained glass, and ceramics and glass, as well as Jonathan Freedman's discussion of American writers and the Aesthetic Movement and Roger B. Stein's consideration of artifacts as "aesthetic text" which should be read through "to their ideological subtexts."[85]

The bringing together of the work of a number of scholars in essays that complement one another in method and observation, hailed by Johns, is an approach which can substantively enrich examinations of one artist. This is demonstrated by the 1982 John Trumbull catalogue and exhibition, which included traditional examinations of the artist's life and work, a discussion of his architectural designs, and Bryan Wolf's deconstructionist approach to several of Trumbull's picturesque landscapes.[86] More recent examples of this approach include the 1987-1988 LaFarge exhibition and catalogue and the current publication on and exhibition of George Caleb Bingham's work.

Other vehicles for innovative scholarship have been the scholarly journals in the field, including the interdisciplinary *Prospects, Winterthur Portfolio, Smithsonian Studies in American Art*, and the *American Art Journal* (the latter funded by Kennedy Galleries), and the university presses. The establishment of graduate programs in American art and American studies has had an equally salutary effect, not unnoticed by the commercial art world, as is indicated by the number of galleries that contribute to the fellowship program of the City University Graduate Program in Art History.

Not only is the interest in art prospering within the academy and in the marketplace, but our museums overflow with visitors of a Saturday or Sunday afternoon. Many observers have noted that the general public's swelling interest in art may be related to rising prices.

I would like to conclude with a few questions prompted by the rise of the price of art and the notion of art as an investment, questions that may be aspects of creative strategies for the future.

Should institutions purchase works collaboratively? Such a strategy might place truly great objects within the reach of more institutions.

Another interesting issue is raised by "B. C. Gardener" in a current issue of *Art & Auction*: should museums be permitted to deaccession objects that "hold no promise of ever being exhibited, or that are redundant or unrelated to the collection," and to invest the resulting funds in their endowments to yield income which could be used for operating funds rather than for the acquisition of new works? Such a policy conflicts with the Association of Art Museum Directors guidelines.[87]

Should laws be introduced to prohibit the sale to foreign buyers, for export, objects that have long been part of America's so-called cultural patrimony?[88]

In light of the clearly interactive relationship between the scholarly and commercial worlds, what is the proper boundary between the gallery and museum spheres—or what might be termed the profit-making and the nonprofit sectors?

The rise in prices and the concomitant view of art as an investment ultimately leaves us with these broad ethical questions, which may affect our work as Americanists. For us, these issues have a particular potency because the opportunity to work in both spheres exists: scholars no longer function in a "separate sphere" but participate in a broad and integrated art world. It is only by adapting to this changing climate and by resolutely speaking out on issues in which we believe that the institutions that embody our commitment to the field will continue to flourish.

NOTES

1. Graham Bannock, R. E. Baxter, and Evan Davis, *The Penguin Dictionary of Economics*, 4th ed. (New York and London: Penguin, 1987), p. 76.

2. *New York Observer* 4 (February 19, 1990): 1.

3. Bannock, Baxter, and Davis, *Penguin Dictionary*, p. 221.

4. At this writing, according to Alexandra Peers, Sotheby's and Christie's are modifying their strategies by planning smaller sales in order to deal with a challenging economic environment; they are readying the art market and their shareholders for a possible steep decline in the fall 1990 auction totals. Dealers, collectors, and other participants in the art market are cautious: New York antiques dealer David Killen observed, "The status antiques, the ones signed by the right artist, or with the right marks or from the right collection, are still bringing tremendous money. Everything else has plateaued, nothing has crashed, and there's still so much money out there" (see Peers, "Art Auction Firms Try Cooling Sales Fever," *Wall Street Journal*, September 20, 1990, sec. C). In "Boom or Bust" (*Art & Antiques*, October 1989, p. 133), Daniel Lazare has noted that "no market goes up forever. Every business has its cycles . . . and there's no reason to think art is any different."

5. Joseph Alsop, *The Rare Art Traditions: the History of Art Collecting and Its Linked Phenomena* (New York: Harper & Row, 1982), p. 74.

6. Wanda Corn, "Coming of Age: Historical Scholarship in American Art," *Art Bulletin* 70 (June 1988): 189.

7. Rita Reif, "Auctions: January Sales of Americana Set Record," *New York Times*, February 2, 1990, sec. C.

8. Judith H. Dobrzynski, "The Picture Is Still Pretty in the Art World—So Far," *Business Week*, December 28, 1987, p. 185.

9. Judith H. Dobrzynski, "Art Collectors May Want to Stay Close to Home," *Business Week*, December 26, 1988, pp. 184-85.

10. Personal conversation between Mr. Reinish and the author, April 2, 1990.

11. For a fine chronicling of the history of *Irises* up to the actual sale at Sotheby's see Calvin Tomkins, "A Reporter at Large—Irises," *New Yorker*, April 4, 1988, pp. 37-67.

12. Rita Reif, "A $27 Million Loan by Sotheby's Helped Alan Bond to Buy 'Irises,'" *New York Times*, October 18, 1989, sec. C.

13. "Alan Bond Says He Bought 'Irises,'" *New York Times*, December 23, 1988, sec. C.

14. Reif, "A $27 Million Loan."

15. Michael Kimmelman, "Getty Buys van Gogh 'Irises,' but Won't Tell Price," *New York Times*, March 22, 1990, secs. A, C.

16. William D. Grampp, *Pricing the Priceless: Art, Artists, and Economics* (New York: Basic Books, 1989), p. 31.

17. Grampp, *Pricing the Priceless*, pp. 163-64.

18. On this last point see Grampp, *Pricing the Priceless*, p. 27.

19. Alsop, *Rare Art Traditions*, p. 16.

20. Peter Passell, "Vincent Van Gogh Meet Adam Smith," *New York Times*, February 4, 1990, sec. 2.

21. "Art Auctions: The Best Is Yet to Come: The Asian art market has grown tremendously, and Asian buyers can be as daring as their counterparts in New York and London," *Asian Finance*, September 15, 1988, pp. 29-30; James Bartholomew, "Fine Art: High-quality Earnings," *Far Eastern Economic Review*, August 24, 1989, pp. 44-45.

22. See, for example, Richard Duveen, "Connoisseur's Corner: Current Art Scene," *Wall Street Transcript*, February 5, 1990, p. 96,169; "Connoisseur's Corner: Today's Art Market [profile of John Marion]," and Richard Duveen, "Current Art Scene: Top Lots at Sotheby's Old Masters Paintings Sale Go To European Trade," *Wall Street Transcript*, February 19, 1990, pp. 96,362-96,363 and 96,406.

23. See, for example, Geraldine Norman, "The Auction Action: An Outbreak of Good Taste? Well, Something Fueled the Record Prices," *Barron's*, December 5, 1989, pp. 16-17, 28; "The Auction Action: Lasting Impressionists: Paintings and Other Art Soar Further in Value," *Barron's*, January 9, 1989, pp. 26-27; "The Auction Action: Old Masters: They Were American Favorites in January Bidding," *Barron's*, February 13, 1989, pp. 20-22.

24. Reif, "A $27 Million Loan."

25. Susan Lee, "Greed Is Not Just For Profit," *Forbes*, April 18, 1988, pp. 65-66.

26. Batholomew, "High-quality Earnings," p. 46.

27. Lee, "Greed," p. 70.

28. Michael Brenson, "Why Curators Turn to the Art of the Deal," *New York Times*, March 4, 1990, sec. 2.

29. Passell, "Van Gogh Meet Smith."

30. "Contemporary Art: There's One Born Every Minute," *Economist*, May 27, 1989, pp. 17-18.

31. Terry Trocco "British Pension Fund Sells $65.6 Million in Art

Works," *New York Times*, April 5, 1989, sec. C.

32. Bartholomew, "High-quality Earnings," pp. 44-46; for a less optimistic view of the Fund's performance see Lazare, "Boom or Bust," p. 134.

33. Joe Queehan, "Not to Everyone's Palette — Will Pension Funds Rush to Invest in Art?," *Barron's*, February 27, 1989, p. 65; conversation between Fraser Seitel, senior vice president and Director of Public Relations, The Chase Manhattan Bank, N.A., and the author, July 2, 1990.

34. Lazare, "Boom or Bust," p. 134; Alsop, *Rare Art Traditions*, p. 141.

35. Matthew Schiprin, "McArt," *Forbes*, March 7, 1988, pp. 123-25; Michael Lev, "Shopping? Don't Forget a Warhol," *New York Times*, July 4, 1989, sec. D.

36. Anthony Sampson, "The Art Boom and the Disease of Acquisition," *Manhattan, inc.* 7 (March 1990): 93.

37. Lee, "Greed," p. 68.

38. John Russell, "Clapping for Money at Auctions," *New York Times*, May 21, 1989, sec. 2.

39. Lee, "Greed," pp. 66-67.

40. Nancy Marx Better, "The Fine Art of the Dealer," *Manhattan inc.* 6 (November 1989): 106, 102.

41. I am indebted to Professor David Spring of The Johns Hopkins University for having shared his research with me.

42. Passell, "Van Gogh Meet Smith."

43. Lee, "Greed," p. 66.

44. Passell, "Van Gogh Meet Smith"; also see Robert Hughes, "Sold," *Time*, November 27, 1989, p. 61.

45. Grace Glueck, "The Mania of Art Auctions: Problems as Well as Profits," *New York Times*, November 26, 1988.

46. Lee, "Greed," p. 69.

47. Stephen Madden, "Investment Strategy and Vehicles: A Rare Seminar on Collectibles," *Fortune 1989 Investor's Guide*, p. 67.

48. "Contemporary Art," p. 17; Glueck, "Mania of Auctions."

49. Reif, "A $27 Million Loan."

50. "Contemporary Art," pp. 17-18.

51. Reif, "A $27 Million Loan"; Lee, "Greed," p. 69.

52. On the rivalry between Christie's and Sotheby's see Peter Watson, "Sotheby's vs. Christie's: Uncivil War," *New York Times*, May 27, 1990, sec. 2.

53. Rita Reif, "Christie's Reverses Stand on Price Guarantees," *New York Times*, March 12, 1990, sec. C.

54. Lee, "Greed," p. 68; telephone conversation between Sarah Miles of Chase Manhattan Private Banking Department and the author on April 17, 1990; and telephone conversation between William Ahearn, vice president, Public Affairs, Citibank, and the author, March 30, 1990.

55. "Rare Seminar on Collectibles," *Fortune 1989 Investor's Guide*, p. 82.

56. Daniel Grant, "A Study in Art Investment," *Consumers' Research*, January 1987, p. 24.

57. William Grimes, "The Antiquities Boom: Who Pays the Price?," *New Times Magazine*, July 16, 1989, p. 17. Grimes observed that Merrill Lynch also believes in the investment potential in ancient art: in 1986, the firm raised $7.3 million for the Athena I Fund, a limited partnership formed to invest in ancient coins, and more recently sold out a $25 million Athena II, which will commit up to twenty percent of its assets to acquiring antiquities.

58. Rita Reif, "Auctions," *New York Times*, April 6, 1990, sec. C; Rita Reif, "Sale of Eakins Work Won't Be at Sotheby's," *New York Times*, April 13, 1990, sec. C. According to Reif, *The Swimming Hole* was withdrawn from the Sotheby's auction after the public strongly protested the sale. Reif states that "the museum now intends to sell the work to a buyer who must agree that [it] will remain on permanent public exhibition in Forth Worth and will never be sold" (Reif, "Fort Worth Strives to Keep Eakins's 'Swimming Hole,'" *New York Times*, April 21, 1990, sec. C). Prior to the withdrawal questions were raised about the museum's choice of Sotheby's to sell the painting, because its chairwoman, Anne Burnett Windfour Marion, is the wife of John L. Marion, chairman of Sotheby's North America. Grace Glueck states that the Modern Art Museum offered the work to the Amon Carter Museum in Fort Worth for $10 million, half of which has been raised with a pledge from two Texas philanthropies (Glueck, "Bid to Keep an Eakins is Rejected," *New York Times*, May 17, 1990, sec. C).

59. Reif, "Eakins Won't be at Sotheby's"; Souren Melikian, "Image Hunting and the Price of Art," *Art & Auction*, September 1989, p. 132.

60. Corn, "Coming of Age," p. 192.

61. Jacqueline Damian, "19th and Early 20th Century American Art, the Boom Continues," *ARTnews*, December 1986, p. 66, cited in Grampp, *Pricing the Priceless*, p. 32.

62. Corn, "Coming of Age," p. 193.

63. Bruce Chambers, *Old Money: American Trompe L'Oeil Images of Currency* (New York: Berry-Hill Galleries, 1988); Douglas C. McGill, "Money Is the Subject, Art the Object," *New York Times*, November 25, 1988, sec. D.

64. Wilder Green, "Acknowledgements," in William H. Gerdts, *Revealed Masters* (New York: American Federation of Arts, 1974), p. 5.

65. William H. Gerdts, *American Impressionism* (Seattle: Henry Art Gallery, University of Washington, 1980), p. 9. For Gerdts's recent work on the topic see *Art Across America: Two Centuries of Regional Painting*, 3 vols. (New York: Abbeville Press, 1990).

66. Robert Judson Clark, ed., *The Arts and Crafts Movement in America, 1876-1916* (distributed by Princeton University Press, 1972); Sharon Darling, *Chicago Metalsmiths* (Chicago: Chicago Historical Society, 1977), *Chicago Ceramics and Glass: An Illustrated History from 1871-1933* (Chicago: Chicago Historical Society, 1979), *Chicago Furniture: Art, Craft and Industry, 1833-1983* (New York: W.W. Norton, 1984); Wendy Kaplan et al., *The Art That Is Life: The Arts and Crafts Movement in America, 1875-1920* (Boston: Museum of Fine Arts, Boston; Little, Brown, 1987); Richard Guy Wilson, introduction to *From Architecture to Object* (New York: Hirschl & Adler, 1989); for examples of regional studies see, for example, *Arts and Crafts in Detroit/1906-1976: The Movement, The Society, The School* (Detroit: Detroit Institute of Arts, 1976).

67. For a definition of a documented or labeled work see Wendy Cooper, *In Praise of America: American Decorative Arts, 1650-1830* (New York: Knopf, 1980), p. 16.

68. Benjamin Hewitt, *The Work of Many Hands: Card Tables in Federal America, 1790-1820* (New Haven: Yale University Art Gallery, 1982).

69. Reif, "Auctions: January Sales of Americana."

70. Elizabeth Broun et al., *Albert Pinkham Ryder* (Washington, D.C.: Smithsonian Institution Press, 1990).

71. David A. Hanks and Donald C. Peirce, *The Virginia Carroll Crawford Collection: American Decorative Arts, 1825-1917* (Atlanta: High Museum of Art, 1983).

72. Lazare, "Boom or Bust," p. 135.

73. Grampp, *Pricing the Priceless*, pp. 39, 157-62. The works cited by Grampp are: John Picard Stein's "The Appreciation of Paintings" (Ph.D. diss., University of Chicago, 1973), which is summarized in John Picard Stein, "The Monetary Appreciation of Paintings," *Journal of Political Economy*, October 1977, pp. 1021-35; William J. Baumol, "Unnatural Value: Or Art Investment as a Floating Crap Game," *American Economic Review*, May 1986, pp. 10-14; Robert C. Anderson, "Paintings as an Investment," *Economic Inquiry*, March 1974, pp. 13-26; Bruno S. Frey and Werner W. Pommerehne, "Is Art Such a Good Investment?" *The Public Interest*, Spring 1988, pp. 79-86; and Geraldine Keen, *The Sale of Works of Art: A Study Based on the Times-Sotheby Index* (London: Nelson, 1971). Also see Bruno S. Frey and Angel Serna, "Is Art Speculation Profitable?," *Art & Antiques*, October 1989, pp. 138-39. Discussing these works, Grampp states: "By the most detailed study, the total rate of return to art (aesthetic yield plus price appreciation) was about 12 percent from 1946 to 1968 when the total return to common stock (dividends plus price appreciation) was about 14 percent. As a spec-

ulation, the only return to art is its price appreciation, at that time 10.5 percent which was still lower than the 14 percent total return to common stock. The prudent amateur—the art lover who is not a risk lover—buys art for the pleasure of owning it. He invests or speculates in other things" (p. 166). Art collecting can entail transaction fees, and inflation must also be taken into account; other hidden costs, including conservation and insurance, exist as well.

74. "Art & Finance: What is the State of the Art Market and How Does It Relate to the World Economy?," *Art & Auction*, April 1990, p. 158.

75. Charles W. Smith, *Auctions: The Social Construction of Value* (New York and London: The Free Press, 1989).

76. See, for example, Carole Troyen, *The Boston Tradition: American Paintings from the Museum of Fine Arts, Boston* (New York: American Federation of Arts, 1980); Carol Troyen and Pamela S. Tabaa, *The Great Boston Collectors: Paintings from the Museum of Fine Arts, Boston* (Boston: Museum of Fine Arts, Boston: distributed by Northeastern University Press, 1985); Judith Zilczer, *"The Noble Buyer"*; *John Quinn, Patron of the Avant-Garde* (Washington, D.C.: published for the Hirshhorn Museum and Sculpture Garden by Smithsonian Institution Press, 1978); Elizabeth Stillinger, *The Antiquers: the Lives and Careers, the Deals, the Finds, the Collections of the Men and Women Who Were Responsible for the Changing Taste in American Antiques, 1850-1930* (New York: Knopf; distributed by Random House, 1980); Calvin Tomkins, *Merchants and Masterpieces: The Story of the Metropolitan Museum of Art* (rev. ed., New York: Harry Holt, 1989); Aline Saarinen, *The Proud Possessors* (New York: Random House, 1959); Colin Simpson, *Artful Partners: Bernard Berenson and Joseph Duveen* (New York: Macmillan, 1986); Harold Sack and Max Wilk, *American Treasure Hunt* (New York: Little, Brown, 1986).

77. "Collector Sues Met Over LaFarge Estimate," *Washington Post*, December 13, 1989, sec. B.

78. Timothy Cone, "Art and the Law: Regulating the Art Market," *Arts Magazine* 64 (March 1990): 21-22; Arnold H. Lubasch, "U.S. Accuses 4 of High Profits in Fake Dali Art," *New York Times*, October 4, 1988, sec. B.

79. Michael Kimmelman, "The World's Richest Museum: The Getty," *New York Times Magazine*, October 23, 1988, pp. 32-35, 63-67; John Russell, "Annenberg Giving Met $15 Million for Acquisitions," *New York Times*, September 29, 1989, sec. C; Michael Brenson, "Curators Turn to the Deal."

80. Michael Kimmelman, "The Case of the Vanishing Art," *New York Times*, May 14, 1989, sec. B; Hughes, "Sold," p. 61. According to both Susan F. Rasky and Jan M. Rosen, the provisions of the 1986 tax code, which over-tightened rules on the tax treatment of gifts by high-income donors, have been relaxed for art works and manuscripts for one year (Rasky, "Senate Panel Adopts Tax Change on Gifts of Art and Manuscripts," *New York Times*, October 16, 1990, secs. A, B; and Rosen, "Minimum-Tax Provisions Expected to Snare Many," *New York Times*, November 1, 1990, sec. D).

81. Fox Butterfield, "Boston Thieves Loot a Museum of Masterpieces," *New York Times*, March 19, 1990, secs. A, C; Michael Brenson, "Robbers Seem to Know Just What They Want," *New York Times*, March 19, 1990, sec. C; William H. Honan, "Masterpieces: Not Usually Vulnerable or Very Vulnerable Indeed," *New York Times*, March 22, 1990, sec. C; Andrew L. Yarrow, "A Lucrative Crime Grows Into a Costly Epidemic," *New York Times*, March 20, 1990, sec. C; Fox Butterfield, "Boston Museum Says It Was Uninsured for Theft," *New York Times*, March 20, 1990, secs. A, C; Irvin Molotsky, "Little Federal Office Has Big Role in Art Tours," *New York Times*, January 16, 1988; and Glueck, "Mania of Auctions."

82. Michael Kimmelman, "Who Else Painted Bellini's Feast," *New York Times*, January 21, 1990, sec. 2; David Bull and Joyce Plesters, "*The Feast of the Gods*: Conservation, Examination, and Interpretation," *Studies in the History of Art* 40, Monograph Series II; David Park Curry, *Winslow Homer: The Croquet Game* (New Haven: Yale University Art Gallery, 1984). Recently, in "Titian and the Perils of International Exhibition," Francis Haskell has called for museums to stop endangering major works by Old Masters by organizing, and lending too readily to, large traveling exhibitions (*New York Review of Books* 37 [August 1990]: 8-12).

83. Elizabeth Johns, "Histories of American Art: The Changing Quest," *Art Journal* 44 (Winter 1984): 338-44; Richard Guy Wilson, Dianne Pilgrim, and Richard N. Murray, *The American Renaissance, 1876-1917* (Brooklyn, N.Y.: Brooklyn Museum; distributed by Pantheon Books, 1979).

84. Jonathan L. Fairbanks, Robert F. Trent et al., *New England Begins: The Seventeenth Century* 3 vols. (Boston: Museum of Fine Arts, Boston, 1982); *The Great River: Arts & Society in the Connecticut River Valley, 1635-1820* (Hartford: The Atheneum: 1985).

85. Doren Bolger Burke et al., *In Pursuit of Beauty: Americans and the Aesthetic Movement* (New York: Metropolitan Museum of Art; Rizzoli, 1986).

86. Bryan J. Wolf, "Revolution in the Landscape: John Trumbull and Picturesque Painting," in Helen Cooper, ed., *John Trumbull: The Hand and Spirit of a Painter* (New Haven: Yale University Art Gallery, 1982), pp. 206-16.

87. "B. C. Gardener," "Art & Finance: The D-Word: The Only Way Out for Institutions May Be De-Accessioning," *Art & Auction* 12 (April 1990): 124, 126-27; on deaccessioning also see Michael Kimmelman, "The High Cost of Selling Art," *New York Times*, April 1, 1990, sec. 2.

88. England, for one, has such a law which stipulates that anything that has been in Britain for fifty years and is valued at over $27,200 is eligible for such protection (see Michael Kimmelman, "Case of Vanishing Art").

Editorial Note *continued from page 1.*

placed to observe the course of events, and for all its rhetorical flourishes his narrative has the authenticity of personal experience. The striking thing about it is the highly charged expression of identity with the generally reviled Communards, which, as Albert Boime points out in his introduction published in this issue, clearly reflects a distinct political orientation.

Warner's description of street battles is remarkably similar to one written by Thomas Eakins in June 1869 when he was a student in Paris. Eakins held the same strong anticlerical and antimonarchical views so vividly articulated by Warner and when rioting broke out against Louis Napoleon's rule he looked on with fascinated attention.

Last night the cavalry charged on the Boulevard Montmartre and Italians opposite Goupils and a great many people [were] trampled and some killed. The night before it was the same thing . . . at Belleville the workmen ripped open the iron railings and armed themselves with bars of iron and drove back the police. The troops came and scattered them. A Paris crowd is ugly to deal with . . . Friday afternoon. Last night it appears the rioting was very bad. The cavalry again charged down the Boulevard all the way from Goupils to the Madeleine. As the crowd went down with a run, the hind ones getting trampled and sabred, the front ones demolished everything that was breakable, overturned every kiosque and omnibus, and tried to make barricades.

Garnett McCoy

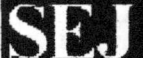

Art Investment: An Empirical Inquiry
Author(s): Bruno S. Frey and Werner W. Pommerehne
Source: *Southern Economic Journal*, Vol. 56, No. 2 (Oct., 1989), pp. 396-409
Published by: Southern Economic Association
Stable URL: http://www.jstor.org/stable/1059218
Accessed: 05/02/2014 13:02

Art Investment: An Empirical Inquiry*

BRUNO S. FREY
University of Zurich
Zurich, Switzerland

WERNER W. POMMEREHNE
Free University of Berlin
Berlin, West Germany

I. A Popular Activity

Investment in art and especially in paintings by the masters is often considered to be highly profitable. Particularly in the United States, but also in the richer European nations, there is an even larger number of investors who believe that buying works of art is not only fun but also a good investment from a purely financial point of view. American banks have recently strengthened this trend toward "art as an investment" by employing "art investment counselors," thus suggesting that it is a financially rewarding activity to engage in, and also suggesting that superior knowledge helps to improve financial success in this market.

Buying and selling art has in fact become an increasingly popular activity since the end of World War II. The auction houses report record turnovers and record prices are paid in increasingly rapid sequence. In April 1987 van Gogh's "Sunflowers" was sold at Christie's London for $39.9 million, only to be surpassed in November 1987 by van Gogh's "Irises", sold by Sotheby's New York for $53.9 million (including the auction house's 10 percent commission). This last painting had been bought by the seller's mother in 1947 for $84,000, less than $0.5 million in today's money, which gives a real rate of return of about 12 percent per year.

These enormous prices that are paid today for some masterpieces create a widespread belief that the rate of return on such investments is in general and on average very high. Books devoted to the subject [40, 385; 27, 24; 12, 215 et seq.] seem to confirm that the rate of return from investment in paintings, at least during the 1950s and 1960s, was far greater than the rate obtainable from comparable risky assets in financial markets. That the financial profitability in the 1970s and 1980s is believed to be, if anything, even larger than before is confirmed by many articles in financial and investment newspapers and journals.

Up to now only very few scientific studies of the subject exist, but they also have serious limitations. The most recent one by Baumol [5] covers a period of over 300 years but ends in 1960. Two other studies by Anderson [1] and Stein [42] extend up to the end of the 1960s but do not go any further. All three studies are practically limited to transactions by Anglo-Saxon auction

---

*The authors are grateful for research assistance by Marina Börkey, Cornelia Haist, Antonia Simon, Angel Serna, Elisabeth Tester, Kai Fürntratt and Alexander Schrader and for helpful comments by George Bittlingwayer, Beat Gygi, Carl-Ludwig Holtfrerich, Jan P. Krahnen, Barbara Krug, Bernd Niquet and Anselm Römer.

houses, i.e., up to about 1920 meaning sales at Christie's and Sotheby's London. Most of the French and German market is thus excluded.

This paper seeks to overcome the limitations and shortcomings of these three studies by (1) covering a period up to 1987, and spanning 350 years; (2) including more countries; (3) taking into account the transaction costs (which may be substantial) involved in buying and selling paintings at auctions, and (4) by checking more carefully the identity and price statements of the paintings bought and sold in different periods. A final, and important purpose is (5) to inquire whether financial profitability of investment in paintings has changed between the periods before and after the last World War.

Section II discusses the peculiarities of calculating a rate of return and risk for investments in paintings. The results are presented in section III, and concluding remarks are offered in section IV.

II. Profitability in the Market for Paintings

In principle, the rate of return and the risk inherent in buying and holding paintings is, of course, calculated in the same way as for investments in financial markets. However, paintings differ significantly from financial assets in various respects.

Prices of paintings bought and sold are not generally available ahead of time; information is restricted to auctions. However, auction prices play an important role in art markets because collectors and professional art dealers take these prices as guideposts.[1]

Returns

We analyze the price development of paintings done by the nearly 800 "best known painters of the world" (only deceased artists), as selected by Reitlinger [37; 38], of whom 305 had at least one painting bought and sold at the well known auction houses Christie's and Sotheby's, as well as at many others in both Europe and North America.[2] Paintings traded in flea markets and the like are excluded because they are not relevant for purely financially oriented investors. The prices chosen for this study refer to paintings of "auctionable quality" only. In addition, paintings with unclear price (e.g., "it is said to have probably been paid," "it is reported to have exceeded . . .") are exluded. As the rate of return is calculated by taking the compound rate of interest resulting from the difference between (gross) buying price and (net) selling price it is important to identify each painting unmistakeably. Whenever there is any doubt, e.g., because the same artist has given the same title to various paintings of equal size, the relevant work has been excluded. This reduced the initial sample of 2070 observations by 133 to 1937 buy/sell transactions.

The rate of return calculated is net of all cost connected with buying and selling a painting in an auction. These transaction costs vary between countries, periods, and prices of the paintings traded, but they are usually substantial. A typical auction fee would amount to more than 10% of the value reached for both buyer *and* seller. In 1985, the sales commission (including indirect

---

1. A more extensive discussion of auction prices is made by Stein [42, 1023–4]. In the meantime, his statement that "very expensive paintings are relatively unlikely to be auctioned" [42, 1024] seems to have been proved untrue as the examples given at the beginning of this paper demonstrate.
2. See the appendix for a more detailed description of the selected sample and the data sources used.

Table I. Real Rates of Return on Paintings, 1635–1987 (in Percent per Year)

mean	1.5
median	1.8
minimum	−19
maximum	+26
standard deviation	5.0
number of buy/sell transactions	1198

taxes) for both sides of the market were at least 18 percent in the United States, 25 percent in the United Kingdom and Switzerland, up to 32 percent in France and about 35 percent in Germany.

In the short run, picture prices exhibit strong ups and downs. As the purpose of our analysis is not short run speculation,[3] we follow the procedure chosen by Baumol [5], that is, we consider only holding periods of 20 years or more. This reduces the sample by 739 to 1198 buy/sell transactions. The reported prices (all expressed in pounds sterling by applying, if necessary, the exchange rate at that time) are then deflated by a price index to transform them into prices of constant purchasing power.

Risks

An investment in the arts market is subject to various kinds of risk beyond the uncertainty of future prices. First, despite all efforts to establish clarity, the attribution problem sometimes remains tricky. An example is Rubens's "Daniel in the Lions' Den," which was auctioned in 1882 for 1,680 pounds by Christie's London, then resold in 1885 for 2,520 pounds. In 1963, having been attributed in the meantime to Jacob Jordaens, it was auctioned for a mere 500 pounds; but in 1965, now acknowledged as a school piece by Rubens, it was acquired by the Metropolitan Museum of Art in New York for 178,600 pounds. Although the attributions of such pictures had changed over time, in all these cases the corresponding transactions nevertheless remained in the sample, because any change in attribution is part of the risk to be taken by the buyer and the seller.

There is a similar problem with fakes and forgeries. Even art experts cannot guarantee that a painting is original. While the technical means for detection continue to improve, the forgers also steadily employ the newest technologies for their purpose. So it has been claimed that there are 8,000 paintings by Camille Corot in the United States alone. This is an astonishing number considering that there are only 3,000 authentic works by that master [17]. The situation is similar for various other painters, in particular for pictures by van Dyck and Utrillo [9; 14]. For the same reason as in the case of a change in attribution, transactions involving fakes and forgeries remained in the sample.

In addition to the financial risks arising from price uncertainty, to changing attributions and fakes and forgery, there is as well a purely material risk: the painting may be destroyed by fire, damaged by war, or stolen. Although during the last two centuries at least most English and American collectors were spared the risk caused by wars and revolutions, art thefts have increased over time as auction prices have risen. Of course, paintings may be insured against some of these material risks; the annual cost of insurance against fire and theft presently amounts to 0.5

---

3. Short run speculation is considered to be financially unprofitable, partly because of the high commission fees and other transaction costs connected with auctions. Therefore Sotheby's recommends strongly that "works of art (be) held for a minimum of 7–10 years to sustain value" [11, 107].

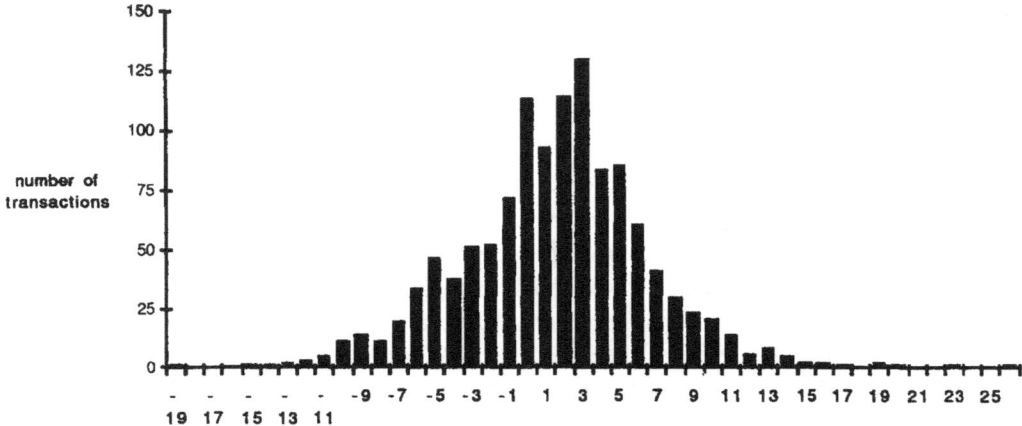

Figure 1. Real Rate of Return on Paintings; Middle of Interval (Percent per Year)

percent of the painting's appraised value on average, with a range between 0.2 percent and 1.0 percent [42, 1028–9; 47], but for earlier periods insurance costs are unknown. Also ignored are the maintenance and restoration costs of paintings, which again are substantial. Nevertheless, although the calculated rates of return on investments in paintings may be biased in the upward direction when the material risk is neglected, in what follows only financial risks are considered.

III. Results

Overall Period 1635–1987

The art auction market does not provide the continuity of data and transactions that would be necessary for an application of sophisticated techniques of analysis.[4] However, a study of less refined aspects is possible, such as an examination of the rates of return on investment in art.

Table I shows a set of measures of central tendency of the rates of return on auctioned paintings with a holding period of 20 years or more at *constant prices* (of 1900).

The mean real rate of return is 1.5 percent per year, and the median rate of return is 1.8 percent. The standard deviation is 5.0. Neglecting transaction costs, the mean rate of return would rise by 0.4 percentage points.

This rate of return seems to be quite low in view of the huge sums that have been paid for paintings. Part of the explanation lies in the representation bias of our memory [26] which leads to too much weight being given to paintings that reach prices that are newsworthy, while the other prices (which most people do not know anyway) receive inadequate weight in an intuitive evaluation. Part of the explanation may also lie simply in the fact that the effects of compound interest and inflation tend to be underrated.

---

4. Such as a test of the so called "diagonal" or "market model" by Jensen [25] and the measurement of the "performance" and the "efficiency" of the market for paintings.

Compared with investment in financial markets the calculated real rate of return on paintings of 1.5 percent per year is rather low. Considering the period from the mid 17th century (due to the twenty year holding period the first resale of pictures occurred after 1650) up to 1987 an investment into best credits, in particular government securities, would have yielded a long term nominal rate of return of 5 percent per year.[5] The rate of price inflation of consumables over the same period is somewhat above 2 percent per year,[6] so that the long term *real* rate of return on financial investment is 3 percent per year. Thus, investing into paintings instead of financial assets implies a (real) opportunity loss of 1.5 percentage points per year for the holder of paintings.[7] This is a sizeable amount: the real rate of return on paintings is half the real return that one could get by buying public securities.

Figure 1 indicates that the financial rates of return on paintings show a large variance: the maximum real rate of return on a painting is as high as 26% per year, which means that the initial value doubles in about two and a half years in real terms. The minimum real return is -19% per year. Of the 1198 buy/sell transactions, 724 or 61 percent yielded a positive real rate of return, 113 or 9 percent nil, and 361 or 30 percent yielded a negative real rate of return. Readers may be interested to know which paintings are among the big winners and losers. The highest real rate of return (26.3 percent per year) in our sample of almost 1,200 transactions was reached by Frans Hal's "Man in Black" which in 1885 was auctioned for a little more than 5 pounds at Christie's London, and in 1913 reached 9,000 pounds at Sotheby's London. There are other pictures by this painter which in this and the last century achieved rates of return of around 10 percent per year. The same applies to paintings by Cézanne, Gauguin, van Gogh, Manet, Matisse, Monet and Renoir, all painters who for obvious reasons are well known to art lovers. It should, however, be noted that in the case of nearly all these painters, there also were transactions with a rather low, and sometimes even negative, real rate of return.

The largest loser in financial terms in our sample with a real rate of return of -19.3 percent

---

5. For the subperiod 1650–1949 the *minimum* nominal rate of return on best credits, including the famous "consols" (with no redemption date), has been calculated from Homer [19, Table 1, 500]. In order to allow a comparison with the activities on the market for paintings the mean rate of return has been compiled as follows: In addition to the United Kingdom and France, from the 18th century Germany has been added, and from the 19th century the United States. The mean minimum rate of return over this period and countries amounts to 3.7 percent per year.

For the more recent period 1950–87 the long run nominal rate of return has been calculated on the basis of data included in *International Financial Statistics* [22, series 61]. The nominal rate amounts to about 7.5 percent per year.

For the overall period 1650–1987, the average long run nominal rate of return on government securities (best credits) is calculated to be 5 percent per year.

6. Based on data collected by Phelps-Brown and Hopkins [35] the average price increase on consumables in the United Kingdom for the period 1635–1949 was a little less than 0.5 percent (0.44 percent) per year in the United Kingdom. The rate of inflation for the period 1950–87 is calculated as an average of the consumer price indices for the four countries, United Kingdom, United States, Germany and France by IMF [23]. The average rate of price increase is 5.1 percent per year. Though these two indices do not conform totally, they allow a feasible deflation procedure. For the overall period 1650–1987 the average rate of price inflation weighted by the share of transactions in each period as before turns out to be 2.1 percent per year.

7. The correct size of the opportunity loss is presumably even larger. In contrast to the calculated rate of return of paintings which tends to be biased in the upward direction, the apparent rate of return on public securities may be considerably biased in the downward direction. One reason is that we apply a conservative long run nominal rate of return for the overall period (see footnote 5). Another, and possibly even more important reason, is that most computations of the rate of return on financial investments—partly those given in Homer, but especially those reported in the *International Financial Statistics*—ignore reinvested yields, whereas such an accounting is implied in the calculation of the continuously compounded rates of return on investment in paintings. Ignoring the interest or dividend yields, as is done, for instance, in Rush [40] and Keen [27], obviously produces an overestimation of the return to paintings relative to the return to government securities.

Table II. Real Rates of Return on Paintings: Levels and Distributions According to Holding Periods, 1635–1987

Holding period (years)	number of buy/sell transactions	rate of return (in percent)				standard deviation
		mean	median	min.	max.	
20–39	493	1.7	2.1	−19	+26	6.3
40–59	286	1.1	1.3	−12	+13	5.0
60–79	165	1.1	1.4	− 9	+12	4.4
80–99	121	1.9	1.9	− 5	+ 8	2.8
100–119	66	1.7	2.0	− 3	+ 6	2.4
120–139	28	2.2	2.6	− 1	+ 5	1.6
140–159	15	1.8	2.2	− 2	+ 4	1.9
160–179	19	1.1	0.8	0	+ 4	1.3
180–199	2	—	1.5	+ 1	+ 2	—
200–219	2	—	2.0	+ 1	+ 3	—
265	1	—	—	+ 2	+ 2	—
Average	1198	1.5	1.8	−19	+26	5.0

per year is John Singer Sargent's oil sketch "San Virgilio" which in 1925 was sold for 7,350 pounds at the Sargent executor sale but in 1952 was auctioned for only 105 pounds at Christie's London. The list of other painters, some of whose works resulted in large real losses, include Sir Lawrence Alma-Tadema, Rosa Bonheur, Carlo Crivelli, William Etty, John Hoppner, William H. Hunt, Joseph Israel, Sir Edwin Landseer, Frederick Lord Leighton, John Martin, Sir John Millais, Jean Marc Nattier, Sir Henry Raeburn, Sir Joshua Reynolds, David Roberts and Constantin Troyon. Most of these are not generally known among art lovers today because they have gone out of fashion. However, this does not mean that there are none among them who have met with increasing interest in the most recent years, resulting in positive real rates of return.

Table II exhibits the real rates of return according to holding periods. It may be seen that large gains and large losses are experienced by those investors with a short holding period. Those keeping a painting between 20 and 39 years, for example, had returns between −19 percent and +26 percent per year, and a standard deviation of 6.3. If, on the other hand, a picture is held for say between 100 and 119 years, the real rates of return are within a much smaller band (−3 to +6 percent), and the standard deviation shrinks to 2.4. The range of earnings narrows as the holding period increases, and approaches around 2 percent per annum.

The empirical evidence presented suggests that for the period 1635–1987 investments in (auctioned) paintings are *not* financially profitable: the real rate of return is clearly lower than a corresponding investment in a financial market. Moreover, the financial risk of investments in paintings, as measured by the standard deviation of the real rate of return (s.d.), is higher than that of investments in financial assets; s.d. is 5.0 for paintings, and 1.7 for best credits (consols). The lower real rate of return of paintings is thus not attributable to a lower risk premium, on the contrary. Our evidence thus suggests that, contrary to what is often claimed, auctionable paintings are not a particularly good financial investment. Rather, consumption benefits of owning a picture which may consist in pure aesthetic pleasure or in the prestige gained, must play a significant role.

The finding that investments in paintings are not financially profitable seems to contradict the observation that *collections* of paintings, such as the one of Thyssen-Bornemisza (near Lugano), have gained enormously in value. However, the sample of collections that one normally knows of is seriously biased: only (financially) successful collections survive while the (financially) unsuccessful ones do not exist any more and are mostly forgotten.[8] These collections are dissipated as the owners or their heirs go bankrupt or are forced to sell. If *all* collections were considered, the successful *and* the unsuccessful ones, it would again show that the monetary rate of return is low, and the financial risk high.

A further factor that tends to bias upwards the rates of return of auctioned paintings is that auction houses have an interest in high turnovers and, for reasons of publicity, in record prices. They are therefore gladly willing to accept works that promise to sell well. On the other hand, they are reluctant to auction paintings whose selling prospects are weak (among other reasons, because the minimum price fixed by the owner is considered to be too high).

Breakdown into Periods

It is often argued that basic conditions on the art market have changed since the last World War because a new type of buyer and collector has entered the market. In order to test whether this proposition holds, the overall period had been broken down into a period of sales and purchases before 1950 (1635–1949), and another period thereafter (1950–1987), wherein the sales at least were affected.[9]

The Period 1635–1949. For the earlier period up to World War II, the average real rate of return on investments in paintings is 1.4 percent per year (the median is 1.7 percent) and the long term nominal rate of interest on best credits (government securities) amounts to about 3.7 percent per year. Since the yearly rate of inflation was about 0.4 percent over this period, an investor in financial assets could have reached an average long run real rate of return of 3.3 percent per year (see footnotes 5 and 6). The opportunity loss of investing into paintings instead of financial assets was 1.9 percentage points per year.

According to the chi-square test, the distribution of the real rates of return on paintings does not correspond to a normal distribution (the empirical $q = 69.3 > q^*(4) = 9.5$, for a confidence level of 95%). The real rates of return on paintings thus do not seem to follow a pure random process,[10] a result which differs from Baumol's finding [5] of a normal distribution for a somewhat different sample over a somewhat different period (1652–1961). Thus, it seems that up to World War II, superior knowledge of art, in particular expert knowledge of paintings, could have helped to achieve a higher return than someone who picked auctioned paintings simply by

---

8. An example is the collection by William Randolph Hearst who, beginning as a young man, spent at least $1 million each year for that purpose. By the end of the thirties, it is estimated that he had spent at least $50 million on his collection. When he was forced to sell a large part of it in November 1938, New York's Parrish-Watson Galleries held an auction which was a failure. The same happened when an auction was held by Marshall Field's in Chicago; less than $200,000 was raised, and considerably more was spent in advertising, salaries and expenses. Finally, the art treasures were offered by the department store Gimbel's in New York, and by the end of 1941 the sales had amounted to $11 million. The objects were offered at large discounts, the most spectacular example being a Spanish Cistercian monastery, built in 1114 by Alphonso VII, King of Castile, for which Hearst payed considerably more than $1 million and which was transported *in toto* to the United States. It was sold for $50,000. For all of this, see the lively account in Hammer [16, ch. 15].

9. A more rigorous test would be to differentiate between the sales and purchases (effected) *before* and *after* 1950. However, with this procedure a substantial proportion of the observations for the later period would drop out owing to the criterion of the minimal holding period of 20 years. The method chosen here is nevertheless meaningful, since in the course of the whole period, there has been a tendency for the average holding period to diminish and for the number of auction sales to increase.

10. The same holds for the overall period 1635–1987 ($q = 48.3 > q^*(4) = 9.5$) and for the period after 1950 ($q = 25.2 > q^*(3) = 7.8$), according to the chi-square test.

chance. However, picture prices are partly influenced by fashions, which cannot be predicted on the basis of an art historian's expertise. Examples of such fashionable painters are El Greco, Vermeer and Turner, who were important in their time but then were practically forgotten, to be rediscovered later and who now would probably be able to reach staggering prices if they were offered for sale. Turner paintings have actually been put up for sale and reached record prices. In 1980, "Juliet and her Nurse" reached $6.4 million at Parke-Bernet's in New York, and in 1984, the "Seascape at Folkestone" was sold for $9.8 million at Sotheby's London. Another example is Jacques Louis David whose group portraits reached huge prices at the beginning of this century but then were largely forgotten. Recently David has met with great interest again. His "Les adieux de Télémaques et Eucharis" painted in 1818 was sold in the mid 1980s for 2.6 million pounds sterling. Examples for receding fashions are artists who were previously highly esteemed but whose work has met with little interest in recent times. Among them are Jean Dominique Ingres, Sir John Everett Millais, William Mulready, Sir William Quiller Orchardson, Adriaen and Isaac van Ostade, Dante Gabriel Rossetti and Frederick William Watts. While such fashions cannot be predicted on the basis of art historians' expertise, they are certainly able to explain *in retrospect* why a certain painter or school of painters wins or loses in appreciation.

Nevertheless, it may be possible to systematically make profits. Those with inside knowledge not available to the general public may have an advantage, similar to those in a normal financial market. Yet this knowledge must especially refer to the future behavior of all other (private and public) potential buyers and sellers, thus going much beyond knowledge about such topics as the quality and scarcity of the works of art involved. Moreover, if a particular investor's expectations with respect to the future behavior of others become important in the market, the equilibrating mechanism in the security but especially in the art market is likely to be very feeble owing to imperfect substitutability, infrequent resales and the monopoly position of the owner (see Henry [18] for a theoretical exposition). Other systematic winners are those who might be able to influence tastes, and thereby create fashions. But so far little or nothing is known of who is in such a position (which may *not* be imitated by other potential investors).[11]

The Period 1950–1987. In the more recent period after World War II, the average real rate of return of investments in paintings (bought before or after 1950) turns out to be 1.6 percent per year (the median is 2.0 percent). A typical investor in the United Kingdom, the United States, Germany or France could get a nominal rate of return on financial assets of about 7.5 percent per year. The average yearly rate of inflation was 5.1 percent, so a financial investor could reap a real return on financial investments of 2.4 percent per year (see again footnotes 5 and 6). The financial opportunity loss in real terms is considerably lower than in the period before 1950, it amounts to 0.7 percentage points per year. (In the period 1650–1949 it was nearly 2 percentage points per year.)

The main reason why investments in paintings have become *relatively* more attractive since World War II presumably does not lie in the fact that paintings would now yield a much higher financial real rate of return: profitability has increased very little, from 1.4 to 1.6 percent per year. The decisive reason why paintings have become a relatively more attractive investment option lies in the fact that the increasing rate of inflation (from 0.5 percent before 1950 to over 5 percent

---

11. This also holds for the argument that art dealers create among themselves a monopolistic sector by forming a dealer ring. By colluding they would then be able to systematically influence auction prices. However, such collusion is unlikely to be effective. First, incentives exist to break out of a cartel. Second, the owners as well as the auction houses may react by establishing "reserve price" or "buy back" strategies. It is therefore not surprising that no empirical evidence exists for successful collusions and persisting monopolistic positions in the long run.

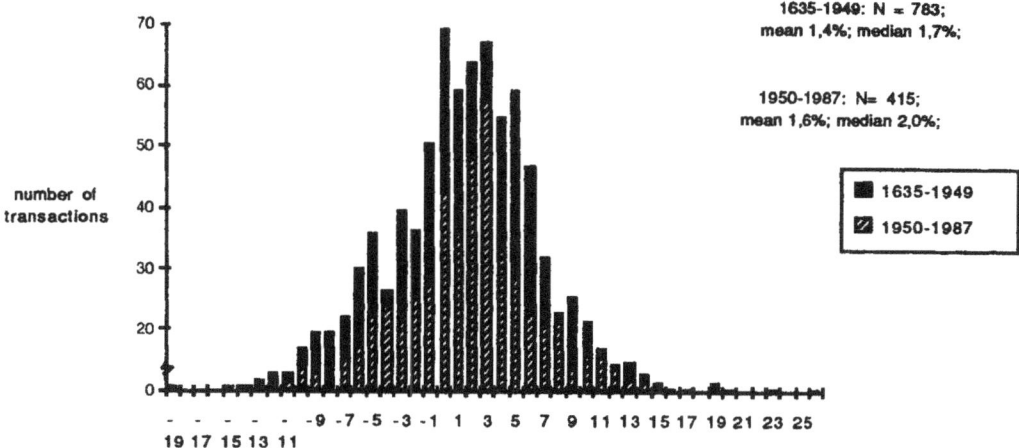

Figure 2. Real Rate of Return on Paintings; Middle of Interval (Percent per Year)

per year after 1950) has not been accompanied by a corresponding increase in nominal rates of interest on long term credits,[12] with the result that such investments have become less attractive (the real return fell from 3.3 to 2.4 percent per year).

Comparison between the Two Periods. Figure 2 compares the distribution of real returns in the two periods. According to the chi-square test (at a confidence level of 95%), the two distributions belong to the same basic distribution (the empirical $q = 9.5 < q^*(6) = 12.6$). This suggests that the profitability of investing in paintings has not *significantly* changed from the pre-war to the post-war period.

Table III indicates in greater detail that conditions in the period since 1950 were indeed somewhat more favorable from the financial point of view. Not only is the real rate of return a little higher (by 0.3 percentage points) but the standard deviation is also smaller. However, the maximum losses were larger, and the maximum gains were smaller, than before 1950. A somewhat larger share of transactions (63 compared to 59 percent) yielded a positive return.

These findings confirm that it is unwarranted to speak of a sizeable rise in the financial profitability of investments into paintings in more recent times, compared with the long run trend. The real rate of return of 1.6 percent per year is slightly higher than before 1950 (and financial risk is not substantially lower), but this return still lies considerably below the return of a corresponding investment in the financial market.

Comparison with Previous Studies

It is not possible to directly compare this study with those by Anderson [1] and Stein [42]. Not only do the periods differ, but also the methodological approach. However, the conclusions are the same: both authors find that the real rate of return in paintings is considerably lower than in financial markets. Anderson calculates for the period 1780–1970 that the average nominal rate of return is 3.3 percent per annum which is roughly half as high as the return for financial assets. The

12. Econometric tests of the Fisher-effect confirm this almost unanimously [43; 50; 31; 3]. The same result is reached for a sample of European countries and the post-war period e.g., by Granziol and Schelbert [15].

Table III. Real Rates of Return of Paintings before and after 1950

Period	number of buy/sell transactions	real rate of return (in percent per year)						standard deviation
		mean	median	positive	zero	negative	min.	max.
Sales and purchases between								
1635 and 1949	783	1.4	1.6	463 (59%)	73 (9%)	247 (32%)	−15	+26	5.3
1950 and 1987	415	1.6	2.0	261 (63%)	40 (10%)	114 (27%)	−19	+16	4.7

Table IV. Comparison of Studies

Authors	period	number of buy/sell transactions	real rate of return (%)			
			mean	median	min.	max.
Baumol	1652–1961	640	0.6	0.8	−19	+27
Present study	1635–1987	1198	1.5	1.8	−19	+26

standard deviation of the rate of return is 56 percent and 12 percent, respectively. Stein estimates a nominal rate of return of 10.5 percent per year for the period 1946–1968 which compares to 14.3 percent in financial assets over the same period. In real terms, a representative investor lost 1.6 percent per year compared to financial assets. He also finds that the prices for paintings exhibit considerably higher fluctuations, suggesting that this form of investment is more risky than in financial markets.

Baumol [5] uses the same approach as that employed here. Table IV compares his results with those derived in this paper.

The real rate of return of 0.6 percent per year computed by Baumol for the shorter period 1652–1961 is roughly one percentage point smaller than the one reached in the present study (both mean and median). The author takes as a representative financial asset the safest securities of the British government with a nominal yearly rate of return of approximately 3.25 percent for the period. The average rate of inflation is taken to be less than 0.7 percent per year. The resulting real rate of return over these 309 years amounts to about 2.5 percent per year. A representative investor in paintings has therefore experienced an opportunity loss of nearly 2 percent per year: this corresponds to our calculations of an opportunity loss of 1.5 percent per year (for the more extended period). It is remarkable that Baumol also finds very similar maximum losses and gains to ours. In his study, 40 percent of the real returns turned out to be negative, while in this study it is 30 percent.

Despite the small deviations in results (which may be due to the differences in periods and countries covered, as well as in the particular paintings included) the results of the four studies come to the same general conclusion: investments in paintings are not financially lucrative. They yield a smaller real rate of return and are exposed to higher financial risk than investments in financial assets.

A unique feature of our study is the result that in recent times it has become relatively more attractive to invest in paintings than in the period before. None of the studies existing up to now has dealt with the often heard proposition that art investment has become more profitable in the postwar years because, so it is claimed, new groups of buyers have entered the market.

IV. Concluding Remarks

A relatively more risky asset (as paintings) should yield a higher rate of return in order to compensate the owner for risktaking, compared to a less risky asset (financial assets). However, the result reached by all scientific studies undertaken so far (including the present one) shows that the real monetary rate of return of paintings lies *below* that of financial assets. This suggests that paintings yield not only a financial but also a psychic reward, or a consumption benefit.[13] There are reasons to assume that the low rate of return on investments in paintings may even be biased upwards, not only because of the already mentioned cost of maintenance, restoration and insurance (here left out of account), but also because of the *inherent selection bias*: in general only successful art is repeatedly auctioned.

Our results suggest that investments in paintings have become *relatively* more profitable in the postwar years compared with the period 1650–1949, which is attributed to the damaging effect of inflation on financial assets, and not to any significant increase of the real rate of return of paintings. Provided this relationship continues to hold in the future, a decline in inflation to historical levels should reestablish the long run real financial opportunity loss from holding paintings of about 1.5 percent per year. A fall in inflation should thus make investments in financial assets more attractive compared with paintings from the financial point of view.

Although our main conclusion is that the rate of return of investments in paintings is not nearly as large as is generally believed, we should note that there are several reasons why individuals may rationally choose this form of investment: provided (1) the owner derives a sufficiently high psychic benefit from looking at the objects, investments in paintings are a reasonable endeavor; (2) paintings are legally or *de facto* only partially, or not at all, subject to property tax or death duties; and (3) buying pictures and after some time giving them to public museums may allow a net reduction of the individual's tax burden. These tax aspects differ considerably between countries and periods, so that little can be said in general.

Appendix: Data Sources

Our analysis is based on the works of "the best known painters of the world" selected by Reitlinger [37; 38] in his compendium of auction sales of art works. He considers deceased artists only, that is, the number of paintings produced in each case is given and quite well known. Therefore, a limited number of intrusions of fakes and forgeries aside, the elasticity of production or supply is zero.[14] These "noted works of noted artists" are the main object of financial investments in paintings.

The selection made by Reitlinger is obviously subjective. There is no way to determine objectively,

---

13. Stein [42, 1029] takes as an upper-bound estimate of the return from viewing services the rental rates in the art-rental market. According to his information, it averages 11 percent p.a. of the appraised value (net). This very high figure may be biased upwards because the clients of art-rental firms are mostly corporations for which such expenses are tax deductable (while buying is not necessarily so).

14. The situation for less well known or lesser artists is somewhat different. If the popularity of pictures from one of these authors strongly increases, there is an incentive to search for his or her works in attics and cellars with the result that the market supply may be strongly increased.

once and for all, who is a "noted" artist, as such evaluations tend to change over time. Nevertheless, de Piles's [36, 489 et seq.] evaluation of the most important living and dead artists of his—he was the advisor of the art-loving Cardinal Richelieu—time corresponds, in 41 out of 55 cases, with Reitlinger's selection. An even stronger correspondence is found with Vasari's [45] evaluation of the leading Italian painters: all but three of the 35 painters there mentioned are also included in Reitlinger.

Building on a vast amount of material collected by other scholars and an extensive own search of auction results, Reitlinger lists the prices paid for each transaction where available. In most cases they refer to auctions held in London because "until 1920 or thereabouts this means with few exceptions sales at Christie's" [37, 242]. This statement, however, is not quite true. Even in the eighteenth and nineteenth centuries a significant proportion of auctions dealing with paintings took place on the European continent, especially in Paris, but also in the Netherlands and in Germany. Reitlinger's sample has therefore been extended by us to cover the results of several thousand auctions on the Continent which could be drawn from the German and French literature and corresponding listings.[15] The period from the mid 1960s up to the present is based mostly on the *Art Price Annual* [48; 49; 21; 10; 20], where roughly 1000 of the most important auctions the world over are listed for each year.

Among the auction results thus collected all those have been chosen where the same painting has changed hands at least twice over the period of roughly 350 years. The average number of transactions for all paintings is 2.5 over the period as a whole; in particular cases a painting has been auctioned up to eight times. After eliminating inconsistent and doubtful cases, these multiple sales and the corresponding prices are used to calculate the continuous compound rate of return for each painting for the period between successive transactions.[16]

The calculation of commission fees and possible (sales) taxes for the seller and/or buyer presented considerable difficulties. For past centuries the literature is rather mute on this question. The few hints have been amended by comparing gross and net sales figures for the buyer and seller in the various countries, for the various auction houses and for the different price levels of the objects traded (which was and still is of particular importance in France). The real rates of return including auction costs and (sales) taxes have been compared with the corresponding rates of return disregarding transaction costs and taxes. It turns out that such additional costs are important for relatively short holding periods of say seven to ten years, but that they are not of much importance for the minimal holding period of 20 years used in our study.

---

15. Of particular help were Smith's [41] "*Catalogue raisonné*" of Flemish, Dutch and French paintings, Blanc's [6] 'Trésor de la curiosité', a collection of auction results of Parisian auction houses extending over one century, and Mühsam [33], Fourastié [13] and Rheims [39]. For Germany, Austria and Switzerland in former times, the works by Koch [28], Brieger [7], Mühsam [32], Bröker [8], Wilm [51] and numerous volumes of the "*Klassiker der Kunst*" were useful. For the first part of this century we relied on Manzl [29], Jaquet [24], Wagenführ [46], Müller-Mehlis [34] and Baumeister [4]. Helpful were also the collection of auction results by E. Mayer [30], by Art Trade Press [2], by Van Braan and Romeny [44] and in specialized journals such as *Connoisseur, Apollo, Burlington's Magazine*, etc.

16. This rate of return has been computed from the standard continuous compounding formula $p_t = p_o \exp r(t - t_o)$, where p refers to the auction prices, index $t(t_o)$ to the year of selling (buying) the picture, and r being the compounded rate of return to be calculated.

References

1. Anderson, Robert C., "Paintings as an Investment." *Economic Inquiry*, March 1974, 13–26.
2. Art Trade Press, ed. *Art Prices Current*. London: Art Trade Press, various years (since 1907).
3. Barsky, Robert B., "The Fisher Hypothesis and the Forecastability and Persistence of Inflation." *Journal of Monetary Economics*, January 1987, 3–24.
4. Baumeister, Peter. "Die Auktion: Zur Preisbildung für Seltenheitsgüter im Versteigerungsgewerbe." Ph.D. Dissertation, University of Mannheim, 1974.
5. Baumol, William J., "Unnatural Value or Art Investment as Floating Crap Game." *American Economic Review, Papers and Proceedings*, May 1986, 10–16.
6. Blanc, Charles. *Le trésor de la curiosité, tiré des catalogues de ventes*, 2 vols. Paris: Vve Renouard, 1857–58.
7. Brieger, Lothar. *Das Kunstsammeln: Eine kurze Einführung in seine Theorie und Praxis*. Munich: Delphin, 1918.

8. Bröker, Josef. "Die Preisgestaltung auf dem modernen Kunstmarkt." Ph.D. Dissertation, University of Munster, 1928.

9. Cole, Sonia M. *Counterfeit*. London: John Murray, 1955.

10. Damrich, N., Honnef, K., König, H. Josef, Madlener, Ch., Weber, I. S. and S. Wolf, eds. *Art-Price Annual/Kunstpreisjahrbuch/Les beaux-arts du monde*. Munich: Weltkunst, since 1985.

11. Dawson, Eileen, "The Art of Investment." *Far Eastern Economic Review*, January 1987, 105–6.

12. Faith, Nicholas. *Sold: The Revolution in the Art Market*. London: Hamish Hamilton, 1985.

13. Fourastié, Jean. *Prix de vente et prix de revient, 14 vols.* Paris: Montchrestien, 1954–61.

14. Graner, Walter, ed. *Antiquitäten als Kapitalanlage*. Munich: Heyne, 1976.

15. Granziol, Markus and Heidi Schelbert, "Ex ante Real-Zinssätze am Euromarkt." *Zeitschrift für Wirtschafts- und Sozialwissenschaft*, 1983, 437–59.

16. Hammer, Armand. *Hammer*. New York: Putnam's Sons, 1987.

17. Harris, R. "The Forgery of Art." *New Yorker*, 1961, 112–45.

18. Henry, Claude, "Indivisibilités dans une économie d'échanges." *Econometrica*, May 1970, 542–58.

19. Homer, Sidney. *A History of Interest Rates*, 2nd ed. New Brunswick: Rutgers University Press, 1977.

20. Honnef, K., Honnef-Harling, G., von Kern, G., Kliesch-Groh, G., König, H. Josef, Madlener, Ch. and S. Wolf, eds. *Art-Price Annual/Kunstpreisjahrbuch/Les beaux-arts du monde*. Munich: Weltkunst, 1987.

21. ———, König, H. Josef, Madlener, Ch., Weber, I. S. and S. Wolf, eds. *Art-Price Annual/Kunstpreisjahrbuch/Les beaux-arts du monde*. Munich: Weltkunst, 1984.

22. IMF (International Monetary Fund), ed. *International Financial Statistics*. Washington, D.C.: IMF, various years (since 1948).

23. ———, ed. *Supplement on Price Statistics*. Washington, D.C.: IMF, various years (since 1975).

24. Jaquet, Christian. *Werte und Preise auf dem Weltmarkt neuzeitlicher Kunst*. Winterthur: Keller, 1962.

25. Jensen, Michael C., "Capital Markets: Theory and Evidence." *Bell Journal of Economics*, Autumn 1972, 357–98.

26. Kahneman, Daniel; Slovic, Paul and Amos Tversky. *Judgement under Uncertainty: Heuristics and Biases*. Cambridge and New York: Cambridge University Press, 1982.

27. Keen, Geraldine. *The Sale of Works of Art: A Study Based on the Times-Sotheby Index*. London: Nelson, 1971.

28. Koch, Guenther. *Kunstgewerbe und Bücher am Markt*. Esslingen: Paul Neff, 1915.

29. Manzl, Franz. "Eine Untersuchung über die Preisbildung im Kunsthandel." Ph.D. Dissertation, University of Vienna, 1956.

30. Mayer, E. *Annuaire international des ventes: peinture-sculpture*. Paris: Editions Mayer various years (since 1963).

31. Moosa, S. A., "Inflation, Non-Neutral Growth, Equity-Yields and the Fisher Hypothesis." *Applied Economics*, February 1986, 237–47.

32. Mühsam, Kurt. *Die Kunstauktion*. Berlin: Verlag für Kunstwissenschaft, 1923.

33. ———. *Internationales Lexikon der Preise von Gemälden und Handzeichnungen aller Schulen und Länder*. Berlin: E. Reiss, 1925.

34. Müller-Mehlis, Reinhard. *Kunst und Antiquitäten als Geldanlage*. Munich: Moderne Industrie, 1967.

35. Phelps-Brown, E. H. and Sheila Hopkins, "Seven Centuries of the Prices of Consumables." *Economica*, November 1956, 296–314.

36. Piles, Roger de. *Cours de peinture par principes*. Paris: Jacques Estienne, 1708.

37. Reitlinger, Gerald. *The Economics of Taste, Vol. I; The Rise and Fall of Picture Prices 1760–1960*. London: Barrie and Rockliff, 1961.

38. ———. *The Economics of Taste, Vol. III; The Art Market in the 1960s*. London: Barrie and Jenkins, 1970.

39. Rheims, Maurice. *La vie étrange des objets*. Paris: Plon, 1959.

40. Rush, Richard. *Art as an Investment*. Englewood Cliffs: Prentice Hall, 1961.

41. Smith, John. *Catalogue raisonné of the Works of the most eminent Dutch, Flemish and French Painters, 9 vols.* London: Smith & Son, 1829–42.

42. Stein, John P., "The Monetary Appreciation of Paintings." *Journal of Political Economy*, August 1977, 1021–35.

43. Summers, Lawrence H. "The Nonadjustment of Nominal Interest Rates: A Study of the Fisher Effect," in *Macroeconomics, Prices on Quantities, Essays in Honor of Arthur M. Okun*, edited by James Tobin. Oxford: Basil Blackwell, 1983, 201–34.

44. Van Braan, Fred A. and A. H. Romeny, ed. *World Collectors Annuary, Vols. 1–3*. Delft and Amsterdam, 1949–51.

45. Vasari, Giorgio. *Le vite de' più eccelenti architetti, pittori e scultori italiani*, 2nd ed. Florence: Giuntini, 1568.

46. Wagenführ, Horst. *Kunst als Kapitalanlage*. Stuttgart: Forkel, 1965.

47. Wellenmeyer, M., "The Money In Old Furniture." *Fortune*, November 1972, 65–6.

48. Wellensiek, Hertha and Robert Keyszelitz, eds. *Art-Price Annual/Kunstpreisjahrbuch/Les beaux-arts du monde*. Munich: Kunst und Technik, various years (since 1945).

49. ——, König, H. Josef and S. Wolf, eds., *Art-Price Annual/Kunstpreisjahrbuch/Les beaux-arts du monde*. Munich: Weltkunst, various years (since 1982).

50. Wilcox, James M., "Why Real Interest Rates Were So Low in the 1970s." *American Economic Review*, March 1983, 44–53.

51. Wilm, Hubert. *Kunstsammler und Kunstmarkt*. Munich: Hugo Schmid, 1930.

American Economic Association

Unnatural Value: Or Art Investment as Floating Crap Game
Author(s): William J. Baumol
Source: *The American Economic Review*, Vol. 76, No. 2, Papers and Proceedings of the Ninety-Eighth Annual Meeting of the American Economic Association (May, 1986), pp. 10-14
Published by: American Economic Association
Stable URL: http://www.jstor.org/stable/1818726
Accessed: 05/02/2014 13:04

Your use of the JSTOR archive indicates your acceptance of the Terms & Conditions of Use, available at
http://www.jstor.org/page/info/about/policies/terms.jsp

JSTOR is a not-for-profit service that helps scholars, researchers, and students discover, use, and build upon a wide range of content in a trusted digital archive. We use information technology and tools to increase productivity and facilitate new forms of scholarship. For more information about JSTOR, please contact support@jstor.org.

American Economic Association is collaborating with JSTOR to digitize, preserve and extend access to *The American Economic Review*.

ECONOMIC ISSUES IN THE ARTS†

Unnatural Value: or Art Investment as Floating Crap Game

By WILLIAM J. BAUMOL*

I shall suggest on the basis of a priori considerations and several centuries of price data that in the market for the visual arts, particularly the works of noted creators who are no longer living, there may exist no equilibrium level, so that the prices of such art objects may be strictly *un*natural in the classical sense. Their prices can float more or less aimlessly and their unpredictable oscillations are apt to be the exacerbated by the activities of those who treat such art objects as "investments," and who, according to the data, earn a real rate of return very close to zero on the average. If the art marketing process really is inherently rudderless, the imperfection of the available information on prices and transactions does not matter in the sense that better information about the behavior of the market really would not help anyone to make decisions more effectively.

I. Supply Response: The Pricing Anchor for Manufactures

The art market contrasts sharply with those for manufactured products, such as steel bolts or ball bearings, in terms of determinancy of equilibrium price level. There the key to equilibration is responsiveness of supply. If, for example, a manufactured product's current market price happens to be well above its equilibrium level, as the text books tell us, capital will flow into the production of the overpriced commodity, its output will be increased and its price driven downward. Thus the equilibrium price comes equipped with a powerful magnet capable of attracting actual market prices to it.

It is this mechanism that imparts value to pertinent information, for data on costs, on the nature of demand, and on the cost of capital are of value primarily because they help the observer to evaluate the equilibrium price, which is of practical interest *only* if there exist reliable forces pulling the actual prices in its direction.

II. The Unanchored Prices of Noted Works of Art

We may well suspect, in contrast with the manufacturing case, that the equilibration process will be considerably weakened in a market where elasticity of supply is absolutely zero, as it is in the market for the noted works of noted but deceased artists (an occasional intrusion of forgeries aside).[1] One may even surmise that, as in stock prices, the market values of such works of art will exhibit random behavior.

Indeed, there are several distinctions between the workings of the securities and arts markets, all of which suggest that an equilibration mechanism is likely to be more feeble in the latter.

First, the inventory of a particular stock is made up of a large number of homogeneous securities, all perfect substitutes for one

---

†*Discussants*: William S. Hendon, *Journal of Cultural Economics*; Harold Horowitz, National Endowment for the Arts; Virginia Lee Owen, Illinois State University.

*Princeton University, 108 Dickinson Hall, Princeton, NJ 08542, and New York University. I should like to express my deep gratitude to the C.V. Starr Center for Applied Economics for its generous support of the research underlying this paper. I am heavily indebted to Michael Goldberg for his analysis of the price data, and to Michael Montias for his very valuable comments, though some differences in views remain between us.

[1] I deal here with noted works by noted artists because the markets for the products of what are considered minor schools work very differently. As Montias has pointed out, a sudden rise in the popularity of such a group can elicit a flow of their works from attics and basements, thereby rapidly expanding their available supply.

another. Widely known paintings and sculptures are unique, and even two works on the same theme by a given artist are imperfect substitutes.

Second, a given stock is held by many individuals who are potentially independent traders on the near perfectly competitive stock market. The owner of a Cranach or a Caravaggio holds what may be interpreted as a monopoly on that work of art.

Third, transactions in a given stock take place frequently, indeed, almost continuously. The resale of a given art object may not even occur once in a century.

Fourth, the price at which a stock is exchanged is, generally, public information. The price at which an art work is acquired is frequently known only to the parties immediately involved. While, as I will argue, the availability of such information is not so helpful as is sometimes believed, it surely is unlikely to impede equilibration.

Finally, in the case of a stock we know, at least in principle, what its "true" (equilibrium) price should be—it is the stock's pro rata share of the discounted present value of the company's expected stream of future earnings. But, for a work of art, who would dare to claim to know the true equilibrium price? Distorting Oscar Wilde to my purposes, even those critics who claim to know the value of everything may know the true price of nothing.

In these circumstances it seems implausible that art markets possess anything like long-run equilibrium prices, let alone that there exist reliable forces that drive market prices toward them.

III. On the Economic Value of Art Market Information

Those economists who helped to achieve it are proud of their role in the unbundling of the services of stock brokers, in good part because, as a result, the securities purchaser is no longer required to pay for research which most economists consider to be useless to the investor. If stock prices do indeed approximate random walks, as the evidence strongly indicates, then there is little that information can do to improve estimates of future prices, the key forecast for the purchaser of stocks.

But, if art prices are no more orderly than the prices of stocks, and perhaps even considerably less so, how can data on past activity in the art market conceivably serve as a portent for the future? If stock market research is worthless for the stock market investor; if the stock purchaser can select as well by throwing darts at the financial pages as by following the advice of professional analysts (see, for example, Burton Malkiel, 1973), how much better off can the investor in art hope to emerge with the aid of similar data on art sales with all their warts and blemishes, or even with the help of someone who conducts some sort of "analysis" of those data, perhaps on the lines of the fundamental or technical approaches fashionable among stock market analysts?

IV. Some Data and their Rate of Return Implications

While data on the art market are woefully incomplete and even those that are available are not easy to come by, there exists a remarkable source which permits analysis going beyond anything I have encountered in the literature. In one book of a three-volume set, Gerald Reitlinger (1961) provides an extensive compendium of the sales of art works by "...the best known painters of the world,"[2] extending over more than five centuries. A price is given for each reported sale, which seems to include every transaction involving the work of a painter on Reitlinger's list for which price data are known to be recorded. As the author describes it, "unless otherwise stated, the items refer to London sales. Until 1920 or thereabouts this means with few exceptions sales at Christie's" (p. 242).

---

[2] It is a noteworthy comment on the haphazard fluctuation of tastes that in the same passage in which Reitlinger ponders on the curiously long period during which Vermeer was ignored, he justifies his inclusion of Turner by the fact that he was a "...Monarch...in the salesroom of [his] day and a very curious chapter in the history of taste, which is so often the history of bad taste" (p. 241).

The art market simply does not provide the continuous data or even the continuous transactions that would be required for a systematic analysis of sophisticated issues such as a random walk hypothesis. However, analysis of simpler issues remains possible. Specifically, I will turn now to examination of the rate of return on investment in art.

Of the thousands of sales recorded between pages 241 and 506 of Reitlinger's book, there are a substantial number of cases in which a given work of art was resold two times and more during a 300-year period. We compiled a complete list of such multiple sales and their prices, and sought to determine what range of rates of return the investor could have hoped for during this period.

Specifically, the following procedure was employed: from the complete list of multiple sales we eliminated all cases in which an interval of less than 20 years intervened between the sales. Approximately 25 listings involved some inconsistencies and were eliminated. In another 25 or so, there were no firm price figures but only word of mouth financial information, and they too were eliminated.

This left us with a total of 640 transactions extending from 1652 to 1961. The reported prices were then deflated by a price index to transform them into pounds of constant purchasing power. For the years 1652 to 1952, the E. H. Phelps-Brown and Sheila Hopkins (1956) index of the prices of consumables was employed. For the period 1955–61, deflation was carried out using the International Monetary Fund Consumer Price Index (1979). The two indices, of course, do not match perfectly but permit a workable deflation procedure.

Finally, from these deflated figures, rate of return figures were calculated for each painting for the period between adjacent transactions. These were calculated from the standard continuous compounding formula $y_t = y_0 e^{r(t-t_0)}$. From these a set of measures of central tendency, that is, the mean, median, standard deviation, etc. were determined and a histogram of the observations was prepared. Let us, then, see what these showed.

V. Results

As a standard of reference it should be noted that, apart from the time of the Napoleonic wars and a few other episodes that were relatively brief, the rate of inflation during the period that encompasses our data was extraordinarily low by current standards. Indeed, by and large the nineteenth century can be characterized as a period of deflation. Over the 300-year span containing our cases, the Phelps-Brown and Hopkins price index rose at an average rate less than 0.7 percent per year. At the same time, according to Sidney Homer (1977), the rate of interest on the safest securities of the British government ranged from a high of some 6 percent near 1800 during the Napoleonic wars, to a low of about 2.25 percent during the Victorian "great depression" of the 1890's in Britain. These include the famous "consols" which have no redemption date and which, literature recounts, were the mainstay of Victorian widows or surviving spinster daughters from financially comfortable families. Probably about 3.25 percent was a representative nominal rate of return for the period, providing a real return of, perhaps, 2.5 percent.

Now it should be recognized that ownership of a painting is a risky affair, aside from whatever financial uncertainty may be involved. A painting can be stolen or destroyed in a fire. English collectors after the restoration were spared the risk caused by wars and revolution (though the affair of the '45 glamorized by "Bonnie Prince Charlie" may have seemed rather a near thing at the time). Yet, London had undergone its great fire in 1666 which left, perhaps, one-fifth of the walled city intact, and organized firefighting techniques only arose well into the nineteenth century. The implication is that whatever the apparent rate of return the ownership of a painting yields, a substantial risk premium must be deducted from the figure to get at the true underlying rate of return.

In addition, the sales commissions charged by the sales agent should of course be subtracted from an art work's resale price in

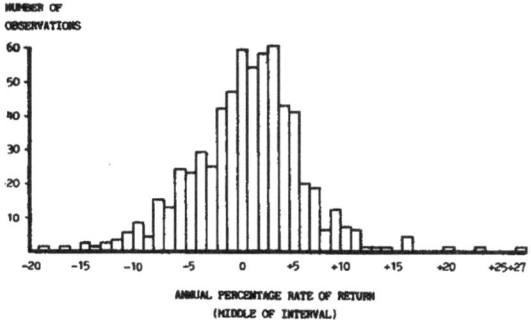

FIGURE 1

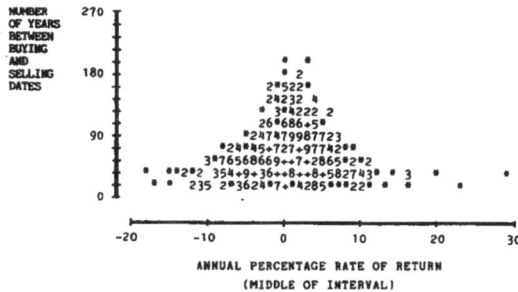

FIGURE 2

Note: Each point is plotted with an asterisk. When more than one point falls on the same plotting position, a count of the number of points falling there is given. When more than nine points fall on the same plotting position, the + symbol is given.

order to evaluate the true rate of return to the investor. Having no data on such selling fees in earlier centuries, we made no attempt to carry out the required subtraction. As a result of the omission of this adjustment as well as that of the risk premium, our calculated rates of return are undoubtedly over-evaluations.

With these observations in mind, what do our data show? To come to the central point they show that, on the average, the purchase and subsequent resale of a painting (making no allowance) for sales commissions, maintenance costs, etc.) brought an annual compounded rate of return of 0.55 percent in real terms. The median was somewhat higher: 0.85 percent. These returns are obviously far from princely. In comparison with government securities they imposed an opportunity loss upon the holder of the painting of close to two percentage points per year. That is, the rate of return on a median painting was about one-third as high as that on a government security, and the average return was only about one-sixth of the latter.

Not only were rates of return on painting as investment remarkably low, they were also remarkably dispersed, meaning that this form of investment was quite risky. Figure 1 is a histogram showing the frequency distribution of the rates of return on resales of paintings. We see that there are cases with compounded rates of return as high as 27 percent per year and others as low as −19 percent per year. In more than 40 percent of the cases returns were negative, and about 60 percent of the cases incurred an opportunity loss in the sense that they returned less than the real yield of government securities.

It may be noted that Figure 1 bears a remarkable resemblance to a normal probability distribution. This conjecture derived support from a Kolmogorov-Smirnov test of the divergence of our observed distribution from a normal distribution. Our calculation showed that the hypothesis that the two distributions are the same could not be rejected at the 0.05 percent confidence level. To that degree we can indeed conclude that art prices do behave randomly.

Figure 2 shows another attribute of our observations. The vertical axis represents length of time that elapsed between the purchase and sale of an art work, while the horizontal axis shows annual rate of return. The graph indicates that large gains or losses are experienced only by persons who hold works for a *relatively* brief period (say, less than fifty years) while as the holding period increases beyond that the range of earnings narrows and approaches very close to zero. This is, of course, what one should expect in a random process whose mean is approximately zero.

VI. More on the Possibility of Profiting Through Knowledge

It is tempting, after looking at the preceding results and the Reitlinger data, to conclude that investment in art is indeed perilous, but that it is dangerous primarily for the amateur who does not know what he is doing. According to this view, people who understand art, who can foresee what works will emerge triumphant from the test of time, can surely do better. Particularly the professionals who have devoted their lives to art can expect to outperform the amateur who ventures into purchasing with the temerity derived from ignorance.

Dispassionate judgement of such contentions can only give rise to skepticism. First of all, the notion that professionals are better than amateurs as prophets of price in anchorless markets is certainly belied by the well-documented performance of stock market analysts.

Beyond the caution with which the analogy with the stock market should imbue us, the evidence of the history of art connoisseurship provides strong warnings of its own. It tells us that the main lesson imparted by the test of time is the fickleness of taste whose meanderings defy prediction. Vermeer, as we know, virtually disappeared from sight for several centuries, only to be resurrected as a producer of works of the most priceless variety. El Greco is another modern rediscovery. Turner, who for a while was a leader of the British art world, is said later to have become an embarrassment to the Tate gallery because of the large collection of his works stored in their cellars; though they are now among the most valued items in the museum's collection. The pre-Raphaelites are "in" once more. Reitlinger's list of painters contains many unrecognizable names such as Wouverman, Berchem, and Van Ostade, who once were anxiously sought after but who were all but forgotten when Reitlinger wrote. Apparently some of them have again become more fashionable. Who knows if that will happen to others and, if so, when that will occur?

It is true, of course, that the profitable investments in our sample were made by those who purchased Vermeers, Turners, and pre-Raphaelites when they were not à la mode, and the heavy losers were the early buyers of Berchem, Van Ostade, and their ilk. But that is only to say that a winner is a winner and a loser is a loser. It is, perhaps, a helpful observation to the art historian, whose very legitimate metier is an exercise in hindsight. It is, however, no help to those who would foresee the future in making art purchases for investment. Only those critics who have succeeded as instruments for the redirection of general tastes seem really to have been in a position to profit from their judgement.

VII. Concluding Comment

I have argued here that if prediction as applied to stock prices is a losing game, it is certainly unlikely to be a winner in the market for works of art. Of course, none of this implies that people should desist from the ownership of art works. It may well represent a very rational choice for those who derive a high rate of return in the form of aesthetic pleasure. They should not, however, let themselves be lured into the purchase of art by the illusion that they can beat the game financially and select with any degree of reliability the combination of purchase dates and art works that will produce a rate of return exceeding the opportunity cost of their investment.

REFERENCES

Homer, Sidney, *A History of Interest Rates*, 2nd ed., New Brunswick: Rutgers University Press, 1977.

Malkiel, Burton G., *A Random Walk Down Wall Street*, New York: W. W. Norton, 1973.

Phelps-Brown, E. H. and Hopkins, Sheila, "Seven Centuries of the Prices of Consumables," *Economica*, November 1956, 23, 296–314.

Reitlinger, Gerald, *The Economics of Taste: The Rise and Fall of the Picture Market, 1760–1960*, New York: Holt, Reinhart and Winston, 1961.

International Monetary Fund, *1949–1978 International Statistics Yearbook*, Washington, D.C., 1979.

Cotemporary American Art as an Investment
Author(s): Evelyn Marie Stuart
Source: *Fine Arts Journal*, Vol. 35, No. 4 (Apr., 1917), pp. 243-257
Published by:
Stable URL: http://www.jstor.org/stable/25603517
Accessed: 05/02/2014 13:05

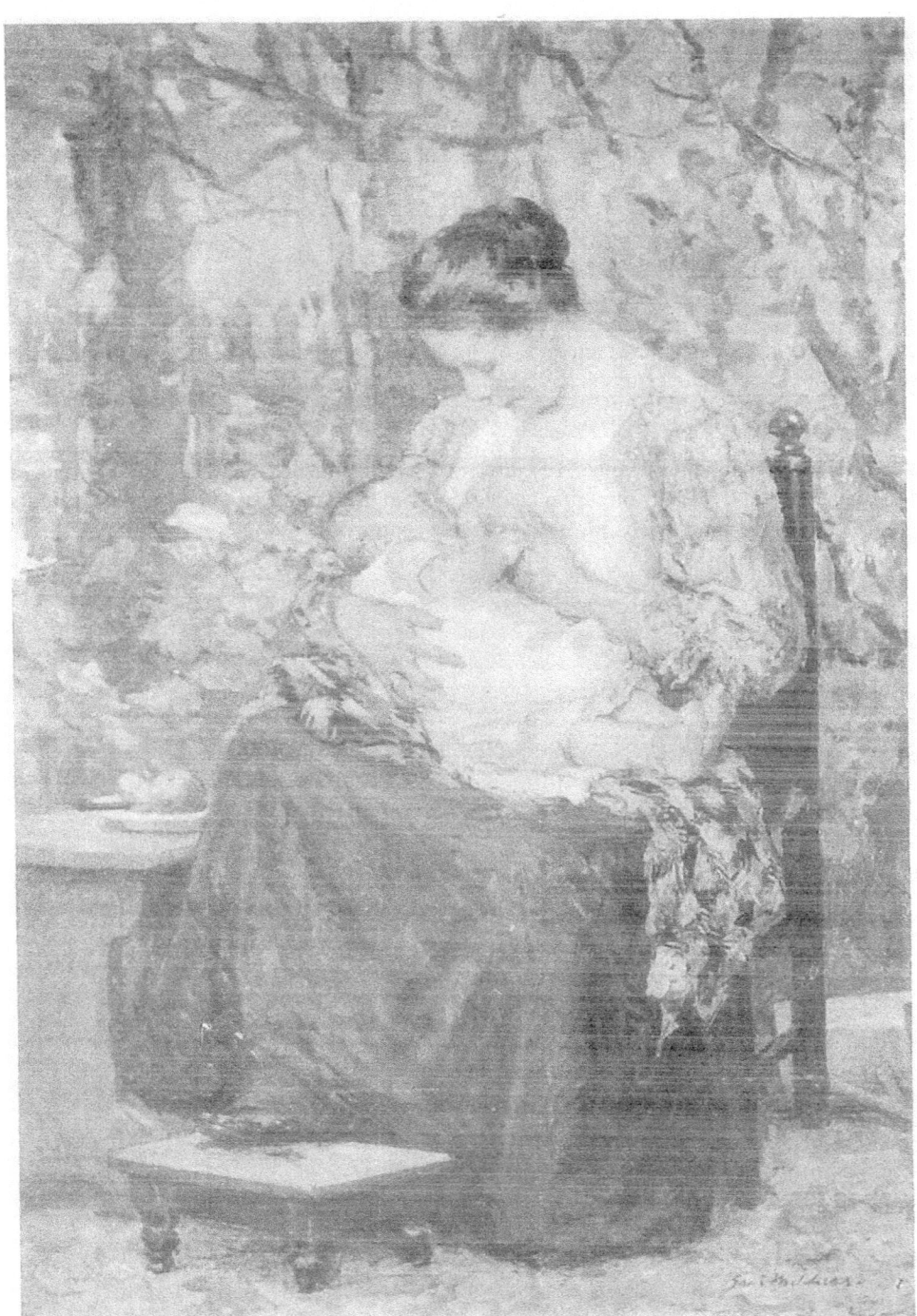

MATERNITY
By Gari Melchers

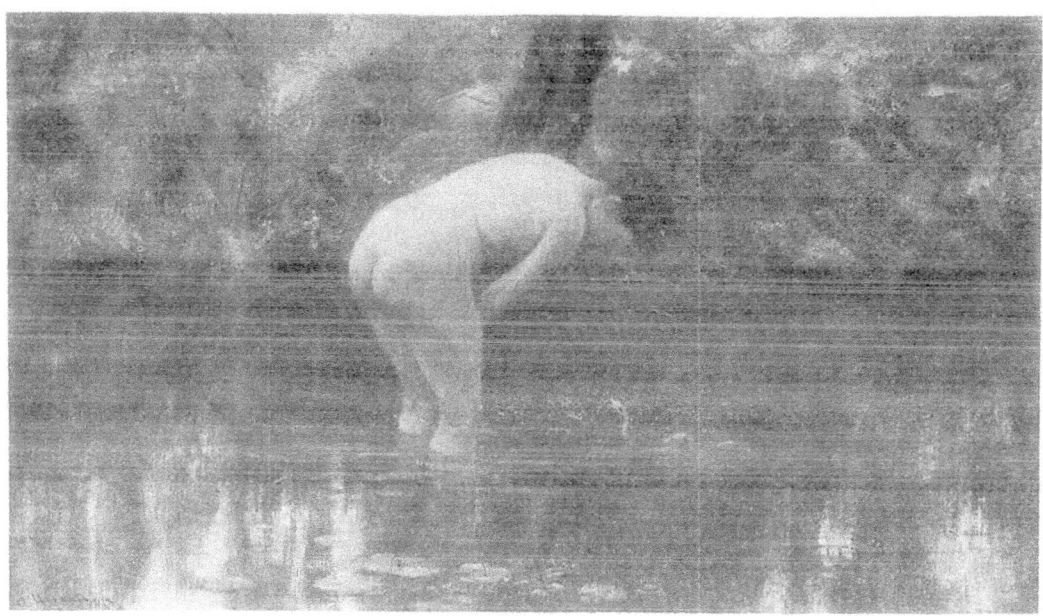

WATER SNAKE
By Alexander Harrison

Cotemporary American Art as An Investment

By EVELYN MARIE STUART

"Be thou the first true merit to befriend
His praise is lost who waits till all commend."

A WRITER in one of our smarter magazines has called attention to the flagrant misuse of the term "art patron" and pointed out that all collectors who pay exhorbitant prices for works of art are not, of necessity, art patrons.

The idea requires not to be enlarged upon for every active mind leaps to the conclusion before it is stated, that the only real art patrons are those who encourage the living, growing art of their own day. Many art patrons so-called are, in reality, only antiquarians whose particular fad happens to be pictures. No one can quarrel with them for this since the lure of the antique is well nigh irresistible to anyone with romance in his soul and a bit of the mystic philosophy of transmigration. Things with a history are almost lovable for that alone; it is as if the souls of former possessions hovered lovingly about them affording spiritual companionship. People will always buy most eagerly and value most highly that which is old and difficult to obtain. Sentiment and pride of possession, urge strongly to the man of means to thus indulge his fancy. Then, too, he buys on established reputation, with the judgment of time to come to the aid of confused or timid taste and furthermore, one must admit that a great work of art by a man long since passed beyond is indeed a priceless treasure.

However, there is the keen joy of developing one's artistic taste and judgment, of helping others and of being a factor in the artistic advancement of one's time in the purchase of works by contemporary artists and added to this, especially in the case of young men just coming to the front, is the zest of

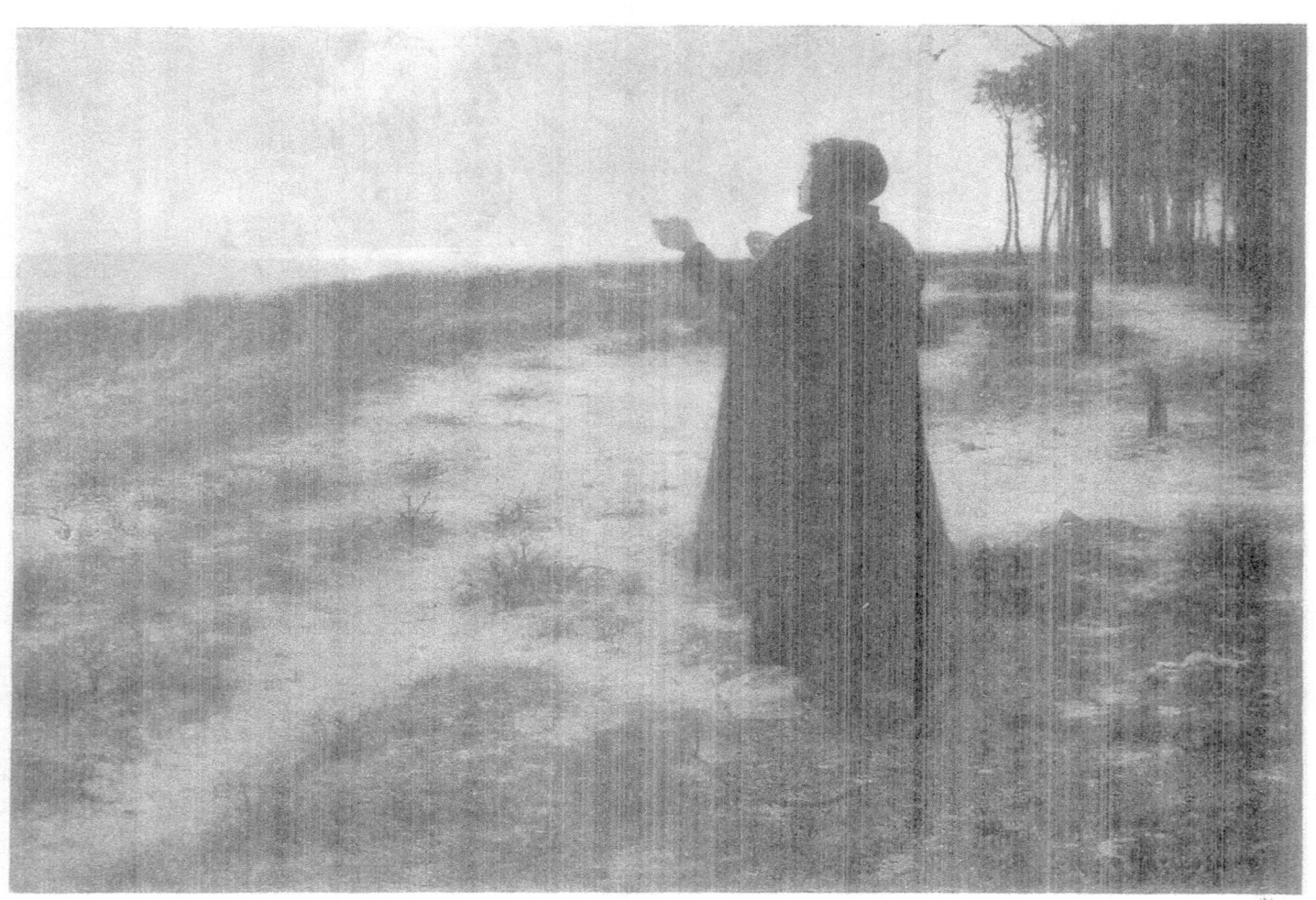

DEPARTURE OF THE MAYFLOWER
By Birge Harrison

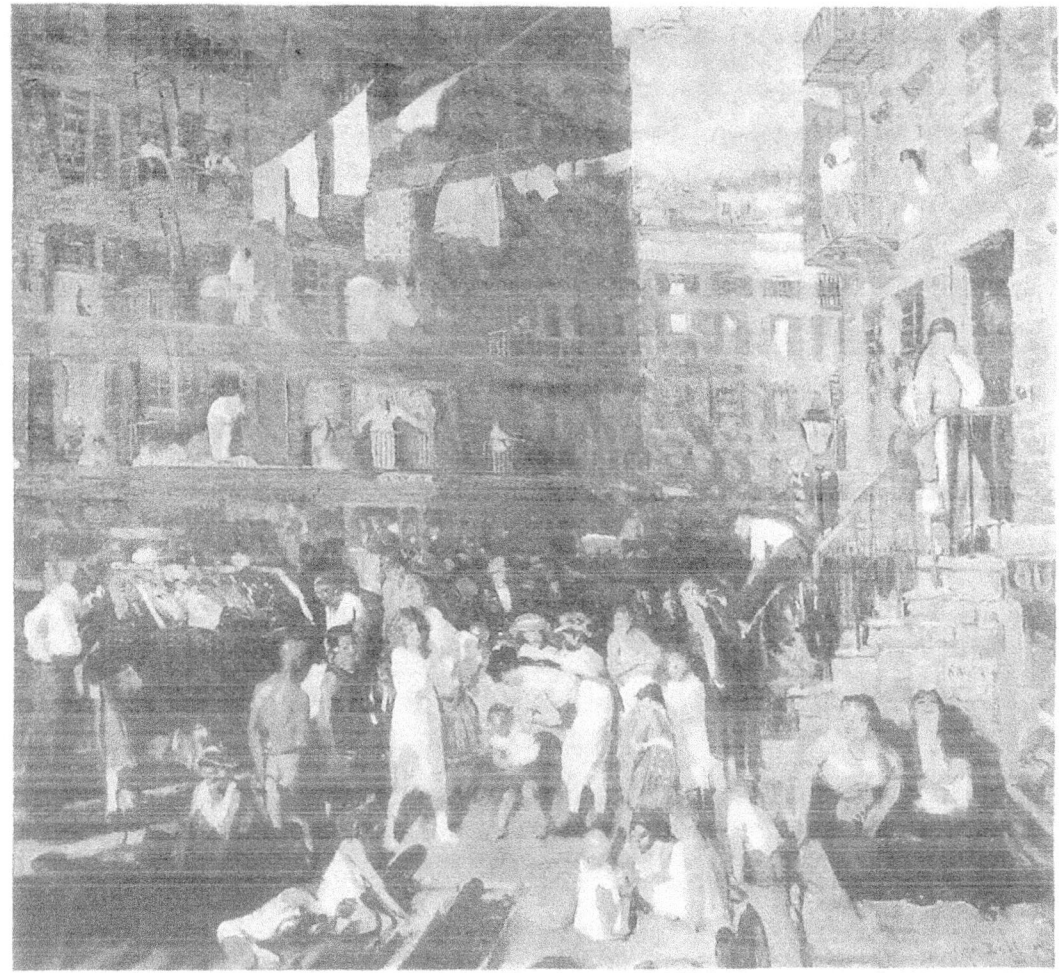

THE CLIFF DWELLERS
By George Bellows

speculation in a commodity that cannot decline in value and is likely to increase no one can say how much.

It is the universal story of great artists that they must pass through an early period of trial and hardships, lack of appreciation and patronage, that their prices advance as fame singles them out for recognition, and that when prominence is once attained their works increase steadily in value.

It therefore behooves a true art lover to learn to recognize true art and hasten to patronize it. Thereby he may make a good financial investment of what is ever the best of aesthetic investments. Viewed from the latter standpoint indeed works of art are with books the most valuable furnishings of a home. A picture or a bit of sculpture like a book, is a companion, a friend, a reflection of life, a stimulus to thought and observation, and further still a satisfaction to the senses through its beauty. To learn to love art is to find a new world, a realm of pleasure that does not cloy, and to find new eyes that shall see more beauty in nature.

Laying aside these higher considerations of the soul there are plain practical reasons why the man of even comfortable means should buy a few good pictures by the artists of his own time, and why the less his means the

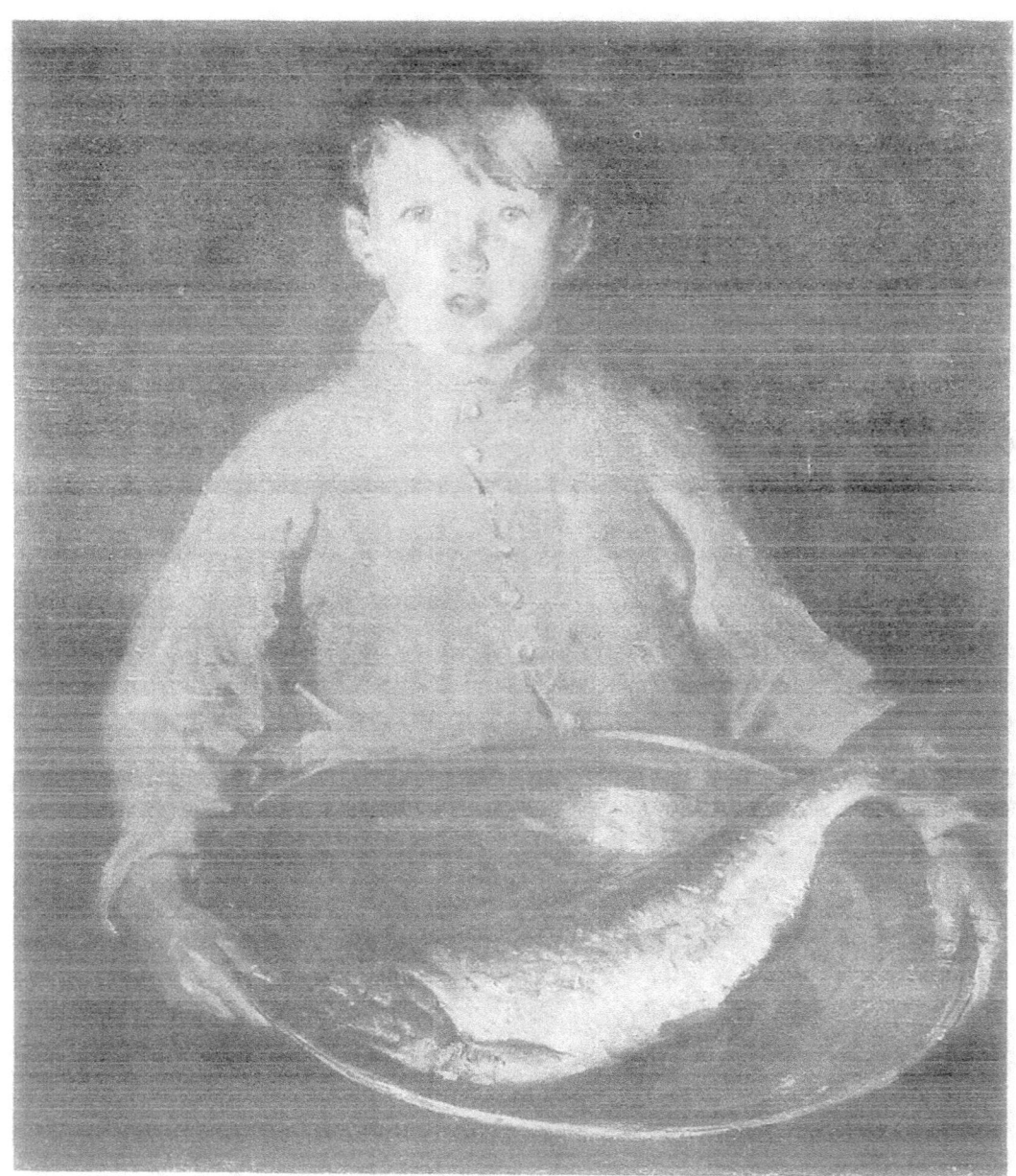

BOY WITH SHAD
By Charles Hawthorne

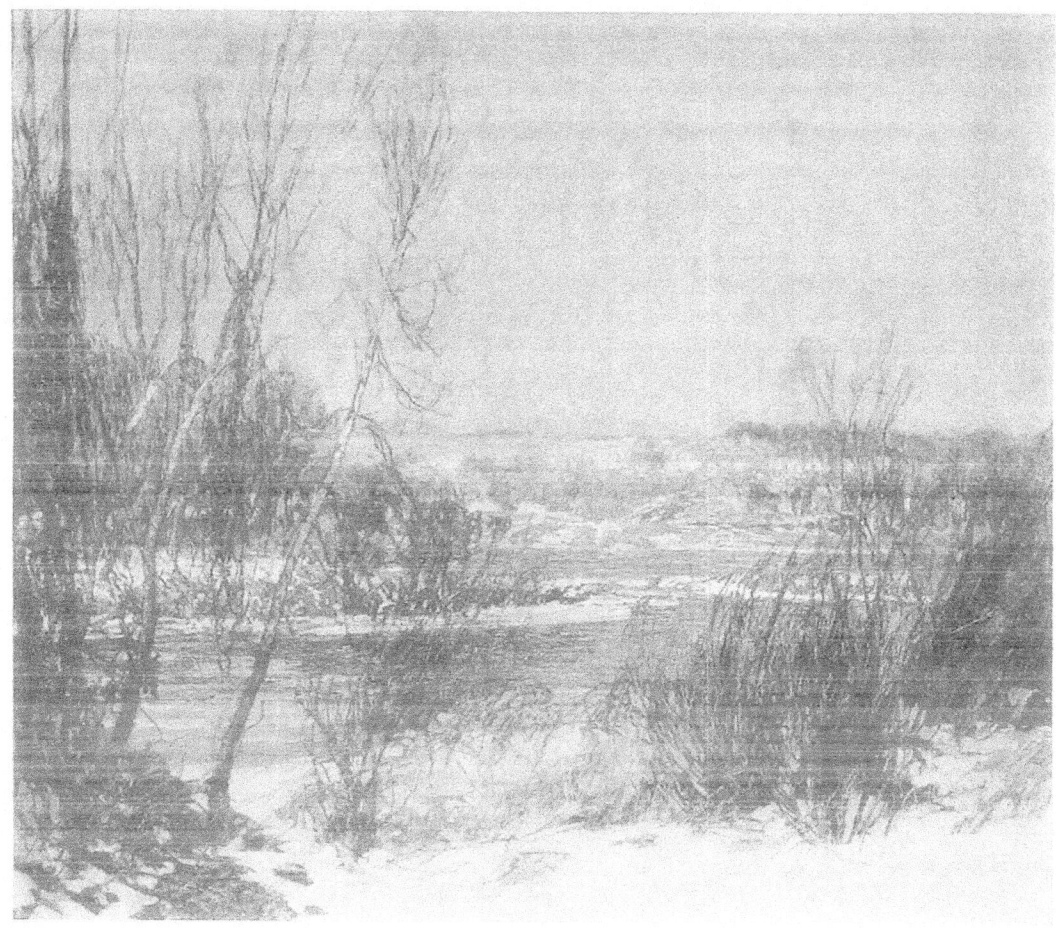

BY THE RIVER
By Edward W. Redfield

greater is his need of cultivating a true taste that he may be able to recognize ability in its first period.

Some idea of the prices brought even at auction by recognized American artists may be gained from the following excerpt from the *American Art News* report of the Humphreys sale:

"All records for a one session auction sale of American pictures, and a number of individual auction records for works of American artists, were broken at the final session Thursday evening, when a total of $143,050 was secured for eighty-three canvases, which, added to the total of $43,255 of the first session, makes a grand total of $186,305.

"The average for each picture in the sale was $1,122, as compared with one of $634 in the Thomas B. Clarke sale of Americans in 1899, of $600 in the first W. T. Evans sale of 1900, and of $700 in the second Evans sale of 1913.

"The highest figure of the session, $15,600, paid by R. C. & N. M. Vose of Boston for the late George Fuller's 'Girl and Turkeys,' was not only the record price for an example of Fuller, but the second highest price ever brought by a modern American picture at auction—the first having been $16,000, brought by a landscape by George Inness at the Combination sale at the Plaza in January. The same artist's 'Romany Girl,' now owned by Mr. H. C. Frick, brought $10,500 at the Ichabod Williams sale three years ago. The so-called 'Vaughan' portrait of Washington, by Gilbert Stuart, brought the highest figure, some $18,000, for an American picture at auction, from Mr. Thomas B. Clarke in Philadelphia three years ago.

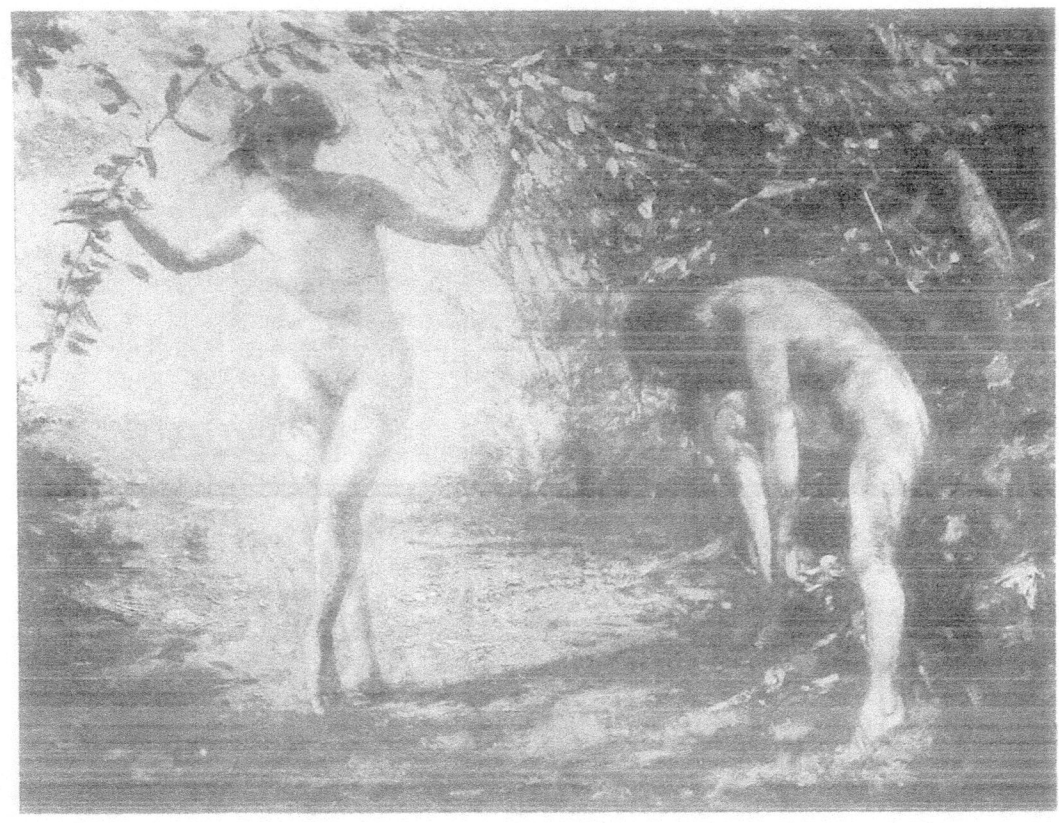

IN GOLDEN DAYS
By Lillian Genth, A. N. A.

"Other records were smashed at the session by the late Winslow Homer, whose watercolor, 'A Voice from the Cliffs,' brought $3,700 from Knoedler & Company, the highest price ever paid also for an American watercolor; Wyant's 'Keene Valley,' $7,500, from Henry Reinhardt & Son; J. Francis Murphy's 'Approach to the Old Farm,' $5,000 from William Macbeth; J. H. Twachtmann's 'Frozen Brook,' $3,000 from William Macbeth; the late Henry W. Ranger's 'Becky Coles' Hill,' $3,200 from Bernet as agent; Louis P. Dessar's 'Changing Pasture,' $2,900 from Marion McMillin, and Paul Dougherty's 'Aisle of the Sea,' $2,150 from Mrs. F. C. Brown."

We illustrate herewith some of the most notable works of s o m e of the greatest of American artists, of yesterday and today. The value of the old school of native painters is too well known and established to require much comment, but the rise in value of the works of living men since they first began to exhibit or receive honors is surely illuminating.

There is probably not one living artist included among those whose works are here shown who cannot, at the present writing, readily command ten times the price for a canvas that he could have asked when his works first began to attract favorable comment. Nor does it necessarily follow that artistic ability has increased in a ratio with prices, for many men do good work, sometimes their best, in their early periods.

Then too for the decoration of the modern home nothing is more appropriate and effective than the modern school picture. It is in the spirit of the time and comports best with modern architecture and furnishings. It is a better influence psychologically also, b e i n g sunnier, more luminous and keyed to harmony with the cheerfulness of our modern

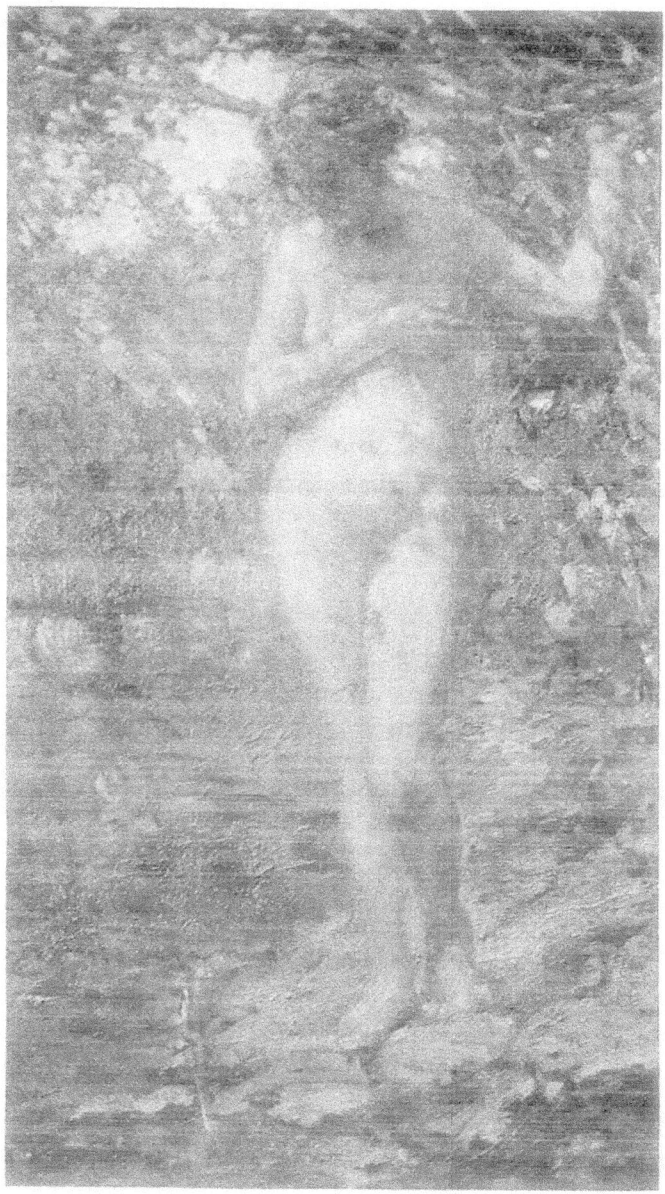

MAIDENHOOD
By Lillian Genth, A. N. A.

optimistic religious and philosophical thought.

Perhaps considerations like the foregoing explain in some measure why the twenty-first annual exhibition of works by artists of Chicago and vicinity ushered in a new order of things with a combined price list and program. This excellent idea was suggested by some of the trustees of the Art Institute who have amassed great fortunes through business acumen. It seems a very sane and sensible measure and one which should bring practical results.

The placing of typewritten lists of the titles and numbers of the pictures at the side of the entrance door was another convenient idea, helpful to those who wish to locate particular pictures. It would be easier, however, to find any given canvas if the exhibition

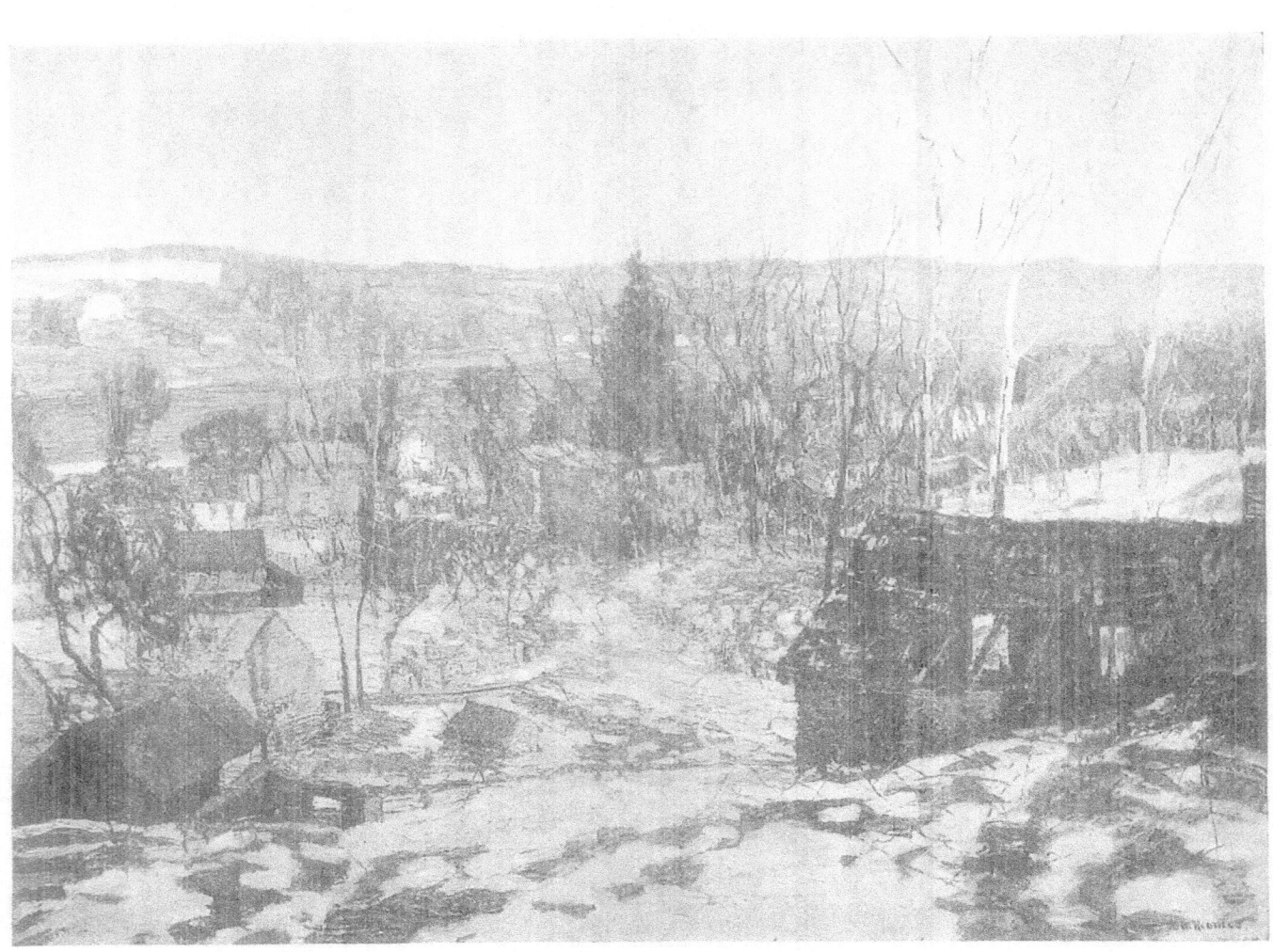

THE VILLAGE IN WINTER
By Edward W. Redfield

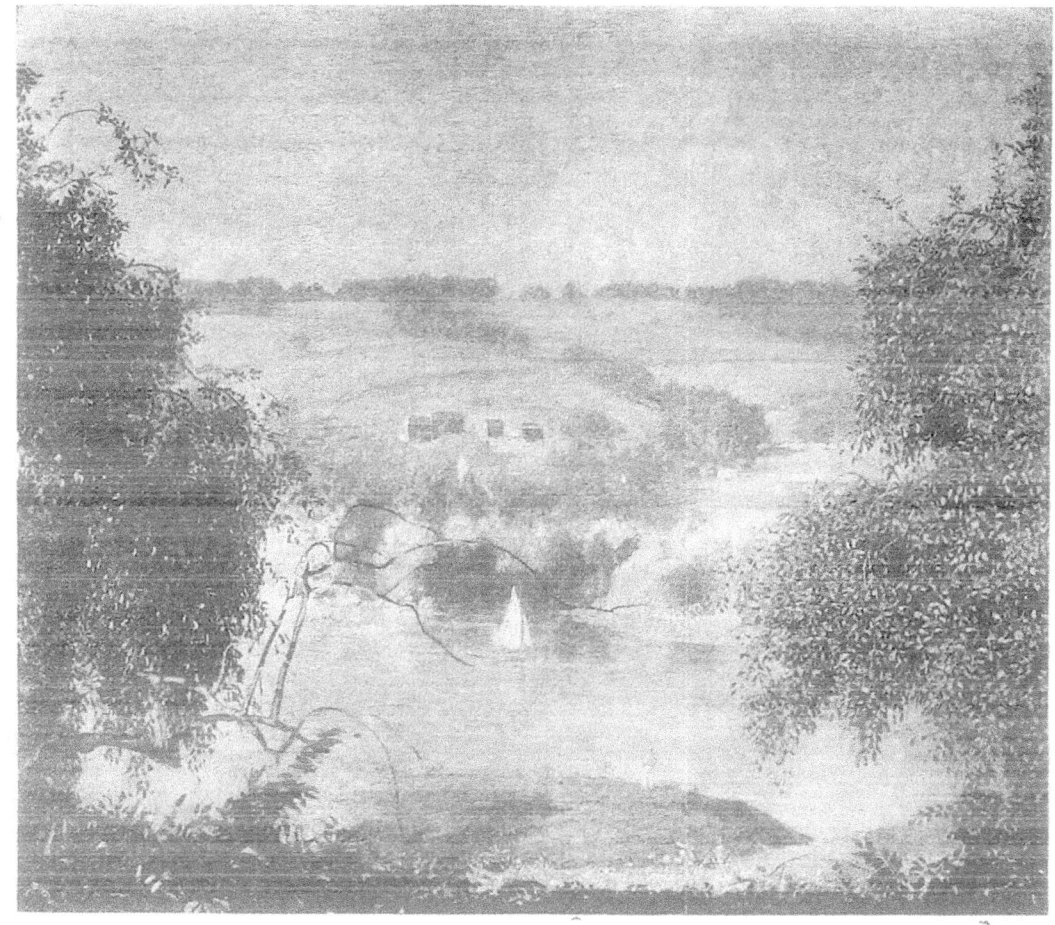

OVER IN JERSEY
By Daniel Garber

could be numbered as hung instead of as cataloged. This, however, is asking too much since catalogs must be printed long before the order of hanging in the galleries is decided. The placing of little red stars upon pictures to mark the ones that had been sold was also a new, unique and pretty notion which aroused curiosity and elicited pleased comment when explained.

To return to the matter of prices: it really requires no justification when one stops to consider how general is the feeling that pictures shown at the Institute are exhibited solely for cultural and educational purposes. Collectors, of course, know better, but alas! collectors are all too rare and that curious cosmopolitan, the general public, is not a collector. Nevertheless, he should be.

One can stand on the Institute steps and watch several million dollars in automobiles roll down Michigan Boulevard daily. What a boon to art if every car owner should aspire to own a picture, or pictures, equal to the value of his car, or add each year a canvas, or canvases, amounting in value to his garage and repair bill. Such a thought, however, would strike the average motorist as wild to the verge of madness and yet, a picture as has been said, is an investment, not an expenditure. It affords joy and comfort without effort or inconvenience of leaving one's home and requires no expense for upkeep. Yet,

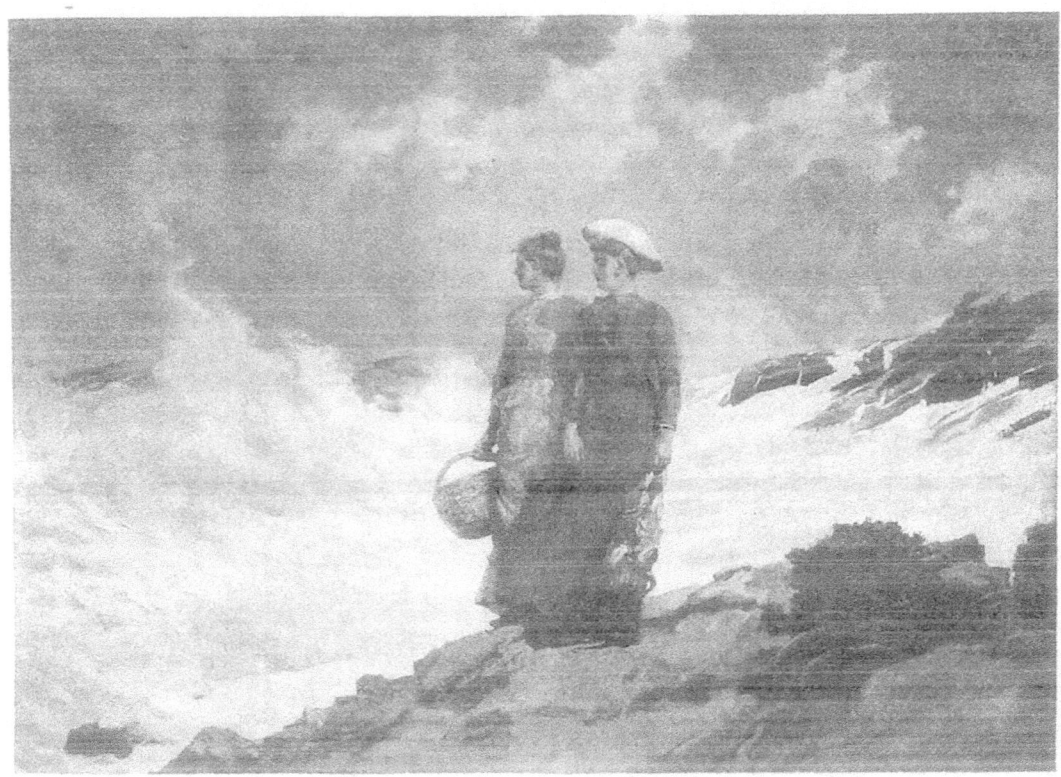

WATCHING THE BREAKERS
By Winslow Homer

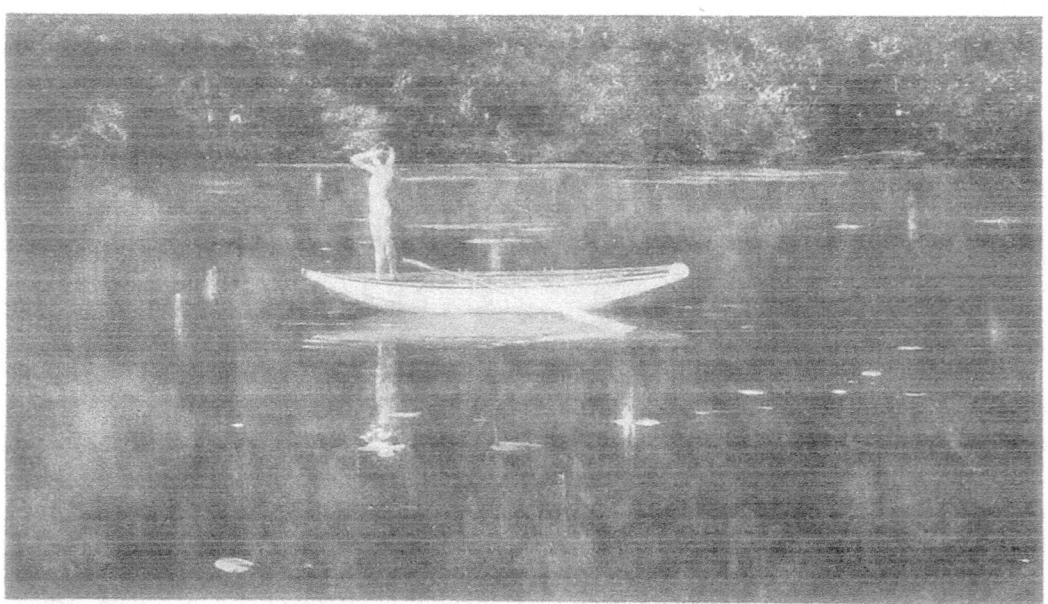

SOLITUDE
By Alexander Harrison

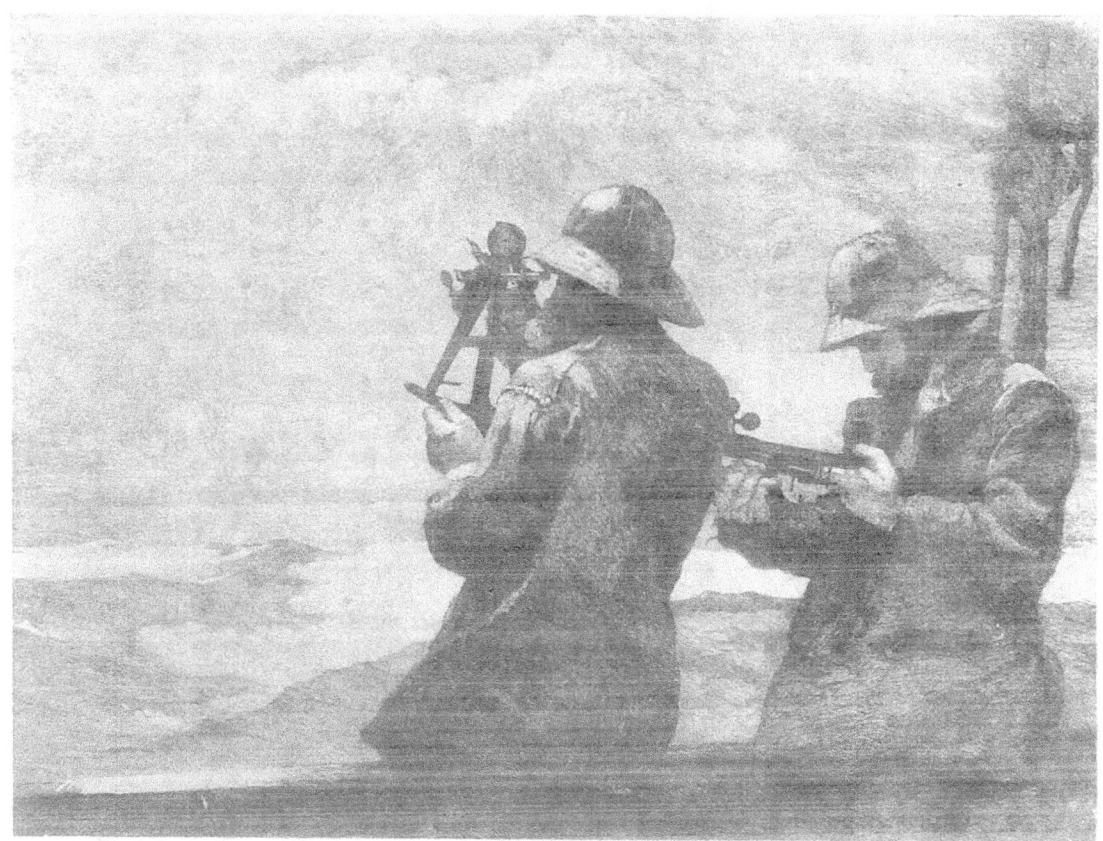

EIGHT BELLS
By Winslow Homer

again, the windows on Michigan Avenue are not lacking for one-hundred to five-hundred-dollar gowns and wraps but the average purchaser of these short-lived lovelinesses would not dream of investing as much in art as she does in dress. Why not? The dress is soon worn out or wearied of, the picture lasts for all time and is always worth what cost, perhaps, in time, much more.

Think, too, of how poorly the value of the pictures in the great majority of homes compares with the value of the rugs. Good Orientals costing from one hundred dollars up are, by far, more common than pictures of the same price. There are, indeed, innumerable houses and apartments without one picture equal in value to one month's rent and some of them are in the one-hundred-dollar or better scale.

Now this should not be; a people so lavish as are we in the providing of physical comforts and luxuries, should not be niggardly about acquiring those things which make for aesthetic development. Art is as refreshing and wholesome to the soul as are sanitation and good heating facilities to the body and the truly good home should not be lacking in either. If every householder in Chicago, who can really afford a few pictures of the price range indicated in the Chicago show, could be led to realize his needs of art there would not be enough pictures in the whole city to supply the demand. Think what it will mean to art if ever the general public awakens to as great an appreciation of pictures as it has of the other good things of modern civilization.

One of the things which has served to delay this appreciation of art has been the fact

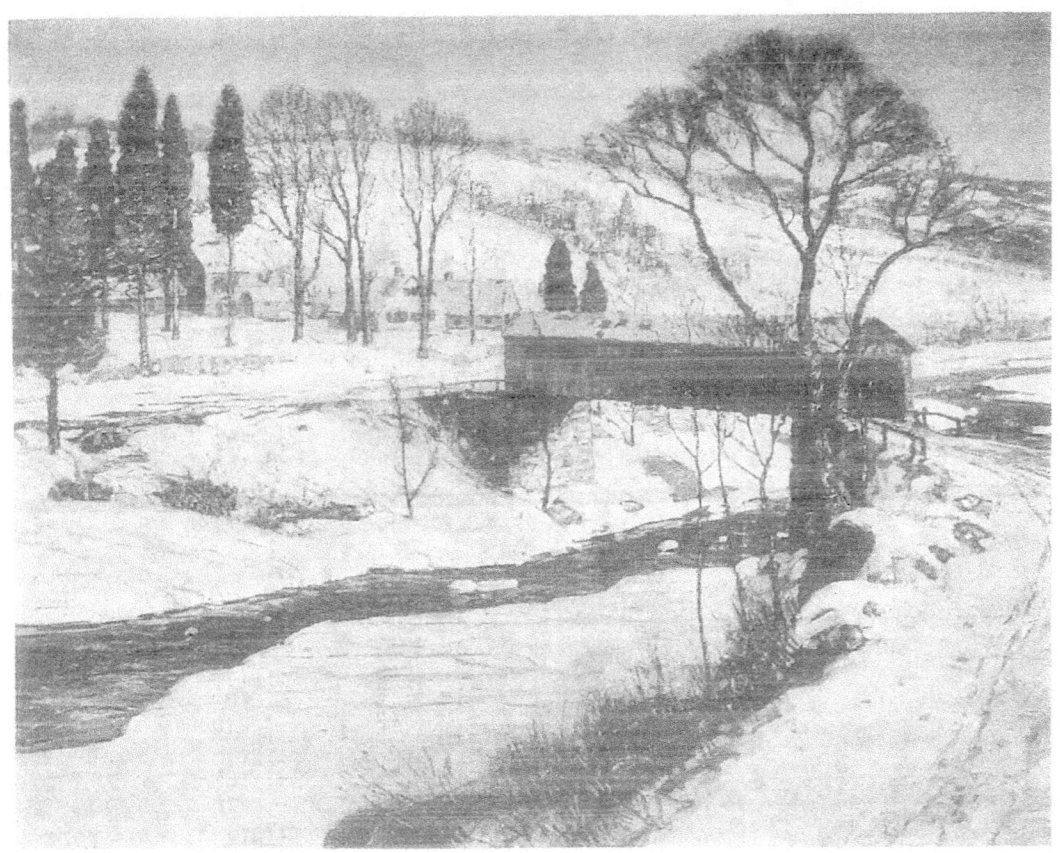

THE BRIDGE AND WINTER SUNLIGHT
By Gardner Symons

that pictures have always lacked publicity. They have not been made the style. Art is not advertised, written about, talked about, pushed as are things of grosser agreeable qualities. Then, too, so much that is written has been of the priceless old masters that people, in general, have come to feel that a really good picture is in the class with the crown jewels and that to be good a picture must be old. Yet the best of pictures were new once and the newest of the pictures may be good, yes even the best for all we know. Many things are being done today better than they have ever been done before. Our passing exhibitions of contemporary art abound in a wealth of great talent and sparkle with many a flash of real genius. Sunshine and air, motion and life are better handled by the modern school than they have ever been by those of other days and there is a strong decorative quality in much of our contemporary art that renders it ideal for the home.

In all the Chicago show there was not one thing that would not have added interest, beauty and delight in some interior, afforded a capital touch of color or a fascinating study of form. In general, it is safe for the would-be purchaser of art to assume that nothing will ever be shown at the Institute which he might not safely purchase. Pictures appearing in these exhibitions have been subjected to a severe competitive analysis by the foremost critics and nothing can be hung that does not possess considerable inherent merit and technical excellence.

For all of these reasons the placing of prices in the catalogs is much to be commended and the general public should attend exhibitions and that ... ut to buy. In so doing a ... consummated and a great ... to the advancement of art. ... recall that a Blakeloch which ... e artist for a few hundred dollar ... hrough a Chicago gallery for tw ... nd dollars during that same ma ... o be reminded of what extremes a ... ible once chance brings a man great fa... Of course this is an extreme example but a raise of two or three times its original value even during the artist's life is not so unusual in a good picture. Who would not bless a grandfather with sufficient artistic taste and foresight to have secured a Corot or any other good Barbizon when the master was young and glad to sell his unrecognized productions for a song? Truly carriages break down like the "One Hoss Chaise," Paris frocks become mere curiosities of the attic, fine homes descend to furnished-room and boarding-house uses, smart neighborhoods become slums and it is only jewels and pictures of all one's personal possessions on which one may rely against time and count upon as constituting an estate.

This perhaps is the one opportunity of the beauty lover, who thinks in terms of personal property, to aspire to that dignity by turning his lavish love of expenditure to a wise end. Perhaps your true financier might scout the idea of an investment which yields no interest, but the same argument would apply to a life insurance policy, which has furthermore no possibility of increase beyond its face value and, speaking of interest, in another sense, nothing is so fertile a source of that one most valuable possession, as interest in life, as is a hobby, and art is the best of all hobbies, ever fresh and exhilarating while life and sight endure.

Our illustrations afford a good apportunity to realize a f r e s h the individuality of the American school. Keith, Inness, Wyant, and the great men of their day might perhaps be thought to have been somewhat influenced by the works of the Barbizon group; still it is just as likely that different groups of men in

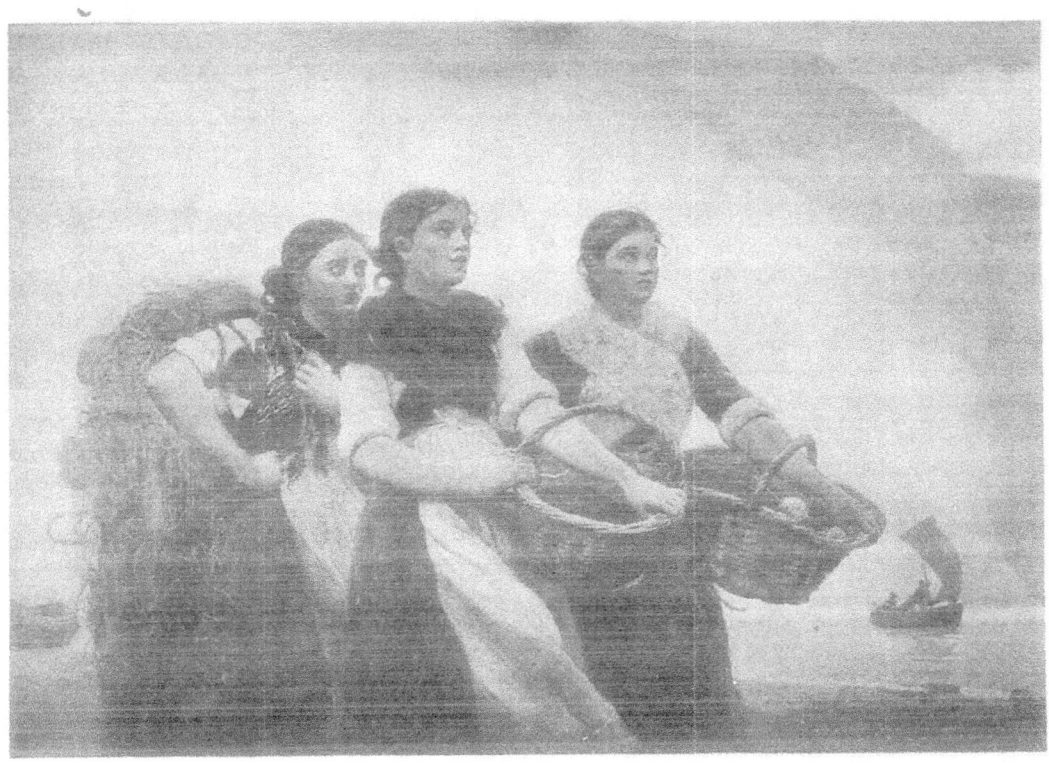

A VOICE FROM THE CLIFFS
By Winslow Homer

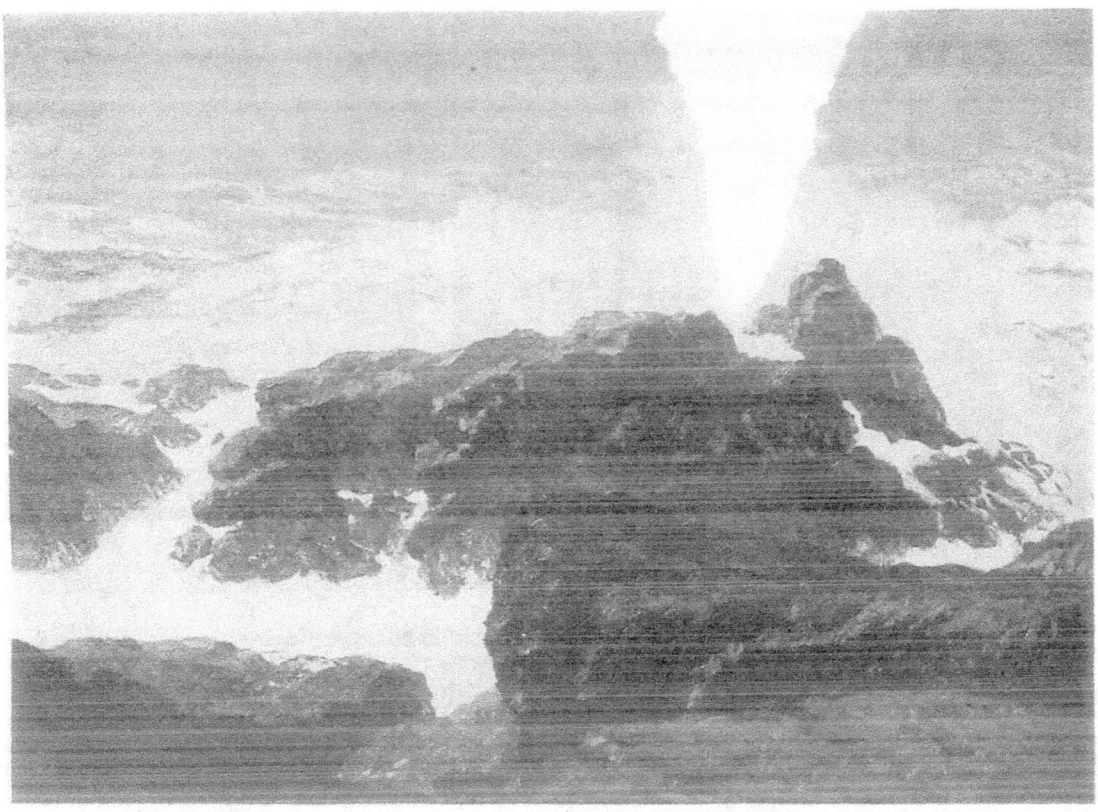

EQUINOCTIAL GALE
By Paul Dougherty, N. A.

Courtesy R. C. & N. M. Vose, Boston

different countries should have attempted independently the solution of the same problems, for, belonging to the same age, they would start with the same fund of previous knowledge behind them and the same possibilities before. Thought will generally be found to go by ages rather than by schools almost universally for this reason. The great American artists of the period just passed were, in large measure, self-trained by interchange of ideas with each other. Their greatest works were studies of native scenery about their own places of abode.

Fabulous prices have been paid, since their death, for the works of these men who, during their lives, never received anything more than fair prices. A single Inness, secured by a school teacher with artistic taste, in the midst of his career, brought a sum last year that was, in itself, a tidy little fortune. Important Keiths are a rarity in the market and Wyants and Winslow Homers are ever in demand at large prices. Yet many of these same pictures once sold at no greater figure than the average scale for works of Chicago artists today. You, who r e g r e t the opportunities o v e r l o o k e d by fathers and grandfathers, should learn to be more keenly alive to those about you than were they to theirs.

Of the modern men, whose works appear herewith, every one is in the zenith of achievement, most of them command as good, as or better, prices than the great men of the old school that has just passed. Some of their works will, in all likelihood, sell for as much a few decades hence as do those of e a r l y American masters now, and the many fine collections, in which they are represented, make famous, as connoisseurs, the men w h o assembled them. This would, indeed, be quite consistent with the usual logic of events.

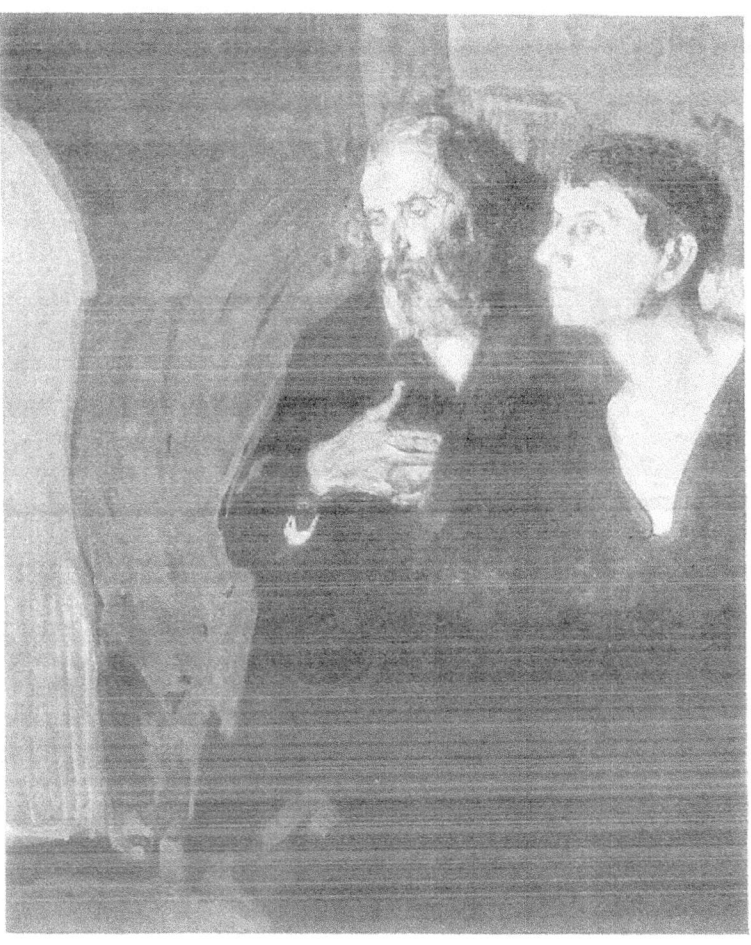

THE TWO DISCIPLES AT THE TOMB

By Henry O. Tanner

Practically every one of the artists represented in our illustrations of cotemporary works is noted for strong individuality. Who cannot recognize a Genth or a Melchers, a Tanner, a Hawthorne or a Garber at sight? Redfield and Symons are sometimes confused with each other but never with any other, possessing a similarity as did Inness and Wyant at times. George Bellows is never to be mistaken, though there are others whom he resembles in some details. The Harrisons are similar in style, as one would expect from relationship and training, but they have no competition, belong to no set school.

Dougherty is among the most noted of modern marine painters and a man whose works can safely be relied upon to withstand the test of time. Everything he does is notably well done with an unusual balance of breadth and detail. One of his most important canvases to date, "An Equinoctial Gale," is reproduced by courtesy of R. C. & N. M. Vose, of Boston, who secured it for a client interested in cotemporary American Art. This picture was given the place of honor in the room devoted to Dougherty at the last International Exhibition at Carnegie Institute, Pittsburgh. It is regarded by connoisseurs as Dougherty's masterpiece.

* * *

These men have securely arrived in the favor of collectors; of whom there are not a few among our men of wealth. Patronage of art, however, should not be left to rich men exclusively. Many more people are able to buy pictures than think they are.